Little White Bull

John Muckle is a fiction writer, poet and critic. He is the author of four books of fiction, including *The Cresta Run* (Galloping Dog Press, 1987), *Cyclomotors*, an acclaimed short illustrated novel set in the early 1950s (available through Shearsman Books), and the novels *London Brakes* (Shearsman, 2010) and *My Pale Tulip* (Shearsman, 2012). His first full-length poetry collection, *Firewriting and Other Poems* appeared from Shearsman in 2005, a late follow-up to *It Is Now As It Was Then* (with Ian Davidson, Mica Press/Actual Size, 1983). Another notable collaboration was *Bikers* (with Bill Griffiths, Amra Imprint, 1990). In the eighties he created the Paladin Poetry imprint and was general editor of its flagship anthology, *The New British Poetry* (eds. D'Aguiar, Allnutt, Edwards, Mottram, 1988). He has been for ten years a regular contributor to *PN Review* as reviewer and essayist. He lives in London, and works as a teacher.

Also by John Muckle

It Is Now As It Was Then (with Ian Davidson)
The Cresta Run
Bikers (with Bill Griffiths)
Cyclomotors
Firewriting and Other Poems
London Brakes
My Pale Tulip

Little White Bull

British Fiction in the Fifties and Sixties

John Muckle

Shearsman Books

First published in the United Kingdom in 2014 by
Shearsman Books
50 Westons Hill Drive
Emersons Green
BRISTOL
BS16 7DF

Shearsman Books Ltd Registered Office
30–31 St. James Place, Mangotsfield, Bristol BS16 9JB
(this address not for correspondence)

ISBN 978-1-84861-305-8

Contents

Introduction

I

Raymond Williams, 'Representation' and British Fiction

It may seem odd to call a study of the British novel in the fifties and sixties after a Tin Pan Alley song. 'Little White Bull' is from a forgotten musical comedy featuring a once-popular cockney skiffle singer—a toothy little chap who made hay for a few years as a family entertainer before being enshrined forever in the early history of British rock'n'roll. It was a song often heard on the radio when I was a small boy. Tommy Steele was a star back then, and 'Little White Bull', written by prolific East End Jewish composer Lionel Bart, is a song that would probably be remembered by anyone who grew up in Britain in the fifties and sixties. This maddening ditty, and its central image of the cockney 'little white bull', became part of a popular memory and of that nebulous, fleeting, ghostly creature once known as 'working-class culture', largely due to its having been inflicted on radio listeners thousands of times. It is a chirpy, hopeful song. The little white bull of the working-class, represented by a young cockney sailor on shore leave in Spain, is determined to show he is just as good as the big black bulls—those arrogant bullying giants bred specifically for combat in the arena of middle-class power, who always seem to believe their pre-eminence has been divinely or genetically ordained.

On the face of it this is a hopeful song about social class, or being an outsider, in tone somewhat reminiscent of Danny Kaye's performance of 'The Ugly Duckling' in another Saturday afternoon favourite. Maybe not. It might well be that the black bulls refer to the African-American boxers who had come to dominate the sport of gentlemen by this time, and Tommy, the brave little white bull, is an East End fighter in the not yet lost cause of white supremacy. Either way, he is just as good as any of them, or so his mother believes, and *Tommy the Toreador* sets out to prove his point: the funny little man (just like Charlie Chaplin, George Formby or Norman Wisdom before him) can and will triumph over the snobs with his combination of unstoppable charm, necessary cunning, and, in Tommy's case, sheer persistence and bravery. It was never easier than in these films to buck the 'little white rule' that holds class society together and puts people like us in our place. Ah, dreams. *Tommy the Toreador* had another song about the power of the imagination to vanquish reality, and in the magnificent opening sequence of Cliff Richard's second feature, *The*

Young Ones, we are again told that nothing is impossible. Cliff and his amazed girlfriend walk up walls, fly over fences, and he effortlessly bends the iron railings that surround the park like so much rubber in order that they may slip through them to joy. Cliff croons to her about all the fools who have scoffed at progress, citing among other indicators the invention of penicillin and the recent achievement of Major Gagarin in conquering space: now the city of London, the world—and the universe itself—is to be the raw brimming oyster of this oh so lucky generation. If only we had kept dreaming.

The story of this strand of postwar British fiction is in large part the story of what happened to those preposterous hopes, retold by someone who for a time believed that the lyrics of 'The Young Ones' and Cliff's other early songs, as well as those of Adam Faith, Billy Fury and others, actually foretold his own future: 'If there is hope, it lies in the proles,' George Orwell had feebly intoned in 1948, and Cliff and Tommy, Joe Brown and Billy Fury were proof positive that young working-class people weren't going to be satisfied forever by bombsites, the cold war and Victory gin. But if this study is *only* a storybook, and in that sense a fairytale, it will have failed. The hopes and social aspirations contained in those early films and songs were after all only the sugar frostings of a time when, in Britain's literary and political culture, definitions of social class, the position of women, race and empire, sexuality and family life, were being fiercely contested across the board. For every vaulting utopian (and these were more likely to be found in advertising and pop music than in serious culture) there was a bevy of nay-sayers who might have been less wholesomely comely than the Beverley Sisters, but often had their fingers more firmly on the pulse of what was actually happening in British society in the Larry Parnes years, and were certainly better versed in the conceptions that it had inherited. The big questions that underlay all the fizz and all the anguish of postwar culture were framed by the generation who had fought the Second World War, later by those who had grown up during it and came of age in the sixties and were to be personally affected by how society was changing to accommodate the higher aspirations of the working-classes. This period, roughly from 1950 to 1970, was intensely preoccupied with questions of social class, social mobility, the meaning of democracy and 'mass society' in a way that no other had quite been before or has since. Furthermore, I believe that it is in fiction more than in popular music, film or any other cultural carrier that the most telling records of this social paroxysm are to be found, and I also believe that the whole period needs to be looked at again and better understood. The strange thing is that in that happy moment when Tommy became a Matador and Cliff ran up a wall and bent the rubber railings, you can always find some book, written by someone, qualified or not, which claims to define the condition and what are seen to this day to be the key problems of the British working-classes.

In his conclusion to *Culture and Society* influential critic and novelist Raymond Williams attempted to come up with an inclusive definition of 'working-class culture', to pin down its palpitating essence under smoky glass: 'It is not proletarian art,' he wrote, 'or council houses, or a particular use of language; it is, rather, the basic collective idea, and the institutions, manners, habits of thought, and intentions that proceed from that.'[1] The real cultural achievement of the working-class, he explained, was the labour movement and the Labour Party: expressions of a co-operative idea or spirit that Williams contrasted with the spirit of competitive individualism in its crudest form, and which he is careful to distinguish from the Victorian middle-class ideal of public service, and its related notion of equality of opportunity, for which he has somewhat more respect. He contrasts his own point of view, or rather that of his Welsh railwayman father, an active trades unionist, with that of the middle class of civil servants, administrators and teachers as respectively the views of lower and upper servants. Equality of opportunity as a social nostrum originates, he says, in an ideal of Victorian philanthropists he calls 'the ladder', and it is 'of course based on the desire to become unequal.' Equality of opportunity and meritocracy were vaunted social ideals of postwar British politics, but Williams dismisses them both as distorting, delusory and, above all, socially divisive:

> Judged in each particular case, it seems obviously right that a working man, or the child of a working-class family should be enabled to fit himself for a different kind of work, corresponding to his ability. Because of this, the ladder version of society is objectionable in two related aspects: first, that is weakens the idea of common betterment, which ought to be an absolute value; second, that it sweetens the poison of hierarchy, in particular by offering the hierarchy of merit as a thing different in kind from the hierarchy of money or of birth.[2]

'The ladder,' he argues, 'is merely an image of a particular version of society' and as such is a substitute for 'the making of a common educational provision; to the work for equity in material distribution; to the process of shaping a tradition, a community of experience.'[3] In other words, social and economic climbing for a few lucky ones had little to do with the needs of working-class people in general nor with the idea of an equally participative polity as he had conceived it: the purpose of meritocracy was 'to sweeten the poison of hierarchy'. But why did he regard hierarchy as inherently poisonous? The anger in that phrase points it up as an important one, in which Williams reveals something of the levelling anarchist who lurked within the moderate reforming socialist he appeared to be at the time. He is echoing the words of St. Paul in Corinthians when he pulls down the vanity of human hierarchies and suggests that people who subscribe to the authority of the earthly wisdom of oppressors deserve no more than to be slaves. God chose the humble and weak to be his congregation and overthrow the existing order, in order to demonstrate the emptiness of earthly power and the wisdom of the great. His tone is like St Paul's and his message is strikingly similar in its call for discipline, fellowship and solidarity amongst those who are struggling together for common betterment.

In other early essays Williams attempts to define what is to be valued and striven for as 'common culture', and in so doing he strikes out at what he perceives to be the counter-forces to such a goal in a way that reveals his impatience for much of what passed as the 'working-class' anger of the group of writers who had quickly won fame as 'Angry Young Men'. John Wain had depicted an alienated working-class academic failure in *Hurry on Down* (1953); the ravings of Jimmy Porter in *Look Back in Anger* (1956) were those of someone who felt that the sufferings and ideals of the thirties had been betrayed; and the travails of Jim Dixon (played in the film by Ian Carmichael, a posh-sounding actor who enjoyed a strange career being cast against class-type as the 'good', aspiring working-class character) in Kingsley Amis' *Lucky Jim* as he tries to make it as a red-brick university lecturer, expressed a new working-class predicament in the semi-feudal world of higher education. Jim Dixon is a pugnacious Northerner whose class on Henry the Fifth is subversively concerned with the role of the poor bloody infantry and who thinks little of the head of department's view of 'Merrie England'. In Kingsley Amis' favour he is the first English novelist to portray a lecturer who had actually risen from the ranks—only John Wain's contemporary *Hurry on Down*, David Storey's *Flight into Camden*, Raymond Williams' first novel *Border Country*, and, decades later, Willy Russell's cloyingly sentimental *Educating Rita* and Malcolm Bradbury's *The History Man* (an acid portrait of a predatory corridor revolutionary) tried to bring the opening up of higher education to ordinary people into the subject-matter of British fiction. But for Raymond Williams, our Virgilian guide to these precincts of hell, any cultural phenomenon was deemed valuable only insofar as it contributed to what he called the project of common betterment:

> The institutions of cynicism, of denial, and of division will perhaps only be thrown down when they are recognised for what they are: the deposits of practical failures to live. Failure—the jaunty

> hardness of 'the outsider'—will lose its present glamour, as the common experience moves in a different direction. Nobody will be proud any longer to be separate, to deny, or to ratify a personal failure in unconcern.[4]

But who was this 'outsider'? Alan Sillitoe's *Saturday Night and Sunday Morning* is a novel which appeared in the same year as *Culture and Society*; its hero, Arthur Seaton, prosperous young lathe operator, a political cynic and philanderer whose attitude to life may on the face of it seem to epitomise what Williams called 'the jaunty hardness of the outsider', and either to give the lie to Williams' vision of community and solidarity, or to embody an alternative 'ethic' of 'looking after number one'. Seaton certainly talks in that familiar way, but he doesn't himself believe in the ladder—after all, he's only been offered a bar stool. Joe Lampton, on the other hand, the social climbing young accountant of John Braine's *Room at the Top*, has swallowed 'the ladder' hook, line and sinker, he just knows that its would-be climbers must forget all about playing by the rules. The subject of John Braine's *Room at the Top* and many other writings by the 'Angry Young Men' was, as I will explain, described at the time as 'hypergamy', a sort of English class equivalent of 'endogamy', marrying out of the tribe, or even of 'miscegenation': a pseudo-scientific term for marrying someone above your social station coined with the intention of making the day-dream of snaring a middle-class woman sound like a crime against nature. Albert, the tally-boy hero of Jack Trevor Story's *Live Now, Pay Later,* is a rebel of the same kind, but lower down the social ladder: a refusenik of social mobility who deliberately failed the 11-plus to avoid the extra work of grammar school, he is nevertheless out for what he can get. Story's tally-boys and their female customers are irresponsible to the core, gleeful consumerists, permanently on the make, or in the case of the local secretarial agency, running a perfectly respectable brothel on the side.

These novels and others like them interest me partly because they appear to contradict what socialist and liberal thinkers and commentators thought the working-classes should be and do and want, because they record dramatic changes in working-class lives and attitudes; but also because, for once, there appears to have been a close fit between the political landscape of a cultural theorist and the rapidly changing society in which he was intervening—it was a context where few people questioned that, yes, culture did actually have something to do with society and many thought it would play an important role in postwar modernisation—therefore a period when working-class people and their predicaments were at the centre of so many films, novels and plays. When the story of the outsider was needed, an insider was often hired to write it, but this is itself a point of interest. There are a few survivors of those times, fewer still who are still creatively active today. Sometimes they can seem like a bunch of imposters around whom a series of once potent but now exhausted myths were woven a long hopeful time ago; but that is a phenomenon in itself and worth investigation by anyone who wants to try and understand how culture works. Is it a reflector of economic power and change, a relatively autonomous construct of the yapping classes or a completely free-floating fantasy world like the flying island of disputing philosophers in Jonathan Swift's *Gulliver's Travels*?

Culture and Society was at the time a breakthrough in the breadth of its considerations on British culture and it is still a genuinely radical book if you look at it right. What may have seemed mildly reformist to the would-be revolutionaries of the sixties and seventies can appear stirringly uncompromising to a supine present; but in later more Marx-influenced writings Raymond Williams distanced himself from his earlier formulations of 'community' and 'common culture'. They had been directed against an elite definition of culture to suggest that culture was more widely produced and meant more things than in current definitions, and served as an argument for redefinition, and expansion in a new kind of higher education. It was an argument for a wider distribution of culture that also pointed to conflicts within culture. He explains his own development from that position to one in which he was drawing more attention to divisions within culture, and to factors that made it impossible to assume a 'common culture': 'community', in his usage, moved from an opposition between a definition of community as 'fellowship' or solidarity against competitive individualism to an awareness that 'community' was widely appropriated by the right in a notion of 'national community' founded on norms and exclusions: on the elimination or subordination of elements perceived as from outside and threatening its own definitions of community, so that the very word 'community' soon became part of a coercive pressure to adapt to nationalism.

Williams told his interviewers at the *New Left Review* in 1977 that he had stopped using the word community once he realised it couldn't be (or never was) used negatively, using a contemporary example of 'a handful of strikers holding the community to ransom': that is, to describe any group as a community tends to positively validate them—a community of strikers holding a handful of bosses to ransom might sound more sympathetic.[5] In more recent years the term 'the paedophile community' has sometimes been used to describe internet child-porn users, partly because it exists precisely as a community—sharing values and information—but also, I believe, because the negative use of the word community is still slightly disturbing and helps in this case to bring home the unpleasantness of what is often being shared by communities. In what may seem an extreme example, but is in fact a completely germane one where the ambivalence about community in postwar British fiction is concerned, William Faulkner's *Light in August* (1932) climaxes when the black-on-the-inside outsider, Joe Christmas, is in effect collectively killed by the community of Jackson, Mississippi, as he attempts to shelter in the house of another outsider, having murdered yet another outsider; and an outsider strikes the *coup de grace* and severs his genitals. But it's the collective assumptions of racism that kill him and a great novel about a small town in the American South reveals that solidarity isn't always such a positive thing and that community values can mean sharing in the fond memories of the most terrible acts imaginable. At the moment of Joe Christmas' death his black blood

> ...seemed to rush out of his pale body like the rush of sparks from a rising rocket; upon that black blast the man seemed to rise soaring into their memories forever and ever. They are not to lose it, in whatever peaceful valleys, beside whatever placid and reassuring streams of old age, in the mirroring faces of whatever children they will contemplate old disasters and newer hopes. It will be there, not fading and not particularly fretful, but of itself alone serene, of itself alone triumphant.[6]

For William Faulkner it's as though this moment is the heart of this heartless community, if it has one, and that its true values lie somewhere between the pontifications of its most vocal and respectable members, the vengeful sense of historical inevitability of its most religiously obsessed, the atavistic hatreds and prurience of its silent majority, finding their truest expression in a culminating act of castration of a shifty outsider, maybe a murderer and white woman raper, which not one of them has the courage to personally carry out. And, somehow, it's this necessary act and this symbolic sacrificial death that has guaranteed the integrity of the community's values and transmitted them towards the future: nigger-lovers may be reluctantly tolerated, but neither they nor any resulting racial impurities will not be suffered to prosper in Jackson, Mississippi.

Raymond Williams' first novel, *Border Country*, is a hymn to the values of his railwayman father and of the community in which he grew up. As economic history lecturer Matthew Price goes home to be at his father's bedside after the latter's heart attack he examines a railway map 'with its familiar network of arteries, held in the shape of Wales, and to the east the line running out and elongating, into England. The shape of Wales: pig-headed Wales you say to remember to draw it. And no returns.'[7] Stubbornness, mapping the ways of a small working-class community, and return journeys are the subject of *Border Country*. Matthew sits beside his father's bed and notices the portraits of his grandparents that hang on his parents' bedroom wall, photographs Williams describes with a loving attention to detail: the women 'in their high black dresses, with the brooches at their throats', the maternal grandfather's 'sharp, dark, inquisitive face… intelligent and cunning from alternative sides of the bargain' and his father's father's eyes 'still with the devil in them, the spurt of feeling and gaiety.'[8] Matthew's sense of solidarity with his family and his sense of the rightness of its ways and values, and also his sense of being its culmination lend great moral authority and seriousness to the opening of the book, but as the action moves away from Matthew at his father's death-bed to a retelling of his parent's arrival in the village and the whole of their subsequent married life, there is an obsessive accumulation of detail—which rooms lead into which in their terraced house, what the pantry was called, every nuance of family speech—which speaks of a lonely rescue operation on memory and identity, of revisited senses of things from childhood that have become attenuated. There's also something rapturously solipsistic about the length at which Williams tells his family story that gradually overpowers his winning sense of loyalty, the attractively faithful Welsh sound of the prose, and the lore and politics of the railwaymen whose voices echo through its pages. Perhaps there is something pig-headed about the Williams who insists so much on the centrality of his family's experience, and even more on his sense of the meaning of that experience, which undermines the novel's ambitions to be a realist text and drags it towards a kind of sentimentalising memoir. Not that the book is without humour, far from it, and it is certainly packed with incident and acute observation, but it lacks the impartiality, the distance, and the ruthlessness a good novel should have. Like most people's stories about their families, it's a bit on the dull side, even the most sympathetic listener might find themselves sneaking a glance at their watch: a shame, because this also suggests that the kind of social and emotional fidelity Williams thinks novels should possess, isn't altogether what makes them run for their historical or present readerships, which as a reader of popular fiction he was in a good position to realise.

Border Country is a meticulously imagined book, with a circular structure that suggests seasonal turning and timeless rhythms: Matthew Price returns to his father's deathbed at the end of this un-novelistic novel and buries him with the community, beginning to let go, as the community itself does, placing this latest death in a collective, agreed past. It is a book of memory and solace: death must be accepted, his father's life must end, but it goes into the weave of memory, and thus stays, and his father's story is subsumed into the ongoing life of the place that has nurtured him. It is both a moving and a slow-moving book, muted, precise, restrained without strongly reaching for, or achieving, strong literary effects; perfect, it is an affirmation of Williams' communitarian politics that hits every nail squarely on the head. He feels it in the deep heart's core: a passionate affirmation of the values of a working-class community he sees overwhelmingly as nurturing and positive. Sentimental? Maybe. It is no *Light in August* but still a powerful, unique novel.

Border Country relates deeply to working-class traditions, where they have been allowed to exist at all, in its sense that it is always having to be begun again, which has also been said of the African-American literary tradition, often finding its truest expression in autobiographical writings in which the writer has the impression of painfully finding a voice and standing at the beginning of something new. For the middle-class cultural critic or novelist the sense of a written tradition is far stronger, and the working-classes are more likely to be examined as an index of what is wrong with society, as evidence of a decline in standards, as an object in social analysis, as a source of anxieties about 'where we are heading' than permitted to speak for themselves, if this is deemed possible at all. Such a genuine working-class recalling subject is relatively rare in the supposed upper echelons of English literature, and its first task is always to explain itself to an all-knowing middle-class expert on its condition. Having said this, these are traditions in English socialism and liberalism that were sympathetic and attempted to contribute to the betterment of the working-classes. If they hadn't existed, would we have all become clever enough to do their jobs and speak for ourselves? This is a question Alan Sillitoe's Arthur Seaton might well have framed, but it is unlikely ever to be properly answered now.

In our wider culture 'realism' is still used as a short-hand for 'telling of reality' and particularly associated with 'telling working-class experience', but the conflation of the two modes—realism has an over-arching world-view in which it places its particular lives and naturalism is concerned mainly with accuracies of surface, whether these are those of upper bourgeois life in crisis in Chekhov or those of the politicised slum-dwellers in Zola—misses something important. Hollywood film is not realist in tendency; it is full of highly symbolic narratives, but is often naturalistic. When at the turn of the last century the American novelist and critic, W.D. Howells, lambasted the sentimentality of popular taste and passionately argued for the socially reforming work of American realists as against 'romanticistic' novelists, he also included the great American allegorists of the nineteenth century out of his conception of the novel, along with Dickens and everyone else who wrote mainly 'for effects' rather than truth to experience. For Howells (and in a way he could remind us of sixties experimental writer B.S. Johnson in this) fiction writers were largely retailers of falsehoods: 'I make truth the prime test of a novel,' he declared. 'If I do not find that it is like life, then it does not exist for me as art; it is ugly, it is ludicrous, it is impossible.'[9]

But it was Howells' own task that proved impossible as the history of 20th century American culture unfolded. Hollywood movies are in general as allegorical as any story by Washington Irving, Nathaniel Hawthorne, Herman Melville, Bret Harte or Mark Twain; but even when this isn't explicitly the case, when films are reaching for a kind of naturalism inherent in a medium based on photography, the symmetries of allegorical melodrama have tended to turn everything into the *Pilgrim's Progress*. Naturalism plus melodrama translated into an early Hollywood in which landlords were always rapacious, priests were invariably hypocrites and the rocky path of love was rocky indeed—so far so good—but was always trodden with ultimate success by lovers who clasped one another under the bower as the last frames shuddered in sympathy and they were seen as if through a closing shutter, an eye closing in blissful satisfaction at the finality of their brief bursting embrace: this is still the ending film audiences will most easily tolerate. Films may have become more morally complex, and Howells may be right that this is in direct proportion to their realism about social conditions, but they are still shaped by the deep strain of sentimental allegory in American fictions.

All this is of relevance to postwar British fiction because for the first time novelists were writing in a context in which, although many thirties writers had been touched by it, American literary and film culture had a very wide currency. Since Raymond Williams last ditch appeals for a realism latter-day proponents of allegory have been in the ascendant; distinctions between 'realism' and 'naturalism' are sometimes lost and realism itself is usually seen by professional critics as an ensemble of codes and conventions—worn out ones at that—as bearers of symbolic representations that should be questioned as figurations of real social experience, largely because of the very persuasiveness of their direct truth claims: the novels of Gillian Freeman, as we will see, are persuasively pellucid, reports from the front lines of domestic class war, although they are not particularly 'authentic'. But need we reject Williams' idea of representation altogether? Can't we somehow simply 'demand' that representations be mandated and criticise them in Howells' light: hold them to account for their supposed truth to experience? Perhaps we do this already: it is part of being a reader and we don't need to have many conceptions or art, realist or otherwise, in order to do it.

Howells, who delivered the essay I have quoted from on the commercial lecture circuit, tells the story of a young woman who praised him for having remembered all the things in his novels, as though he had not invented them, which he admits he had. It might be possible to demand mandated representations from writers of contemporary fiction if they really did represent, or make present, their real spontaneous social experience rather than recycling the definitions of sociology (whether overlaid with Marxist definitions of social class or not), playing to markets for writing and their various controllers and constituencies, and by partaking of the nebulously defined state of cultural play manifesting itself in the agendas and atmospheres nurtured by different governments and the public language of the moment, or simply all the happy recycled approximations of history and national character that float around, half-discredited phrases, in flux beneath all this stuff—'a nation of shopkeepers', 'imperial nostalgia', 'a feudal infrastructure'. Language considered ill-fitting to the new interest groups who must continue to deploy it in order to be heard in our contested consensual cultural polity, which is more likely to be driven by market forces than by the notion that any particular group should be given a fair shake of the stick.

These senses of things are a kind of logos or imaginative pool into which anyone might be expected to try and dip their cup, and may therefore be easily seen as modes in writing only, and in practice they represent places on the back benches of culture for which there is powerful social competition. In other words, it is impossible for writing to be 'democratic', 'representative', or indeed a socially and historically reliable account of anything in our historical moment, and realism's fading claims were therefore always false. Novelists can neither be mandated nor made subject to recall, whether instant or otherwise. 'Tell all the truth but tell it slant,' wrote Emily Dickinson. 'Success in circuit lies.'[10] She seems to know cunning and indirection are essential tools if the truly marginal social experience is to be articulated, and might be heard, even if sometime in the far future. My own approach to these questions stems from a hard-to-shift belief that novels, many novels, do indeed contain such slanted truths and if the worlds and conceptions of those worlds revealed in their scrabbled or artful pages is an inherently partial and hemmed around kind of truth, it still comes through to the right kind of attention however slant the novelist may be trying to tell it. W.D. Howells, in his own novels and his prostelytising for the great Western realist short story writer Hamlin Garland, was indeed a radical writing against the grain of his society.[11]

The category of experience—which names something that is both immediate and typical, close and far away—appeals to 'direct knowledge', but in some very different senses: we might say 'she's an experienced liar' or 'such is the experience of the working-class', and mean in the first case merely that there is a precedent for her lying, and in the second be referring to a certain historical kind of knowledge, yet when we seek 'experiences' it is their immediacy that is imagined as gratifying. 'Experience' has both a supreme cultural authority, that takes precedence over book learning, or other kinds of knowledge, but it is also most insecure and open to question—one is trapped in, or by, ones experience—'that's just your experience, mine's different.' Experience is both particular and ineffable, concrete and hard to pin down; it is the very stuff of life, but it is not in itself seen as valuable. The truths of experience may have been hard won and incontrovertible to those who have acquired them, but they are worth little to those who don't share in the same circumstances or point of view. This authority (and insecurity) is what enables realist novels to be written, often what motivates them, and also what makes them vulnerable to subsequent identification as particular, partial, or wrong in the light of other 'experiences'. We want to know how the other half lives, but having experienced it vicariously are unlikely to surrender much of our own previous sense of things. For in reading from and for 'experience' (as much as in writing from it) we are particularly likely to reproduce unexamined attitudes and assumptions towards characters and their worlds, to read in 'stereotypes' and in attempting to encompass uncharted experience revert to the same timeworn ways of looking at things. It's just the same for the writers of realist fiction, except that they needed far more commitment, as well as an eye to the double-game of satisfying more than one constituency, to see their inventions into print.

When Enoch Powell made his infamous 'Rivers of Blood' speech in response to the introduction of a race relations act outlawing discrimination against immigrants, it was in a context where what was to become 'multiculturalism' was already being mooted by the Labour Party: that immigrants should be accepted not on the condition of total integration into British ways of life, but as an element of cultural diversity. For Williams, writing in a context of British working-class politics, ideas of community and solidarity remained essential; they just needed to be redefined in order to continue to be useful. Once a particular definition of community became dominant, he argued, and any variants were subordinated, then the value he saw in solidarity turned in an opposite direction: 'The whole notion of the common and community is precisely what all this work has been analysing. So, if one says, does the use of this idea create problems… it isn't a matter of defining the problem; this is what the analysis has been about. Certainly, the project is something "common" in that sense, something in the sense of *a shared culture includes diversity*.'[12] But this idea of diversity within commonness is one that will bear a bit of further examination. An opening up of formerly elite definitions of culture was certainly a priority of the British cultural left in the fifties, and in this senses it was a period in which the terms of a new 'diversity' were beginning to be defined. One problem that a notion of 'diversity within commonness' ran into is that such diversity isn't necessarily, and cannot altogether be described in terms of, a freely-associated harmonious plurality and richness, but must—always does, anyway—include conflict, antagonism, mutual exclusion, fierce competition, and an all-important power to define what its parameters should be.

The political sense of the desirability of 'diversity within commonness' that was beginning to emerge in the fifties and was consolidated and extended in the sixties was one that usually wished away conflict, that fudged uncomfortable realities while promising to repair social inequalities and divisions. Most importantly it was—and is—a consensual model: inclusion as an element in diversity is always on the terms of acquiescence to a shared notion of culture in which difference is possible only where ranged around a defining class authority (that's if you get to be included at all): in Britain middle-class mores and values and aspirations were and are the centrally defining ones, and, as Powell pointed out, these were far more sympathetic to new British communities of immigrants than to the native working-class, particularly after Powell's speech. Invoking a threat to white women, with references to 'excreta' being pushed through the letterbox of one of his elderly Wolverhampton constituents and to 'grinning piccaninnies', had stirred up working-class protests in his favour. Even when expressed in far more moderate and reasonable terms, everyday views found amongst the British working-classes, whether socialist or conservative, simply did not fall within the terms of any liberal consensus. Inclusion was always inevitably at the cost of a heavy distortion of what was to be represented, and Williams' discussion of 'representation' makes much of a contrast between the meanings 'to symbolise' and 'to make present' which he finds latent in the word 'representation'. This he traces in controversies about political representation, particularly the claims of representative democracy and the question of whether representatives speak 'in the name of' those they stand for, or are to be merely taken to be 'typical' of them. In either case they stand in the place of the constituents themselves. Williams believes that representatives and representations should be somehow mandated and potentially recallable like Trades Union delegates, shop stewards, the officers of a tenant's association, the kinds of recallable parliaments envisioned by Gerard Winstanley or Thomas Paine, in the Soviet ideal of local and work-place assemblies, or indeed in any other vision of a direct, flexible democracy. He traces a similar history in aesthetic uses of representation, where the meanings of 'symbol' and 'reproduction' are also both in play in a series of historical transactions between Realism and Naturalism. Williams makes this hinge on the contrasting meanings and difference between 'representational' and 'representative' art. The former reproduces surfaces, observed forms; the latter deals in types or 'ideas' or symbols. In both cases, political and aesthetic, there is a cleavage, which is to say both a sharp distinction and a connection, in the word 'representation' between the ideas of a group speaking for themselves and a group spoken for, or pictured in a certain light, whether by politicians or artists.[13] This is no longer a remotely fashionable view of representation; but, half a century later, we are seeing the frightening electoral emergence of a right-wing populist party, isolationist and anti-immigrant, which claims to speak for the misrepresented working-classes.

II

The Good Old Working-class and the Bad New Working-class

Do enough research and you could probably track down a quote from King Harold to the effect that 'ye peasants are not what they were in my young day' shortly before he got it in the eye on Hastings beach. A contrast is often drawn between the communitarian ways and values of an old working-class that is being supplanted by the rapaciousness, anomie and thuggishness of a newly affluent one is a theme in British culture that can easily be traced back to the industrial revolution but probably made its first appearance long before.[14] It's there underlying all forms of golden ageism of left or right: William Morris' vision of unalienated labour in the middle-ages, Edward Thomas' celebration of the elusive 'Lob', Yeats' disdain for the money-obsessed shopkeeping classes as opposed to the story-keeping peasants of yore and his amiable fantasy of turning them all into busy-bees in his personal honey factory, Ezra Pound's denunciations of 'usura' and Vita Sackville-West's hymns to old ways in poems like 'The Land' and 'A Saxon Song'[15] as well as in F.R. Leavis' contrast between an old rural culture of 'experience' supplanted by a degraded commercial culture; his ideal artist, D.H. Lawrence, lauds aristocratic virtues over democratic ones (there are no such things so far as he is concerned) and is more likely to see a peasant-like stolidity in his Nottingham miners—he has too much first-hand experience to idealise them—than to see in them the potential vanguard of a revolutionary working-class. Indeed, his saving grace is that in his poetry he thinks they should repudiate work altogether. When he is not lamenting the dumbing down that further democratisation of cultural life will inevitably bring he hankers after believing in aristocracy for everyone.

But nothing could illustrate the difficulties and paradoxes of D.H. Lawrence's view of the class he had come from, nor why critics of Leavis' stamp could so readily accept a radical working-class writer, better than the chapter in *Women in Love* when one its pairs of lovers, Birkin and Ursula, visit a Nottingham street market, buy a pretty chair they quickly decide they don't want, and attempt to give it away to a young couple who are also browsing. Experiencing the travails of many a would-be philanthropist, Birkin and Ursula find the couple distrustful of this sudden bounty. The young woman wonders why they are giving it away: if it's not good enough for them why should she and her husband-to-be be satisfied with their cast-off? Lawrence describes the couple with fascinated disgust—the woman is blowsy, heavy with child, the man insolent, leering and sexually magnetic: a rangy, slimy little rat. It's clear they have no aesthetic appreciation of the chair, they are unable to see any intrinsic value in it and find Birkin and Ursula's act of spontaneous generosity incomprehensible. But they are attractively unselfconscious, self-defining characters whose autonomy is dented a little by their acceptance of Birkin and Ursula's wedding gift. Lawrence closes the scene with Birkin's doom-laden prognostications on democracy: it is common rats such as these who will inherit the future when people like Ursula and himself, appreciators of high culture, life's natural aristocrats, are forced to hide in chinks and corners and live on society's leavings.[16] This couple walking away with such carelessness, carrying the pretty chair in such a way that Rupert Birkin fears they may destroy or discard it without a thought—are in effect the bad new working-class in waiting. They are the ignorant spawn of the base beds of democracy: great-grandparents to Harry Enfield's Wayne and Waynetta and all the stereotyped media offerings of the chavs of Basildon and Ipswich and Chelmsford.

A strong element of nostalgia—usually combined with disdain for a degraded present—has very often found its way into leftward accounts of the working-classes. Indeed, it seems always to have been there, and may be understood partly by looking at the origins of such thinking, partly by the social complexion of its proponents, and partly by a generally backward looking 'structure of feeling' (to use Williams' term for a popular ideology) that is rightly said to pervade English culture. At the same time there is a rich literature of dealing with the lives of ordinary people, including the great realist novelists of the nineteenth century, the writings of historians like A.L. Morton, Eric Hobsbawm and Edward Thompson, socialist commentators like George Orwell (about whose paralysing effect on the postwar left Amis is astute), and earlier (perennially neglected) working-class novelists like Arthur Morrison, Alexander Baron, James Hanley, Jim Phelan and Jack Common, and left-leaning middle-class low-life writers with connections to bohemian Soho like James Curtis and Patrick Hamilton—all those writers whom Hanley refers to in his essay 'Don Quixote Drowned' as 'a peculiar flight of proletarian duck' which alighted briefly in the thirties: rarely acknowledged predecessors of some of the sixties novelists whom I shall be examining in this study. James Hanley is probably, with Hamilton, the most prolific, ambitious and interesting of the novelists of the thirties; but although these two writers continued to produce fiction during the sixties, their time had gone, to paraphrase Hanley, and a writer like James Curtis, silent since his heyday, articulated more of the glamour and violence associated with the bad new working-class, or the criminal classes, and in his attempt to develop a 'working-class' fiction in a popular fictional form seems closer to some of the sixties writers than most of his contemporaries.

Raymond Williams has a more agile and sympathetic take on modernity than most cultural commentators. Nothing could be more clear-sightedly democratic than his early essays 'Culture is Ordinary' and 'The Idea of a Common Culture', where he declares that working-class people don't want to be middle-class, they simply want what more affluent people have; but some of his immediate followers fell straight into the same old sub-Lawrentian formulas, most strikingly and crudely Richard Hoggart in his influential book *The Uses of Literacy*, where newly affluent working-class consumers are described quite luridly as the bovine masses, 'their faces bloated by cheap confectionary' as they listen to their music with 'the hollow cosmos effect' (early audience shots in *Oh Boy!* and *Top of the Pops*?) and unfavourably compared with the whippet and pigeon fancying denizens of real Northern working-class communities or the female factory hands who had heroically got up at dawn to participate in Shakespeare reading groups before clocking-on for their twelve hour shifts in the mills.[17] It was attitudes like these that Kingsley Amis was pointing to in his 'Angry Young Man' essay about 'Socialism and the Intellectuals'. With no Spain, no Ethiopia and no mass employment of the thirties around which to focus their dissent, many intellectuals turned to the right and those on the left turned nostalgic-romantic and lost touch with the grass-roots of the Labour Party, which was anyway pragmatic and managerial and compromised by its foreign policy in the service of a failing, fading British imperialism:

> Everyone, from Dr Leavis at Cambridge to Mr Priestley in Reynolds News is saying that our values are perishing before the New Barbarism—which used to mean Hitlerism, but now it means the Welfare State and commercial television (...) It was all very well to press for higher working-class wages in the old days, but now that wages have risen the picture is less attractive; why, some of them are actually better off than we are ourselves. We never contemplated *that*. And now the Labour Party have the confounded cheek to press for more equality still. They are out to make everyone the same, you see. Levelling down.[18]

If I were to set up another polarity in accounts of the working-classes in British cultural writings to apply and return to in my readings of postwar fictions, it might be to draw a contrast between the anthropological and the sociological as approaches to working-class life. It might be objected that these often amount to much the same thing. But in general the sociological approach is improving and tends to focus on the impact of modernity and social change on the working-classes; it is functionalist in flavour and directed towards seeing the role of the working-class role within capitalism, whether to make conditions more humane or to make workers more efficient. Mass Observation most famously exemplifies the anthropological approach: the habits and ways of living of the people are documented in a non-critical way, as elements of tribal tradition, as though they were unchanging. Sometimes patronisingly, sometimes not, they are accorded a certain value in themselves, much as the coming of age rituals of the Samoans or the tribal customs of what were collectively known as 'Bantu' peoples by field-working anthropologists. Sociology tends to be urban, anthropology rural. Sociology attempts to reform and is concerned with adaptation; anthropology is looking for the old ways, the untouched past, and is interested in preservation. Anthropology has a universalising tendency with its generalisations about the primitive mind and its discovery of trans-cultural linguistic and narrative patterns as in the work of Claude Lévi-Strauss. Sociology is generally concerned with the workings of particular societies at particular moments, in particular times of cathartic development such as those that gave birth to it. Auguste Compte's early 19th century Positivism is usually taken as modern sociology's main starting point, but as the social sciences developed a contest of theories of society became its main preoccupation as an academic discipline. Karl Marx versus Max Weber, post-modern Economies of Signs and Space versus 'third way' sociologist Anthony Giddens' (influential on New Labour) ideas about the re-embedding of traditional practices within a compelling modernity.[19]

Michael Young and Peter Willmott's *Family and Kinship in East London* (1957) is a classic sociological study of an urban working-class community, that of Bethnal Green, poised between old and new ways of living. On the one hand everyone knows one another, kinship ties are close and supportive; more negatively girls passing the 11-plus and going to grammar school are regarded by their contemporaries as outsiders, traitors, stuck up, and are painfully ostracised. A passionate plea is being made on behalf of the traditional values of a three-generation community of 'turnings' and 'back-doubles'[20] but the process of moving out into new high rise housing and council estates in Essex is an unstoppable one. However immutable the ways of life of the working-class East End might seem, they are coming to an end, and for some members of the younger generation the dispersal of traditional values this entails might not be altogether a bad thing. It's fantastically useful, if you are a young working mother, to have your old mum on hand to mind the kids. On the other hand her ways of nurturing might be shockingly harsh and inappropriate to the modern world, as might be many of the values she tries to pass on—like many younger generations, and like their contemporaries in the middle-class, young adults coming of age in the late fifties East End may well have felt that the past was better forgotten.

We might be tempted to ask of novelists who write on the working-class whether they are sociologists or anthropologists, but it is a distinction that tends to break down since so many are a little of both and neither. Dickens for example would be an anthropologist in the way he so lovingly documents the speech and manners of his working-class characters; their patterns of life and basic character is as unchanging and unchangeable as the repeated tics of speech and thought by which they announce themselves. But in his unmatched reforming zeal, as a crusader, and as he records the impact of city life on them he is a radical sociologist. Raymond Williams finds something unique to modern city life in the flaring vividness of Dickens' character sketches, his urban types. Italian critic Franco Moretti finds Dickens' outlook to be an underlyingly feudal one in which a person's social place is taken to be utterly fixed unless, like Pip in *Great Expectations*, you are lucky enough to have a mysterious benefactor, an escaping convict you once tried to help, to buy you a place in the legal profession: unless, that is, you are the beneficiary of the sort of miracle without which the action of such novels of vertiginous upward mobility can't begin in nineteenth century England. Moretti contrasts *Great Expectations* with Stendhal's *Le Rouge et le noir*, whose upwardly mobile Julien Sorel rises purely by ability and cunning. But who can say who is the social realist and who is the mythmaker: England's revered purveyor of fantastic coincidences or the European believer in a possible way up in the world for a young man of peasant stock with abilities?[21] Sorel has only to look up from the gutter to be offered two professions; Pip is lucky, but he has to prove his own worth by the end of the novel, in order to win Estella, who would never have married him if she had been who she thought she was and not the daughter of Abel Magwitch: both their illusions and their expectations are the helpful sport of an escaped convict, his lawyer and a mad rich old snobbish woman, all of whom know the ways of the world, and they find out their true destiny despite the latter's dusty charades, which burn and blow away in the sunny breeze of fulfilled love in the novel's final pages, when Pip finally has the authority to rescue her from the mantle of crispy Miss Haversham. By this act Pip inherits Magwitch's wealth after all; but does he tell her about her real living mother, the murderess who is Jaggers' servant? We are never told.

But the kind of magical coincidence out of which romances are made isn't unique to the English popular novel, nor did it die out in the nineteenth century. Near the beginning of Faulkner's *The Wild Palms*, a book which is composed of a pair of intertwining novellas of Southern high and low life, there is a celebrated incident where the impoverished law student protagonist suddenly, miraculously finds a wallet full of money in a sidewalk trash can. This fortuitous event occurs a few moments after the restless artistic wife of a wealthy New Orleans businessman has expressed her interest in him: it is an implausible moment of contingency about which sensible readers of Faulkner have bitterly complained, but it is not without a certain instructive value about the underwhelming likelihood of romance without finance. It's a nuisance, as Slim Gaillard sang, but it just don't make sense.[22] And social novels don't necessarily make that much sense either, at least not that which is most loudly claimed for them in the never had it so good white heat of their moment.

Fifties British fiction is often about social mobility and, along with its sixties development, it is often also about what I have called 'the bad new working-class', but it seldom asks why they were like that, and what (if anything) is to be done about this. It is, by and large, content to record and sympathize on various terms and tends to justify and even to celebrate what might be seen as anti-social attitudes. Nell Dunn makes rebellious young working-class women into heroines of matriarchy and Lynn Reid Banks celebrates a new female consciousness. Other writers, John Berger and Raymond Williams for example, suggest some sort of remaking of collective traditions is needed—a communitarian movement towards socialism, or other connections with what is seen as a wider historical movement. Social mobility itself is most often explored in a negative way, while writers whose terms of reference are rooted in a working-class 'as it is' celebrate work dodging and fantasy in a humorous vein. This is true both of Samuel Selvon—although his is a different 'new working-class' of West Indian immigrants—and Essex's Jack Trevor Story. Story and Lancashire's Bill Naughton both create 'new' roguish folk heroes. Another kind of writer taking bearings from the period of Colin Wilson's *The Outsider* and the Angry Young Men, psychoanalyses them as artist-heroes, as versions of himself. In different ways this is true of B.S. Johnson, Alexander Trocchi, and Paul Ableman, whose first novel, *I Hear Voices*, creatively explores the world of the schizophrenic. The outsider—who is not seen to enjoy a 'jaunty hardness' although he is often a failure—is still quite likely to be celebrated in these books as someone who is kicking against the pricks or bucking his or her allotted place in society; but there are always, as Samuel Beckett said, more pricks than kicks, and in real life it tends to be the pricks who do the kicking.

British social realism has certainly had a hard time critically in the past few decades. Claims to show 'real life', to 'tell it like it is', or was, have been gleefully demolished, deconstructed by cultural theorists, gleefully revealed as ideologically driven 'representations', discursive constructs, saying the opposite of what might be supposed, failing to address a wider world in which they are enmeshed and victimising those it would seek to celebrate. Its legacy, in the nineteen eighties, turned into what were characterised as a series of increasingly dreary and repetitive indictments of 'Thatcher's Britain', as aesthetically conservative and politically played out as market forces and the concomitant politics of consumption and desire were dynamic and forward looking. A political and aesthetic style that reminded fashionable Londoners uncomfortably of what was happening elsewhere (since our sense of the working-class North, and of Northerners as automatically 'working-class' derived in large part from films about it); on the plus side the black-and-white early sixties were recycled as poetic miserablist bedsit style by The Smiths, and more negatively were parodied as 'it's rough up north' by Harry Enfield, and it seemed for a while that the people, ways of life, 'structures of feeling' that such films alluded to could never again be referred to without irony, without quotation marks, without, finally, succumbing to an omnipresent anxiety about identifying with the losers in these struggles.

On a political level I want to argue that late fifties and early sixties British fictions such as Sillitoe's *Saturday Night and Sunday Morning* and *The Loneliness of the Long Distance Runner*, Lynne Reid Banks' *The*

L-Shaped Room and Nell Dunn's *Up the Junction* and *Poor Cow*, were in themselves the beginnings of a politics of representations that continues to dominate both our academic and especially our mainstream media culture, and that, by analysing how specifically this is the case, we can reveal much about the current state of play in the circulation of such cultural meanings: culture's claims to be multi-vocal, to represent 'us' in our diversity may fall apart more easily if we look at their clumsy beginnings. The study of the sixties is important because paradigms established then still inform British cultural life. On one hand there is a legacy of sixties political movements, their commentators and theorists, and the influence they have exerted on the liberal intelligentsia, on the other the negativised, demonised sixties of the right: its woolly liberalism, social experimentation, looney leftism, false egalitarianism, the social consequences of the sexual revolution, the rise of welfarism and 'the dependency culture'. These two versions of the sixties mirror one another, are recognisable in one another. In addition, there is the by now perennial status of the sixties as revolutionary golden age in the eyes of the young as well as some people who were actually there. This started, arguably, in about 1969 or 1970, about the time that John Lennon crooned wistfully that 'the dream is over'; but the sixties was and has remained an indefatigably self-mythologising period, the first to refer to itself, typically, as 'the sixties', the first 'post-modern' period, or 'period': the moment when 'periodisation'—the construction and enforcement of time periods in terms of style decades emerged to an obsessive degree ('the twenties', 'the thirties', 'the seventies', 'the eighties') in the making of modern mass 'history', although it is equally arguable that nothing much was invented in the sixties unless it was an attempt to escape from the exigencies of social being and mundane time-consciousness by chemical means.

For many such interest groups (or 'interpretive communities' as Benedict Anderson has called them[23]) the sixties is a mythical point-of-origin for what they love or hate. The sixties as we know them politically is their collective invention, albeit a continually contested one. But what was invented in that decade? What is contested? And is it all a myth? I will argue that one of the crucial inventions of the sixties, emerging from the social agendas of the left in the fifties, was a politics of representations, and a genuine attempt to map new social territories in new ways, and that this is why it is our most contested and obsessively rewritten decade. The structuralist-influenced Marxism of the 1970s produced a critique of what had become known as the 'Culture and Society' tradition based on enthusiastic importations from European Marxist thinkers, but whatever its overall intellectual validity constituted in effect a withdrawal from the radical cultural interventionist tendency of Williams to a more purely institutional focus, and it was there, in universities, in the space that Williams had helped to open up, that it survived until its thinkers and political agendas were first marginalised and then swept away by the Thatcher decade. The nineties and the early twenty-first century have seen the beginnings of some refiguration of accounts of British history and literature in terms of postmodern critical vocabularies, and all but a few specialists have forgotten Raymond Williams, a seemingly moderate figure whose ideas still carry a radical charge after five decades. But now might also be a good time to re-evaluate Williams' work, re-examine its project of social equity and to ask if his approach still has anything to say to us in the early twenty-first century.

In British society there are ways of life that involved and continue to involve millions of people yet which remain relatively marginal in our culture, appearing only in novels of the fifties and sixties working-class fashion moment and a number of haunting films of the same period, then popping out of existence forever, or at least until the next retrospective. The moment they appeared in remains an important one, and could be presented as a lost golden age, because of the sympathy, dignity and centrality working-class people were accorded in these fictions. These films and to a lesser extent novels are remembered with such affection because in them working-class experience was accorded an importance that it always had and of course still does for people who are actually living it, although whether or not many of us wish to consume representations of ourselves in leisure hours is a moot point, especially now that we can all be authors of self-produced self representations.

Many of the books I will discuss have an intimate connection with the films and television of their era; a large number of them were filmed, many were made to be filmed—that was their authors' hope—and in this sense they are very much part of the film moment of the British fifties and sixties. Bill Naughton's short story, 'Late Night on Watling Street', for example, could easily have been made into a two-fisted trucker (or lorry-driver) film like *Hell Drivers*, which starred Stanley Baker, perhaps the ultimate intimidating working-class actor of the period. Unfortunately, it's not quite two-fisted enough. But this book isn't about British films, or plays, or TV, or songs, or poetry—it is primarily a book about novels and short stories, because I believe it is in these that counter-stories, counter-myths are told, and here that the true preoccupations of the period appear most freely—more can be tucked between the pages of a cheap paperback than the committees who decide what will be a commercial film, or is good enough for the nation to be nationally broadcast, will ever countenance, and in novels the rough edges haven't yet been rounded off experience. Not many of the books I will discuss are mainstream novels by the most critically respected writers of the period. Some are written in a realist vein, or in a mode I call poetic naturalism; others counter the claims of realism to tell satisfying truths or produce satisfying modern art, go back to modernism, import from the European novel, attempt to invent new forms of their own—or create new forms of speculative fiction by employing and transforming popular fictional forms: science fiction and swords and sorcery.

Chapter One

Scary Monsters and Super Creeps: Alan Sillitoe and the Angry Young Men

'Angry Young Men' is an appellation often disparaged, and often repudiated by those to whom it was applied, and those so-labelled have in turn been dismissed by many others as an invention of journalism, as a group of apostates or class imposters remote from the social group they supposedly represented, as well as for being miserablists and aesthetic conservatives. Nevertheless, they had a giant impact on postwar English writing. They emerged in the early fifties with a supposed left-wing agenda and a claim to be sweeping away the cant of middle-class English society. They were soon to become a new establishment of their own—and were roundly despised for it by many sixties upstarts. Less glamorous than the Beats and offering little in the way of spiritual upliftings, adventurous sight-seeing or revolutionary hopes, they nevertheless had a giant impact on the flavour of English fiction and poetry in the decade that followed and in which, of course, they were still active as the bad guys. They opened the way for a wave of writers on working-class subjects, for women writers, and, more reactively, for a wave of poets who took their bearings from American modernism, and for a group of innovative, serious minded SF writers who found them limited and parochial, and a few experimental novelists and poets who felt the much same way about their obsession with class. These negative views of the Angry Young Men are not without validity and should not be too lightly dismissed.

Read at a historical distance they are mostly good writers—particularly in the writings by which they were first defined. The name was taken from Leslie Paul's *Angry Young Man* (1951), a book about left-wing youth in the thirties; but the main figures have usually been taken to be Kingsley Amis, John Braine, John Osborne, John Wain, Colin Wilson, autobiographer George Scott—and a few others, including theatre and later film director Lindsay Anderson, novelist David Storey, as well as the poets known as 'The Movement'. Many of the novelists in this study began writing in a context supplied by the Angries. One of these was Alan Sillitoe, a Nottinghamshire writer who had left school at fourteen to do factory work, and who began publishing towards the end of the fifties.

An indication of how fine a writer is Alan Sillitoe may be seen in how little plot he needed to contrive in order make Arthur Seaton's perambulations around a few Nottingham pubs and a few willing women into a novel that bursts with dramatic intensity and world historical sweep. The rangy, anarchic young lathe operator and anti-hero of *Saturday Night and Sunday Morning* constructs a compelling world-view out of what he gleans from the daily paper, conversations with his workmates and jeering competitions with the TV in his mother's house, a bedroom of which, like many young men, he occupies, touches down in, but never finally vacates in favour of a married life into which he is being coerced. Asked what he knows about any given subject he replies shortly: 'Only what I read in the papers.' Arthur takes in the papers very well and sees them for the ill-woven skeins of half-truth, fantasy and downright lies they really are. He reads with a kind of gleeful absolute authority. His sense of the fun of spontaneous ridicule and keen eye for a conspiracy is utterly convincing and it is in the theatre of his restless intelligence that his town and predicament spring to life. This novel and its impact (and that of the film in which Arthur was played with swaggering conviction by Albert Finney) created the context in which many a working-class novel of the sixties appeared and it is better than most of them.

Late in the book Arthur decides to wind up his pint-cadging uncle by offering him tips on a few horses that have been mysteriously passed to him by an authoritative source: 'Lord Earwig rang me up today from Aintree.' Uncle George has been having thoughts on a coming nuclear war— 'A bloke told me in the market that he's read in the paper as a war was goin' ter start in three months time'—containing an unspoken hope that he might clean up with produce from his allotment if rationing comes in again, as he did in the last lot. But it is Arthur who really knows about such things as the effects of radiation, from 'a talk on the wireless', and he is soon spinning a few horror stories about its long-term effects according to 'This bit I'd read in the paper as well, by a doctor who's bin six months testin' lettuces from the places that have bin atom bombed.'[1]

Saturday Night and Sunday Morning sits squarely on the shoulders of D.H. Lawrence's *Sons and Lovers*: Nottingham setting and dialect; a sensory descriptive poetry and immediacy in presentation of characters; protagonist's allergy to marriage and his questioning attitude to the world into which he has been born—not to mention his tempestuous involvement with a married woman. But here the two books diverge. Paul Morel is priggishly moralistic and a bit of a snob; Arthur Seaton is the opposite; Paul is articulate, highly educable and clearly on the way up. Arthur may be intelligent but accepts his place in the working-class as a lathe operator. *Sons and Lovers* essentially tells the story of Lawrence's early life, intensely revisited following his mother's death. Sillitoe's decision to make his central character one of those who stayed rather than one who travelled far away distinguishes his novel from Lawrence's and enables him to be more than an imitator, to draw heavily on Lawrence yet to quickly step from his shadow and address a new and contemporary working-class experience. He places the insolent young male whom Lawrence describes in passing in *Women in Love* at centre stage. Yet both are meditative, retrospective books as well as *bildungsromans*. Sillitoe's novel was written over a seven year period, distilled out of many drafts and writings; Lawrence's composed rapidly and reshaped in progress, a capability that accounts for much of the unfolding flow and ride of his novels. Sillitoe's method results in his book's density, focus, an epic quality and a sense of many voices that frames and displays Arthur's overbearing manner and helps to make it more palatable to the reader.

Arthur is full of bravado and big lies, exhibiting most common tics and tropes of working-class male personality and attitude—he is a distillate who smells like a distillery, a careful mockery of a particular (and particularly charming) animalistic braggart Sillitoe had once known, constructed out of his memories of a man who was in real life, Sillitoe has said, 'a plank'. We first meet him at the tail end of a Friday night drinking contest: 'Arthur didn't like being called "matey", It put his back up straight away'; follow him back to his married girlfriend Brenda's place and wake up with them as her children clamour to play with the 'Uncle Arthur' they love more than their dad. He is a champion in every respect, but we are not, as with later versions of this avatar of working-class manhood, invited to laugh at him. Far from it. We are kept wary of Arthur. He might just lash out at us from the page. His derogatory opinions of everyone and everything, from Jack, Brenda's husband ('the nit-witted, dilatr'y, unlucky bastard'), to the war ('a marvellous thing in many ways, when you thought about how happy it had made many people in England.') and television ('It can't be good for yer. You'll go blind one day. You're bound to.') are offered to be treated with the utmost seriousness by armchair diagnosticians of the state of the working-class. Sillitoe may well be laughing at him, but we are not allowed to crack a smile, unless of solidarity with this paradigmatic paragon of the essence of the new worker: a Stakhanovite with plenty of stamina but few social niceties, let alone social commitments to anything. Yes, he has raised productivity; no, he has not been awarded a medal for it, only a bonus, which is always going to go straight down his throat; that's when he isn't forcing his opinions down yours.

'Liars don't prosper,' says Brenda. Arthur knows better. They have prospered so far, why shouldn't this continue? Anyway, his talk is 'for nothing, taking words out of the air for sport, ready to play with the consequences of whatever he may cause.' It is this gratuitousness of Arthur's that quickens our sympathy. He is arrogant, brave in a way, and we want to see him deal with the consequences of his word-play. We want to hear more of it, because in speaking to provoke (and he has noticed that only extreme statements are likely to elicit a response) he will be targeting, honing in on and trampling down shibboleths in such a way as to reveal the nature of the community he is part of and at the same time address a wider set of moral, political and social attitudes. Arthur's lies reveal his contempt for his listeners but are the means by which he addresses a larger world, a world he is of course naïve about, and sees it composed of just such fantastic digressions as his own. His teasing of his father's TV watching leads to this:

> Anyway, I know somebody who knows this kid as went blind, so the papers was right for a change. They said they saw this kid bein' led to the Eye Infirmary by 'is mam. It was a rotten shame, they said. A kid of seven. She led 'im along wi' a lead, and the kid had a stick specially made for him painted white. I heard they was getting him a dog as well to help him along, a wire-haired terrier. There was talk o' standin' him outside the Council House for the rest of his life wi' a tin mug if he don't get better. His dad's got cancer, an 'is mam can't afford ter keep him in white sticks an' dogs.[2]

Arthur has 'allus bin a liar' just as his eyesight has 'allus bin good, and allus will be.' He is as self-congratulatory about his clear-sightedness as about everything else, and that is our guarantee of his strength and purity. As we follow him into work on Monday morning we discover the world where his confidence in his own judgements has been forged, and we soon see his mastery of it, as well as the sources of the explosive cocktail of personal anarchism, 'communist' attitudes and plain selfishness that go to make up his view of the world and his place in it. The rhythms of the factory and of lathe work are there to be managed by Arthur as surely as the foreman, Robboe, and the hated rate-checker who sometimes stands at his shoulder try to manage him. Just as he calibrates his lathe he must measure his rate of work—not too fast and not too slow—for although Arthur is the quickest and most accurate of workers, and has on occasion produced four hundred pieces in an hour in the race to finish on Friday afternoon, such a rate produced regularly would soon result in his own hourly rate being reduced. Thus, in his head, Arthur imagines he is forcing the factory to run at a pace dictated by himself. As a frightened fifteen year old he had been in awe of the overhead belts and pulleys and the complex interlinkage of machines; now he stands casually at the centre of the levers that move the world like the universal worker in Diego Rivera's famous mural of the thirties, and just as his accuracy and speed of judgement is crucial to his success as a worker and his sense of self-worth, so his judgements of people in the factory—'a world of enmity that demanded a certain amount of trust'—are emotionally-based and intuitive but grounded in an engineer's model:

> Arthur did not assess men on their knowledge and achievement, but by a blind and passionate method that weighed their more basic worth. It was an emotional gauge, always accurate when set by him, and those to whom it applied either passed or did not pass the test. Within the limits of its narrow definitions he used it as a reliable guide as to who was and wasn't his friend and up to what point he could trust a person who might become his friend.[3]

Arthur himself is of course not to be trusted at all, but part of his calculation must always be to what extent he must appear to be a good bloke, or at least a harmless one. Sillitoe's method for defining is one of definition and cross-definition: to show how he fits into a world of precise measurements that is the measure of him by means of a calculation of measure or worth that is his own. His abilities in this respect, and the casual rapidity with which he applies his moment to moment judgements are the principal means by which Sillitoe shows us Arthur's intelligence and his limitations. His technique for placing Arthur in his world and outside is free indirect style: a form of third person narration, defined by Hugh Kenner in his study of *Joyce's Voices,* whereby we move seamlessly in and out of a character to see how the objects and relationships that define him or her are registered in consciousness. In other words, Sillitoe's method in this book owes as much to James Joyce as to D.H. Lawrence, albeit that his techniques are applied in a way that is more explicit, immediate and suitable to the presentation of character and action in a popular novel. Sillitoe recycles what Joseph Conrad and Ford Maddox Ford learned about *progression d'effet* in the novel when they were working on their turn of the century collaborations and trying to import the techniques of Flaubert into the English novel—his early version of the novel of working-class life incorporates a kind of hybrid, popularised modernism.[4] Molly Bloom's soliloquy or Gertie MacDowell's unreflective reflections, Joyce's deployment of magazine articles and advertisements to define their inner worlds, are very much grist to Sillitoe's mill as a novelist and a means of lending weight to characters who could only otherwise be defined by an overarching narrative voice that would diminish our sense of them as autonomous beings. Arthur's stream of consciousness fantasy is consciously arrived at by himself though, partly suggested by a corporal he met in the army who remarked, in a Joycean kind of way, that it was funny what you thought about while sitting on the toilet. For the factory worker these techniques are a means of making oneself absent during periods of repetitive work on the production line and this continual interplay of absence and presence is something that defines Arthur Seaton's consciousness:

> You began the day by cutting and drilling steel cylinders with care, but gradually your actions became automatic and you forgot all about the machine and the quick working of your arms and hands and the fact that you were cutting and boring and rough-threading to within limits of only five-thousandths of an inch… It was marvellous the things you remembered while you worked on the lathe, things that you thought were forgotten and would never come back into your mind, often things you hoped would stay forgotten. Time flew while you wore out the oil-soaked floor and worked furiously without knowing it: you lived in a compatible world of pictures that passed through your mind like a magic-lantern, often in vivid and glorious loonycolour, a world where memory and imagination ran free and did acrobatic tricks with your past and with what might be your future, an amok that produced all sorts of agreeable visions.[5]

Arthur's vision, and he definitely has one, is one of a kind of vertical transcendence in which he is both in his place in this world and floats high above it. Not a social transcendence by means of finding his way up in the world—that is impossible for him—nor a political transcendence through collective identity and joining the cause of common betterment (much as he enjoys the rhetoric of the soap-box reds at the factory gate), but a physical transcendence through his sexual love with Brenda. His drinking and his working life are only periods when he is marking time, distractions from this core, which is the defining purpose of his being and a higher reality than any other he knows. He would gladly blow up the factory if offered dynamite and a plunger, not for any political purpose but because 'that'd be something worth doing. Action.' In this he is a kind of proto-punk, an inspirer of John Lydon as well as John Lennon, a soap-box nihilist who doesn't like soap boxes and couldn't care less if the world blew up tomorrow. His overarching conviction is of his own immortality and power: and yet it is not personal survival that he is thinking of but the endurance to the end of time of people like himself and his Molly Bloom whose thoughts and acts would flow on in a great river to the end of time:

> The factory did not matter. The factory could go on working until it blew itself up from too much speed, but I, he thought, already a couple of dozen above his daily stint, will be here after the factory's gone, and so will Brenda and all the women like her still be here, the sort of women who are worth their weight in gold.[6]

Is Arthur Seaton a potential Nietszchean superman driven by the will to power, or a follower of anarchist Max Stirner, author of *The Ego and Its Own*?[7] In early interviews Sillitoe was often described, and self-described, as a pipe-smoking anarchist, a pose more agreeable to the English press than what he became later, a Communist sympathiser of the Soviet Union. At the time of writing 80 years old, Alan Sillitoe was last pictured holding a pipe in his hand as though it were an Edwardian railway clerk's pen: my grandfather Leslie Fenton's pen. I still love the pride with which he holds it, as a sixteen year old at his desk, in his railway uniform. Arthur is none of these things, we object, in real life, although manual workers are often said to be a bit anarchic and a bit fascistic, but his creator has served him up to us with measures of both, a cocktail shaken not stirred, with his own self-definition: 'Whatever you say I am, that's what I'm not.' He is certainly not quite the raw slice of life as which he is presented in the filmed version of *Saturday Night and Sunday Morning*. Sillitoe's lends him an explanatory conceptual framework that reveals his own literary and philosophical underpinnings and thus gives a coherent voice to working-class alienation as well as creating something beautiful out of physical arrogance. But like all such fabrications of petit-bourgeois intellectuals, Arthur is a paper tiger. *The Loneliness of the Long Distance Runner* is the longest short story in Sillitoe's second book, and like the book that preceded it, was quickly made into a film, this time starring Tom Courtney. It is another story about the refusal of authority, and soon became another famous piece of writing that was once seen to define working-class rebellion. A young borstal inmate deported to Essex from Nottingham for his part in a robbery, decides to lighten his time inside by getting into long distance running and proves good enough at it to get into the governor's good books. He is the great hope and champion of the Borstal in their annual cross-country competition with a nearby public school. Sillitoe cuts between daily life and the runs themselves, in which Smith, like Arthur Seaton at his lathe, dreams and plots and remembers. The life he remembers is one of carefree teenage rebellion, the joys of unpunished guilt-free crime. He elaborates an outlook very similar to Arthur Seaton's, but in a language nowhere near as richly regional, and in a structure neither as inventive not as convincing as that of *Saturday Night and Sunday Morning*. Smith seems more of a character invented to exemplify a certain set of attitudes; his more rebellious acts bear out the half-truths of sociology in studies like Paul Willis' *Learning to Labour*[8] which argues that working-class rebellion often takes forms that are self-defeating if social mobility is one's aim: if not they are self-protective and will reinforce a sense of pride and independence.

Smith is an articulate and self-conscious class-warrior in a way that is emotionally powerful in the film, but fails to quite convince in the story:

> You see, by sending me to Borstal, they're shown me the knife, and from now on I know something I didn't know before: that it's war between me and them. I always knew this, naturally, because I was in remand homes as well, and the boys there told me a lot about their brothers in Borstal, but it was only touch and go then, like kittens, like boxing-gloves, like dobbie.[9]

As is well known, the long distance runner defies authority by winning the race by refusing to cross the finishing line, a symbolic act of defiance that enables him to eat the cake of victory rather than the humble pie of compromise. Sillitoe's handling of authority in the Borstal and the attitude to it of this particular young prisoner is interesting to compare with that expressed in Brendan Behan's autobiography *Borstal Boy*, a contemporary hit which may have helped to make youth offenders a subject worth considering for fiction. Behan was a famous writer and television personality in the fifties and many aspects of his personality and the way he incarnated and enacted a kind of working-class rebellious hero in the media—and his popularity for doing this—will certainly have influenced British writers of the period. Behan, imprisoned for his IRA activities (planting a bomb in a pillar box) fared well during his time in Borstal, similarly excelling at sport and impressing governor and screws with his intellectual prowess. He seems to have been greatly liked by everyone and developed as a writer under the tutelage of some unlikely representatives of the state he was dedicated to overthrowing.[10] Behan is winning, and a winner, in that he sticks to his guns and apparently adapts to the authorities without really losing face. It's almost certain that Sillitoe read *Borstal Boy* and it's possible that *The Loneliness of the Long Distance Runner* was written to cash in on Behan's success, as a kind of response to it and also a riposte to Behan's sunny view of prison, although Smith has also done what he could to make himself comfortable and says he has 'no complaints'. The main difference between them is the overwhelming negativity of Sillitoe's depiction of the prison authorities and of the reaction of his young hero to their efforts to help him when compared to Behan's realistic approach to his situation; surprisingly since he was a political prisoner of a state he had sworn to destroy. Alan Sillitoe's long-distance runner has inherited his personal bloody mindedness from his father, who died refusing medication and chased the doctors out of the house, and upon his release Smith defiantly returns to crime, writing his story in order to have a last laugh on the governor.

Joe Lampton is a working-class archetype as potent as Arthur Seaton and this ruthless social climber was cloned as many times in the fiction of the sixties. He is most easily understood as a more intelligent Seaton with greater social reach, just as ruthlessly self-seeking but with more far more cards to play. His predicament is that of the rest of the anti-heroes of the loose group of writers quickly dubbed 'The Angry Young Men'. The desirability and dire consequences of bedding the boss' wife or daughter go back in popular art to the fourteenth century or earlier where they are explored in such songs as Matty Groves or the Raggle-Taggle Gypsies. John Braine's *Room at the Top* is a novel built around the revolutionary proposition that, in the modern world, such liaisons can lead to social advancement rather than summary execution. John Lennon was probably a fan of anything in story or song that suggested we could prove we were just as good as our masters by bedding their women and taking their place. The trouble is, even if the lady is willing, her father is liable to scotch such a plan; and even worse if she happens to be the property of the King of England, as in Sir Thomas Wyatt's poems relating to his alleged affair with Anne Boleyn, in which he is a proto-hypergamist, giving fair warning to all those who would follow in his faltering footsteps:

> Whoso list to hunt, I know where is an hind,
> But as for me, helas, I may no more.
> The vain travail hath wearied me so sore,
> I am of them that farthest come behind.
> Yet may I by no means my wearied mind
> Draw from the Deer, but as she fleeth afore
> Fainting I follow. I leave off therefore,
> Since in a net I seek to hold the wind.
> Who list her hunt (I put him out of doubt)
> As well as I may spend his time in vain.
> And graven with diamonds in letter plain
> There is written her fair neck round about:
> 'Noli me Tangere, for Caesar's I am,
> And wild for to hold, though I seem tame.'[11]

Whilst there is a certain amount of female flightiness in mid-century British novels exploring working-class romance, it was still far more likely to be the man who was the sinner in this respect and the woman ruined: as in an equally strong and deep tradition of folk-song stretching from 'Mary Hamilton' and 'The House Carpenter' to songs recorded by the Carter Family, like 'Wildwood Flower' and 'Little Darling Pal of Mine'. This might suggest that the novel lagged way behind the libidinous popular song of the day and tended instead to hark back to the social relationships and traditional values implicit in old folk-songs, where the minx-like behaviour of upper-class women invariably led to sudden death for men bold enough to take advantage of it.

O well I like your feather bed
And well I like your sheets
But better I like your lady gay
Who lies in my arms asleep [12]

But is Joe Lampton usefully compared to Matty Groves? In a contemporary piece combining supposedly objective social analysis and good old fashioned snottiness, called 'The Perils of Hypergamy'[13] and published in the *New Statesman*, anthropologist Geoffrey Gorer makes upward marriage the main theme of the Angry Young Men, citing John Wain's *Hurry On Down*, Kingsley Amis' *Lucky Jim*, John Osborne's *Look Back in Anger* and John Braine's *Room At the Top* as examples of what might easily go amiss in marriages that crossed the English class barrier. He offers a wealth of illustration from sociology and literature that female hypergamy has always been relatively commonplace and that women have often raised their social status by marrying upwards, but says that the male equivalent, if not entirely unknown (he cites the writings of D.H. Lawrence as an exception) is more likely to result in the woman being declassed—a teacher becomes a miner's wife—than in the man being raised above his social station: a miner doesn't often become a teacher. Access to higher education by men of working-class origin both threatened this status quo and was likely to result in abused women, as these works illustrated. Whereas the permeable barrier of class was previously penetrable over a couple of generations, the 1944 education act meant that some working-class men had leapt up several rungs in one go. The problem was that working-class men expected their women to be drudges. Not only did they have more traditional expectations of marriage, their early years left them with a radically different emotional make-up: they were needy, belligerent and insecure—and likely to take this out on wives of a higher social class. Gorer advises nice middle-class girls to steer well clear of them, and socially mobile working-class men to find brides amongst similarly mobile women, or alternatively, to try foreigners. This last suggestion seems to give the game away: either foreigners don't have the English feudal attitude to class, or Geoffrey Gorer didn't really care what happened to the aspiring socially mobile working-classes.

This is, to be fair, an important theme with the Angries, and we can't help but wonder (although *Look Back in Anger* is still a powerful play, *Hurry on Down* an emotionally truthful novel and *Lucky Jim* a funny one) if their sudden ascendancy wasn't the crassest possible take on social mobility and egalitarianism: one that unhelpfully spoke to middle-class anxieties and working-class fantasies rather than to any pressing social reality. For most working-class people who went to university in this and succeeding generations the social gains were more moderate: you were more likely to find yourself qualified as a school teacher or clerical worker than leap straight into the horse-riding set. *Hurry on Down*'s Charles Lumley has left university with a mediocre history degree. He has failed to take full advantage of his golden opportunity to rise in the world, and soon finds himself judged harshly both by his own parents and by those of the woman he has been hoping to marry. Unable to make plans for the future or to fit in anywhere, he does have a considerable facility with fantasy, telling his landlady that he is a private detective investigating the Jehovah's Witnesses and wondering if he can get a job working the 'totalisator' at a dog track. Returning to his hometown in defeat he has the ill-fortune to meet the parents of a more successful fellow working-class student on the train, a young man he regarded as a creep:

> 'I s'pose you've heard all about George's success,' said Mr Hutchins; his voice was bright and confident, but with a curious undertone of bewilderment and pathos. 'He's got a Fellowship,' he added, using the strange word in inverted commas, grafting it like some strange twig onto the stunted trunk of his artisan's vocabulary.[14]

But Charles himself has a curious way of talking: a clipped, stripped down muttered speech ('Mind if come in perhaps cup of tea? Or when Sheila be back wanted to see her if I could?') which expresses his social unease and an apparent desire for invisibility as well as conveying a certain contempt for his listeners, compounding their disapproval of him. When he arrives in his hometown his girlfriend's parents invite him in frostily and berate him for his ingratitude to those who have helped him and also towards his parents, with whom he has broken off contact following his shameful failures. He reflects bitterly that he will never fit in to the middle-class world of Sheila's parents, but is convinced they don't dislike him merely for being unsuccessful, which is not a crime in itself merely a legitimate reason for social ostracism by the middle-classes, but because he doesn't appear to be trying—and doesn't even look right. Such is the iron rule of conformity:

> In their world, it was everyone's duty to wear a uniform that announced his status, his calling and his ambitions: from the navvy's thick boots and shirtsleeves to the professor's tweeds, the conventions of clothing saw to it that everyone wore his identity card where it could be seen. But Charles seemed not to realise the sacred duty of dressing the part. Even as an undergraduate he had not worn corduroys or coloured shirts.[15]

By failing to notice or deliberately flouting such conventions, Charles appears to create a feeling of vertigo and instant anger in everyone he encounters. He feels he understands them perfectly, but they don't grasp what he is all about in any sense. For example, his emotional reasons for not contacting his parents. Charles is guarding his detachment against 'the emotional midden that his parents had spent twenty-two years in digging' but as he contemplates his girlfriend's mother, 'fixing her absurdly small eyes on him as she stood squarely beside the sink, a Woman on her Own Ground, in her hideous dress and splashed apron', we feel it is Charles who is snobbish and quite unable to see others apart from the parts he sees them as playing, uncaring except for Sheila, although not unfeeling exactly—every human encounter brings him out in an emotional rash. He is seriously out of kilter, we realise, when in the scene which may have given kitchen sink writing its name, Charles heaves the washing up bowl out of the sink and throws its contents over her irritating parents. He rushes from his encounter with them, feeling their judgemental eyes still on his back, eyes and values that will be judging him as he hurries down all the days of his life. In *Hurry on Down* John Wain creates a brilliant portrait of the desperation of failure rather than trying, as Raymond Williams put it, 'to ratify a personal failure in unconcern', although he is undoubtedly trying to ratify it as something. As so often with Angry Young Man writing, there is an equal and opposite tendency to undermine the social criticisms it is purportedly making by putting them into the mouths of semi-dysfunctional people: men who are making excuses represent no threat to the established order. To recover from their feeling of distress would in every case be to conform utterly to the middle-class values they despise. In John Wain's case his sense of estrangement came from growing up middle-class in a Northern industrial town in the 1930s—and being hated for it by working-class boys: 'I was frightened and never concealed that basic fact from myself, though to the best of my ability I hid it from others.'[16]

John Braine's *Room at the Top* wraps up its avatar's thirst for social mobility in so much guilt and betrayal that most aspirational working-class readers would have been likely to reach for the cloth cap, the pint of bitter and the whippet in unhealthy relief. Faced with a choice between an older married woman and a younger, prettier one who worships him and is the boss' daughter, Lampton chooses the latter and apparently condemns the woman he has rejected to her death. The scenes in which Joe's life and decisions take the direction that they must if he is to rise in the world are worth examining in detail for the vivid picture they paint of a Northern social world and its middle-class hierarchies—to enter them and to climb them requires greater resources and a greater honesty than Joe Lampton has found amongst the working-classes he so plainly despises: he is in no doubt as to who is superior, and depicts the Northern factory owners as self-made and solidly meritocratic in outlook.

Lampton is a town hall socialist and trainee accountant when the factory-owning father of his teenage girlfriend summons him to the Ledderfield Conservative Club for luncheon. Braine has him noticing the light Italianate architecture of the building with which the self-made nineteenth century Northern capitalists had signalled their inheritance of Renaissance values, but he notes that 'a hundred years of smoke had given it an unhealthy mottled appearance.' Lampton is impressed by the portraits of grim-faced conservative potentates, their mouths 'clamped hard on the juicy steak of success'. Braine describes the ostentatious furnishings with relish and Joe, a large fit man who has distinguished himself in military service, is impressed by the sheer physical size of the rich, many of whom seem to dwarf him. Healthy specimens indeed. Enjoying the waiter service and the free double scotches, he waits with some trepidation for the arrival of Mr Brown, who strikes him upon his advent as fully the equal of the portraits and the lush décor of the club:

> He had very heavy black eyebrows and in conjunction with his grey hair and red face they were a little alarming; compressed over his deep-set eyes the effect was that of a hanging judge, a jolly old *bon viveur* sentencing some poor devil of a clerk or a labourer to death by dislocation of the neck as an aperitif to a good dinnah with a bottle of the best—the very best, waitah—port.[17]

Mr Brown immediately puts Lampton to the test—by offering him a well-paid managerial job on condition that he stops seeing his daughter—to which he responds with an angry refusal and declaration of his love for Susan, in which, to his horror, he finds his accent broadening into the working-class brogue it once was, and to his surprise Brown admires him for his anger, his roots and his stubbornness and consents to his marriage to Susan, informing him that she is pregnant. Lampton leaves this meeting a made man who has won his heart's desire, but at the moment of victory he is assaulted by a disturbing memory from his airforce days, which recurs with Brown's resonant words: '*You're the sort of young man we want. There's always room at the top.*' Over Cologne the bomb-aimer in his aircraft had been hit by flak, and a small chunk of metal had neatly 'scooped out his eyes and most of his nose' at which the sergeant had only grunted and said 'Oh no. Oh no.' Again and again. 'Until the morphine silenced him.'

One of Brown's conditions for offering his daughter and the riches of the earth is that Lampton severs his relationship with the married woman with whom he has been having an affair. Alice Aisgill is nothing but an old whore, he says, and he won't risk the scandal of a son-in-law of his in the divorce courts. Furthermore she has also 'gone with' his hated posh rival Jack Wales. The fearful image of success (a successful raid) being suddenly punished by a physical wound seemingly from heaven, a disfigurement and loss so complete that one can only mutter the same baffled words over and over again, is a powerfully disquieting one: *thanatos* exacts its dreadful psychic toll on the upwardly mobile man who feels he is unworthy, inadequate, will surely be found out and may as a result sabotage himself. But he is also being asked to betray a woman he loves as a friend, and in his own psychic world as well as the 'real world' of the novel, to exact another's death as the price of his own success and happiness. Equally disturbing is that Lampton does not hesitate to do as he has been instructed, disposing of his ties to her with 'a sufficiency of dignity and a minimum of pain'.[18]

Unwilling to accept his ending of what is to him their semi-defunct affair as just one of those things, and unable to see Joe as he sees himself—as motivated by his love for Susan rather than greed, selfishness and lust—Alice goes out and gets blind drunk after he leaves her, and on the way home she crashes her car at high speed. She dies in the accident—if it is one—but not before crawling around on the road for a considerable time with her scalp ripped off, injured by the steering column and still living for a while. The cruelty of the workmate who callously shares these details with Joe goes unpunished; for Lampton and for us they weirdly echo the terrible experience of the bomb-aimer and they are evidence that he has inflicted something on her that is worse than a clean death. Joe's response to her death—and the impulse of others to blame him for it, as he does himself, are the most powerful scenes in the book and summate his character and his dilemma as an upwardly mobile working-class man.

In the first minutes of being told Joe experiences a familiar sort of psychic splitting as the character called 'Joe Lampton' spouts a series of platitudinous and priggish rote responses to the news of Alice's death—the evils of drunk driving, she was always reckless—through which he tries to protect himself and his position: a betrayal as terrible as Peter's denial of Jesus. Inside the real Joe Lampton squirms and looks for a way out of being implicated in her death, which he obviously is. It is the gratuitous offering of the horrific details of Alice's death by his colleague Teddy that drives him out to the toilets and towards the next stage of his attempted expiation of what her old friend Elspeth will soon accuse him of: her murder. Unable to work or face people who will talk about Alice, Joe leaves the town hall at lunchtime, and on the bus he experiences a kind of negative epiphany:

> Then there were fields and cows and narrow roads wriggling like tapeworms into the new Council estate. But Alice had been killed, and what I saw was the components of a huge machine

> that now only functioned out of bravado: it had been designed and manufactured for one purpose, to kill Alice. That purpose was accomplished; it should have been allowed to run down and then stop, the driver asleep at the wheel, the passengers sitting docilely with their mouths wide open, waiting for the bus to fly away, the estate left unfinished, the shops shuttered and overrun with rats, the unmilked cows lowing in agony with swollen udders, the dogs and cats running wild and bloody mouthed, and then a great storm to scour the whole dirty earth down to clean rock and flame.[19]

Joe tells Elspeth that he will punish himself, a process that involves a great deal of drinking, being bought drinks by poufs, picking up a young woman in another pub and getting into a fight with her boyfriend. But like his vision of a merciless world, his attempts at expiation are self-centred, and deflect his own responsibilities onto God for failing to exist. The process of expiation is therefore one in which Joe comes back to his familiar heartless self, insulates himself from himself with alcohol and indulges in his usual role playing and assumption of false identities, including that of his rival Jack Wales. He oscillates, prevaricates, eats fish and chips to get a second wind, and plunges onward. It is clear that Joe is trying to hurt himself, but becomes clearer in the course of his binge that he cannot truly accomplish this. After a few drinks 'a slatternly happiness sidled up to me,' but at other moments he thinks of throwing himself under a tram 'to make all the bovine pay-night faces sick with horror': he cannot settle to guilt but must strike back at the inadequacy of humanity in general, the drunken working-classes in particular. He comes to rest for another moment in contemplation of a warehouse with missing letters in its sign: 'Umpelb and D kinso are the three most terrible words that I have ever seen.' Vertiginous words that fail to signify, apparent signposts offering no shred of wisdom or comfort in the carnival of meaninglessness of his nighttown. Drinking with the girl Mavis in the last pub of the day he peers into her open handbag whose familiar contents 'gave me an intolerable feeling of loneliness.' They have ecstatic sex in a cheap hotel, but when he is later confronted by her boyfriend and an accomplice he seems at first almost pleased to take a beating, only to remember his military training, his strength and his survivor's instinct at the last moment and leave both of them broken and bleeding. Joe Lampton appears to be indomitable, or at least unable to suffer enough, and when he finally makes his way home to find that others have been worrying about him. 'Nobody blames you, love. Nobody blames you,' he is told by Eva. 'That's the trouble,' he replies.[20]

Guilt is on his trail like the relentlessly pursuing hound in Francis Thompson's poem 'The Hound of Heaven', where Christ's all-seeing love is in slavering pursuit of the sinner:

I fled Him, down the nights and down the days:
I fled Him, down the arches of the years;
I fled Him, down the labyrinthine ways
Of my own mind; and in the midst of tears
I hid from Him, and under running laughter.
Up vista'd hopes I sped;
And shot, precipitated,
Adown Titanic glooms of chasmed fears,
From those strong Feet that followed, followed after.[21]

'All things betray thee, who betrayest Me.' Christ is a fearful figure in Francis Thompson's poetic masterpiece of Christian mysticism, but for John Braine's Joe Lampton there is no promise of redemption to accompany the consuming fear of God's inescapable justice; or in his case, the sense of his having betrayed his origins and his politics as well as his former lover. Braine follows him in a sequel, *Life at the Top*, set ten years later in time. Joe is living in the home counties, a two-car middle-class family man who is still wondering where it all went wrong, hoping for rebirth through an affair with a younger woman. The book is a creditable attempt to write honestly about where Lampton's kind of social mobility leads: its bland surface teeming with Ronson cigarette lighters, dark suits, large whiskies, gravel drives and social anxieties; its depths with emotional confusion, hard business decisions and middle-aged lust, and a sense of ultimate rootless vacuity. His third novel, *The Jealous God,* announces his theological preoccupations more explicitly, in another tussle between the claims of religion and duty and those of romantic love. The romance of social aspiration and ideas of progress breed uncomfortably in Braine's early fiction; and in the end Joe's (or anyone's) lust for the good life defeats the values which had given him edge and his aspirations their validity.

George Scott, whose autobiography, *Time and Place* (1956) was written when in his late twenties, records a slow disillusionment with the socialist writers of the thirties, as well as an originally similar desire to keep faith with their politics as John Osborne's in *Look Back in Anger*. Scott was a working-class boy who went to Oxford (which his father had rightly thought was 'for the Nobs') and later became a *Daily Express* journalist, but he understands the stymied emotional centre occupied by Jimmy Porter and offers a commentary on the conflicting senses of class at play in fifties Britain. His father thought his youthful socialism amounted only to trying to change people who kept coal in their baths, people who were essentially ineducable: 'If you put them in a slum they'd make a slum of it.' His parents had both admired George Lansbury, the radical Poplar councillor of the thirties, as 'a good man' with sadly deluded politics; their son makes a painful circuitous journey towards what he hopes will be something else, but which sounds like reborn working-class Toryism. His problem is that he has an intellectual culture based on prewar socialism, and is trying to make his way in a postwar world in which social mobility is available on quite different terms. This entails a wholesale rejection of the previous generation—of which he offers the following characterisation, suggesting that is was they who were angry and wanted to change things, whereas he and his contemporaries are justifiably cautious about embracing their lost causes. He writes with the urgent condescension of youth: he is angry that it is older people, especially socialists, who expect him to be angry when he isn't particularly:

> It is just one of the curiosities of the modern world that age and experience have brought to so many only the sickness of self-despair and the desire to escape from the realities of existence if not through suicide then by bolting down a variety of intellectual and emotional hidey-holes. It is the claim of my generation that we can understand the causes which have driven our elders to this situation and can pity them. We can sympathise with their torments and admire the original courage and enthusiasm which brought them into peril. We do not condemn them for their inability to make the transition to the present day. Yet strangely these same men who have lost their own way and are so publically conscious and even proud or their stigmata are quick to castigate us for our lack of violent enthusiasms, for failing to 'commit' ourselves, for not wanting to turn the world upside down. Surely we are not to be blamed for learning from their mistakes?[22]

If the so-called Angry Young Men often wrote about the pains of social mobility, they were also writing about a collision between working-class values and the conceptions of class and culture then current in education, and might also be seen in retrospect as recording a moment of disappearance of the possibility of an independent working-class view. Seen by many as a handy media creation but nevertheless a kind of affinity group, they were a lightning rod for the anger of others (who were often angry with them) and presented as a centre of gravity for the preoccupations of the time; but were themselves disappointing politically. Kingsley Amis was soon denouncing socialism as a romantic myth, John Wain became an academic poet, John Braine veered to the right. John Osborne, instantly assimilated, continued to reach intuitively for the nerve of anger out of which his best writing came. Alan Sillitoe's anarchist tendencies (he was not really an 'angry young man' although certainly angry) resolved themselves into a more orthodox Communist political stance and a continued affiliation with traditional working-class (labour movement) politics. Inherently unstable and brief though it was, the moment of the 'Angry Young Man' did open the floodgates to writings about working-class and other hitherto marginalised groups, setting a tone and an agenda of fearless truth-telling in early postwar British fiction. Their writings are still powerful, without exact precedent and can be exhilarating in their ruthless questioning and sincere desire to shake things up. They were certainly not emptily optimistic. If anything, they are underrated, and worth rereading today in the early twenty first century at a moment when British politics and culture seem rather bland, compromised and at a loss. All the more interesting in that they themselves were at something of a political loss; they asked all the right, sceptical questions about easy political solutions to something as deeply engrained as the English class system.

But it seemed to some that the whole phenomenon had more or less run its course by 1960, its writers co-opted by the establishment and whatever they had to say traduced by the gimcrack label. This is certainly the view expressed by a 22-year-old unpublished poet, Tom Raworth, an angry young man himself, in a contemporary letter to the American Black Mountain poet, Edward Dorn:

> The angries over here have been turned into a joke. Of course there was no group calling themselves 'angry young men' but give something you don't like a label, and it's very easy to dismiss it. After all, who are the angries? Osborne, Chris Logue, Colin Wilson, Kingsley Amis, John Wain, Lindsay Anderson etc. etc. all are lumped under the heading. The only one who was a danger to the established order, Osborne, was assimilated by it. 'Look Back in Anger' expressed what a whole generation over here feels. It changed the English Theatre nearly overnight. They couldn't let it go any further, so what happened… he was praised by everyone… loaded with this that and the other… smothered with glory. His plays got worse. 'The World of Paul Slickey' was so bad it was unbelievable. However, I have always had a sneaking feeling that the last play was a gesture, a blow against the whole cult of personality as if he said 'look, I've got such a big name here now that they'll put on anything I write without even reading it' […][23]

Dismissive as this letter is of the whole phenomenon of literary fame, it also shows that some young people in Britain were stirred by what the 'angry young men' were supposed to be, and cared enough to be highly critical about the whole process of turning social and political dissent into a literary commodity. Raworth was at the time a young father sharing a cramped basement flat in Hackney with his wife Val and their two small children, and he does seem to feel that the slew of 'working-class' novels and plays that appeared in those years in some way expressed the way 'a whole generation' was feeling. Probably like many others, he didn't necessarily feel that they spoke for him, but his unappeasable tone suggests that, whoever they were, the Angry Young Men had accidentally got it more or less right. Kenneth Allsop's *The Angry Decade* (1958) is an on the spot account of this sea-change in British literature, centred on the moment of its first impact. Journalistic, first-hand, and highly effective, his technique of novel summaries and catalogues of the era's preoccupations in lists of famous names and media buzzwords, captures a time of prosperous conformity, infant consumerism and the search for something new, perhaps a pan-European phenomenon as well as a strongly transatlantic one, the hinterland of a new age which the New England poet Robert Lowell was to characterise succinctly a couple of years later, in a poem about Boston, as a place where 'a savage servility slides by on grease.'[24] Allsop's is the most perceptive account of the Angry moment, firstly as a publicity phenomenon, and secondly, for its descriptions of novels and of the social and cultural torsions that their writers were articulating; he is a brilliant first reader of novels and plays, many of those discussed here and more besides. He is good at defining writers as characters, and in intellectual cast (as emotionalists, neutralists, and lawgivers) although it must be said that these were writers good at defining themselves.

His account of Colin Wilson's sudden catapult to fame and equally abrupt crash landing as the establishment spitefully turned on him is fascinating, and illuminates much of the character of this duffle-coated crusader for Nietszche and psychopathic peak experiences. His self-opinion that he was the greatest genius yet of European literature must have been hard to take, especially from the author of one book that was largely a collage of quotations, but the verve with which Wilson tried to wing it in this role speaks of a brave twenty-four year old self-educated writer. Wilson clearly identified with other rapid cult celebrities, not least rebel-without-a-cause James Dean, recently dead in his Porsche, drily remarking that he hoped to escape paying the price of death himself. But Allsop is also somewhat heavy-handed and offensive in his slanginess and plain-speaking about the working-classes, in a manner that is revealing about prevailing middle-class attitudes. He is snobbish in his turn, for example, about the racy home counties roadhouse types that Kingsley Amis' characters seem to mistake for the upper class. Of the Angries' predicament he says: 'They feel a mixture of guilt about renegading from their hereditary background and contempt for the oafish orthodoxy of their parents.'[25] A moral no-win situation then for these disgruntled recipients of scholarship-aided social mobility, abusers of the nice middle-class women they don't deserve anyway:

ungrateful slobs whichever way you look at it. Except that Allsop might have said more sympathetically, and accurately, that their loyalties were divided and that there was as yet no social group with whom they could easily identify.

Chapter Two

Moving Up, Dressing Down: Edna O'Brien, Lynn Reid Banks, Nell Dunn

The early sixties was a time in which a relative honesty about sexuality, or the promise of it, was enough to make many books successful, particularly if they were by a young woman; but young writers with the verve and honesty of Edna O'Brien were never commonplace, and in this case helped to define a genre in women's writing that is still going strong. Near the end of her *Girl with Green Eyes*, the second volume of her highly popular Country Girls trilogy, Edna O'Brien's heroine Cait (or Kate) loses her virginity to Eugene, an older man, a film-maker and a dangerous atheist who is separated from his wife, whom everyone except her friend Baba has warned her against. Her father, a devout Catholic whose idea of a useful gift to his daughter is a gilt-edged copy of *The Imitation of Christ*, has been in receipt of an anonymous letter tipping him off to a plot to 'dope' and 'ruin' Cait by this 'dirty foreigner', and after a great deal of toing and froing, ruined she is, on a night she has to engineer herself, wearing a gold mock-wedding ring to satisfy the hotel authorities, by a man who thinks at first he might get away with a half bottle of champagne. Details that might have been thought sordid are relished and celebrated by O'Brien. After the deed has been done and Kate has pocketed the cork as a souvenir, marvelled at 'the tender limp thing like a wet flower between my legs' and begun to cry a few preliminary tears, she muses:

> I felt different from Baba now and from every other girl I knew. I wondered if Baba has experienced this, and if she has been afraid or if she had liked it. I thought of Mama and of how she used to blow on hot soup before she gave it to me and of the rubber bands she put inside the turn-down of my ankle-socks to keep them from falling.[1]

That last sentence, both in its directness, its telling detail and its precise turn of phrase, 'the turn-down', defines what is so attractive in Edna O'Brien's writing, and perhaps also offers a clue as to why so many young women, or girls, continued to read her books for decades after their shock value had passed. She has the confidence and ability to try to define a common experience fully yet romantically, and with a sense of ironic detachment that seems to fit this one like a damask glove, to fit everything. Losing your virginity. The sense of a threshold definitively crossed and paused at a moment, the end of girlhood, the everythingness of it, the cliché, and the poignancy that no-one will ever take the trouble to keep your ankle socks from falling again. Who cannot remember something a bit like this, whatever end of the wet flower you were on? Then there is Eugene's jocular throwaway casualness, doing it again, washing together, breakfasting, and, a few pages later, fleeing Ireland and moving to a flat in Bayswater with Baba. There you have it: a knowing sigh, a catch of the breath and a turn of the page—the secret of Edna O'Brien's wealth and her continuing favour with so many women readers. She is the progenitor (with the equally saucy Françoise Sagan) and doyenne of what has become the genre of bad-girl chick lit. But surely, surely there must be a lot more to her than that?

Edna O'Brien's acerbic wit, her sense of the gothic, and of outrage, and her relentless female eroticism must have done a great deal to cheer up young Irish women in the late fifties and early sixties (if they were able to obtain her books) and also provided a role model for English women who were still labouring under the yoke of the Good Housekeeping view of femininity. A middle-class woman's dutiful place was to be the adjunct of a mighty suburban warrior whose battles up and down the tracks to Waterloo were to remain forever beyond her comprehension but deemed to be the whole of her sky, as shown in these excerpts from a 1955 article, 'The Good Wife's Guide', from *Housekeeping Monthly*:

- Greet him with a warm smile and show sincerity in your desire to please him.
- Listen to him. You may have a dozen important things to tell him, but the moment of his arrival is not the time. Let him talk first—remember, his topics of conversation are far more important than yours.
- Arrange his pillow and offer to take his shoes. Speak in a low, soothing and pleasant voice.
- Don't complain if he's late home for dinner or even if he stays out all night. Count this as minor compared to what he might have gone through that day.
- Don't ask him questions about his actions or question his judgement or integrity. Remember, he is the master of the house and as such will always exercise his will with fairness and truthfulness. You have no right to question him.
- A good wife always knows her place.[2]

But perhaps we shouldn't altogether take this at face value—it may have been written by a mischievous feminist offering tongue in cheek advice to her readers, by somebody who has failed to completely live up to its wise dicta of womanly behaviour and is having a laugh about it, if not by a hopeful man. I suspect it was probably written to be ridiculed. It should continue with an instruction to hide any reading matter with the names of Doris Lessing or Edna O'Brien on the cover. But however remote or silly it may now seem, this sort of thing remains a staple of women's magazines in some parts of the world, and is certainly a fair approximation of the background (and foreground) of expectations about women's role in marriage and society against which the rebellious young writers of the fifties and sixties were pitching their hopeful fictions. Edna O'Brien seems to differ from most of them in her sense of effortless transcendence of the circumstances of her family and community, and a sort of breezy indifference to what was expected of her as an Irish woman of her time. English women writers of that moment, as we shall see, were struggling with a quite different set of patriarchal attitudes.

Edna O'Brien's version of married bliss is offered in the last volume of her Country Girls trilogy, in which the plucky pair, Cait and Baba, the latter's Pink-Witch bicycle, their convent sacking and the purple died underwear of their early bohemian days in Dublin left behind, follow the immigrant trail to London and are getting to grips with the next stage of their careers of exemplars of middle-class Irish womanhood. By this stage her first book, *The Country Girls*, had been banned in Ireland as a slur on Irish womanhood—Cait has sex before marriage, Baba induces a miscarriage—had been ritually burnt in the churchyard of her hometown in County Clare, and the second volume, *The Lonely Girl*, had been filmed as *Girl With Green Eyes*: good publicity, but also wounding to a young writer however beneficial being made such an example of might turn out to be for others. All Edna O'Brien could do was brazen it out, which is what she did with great relish. *Girls in their Married Bliss* is taken over by Baba as narrator, by far the less romantic of the two women, and as if in defiant revenge against the savaging her lyrical eroticism and tart humour at the expense of the Catholic Church and male authority in general had provoked, O'Brien seems determined to plumb the depths of filth by letting them all know what a really unvarnished woman's point of view sounds like. Enduring a domestic cold war after cheating on your loyal husband. Marrying a rich but stupid and sexually dysfunctional building contractor for the money. Shagging incompetent men you picked up at parties and holding their sexual vanities and risible conversational gambits up to ridicule in blow-by-blow bedroom scenes. It is the lives of shameless and high-rolling arrivistes that she documents, in a country where the servants were likely to hit the brandy and call you 'Jumped up Irish scum' if they decided that they don't like your morals. Cait and Baba's heels climb up more than a few broad majestic backs and many which prove too narrow, and their own tender, antagonistic relationship all but dissolves in a welter of cynicism, sixties party scenes, slipping your knickers in and out of your handbag, and some withering, somewhat bilious accounts of a sort of distended, unanchored pub identity that is, or was, seemingly the dominant Irish experience of living in London:

> The Jew looked interesting and sort of wronged, so did a small pale boy—you couldn't call him a man even though he was about twenty-five or six—with a girlish face. Dead wrong for a man of course, but still… His complexion was blue, as if he'd been left out nights when he was young, and his lips had no colour, and his hands were about as big as a child's. I never got near him because Frank said the actor was hungry and the muses must be fed. You know the sort of faker, faker than fake talk. Before leaving he stuffed pound notes into a couple of collection boxes that were on the counter.
>
> 'Poor hungry devils,' he said, meaning neglected dogs or kids or whatever he was financing. Charity! He and his brother sack men on Christmas Eve and rehire them on St. Stephen's Day to escape hoiday pay. He dropped about ten quid in all.[3]

'I can't stand serious people,' Baba remarks of her friend, and as the more pleasure-seeking half of the duo she leads her long-suffering, bank-rolling husband a merry dance indeed, betraying him unceasingly (he suffers from the male Irish ailment of brewer's droop) and berating him with what once had been girlish impudence and is now a nasty vein of relentless snobbery: 'I knew that he'd take revenge by yelling at bogmen that are no better than himself.' [4] O'Brien's comments on the ways of the Irish in London and the building trade in particular are offered in her passing scattershots revelling in her super-disloyal truth-telling that, in the absence of any contemporary novels dedicated to this experience, will have to serve as a snapshot of the Irish working-class way of life in England:

> The thing about Frank and the brother is they hire nice people. They have boys who would sit up all night on that building site just to make sure that buckets aren't stolen. Now and then they get what Frank calls a hobo on the site. Someone with a bit of common sense that knows about unions and strikes and things. And boy, do they have *him* fall off a scaffold![5]

Estranged from her own husband—the once-glamorous man who had desultorily deflowered her at the close of *The Lonely Girl*—Cait finds herself assisting her friend in an attempted bathtub and castor oil termination that doesn't wash. Baba's husband accepts her baby, accepts her too, along with her unstoppable propensity for playing the game of 'sticking the soft anvil under the hedge'; Cait herself is unable to quite cure herself of hoping to meet another Mr. Right, her party ears hyper-tuned to the phoney ring of people who say things like 'You must be a very real person.' And later wish to pejoratively discuss the female demand for orgasm and dress up in supposedly enhancing sex gear that appears to replace the act itself. A vein of homophobia a mile wide runs through Edna O'Brien's descriptions of the attitudes of men she finds inadequate between the sheets. All of which leads her into analysis, where, free-associating, she compares herself to the starlings who cause an air crash she has read about by nesting in the engine. She tells her analyst that she feels she destroys people through her weakness, those people including her children—her son is named Cash, possibly after one of the sons who attend Addie Bundren in William Faulkner's *As I Lay Dying*, a favourite book of O'Brien's, on her way to be buried in Jackson Springs. The result of all her unassuagable guilt and romanticism and sexuality, it seems, is just such a journey. Cait has herself sterilised, and in an epilogue written twenty years later, Baba, still swearing like a trooper and suffering from 'minnows in the cunt' tells us of her childhood friend's dark final destination.

'Far away and lost, all those moments. Part of her had died in them.'[6] The halting, pregnant music of those lines is O'Brien's signature as a writer, but there is the significance of that music for her to consider—it is a remembered song, a song with a catch in it, as is most of her work, in common with so many expatriate Irish writers (it is a cliché) the conjuration of a lost country, very seldom the mapping of a new one. Phrases and phrase-making are desperately important to her (being good at it is perhaps the source of the windswept imperious pride with which she looks out at the viewer in her sixties photographs) and to her heroine: 'She thought that phrases were like melodies, they went on appealing long after one had stopped listening. Then one day they fell out of favour.'[7] As the Country Girls trilogy wears on, the finer distinctions of her girlhood and adolescence, although intensely remembered, gradually give way to a sense of moral chaos and confusion and a mistaking of that for a Catholic sense of being an evil woman, and a kind of indifferent embracing of that role. The world is contingent and O'Brien's women (of whom she is a harsh judge in the end) are at best morally indifferent:

> Don't ask me to say crime does not pay because I'll say it, but I'll also say virtue does not pay, it's all pure fluke, and our lives prove it. Kids, I thought. God help them, they don't know the bastards they're born from.[8]

Her characters rebel against the Catholic Church but seem to have spontaneously fired up within themselves a death-seeking, self-destructive and blood-soaked culture of permanent revolt and a kind of hypersexuality, a guilt-ridden impetus to guilty pleasures, freely indulged in, that will ride them to their graves. They are never far from a message on the Banshee telegraph—an early form of Irish mobile phone on which ancestral messages are received. There is a final act of contrition or loyalty and a bony hand stretches back from the past to write how it is and always will be for women in the sand before the sea inundates their girlhood sandcastles. They are haunted by melodies that may not have any meaning, that she fears may be best forgotten, and the Irish women in her books are intelligent, cynical but mainly driven by sexuality and hopeless longing. Her writing is an acute flaring of consciousness, of overwrought sensibility: it is a seeing through of things—to the truth maybe, but to inescapable ends and a doom-embracing Celtic twilight. Whether or not hers is an accurate picture of Irish womanhood, I am absolutely certain she has influenced many a Catholic rebel girl, and in the freedom and honesty of her writing about women's sexuality she set a benchmark that had to wait many years for anyone to attempt to stretch above it. She is desperate, an Irish girlfriend used to say, meaning just terrible or desperately bad. She is matchlessly candid on the subject of female sexuality. For English women it all seemed a little different, but they read her and some of them wanted to be as bold as she was herself—and not many English writers of either sex had the sheer writing ability and nerve to get away with being Edna.

Lynn Reid Banks is positively respectable by comparison, or perhaps negatively respectable would be a more accurate description of Jane Graham, the wan leading lady of *The L-shaped Room*, who arrives in her seedy Fulham boarding house freshly pregnant, at odds with her father, and determined to make it on her own in an area where 'most of the windows lacked curtains and that gave the houses a blind look, or rather a dead look, like open-eyed corpses.'[9] What makes Jane strikingly different from Kate and Baba is her attitude to her predicament. Her half-horrified, half-interested reactions to her fellow denizens of bedsitland combine niceness and snootiness, and at this distance seem to assemble a gallery of urban prototypes—designed to make the novel sexy and dangerous—who are to recur time and time again in England as 'the other' to middle-class culture. Stung by her father's rejection of her as no better than a whore, Jane visits the colourful prostitute downstairs (come in, dearie) to discover that she is a woman 'just like herself' (or is she?); a fearsome West Indian jazz musician turns out to be just a big cuddly child-like fellow 'like a chimpanzee' with a 'pungent negro smell'; the gruesome little chaps who run the local sweetshop and caff aren't such bad sorts really, if you ignore their racism; the Jewish hotel owner for whom she works turns out to be only human after all, even though he apparently sacks her for being a gentile. Jane is sympathetic to Jews, but this in a context where anti-semitism is commonplace. A perpetual not-so-innocent abroad, we see her struggling to overcome her prejudices, but these are always waiting in the wings to ambush her and the reader whose sympathies Lynn Reid Banks has painstakingly won over. It is her consciousness that frames the appearances of her urban types, her terms of reference and standards against which they are measured, and her notions of what they are that dictate the vocabularies in which they speak to us. How could it be otherwise?

'You mustn't mind old John,' says Toby, the Jewish writer who is to become her friend and lover, speaking of the resident West Indian jazz musician: 'He's just naturally inquisitive. Like a chimp, you know, he can't help it. He could no more resist having a look at you than a monkey could resist picking up anything new and giving it the once over.' Jane replies: 'Yes, and then when he's picked it up he'll probably try to eat it.'[10] *The L-Shaped Room* may seem a naïve book now, but it is self-consciously a novel about naïvety, has never been out of print, and has doubtless been enjoyed by generations of young girls dreaming of futures of independence and fun in the big city. Unfortunately there's not much fun on offer—in fact the book's underlying message is something of a dire warning of the consequences of liberation and an affirmation of traditional middle-class values. Lynn Reid Banks' heroine has become pregnant from reluctant first time sex and any future contenders for her affections are left in no doubt that sex is not to be taken lightly, is only permissible as an anguished expression of love, and as part of an ongoing commitment probably leading directly to marriage. Again, we see her struggle to throw off the attitudes of her parents' generation, but contemporary readers (at least this one) and in particular those who somehow manage to withhold sympathy from this central character—can't help but notice that those attitudes are being replicated again and again. The naïve eye of the narrator reveals more unconsciously about her symbolic universe than about the working-class and immigrant lives she has decided to share as a self-punishment and to strike out at her middle-class father.

Anthony Giddens' *The Transformation of Intimacy*, a sociological account of 'the sexual revolution' and its social implications draws heavily on the literature of self-help and tends to promote a Mr Fixit approach to dysfunctional relationships, but his account of the sixties as a period when settled sex roles were being renegotiated has an interesting focus. He points to an intense, hopeless and rather unanchored romanticism in sixties culture—in the Beatles' songs, for example, super-sweet and sexually urgent by turns, looking for a new understanding—and demanding it—in a way that both young women and men could identify with. Giddens might handily locate Lynn Reid Banks as an early moment in the passage from 'romantic' to what he calls 'confluent' love, which he optimistically sees in the process of emerging as the pure negotiated love relationship of modern capitalist societies.[11] This may be one useful general context in which to look at her first novel: it is an archaeology of postwar British conceptions of womanhood. Seen in sociological terms Lynn Reid Banks' heroine is a precariously financially independent woman and therefore has a new bargaining power. She is able to make up her own rules, and, in that her apparent range of options was without much precedent in previous generations, is driven to do so out of pure necessity. In *The L-Shaped Room* we see that freedom involves a continual struggle to cope and to live up to it, and it is this earnest struggle for development that engages our sympathies for her and that made her author's books so engaging for many female readers.

Jane Graham also has Doris Lessing's female characters as a precedent; Martha Quest, heroine of her *Children of Violence* series of novels, had appeared a decade earlier: both are struggling independent women and both writers tried to speak to a female readership looking for political and spiritual direction. Lessing had arrived in London in 1949 from Southern Rhodesia, soon to become a highly successful novelist; Lynne Reid Banks was evacuated to Canada during the war and returned to build a successful career in TV journalism before writing her first novel, *The L-Shaped Room*. Lessing's book about her first year in London, *In Search of the English*, was published in the same year, and though subtitled 'a documentary' is also a sort of non-fiction boarding house novel and tour of the London working-classes. These books were about women changing and growing and eating the old meat with the new forks, and part of the early kindling of a new feminism; both writers strove for connection to ordinary preoccupations and to everyday life, but Lessing's politics were more sophisticated and her sympathies seem to run deeper. But where Jane Graham differs sharply from Lessing or one of her female characters (a hard distinction to make) is that she is thoroughly racked by guilt and messed up about sexuality. Lessing by contrast is sexually fearless, unshakeable (if wryly detached) in her Communist politics and her sense of adventure, eager to learn and with good judgement: a sympathetic observer and commentator on London people she meets, who accept her as a single-mother and are for the most part helpful to her.

Paroxysms of guilt aside—and these may be her way of punishing a father who has been overly sceptical about her acting talent and secretarial capabilities—Jane Graham must be one of the most repellently smug middle-class female characters in fiction, I mean who is not a caricature created by a misogynist, and whom we are expected to identify with rather than laugh at or vilify. We soon hear of her penchant for comparing people to animals. Jane resigns from her career in provincial rep after a queer who reminds her of 'A female cat, soft and affectionate, with something hidden deep that you couldn't get to know' shows his sharp claws and tries to scratch her eyes out for sleeping with an actor with whom he is in love. She quickly gets a job in a Yorkshire café as a waitress, attracting new customers because she is a pretty actress and because they have never seen anyone middle-class close up. Soon she is all but doing the sick cook out of a job by acquiring instant culinary expertise, turning out to have talent as well as reforming zeal, and further boosts business by adding garlic salt to the baked beans. Not major crimes against humanity, I grant you, unless you were the cook, but this is only a beginning of her relentless, eager demonstrations of her superiority to everyone she meets. It might be argued that it is only weakness that makes us male readers sympathetic and female strength is unattractive to us. Jane seems acceptable when she's crying and abasing herself, but as soon as she rallies we are treated to yet another dose of middle-class self-righteousness.

The Fulham working-classes (or at least, the sweetshop owner) speak a curious slang all their own, or at least I'd never heard it before, in which black people are 'bobos', landladies are 'faggots' and prostitutes are 'chippies' (American idioms?) and apparently the communists are to blame for everything, as we hear in this obsequious rant:

> He stared at me a bit longer, sucking his teeth. 'Bloody Commies,' he said suddenly. 'Why couldn't they leave the middle classes alone? Never did no real harm as I could see. Live and let live, I say, all except the bobos, you have to keep them in their place. And the old faggots with their bleeding houses. Sorry, miss.'
>
> I realised with surprise that he was apologising for saying bleeding. It was as if he was in the presence of a corpse—the corpse of the middle class. He was looking at me as if I were its last twitch.[12]

We are told that Jane's mother had died in childbirth, and this may be intended as part of the explanation of her difficult relationship with her straitlaced father and her difficulties with sex: 'He's a civil servant. The only time he ever stayed away from when my mother died. Even then he worked in the afternoon; he went straight from the crematorium to his office. He told me that himself; he was very proud of it, for some reason.'[13] When she becomes pregnant he angrily throws her out, but not before she has visited a doctor who assumes she wants an abortion. Backstreet abortion is an important subject in sixties fiction—abortion was not legalised until 1967—and there are many depictions of sordid, dangerous operations in the fiction of the first half of the decade. In *The L-Shaped Room* we see what it was like for a middle-class girl such as her: she is immediately offered what can only be described as a front street abortion:

Dr Graham took off his glasses again and looked at me with his small, short-sighted eyes.

'A hundred guineas,' he said.

Then he took out a cream silk handkerchief to polish the lenses. I could see his monogram on the corner, J.G., the same initials as mine.[14]

But Jane Graham is fiercely anti-abortion and promptly locks horns with the doctor for his assumption that she wishes to terminate the pregnancy. She accuses him of greed and immorality with the self-righteous moralism we will come to recognise as her leading characteristic:

'Life is precious once you have the realisation of it. Even the vilest sort of existence can seem better than nothing. But I think a woman, when she finds she's going to bring a human being into the world, has the right to judge in advance.'

'Well, I don't. That's sheer sophistry. Those women are rationalising their own fear. They're judging for themselves, not the child.'[15]

She is hounded by an inner voice which will sometimes tells her to conform to inherited moral precepts, and at other moments to follow her own self-interest, but although often diffident towards those who try to help her, she is painfully moral and always seems to act out of her own ethical, or at least ethically presented sense of right and wrong. Later on in the novel she muses:

There couldn't be anything wrong with disposing of it. It wasn't a baby yet, just a potential; not much more than a seed. The chief reason I'd always been against abortion was that it seemed like tearing up a bill instead of paying it. What a piece of high-flown theorising that seemed now! Why should one pay a bill that was out of all proportion to goods received? It was absurd.[16]

Once she has made the decision to have the baby on her own, she is plagued by misgivings and second thoughts. The difference between working- and middle-class attitudes to abortion and ways of dealing with it are pointed up by her visit to Mabel, her downstairs neighbour, who offers her a Nescafé tin with some dubious pills in it and a bottle of gin: 'Mother's ruin. Now you know why they call it that, one reason anyway. Of course, you have to drink lots of it—"lots and lots, no tiny tots", as they say.'[17] Jane decides to try curry instead, and when she nearly miscarries as a result of her overindulgence in hot food, she is soon rushed into hospital where Dr Maxwell (whom she has been referred to by the doctor who wanted a hundred guineas) expresses concern that once recovered she will have to return to 'that place'. 'Damn it,' he expostulates, referring to her father's attitudes, 'we're not living in the middle-ages.' But it's clear that if she had been a working-class girl the middle ages were indeed where she would have been living, and that nobody—least of all him—would have given a damn about her predicament. But Jane is obviously living in a context where being pregnant, or even having sex with more than one person, implies that you are a whore, hence her investigation of the ladies down in the basement. A more touching aspect of her naivety is this passage about certain items of female underwear which, in their day, apparently had most men slavering with lust, and we can imagine it must have been revelatory stuff in 1960:

> I'd always thought it would be embarrassing to have a man undress you, especially the suspenders which are so ugly and comic, but I helped, and except for the girdle which must be the most resistant, unromantic garment since the chastity belt, it was all easy and delightful.[18]

For much of the book Jane's tour of the lower depths is offset by her working life as a PA to the manager at Drummonds, a Jewish-owned hotel that caters for celebrities, and by her relationship with her admiring, sympathetic boss. Here we see her at her most confident and competent—in a sense we see who she really is, why she is able to take the vicissitudes of boarding-house in her stride and why everyone is so sympathetic and helpful to her. She is extremely posh, from another world, and when she returns to work following disasters and periods of inner torment, we see her put on the brave face that is necessary to survive in such employments. We see the person she should be, and that her father, perhaps without knowing it, has equipped her to be, and we see that she is an consummate actress. A month or two after throwing her out, her father writes her a dutiful but unapologetic letter, and Jane throws it away in tearful disgust:

> It hurt for a while, then stopped. I thought how quickly all the ties of one's life could be broken and those of a new one built up… It was sad to reflect that the new friends were probably just as transitory, and the links with them just as fragile… Stupendous days—turning-point days—come without warning, and start as innocently as if butter wouldn't melt in their mouths.[19]

Whether they are 'true' or not, the warp and weft of Lynne Reid Banks' fiction is made up of such observations: they roll on and on, cumulatively building up her sense of the world. They are usually not arresting enough to be quotable, and not particularly memorable in themselves. She's dedicated to the thought that isn't really a thought, the intimation, and through their notation to building up a sense of her character's predicament that she knows readers will identify with, which blithe confidence is how she manages to regularly offend a modern reader. In her Fulham room, she copes with morning sickness and depression, and aided by carpenter John, the jazz guitarist, and by confidence-lacking writer Toby, she engages in a little nest-building, each stage and banal incident in the transformation of her bug-ridden room into a viable living space documented with a kind of excited love of banality. Despite her earlier acting career and her apparent sophistication, Jane has only just left home and has never before defined a space of her own:

> I started moderately with small, necessary items like a potato peeler and a kettle; then I branched out a little and acquired a small casserole dish and three coffee mugs; and finally I got really reckless and bought material for re-covering the chair, a three-layer vegetable rack, two cushions, a burgeoning pot of ivy and a totally unessential object called a sink-tidy which I fell for in a bargain basement.[20]

Will she find love in the L-shaped room? This basic question and the simple metaphor of life as a poorly furnished, inherited space that one must redefine as one's own but can only do so with the help of others, is the premise of the book. Jane is empty, broken down, loveless. Love in her life is an L-shaped blank. One of the prostitutes in the Fulham basement is also named Jane, and this kind of coincidence is one of Reid Banks' ways of flagging up Jane's sense of her predicament, which she tries to define by means of these grasped at affinities: objectively meaningless but subjectively important details—a kind of pathetic fallacy of human encounter that not many people would set much store by: the doctor has her initials, the prostitute has her name. Jane's inquisitiveness is that of someone who is looking for some kind of measure of her own experience. 'Come on, tell me the truth and shame the devil—what are you, one of these writers? Or an actress, going to play a prossie or something, is that it? I've met your sort before.' But she didn't seem at all angry, just amused.'[21] Jane interrogates her about sex and is rewarded with: 'What f—ing? Doesn't mean a thing, ducks, one way or the other. Lumme, you'd go mad if it did. Have another cup?' And this gem of folk-wisdom: 'Hungarian's a funny language—sounds like a mouthful of peanuts. Listen to this.' She stood with the teapot in her hand a recited carefully: 'Ha-yoke-lesteck-cop-toke-chock. Know what that means? "If you're a good boy, I'll give you a kiss." Isn't that a scream? Son taught it to me, in case I ever got a Hungarian.'

But most important, and closest to Jane's ambivalence about men is the prostitute's attitude to marriage:

> 'Fancy promising to love, honour and obey—some man. That's what'd stick in my throat.' She picked up her eyebrow pencil and eyed me shrewdly. 'Now you're going to ask if I hate all men. Well, I don't. You can't hate what you don't respect. I'm sorry for them—I don't suppose you believe that, but it's true. Even the queer ones, the ones that want a bit off the other side of the cake, well you can't help but be sorry for 'em. And some you can only laugh at—only you mustn't let 'em see it of course.'[22]

Eventually the novel circles back to her abortive affair with an actor when she was in rep, and how she was glad they hadn't actually had sex, 'still being at that age to believe that there is something intrinsically precious in virginity, and I decided to carry mine intact to the altar. But I didn't go to the altar; to be honest it wasn't for lack of offers, but because they always seemed to come from people I wouldn't have been caught at an altar with. (…) I never again saw an ordinary face change and become Apollo-like though the intervention of love.'[23] Seven years on her own has been the result—but strangely she pursues Terry again and gets pregnant by him after unsatisfactory sex, although, she tells us, she would never call any child of hers Terry, a name 'too bloody weak-kneed by half'. Jane's self-lacerating honesty cuts away at any sympathy we might be feeling for her when she admits: 'I was not in love with Terry, never had been; I went after him, deliberately, because I was ripe for an affair and I thought with him I could have one and enjoy it and still feel like the nice clean girl-next-door afterwards… I also recognised that it was more my fault than his. That didn't stop me from thinking bitterly that he'd got away scot-free.'[24]

Jane's basic emotional problem, we might be tempted to object, is that no-one is good enough for her. She has been indulged and over-protected by her father rather than, as she believes, blamed for her mother's death—that's my verdict early in the book. She serves herself up to us, hoping to win our sympathy with her charm, which has always working in the past—and it works again, her book is definitive in a way, its still in print, and here I am writing about it forty five years later as a record in the inception of popular middle-class feminist consciousness. One of Jane's characteristics, what she takes to be her 'sturdy self-righteousness', may she believes turn out on closer self-analysis to be only 'common-or-garden cowardice'. She feels that her actions must be 'justified', including her decision to have her child, by reference to some higher court of morality that is shaped by her father's attitudes but obviously transcends them. So she worries about whether she is a self-righteous coward, but Lynne Reid Banks the writer never has any doubt that her feelings, attitudes, misgivings and prevarications are representative ones, and that to record and represent them in a soul-bearing novel is to represent women and speak on their behalf—and she was obviously right. Jane's comments on how to be a writer to Toby can be taken as Reid Banks' own aesthetic credo, and it is a good one that obviously worked for her:

> ...you shouldn't need to submit your ideas to anyone for approval. If you do, you'll get as many reactions as there are people. In the end, if you're stupid enough to try and please all of them, you'll tinker and adapt and mess about until there's nothing of your original idea left—it'll just be a disgusting hotch-potch product of a lot of people's brains where it should be the pure product of one. Whether the finished product is good, bad or indifferent, the very least it should be is yours.[25]

Another book becomes important in the last third of *The L-Shaped Room*—a novel of letters to an imaginary man written by Jane's kindly, spirited aunt Addy, which this lady employs Jane to type for her on an old machine she owns. The letters of her aunt are given force and cohesion by the need that has conjured up its addressee and ideal reader. Such men don't exist in real life, especially not for the independent, eccentrically intellectual Addy, but the imagination of an understanding, sympathetic listener/lover enables Addy as a writer. Jane herself becomes its ideal reader—it helps her to understand herself and also communicates with a female literary agent who takes it on. The ideas about writing expressed by Jane are simple, hopeful, and lead Reid Banks to an emotional honesty and occasional profundity in her writing of a kind of female consciousness she believes is being expressed or the first time. But Jane's predicament is different from Addy's as it is different from that of the prostitutes in the basement, although she also accumulates a train of hopeful men wherever she goes. It is fairly easy to take pot-shots at Lynne Reid Banks in this early book; it is a relentless compendium of middle-class bigotries and privileges retailed as virtues from beginning to end—especially the virtue of speaking as you find, which covers a multitude of sins, not least racism. Finally, her queasiness about poor old helpful childlike chimp John is crossed with her previous ill-experience of homosexuals in a passage of luminous explanatory force:

> Even in that very emotional moment, I felt a little twinge of uneasiness at being embraced by this huge odd-smelling, odd-coloured man. It was a very strange feeling, and the strangeness didn't come entirely from his being of a different, a 'forbidden' race. It came from there not being even that trace of sexuality

> which there always is between men and women, even those who are just friends. I tried to remember when I'd been held like that before, and by whom. Then I did remember—it was Malcolm, the little queer who had scratched my face all those years ago.[26]

Jane's concealed pregnancy, her sexual dysfunction, her problems with her father, her daft misadventures: all ring true enough and are still contemporary in the sense that these are not problems that young women have stopped having. Penguin describes this novel as 'tender, compulsive, contemporary' on the front cover of the 1985 edition. And here we probably have one explanation as to why the book continues in print: it has a 'look into your heart and write' quality; it is highly identifiable with, is still going strong and on some levels is almost impossible to criticise except for being frank and of its time: and what she is saying is that, having thrust herself into the lower depths, with all her faults and prejudices, most people were kind and supportive of her. At the time it appeared in 1960 *The L-Shaped Room* was an advanced book about being an independent woman, racy but starkly honest, and soon afterwards became a must-see film. I remember being sent to bed when it came on television. It was a book that tried to explore and overcome English middle-class prejudices. It certainly stood at the beginning of something. A novel like Margaret Forster's *Georgy Girl* (1966) stands in a similar relationship to Lynn Reid Banks' *The L-Shaped Room* as Barry Hines' *A Kestrel for a Knave* does to Keith Waterhouse's *There is a Happy Land*: in both cases a kind of permission has been given by the earlier writer, as well as some elements of a format. Georgy's room is a dance studio in the well-appointed Kensington house of her parents' employer; the room she escapes into from his advances is a ricketty shared flat, complete with jazz musician potential boyfriend, his callous girlfriend, pregnant, and a batty neighbour: best-avoided, but any port in a storm. The engaging manner and technique of this book is a kind of perfected version of *The L-Shaped Room*, as young female options and identity are explored, still freshly, but more fruitily, for a now established market. The theme of how to buck a life that has been laid down for you and achieve independence is identical, although Forster's resolution to her character's predicament is shocking and perverse. Like Reid Banks' heroine, Georgy ultimately gets what she wants; but we are left feeling queasy rather than optimistic about likely outcomes for an intelligent female misfit. Lynne Reid Banks later lived in a kibbutz on the shores of the Sea of Galilee with her Israeli husband; I wouldn't be at all surprised to hear that Jesus of Nazareth walked across its waters a few times to ask her advice, irresistibly drawn by the fragrant odour of her baked beans with added garlic salt.

When rebellious Chelsea convent girl Nell Dunn crossed the river to Battersea to work with the South London working-class girls whose voices are heard so vividly in her first book, *Up the Junction*, she was rather in the position of anthropologist Margaret Mead when writing her *Coming of Age in Samoa* in the late twenties—investigating local customs as a sympathetic observer, with few independent sources, and having won the confidence of her subjects, she was left with little choice but to trust that everyone was telling her the truth. Like Mead she also had the evidence of her own eyes, and her own participation in their workplace and recreational rituals, and the advantage of a more-or-less common language. On the other hand she was investigating a notoriously unreliable group—teenagers—who may well have noticed, as Mead's young Samoans did, that the lady liked to hear about sex, and helpfully slanted their talk in those directions.[27] Did the young women of Battersea routinely slip off their knickers and put them in their pockets on their way 'up the junction' for a Friday night on the tiles? Dunn's results were first published in *New Society* and I suppose they're not that hard to swallow. But in not examining her induction of her 'results', it may also be that she gets a version of coming of age in Battersea in which a group not regularly asked their opinions by a young sympathetic outsider, gleefully elaborated on their own lawlessness, and Dunn—and her concerned readers—as it were lapped it up. Many women if asked about their teenage years will laugh and say, 'We were terrible, really terrible.' But how terrible were they?

Nell Dunn was a participant observer with an agenda. Her own background has been described as 'outrageously posh': her mother was the daughter of the Fifth Earl of Rosslyn, 'the man who broke the bank at Monte Carlo', and she is descended from the liaison between Nell Gwynn and Charles II. She has described her own family as bohemian and said that her mother, like her, was always fascinated by the working-classes. Married to Old Etonian TV playwright Jeremy Sandford, the young couple shared a passionate reforming zeal where working-class poverty and living conditions were concerned, and decided to buy a terraced cottage in Battersea to further their contact with working-class Londoners.[28] Dunn wished to celebrate women's autonomy and sexuality, and any sign that a previous generation's modesty or repression are being thrown to the winds that blow down from Clapham Common were more than welcome so far as she was concerned. However, she forcefully depicts the cruelty of girls as well as their joyfulness, and she also depicts the local reaction to herself, particularly of boys who hope she is 'easy' (aren't their own girls after all?)

and plainly have little or no respect for women in general. There is hopeful utopianism in all of this, a new hope that a repressive patriarchy whose conventions and customs that have held back women for millennia was soon to be dissolved in what Norman Mailer was to call the suck of the orgy as an empowered matriarchy rapidly gained ground, its vanguard a phalanx of knicker-waving teenage girls. Perhaps young women like those she celebrates had always been a bit wild, or perhaps she was genuinely witnessing something new, or perhaps she was excited by the thought (untrue or not) that working-class people were more sexually liberated than anyone from her own background—except her. But I can't help but wonder if any of her correspondents, once her sketches had made it to the small screen via the beautifully structured oral poetry of Ken Loach's television play, got a parental clip round the ear for their troubles. What can't be stressed enough about *Up the Junction* on the page is the poetry of its construction, its counterpointing of speech, social observation and everyday cultural detritus to create a rich sense of working-class women's lives in the sixties. At this moment Nell Dunn is writing a kind of newly-minted—and funny—populist modernism of women's consciousness:

> Rube looked up.
>
> 'Well, the council sent his dad a bill for five pound for the eight buckets of sand they used in clearing up the blood.'
>
> Joe Brown sang on: 'Then you were gone like a dream in the night. With you went my heart, my love and my light.'
>
> We walked back to the court. They found Dave guilty. In the underground cells we went to say goodbye to him. Through the grating I could see a Milky Way paper, a blue plastic bottle and a Spangles packet. Dave kicked at the iron door and screamed, 'I'm bloody well going to get out of here.'
>
> Rube and I cut down a side-street past a baby in a pram wrapped in a khaki blanket sucking at a teat stuck on a lemonade bottle, and headed for home. Towards us glided an apparition, a huge pink Cadillac pulling a pink caravan on which was written: MISS CAMAY IS HERE! WIN THIS CAR AND CARAVAN. ENTRY FORMS HERE. Music blared out of a loudspeaker. Inside the car sat a sulky blonde. The car drove dead slow and behind swarmed kids on roller skates or running, lollipops in mouths.
>
> 'Shame about that. Now you'll have to find yerself another bloke.'
>
> 'Yes.'
>
> 'That's the thing—what you don't get caught for you're entitled to do.'[29]

Poor Cow, her first novel, was also Ken Loach's first cinema release, and according to a recent television interview, it now embarrasses him for the sexually exploitative way it was sold. But the novel is superior in this case in that Joy's inner-life is far better represented than in the film. She can't altogether be turned into a sex-object on the page, and Dunn's agenda is again to celebrate female autonomy and sexuality. Her technique is to counterpoint Joy's letters to her imprisoned boyfriend with a form of what the great critic of modernism, Hugh Kenner calls 'free indirect style', close to stream of consciousness, in the narrative voice. This gives real dimension to Joy as a character and enables Dunn to explore the gaps and contradictions in Joy's evolving consciousness in a way that approaches the James Joyce of the Gertie McDowell chapter of *Ulysses*: her self-presentation in romantic letters to prison, her self-justifying thoughts as she descends through bar work, glamour modelling and prostitution—through which she becomes ever-more affluent, self-defining and confident—and the intrusion of various harsh realities of her situation. Donovan's plangent folky soundtrack contributes to the film's steady drip of romanticism and male sympathy for Joy. Nell Dunn's novel is of course highly sympathetic to her as well, but not in quite the same terms. Joy's eventual comeuppance is harsh and unjust and in it Dunn exposes the everyday counter-forces to women's sexual liberation and the revenge they will exact against transgressors like the joyful Joy. Dunn's novel depicts the loops, repetitions and elisions of consciousness of a central character who is all at sea in enthusiasm and desire—and in this Joy somewhat resembles Gertrude Stein's far more modest and innocent African-American servant girl, Melanctha, in her own first book *Three Lives*.[30] Both characters live in an unarticulable soup of desires, drives and sustaining self-delusions and in her first two books Nell Dunn avails herself of some breakthrough moments in modernist narrative technique and brings them to bear on the sympathetic depiction of a young woman's decline, the routine violence she must endure and her pitiful fantasies of escape with only ephemeral consumer goods as materials for self-redefinition:

> If I could get rid of him I could go out—have my false piece on top like a cottage loaf. I might win on the spastic shilling-a-week and if you win you can choose anything from a book: Prestige Happymaid; Dish Drainer; a Bex 'Decorair' and four tea towels; Kitchen Timer and Hand Towel; Gents winter weight Pyjamas; Six Table mats; Four pairs of gents socks—I'd be well away.[31]

What makes Nell Dunn's early writing especially interesting is its clarity of focus and her careful avoidance of making herself a protagonist, a decision reinforced by her relationship to other modes of writing: film and television, the British documentary as well as French and Italian films of the thirties and forties—and radical television of the sixties. Nell Dunn's relationship with Jeremy Sandford and to Ken Loach and through them to a new incarnation of 'socialist realism' was obviously an important influence on the shape and focus of her first two books. Fly-on-the-wall and *cinéma vérité* were newly minted and popular forms. John Berger's and B.S. Johnson's 'documentary' books partake of this moment, as do various others, like Doris Lessing's *In Pursuit of the English*, all of them harking back to George Orwell's *The Road to Wigan Pier*. There was also the new kind of documentary novel that had been invented on the other side of the Atlantic by Truman Capote in his *In Cold Blood*, and all the 'new journalists' who followed his example, including Norman Mailer and Thomas Wolfe. But however literary these big name writers were seen to be, their work is also related to the directness of the relatively new medium of television. And in various ways all attempt to answer the objections to naturalism made by Raymond Williams: a flattening out of the social world, and a restriction of focus are amongst its major distortions. Naturalism is unable to show wider social processes and properly relate the individual subject to them.[32] They were anxious to leave the nineteenth century novel far behind, they had no choice, but in this sense the realist novel remained an underlying cultural model yet to be surpassed (except, where it was allowed to be, by television) as a vehicle for social reflection and criticism that could make sensuously present that upon which it was attempting to reflect.

Talking to Women (1965) is a fascinating book of interviews by Dunn that does much to define the predicament of a group of sixties women, largely educated but with one working-class exception, who felt themselves to be on the cusp of a new consciousness of themselves. All of the women (they are in their mid twenties to early thirties) describe themselves unaffectedly as girls. Most of them are middle-class women, a preponderance of writers, artists and actresses, and one working-class girl from Battersea, Kathy Collier, pictured on the book's cover lighting a cigarette with Nell Dunn, who may well have been one of her main informants for *Up the Junction* and *Poor Cow*—she is an articulate and open-minded commentator on her area and her contemporaries and Dunn obviously has a strong, sympathetic bond with her. The unique woman pop artist and actress Pauline Boty speaks of her enjoyment of pot and purple hearts, her fear of having an 'ugly cunt' and her feeling that she is not really herself until she has 'put her eyes on'. Edna O'Brien is a magnificent interviewee, full of dramatic intensity, effortlessly spun erotic tales, dark intuitions, strikingly archaic attitudes and thrilling candour. Orgasm for her can be triggered by being touched on the heel, 'arse-probing' (of male homosexuals) is a probable crime against the almighty as well as an unsatisfactory flight from fusion with the Great Mother; she is a self-confessed guilt-ridden poor mother herself and yet she leaves us in no doubt that she is totally self-defining as a woman. If the expression of a new female subjectivity is the basis of the emergence of a distinctive postwar feminism, Edna O'Brien defines and is its exemplar. Her attention is all to her own petites sensations and her inner life, and she freely admits to embarking on relationships with the noble purpose of writing about them. Emma Charlton talks of being an early postwar bohemian, a pre-beatnik, and the frustration of seeing your once unique anti-style (circa 1951) become a mass phenomenon. She describes being in the queue to see the James Bond film *Goldfinger* at Hammersmith, and the depressing experience of everyone having her beat look—and the equally dispiriting outcome of her rejection of the middle-class way: she imagined no possessions and it was so. The book is engaging for its freewheeling talk about the expectations of men and their attitudes to men, mostly sympathetic. and the competing demands of art and emotional and family relationships. One of the most notable things about these women from an era where the feminine was still considered to be mysterious and intuitive is that they appear to be mysterious to themselves—they, including Kathy Collier, feel they have no real templates for their ways of being, are mostly happy to 'live for the moment': almost everything they have to say about themselves sounds excitingly spontaneous, tentative and exploratory: it is as though their version of female consciousness is a new place, one just arrived at.

One of the most interesting encounters is with her fellow novelist Ann Quin, a highly sensitive experimentalist writer from the stable of radical publisher John Calder, who responds angrily to Dunn's question as to whether the concept of class means anything to her, leading to an interesting exchange of views on the subject:

> ANN. No. Class has never bothered me only inasmuch that I get sick to death of it being—well, ever since the novel in England has been concerned with class, Osborne and so on and Wesker. I think it's been overdone. I don't think it amounts to that.
> NELL. I think it's interesting insofar as it still to a certain extent activates the way people behave, in many little detailed ways.
> ANN. Yes. I'm writing about it at the moment, two people who have always had money and have always known a certain side of llfe and never gone beyond and the girl has never known a family life as such and she's very intrigued by it, although she hates it, she's also intrigued.
> NELL. But certainly something that struck me, again when I was about seventeen and I began to meet working-class people, was I had no idea how to talk to them, get through to them or they to me.

> ANN. I hate this sort of thing of setting up working-class people and so on I really do. People are people to me.
> NELL. They're individuals?
> ANN. Yes. It's never really bothered me that.
> NELL. But it does bother a lot of people.
> ANN. Yes I'm sure it does. It exists. There's an awful lot of snobbery. I mean as much in people, as you would call them working-class, as in people who aren't. There's snobbery in all these stratas of society.
> NELL. Are you interested in politics?
> ANN. No.[33]

Ann Quin is clearly hostile to the social preoccupations of the English novel of the previous decade and feels that these books have traduced reality, yet she is defensive enough to be browbeaten by Dunn into admitting the existence of precisely the social phenomena that Dunn is so intent upon documenting. Nor is it precisely a matter of Dunn's conceptions of class, which are only vaguely and mildly expressed here. Quin seems to insist that even to speak of working-class people as such is to impose an oppressive category on them, yet her own interest is clearly in the social problems of people who have always had money. Dunn convicts her of being apolitical and is equally clearly highly class-conscious in a way she believes to be honest and sympathetic. Her talk with Kathy Collier shows that she has indeed learned how to talk to working-class people: she gently pumps her for attitudes and information, butters her up, and assumes a working-class way of speaking herself. She is to some extent a social chameleon, as Edna O'Brien and Pauline Boty also admit to being, in a way upper-class Chelsea socialite Suna Portman can never be. Nell Dunn doesn't ask her, or any of the other women, what their attitudes to class are. Ann Quin's *cri de coeur* that she is sick of hearing about class and that much of what has been said about it is false is far from being totally ridiculous: although offered naïvely it remains the dominant view and, then as now, is generally asserted with great confidence.

Despite what might be said to undermine her authority to speak of her class subjects—and they are no more than the liberties all creative writers have taken—Nell Dunn's subsequent writing never retreats from this moment of intense loving solidarity; but is arguably less effective because Dunn's own feminist consciousness takes centre stage. She loses her sense of the otherness and difference of her characters and their social milieu and the magic and tension is lost. She has also told the stories she wished to tell—told them in a manner that ensures they still live in the collective memory of film. Some might say she is a more honest writer in later work, but to me it seems she treads the path of so many middle-class writers on working-class subjects, of replacing their voices and aspirations with her own. She appears to believe that she, if anybody, is the people she represents, or at least a role model for them, rather as the communist party substitutes itself for the working-class in Lukács' *History and Class-Consciousness*. As the women's movement gained ground, she published a further book of autobiographical reflections and interviews about her interest in communal lifestyles called *Living Like I Do*.[34]

Lynn Reid Banks' *The L Shaped Room* and Nell Dunn's *Up the Junction* and *Poor Cow* are congruent in many ways in their treatment of young women's economic status, sexuality, language—but less so in the literary techniques they employ. Reid Banks' realist mode and Dunn's populist blend of naturalism and modernism impact on the kinds of social picture of young women they offer. I think we could say that Lynne Reid Banks' is a more 'natural' novel than Nell Dunn's early books: it is a female *bildungsroman* that charts its heroine's development with honesty and little attempt to distance itself from her autobiographical persona's point of view. Dunn is playing a more devious and complex game with her characters: at first she is included as observer, then excises herself in the later book, remaining immanent like Flaubert's notion of the novelist as the God of the creation. Her main purpose is to define another point of view rather chart the development of her own; this she continues to do in different kinds of documentary books, again, often through exploring the lives of contemporaries. Lynne Reid Banks has a thorough-goingly middle-class point of view, but has often been understood as a working-class writer. She speaks to a middle-class girl who is hoping to find out what its like out or down there, or to an aspirational working-class one; Nell Dunn tries to sympathetically document the ways of life of a class of young women remote from her own background; and it is clear that, in terms both social and geographical, they will be staying exactly where they were put.

Nell Dunn's hallmarks as a writer are inquisitiveness and generosity; but there is always a nagging version of Ann Quin's objection ('I don't think it amounts to that') to be encountered in her account of working-class women. The voices that still live in her books played little or no part in framing their own stories: their processed talk clatters on and on, their hopes long expired in a format that seems as built in obsolete as their discarded teetering heels, crispy beehives and Magimix packets, their clapped out chocolate wrapper Minis bound for the British museum of happy motoring: as case-histories they are long despaired over and perhaps justly forgotten; but they are still vivid to us insofar as Dunn has found something to celebrate about their attitudes and their way of life—a perennial segment of the female manual working-class who are as rough and ready nowadays as they were in the early sixties.

The Incurable (1971) was Dunn's next published novel, and in it she gives the Battersea girls a break and focuses on her own kind of life as a young mother. Dedicated to her sons, these three shaggy-haired young boys adorn the front cover, gambolling black and white lambs before a limitless pale grey sea, while on the back of the wraparound jacket, Nell Dunn looks out at the camera, fag in hand, still defiant in her pushed back fedora, her afghan cut-off and spectacularly flared jeans: a hippie mum, living as she does. Love is a disease as incurable as multiple sclerosis in this novel of illness, marriage, bringing up small children and unquenchable hopes that have taken a good dousing. It is a hard story to make exciting, and she doesn't really try: just to carefully record a woman's sense of the demands of marriage and child-rearing and a necessary retreat into an inner world by the girl she once was—and still is, in a way.[35] It reveals some of her limitations as a writer—she is unable to freely invent—and shows that her working-class sources and her relationships with them, both their language and their spiritedness, were what pulled the lyricism of her first books out of her. But she also shows an incurable fidelity to her original project, recording her own inner speech this time: affirming a sense of felt autonomy without which women's care could not take place. We are returned to the interviews of *Talking to Women* in which the talk of a number of relatively young women attempts to refract and reflect upon the concerns of women in society, and to a problem at the heart—and at the beginning—of feminism's idea of representation: the very different attitudes and expectations of middle-class women and those whom they have particularly sought to help up the ladder of consciousness.

Chapter Three

Looking for a Brand New Start: Colin MacInnes

Colin MacInnes' first novel, *To the Victors the Spoils* (1950), is mined out of his experiences as a soldier at the end of the Second World War in Europe, and shows that he was always intensely interested in what was going to burgeon out of the ruins of that apocalypse. Like Norman Mailer's near-contemporary *The Naked and the Dead*, it is a book written by a young demobilised soldier with a lot to say, many experiences to recount, even more so in MacInnes' case. *To the Victors the Spoils* is a long book, with a panoramic sweep across Holland and the Rhine, a novel which sees it responsibilities as partly documentary: this is how the victorious armies of democracy behaved in the defeated countries of Europe, and this is what those countries looked like after five years of pounding by the allies, after Nazism, after the Jews has been disposed of. The book's style is very assured, so assured in its descriptions and the acuity with which he captures the class relationships of British Army life that, for all the density of detail and incident, it is not really a vivid or involving or dramatic novel at all, but one which rather reduces the rubble it witnesses to a sort of affectless, bureaucratic uniformity. This, characteristically, is part of MacInnes' subject. His officers and sergeants are so preoccupied with their own morality, with judging one another—too vulgar? too cynical? too soft? too gullible?—and relating these judgements back to a chain of command, that the war-torn peoples of Europe become a kind of backdrop to a cosily hierarchical and morally preoccupied military life.

It is a novel that explores the contradictions of working in an intelligence unit charged with uncovering collaborators and black marketeers, discovering who were the Nazis and their collaborators and breaking down the last psychological defences of a defeated people. Cynicism is in order if you are continually being lied to, but one's own humanity is put at risk in the process of uncovering the truths of human weakness and amorality. In this work it is vital to be a good, accurate judge of character, but are the less well-educated and more down-to-earth sergeants possessed of a greater clear-sightedness, and better able to smell a Nazi rat, than their more sympathetic, sophisticated officers? For MacInnes intelligence work offers an unparalleled opportunity to see a lot of duplicity in action and is obviously excellent training for one who would be an observer, psychologist and fiction writer. However, he hopes to be able to farm out the dirty work to those who most relish it, and to continue to cultivate his humanist sensitivities:

> I was fascinated by the human weaknesses this work disclosed (in oneself and others), and eager to understand the motives and methods of those involved in it. But all this was equally disgusting… I was hoping the Depot would send one or two hard-headed men who would do the dirty work that would have to be done. Not just strong arm men like Walker, but men crooked and capable as those they would be hunting… And I would be able to see the sights our life uncovered, without being implicated in all the acts that made them visible.[1]

To the Victors the Spoils is a highly impressive book that sweeps across Europe with the Allied armies and sympathises both with the conquered Dutch and especially with the Germans themselves, whom the narrator and various other English characters regard as racial and cultural kindred. Far from being seen as the defeated Hun, they are seen by the Unit, many of whom have German ancestors or sympathies, as perhaps the only people in Europe that the English could believe to be possibly superior to themselves. Moving from place to place in the wake of the victorious allied infantries, the Intelligence Unit to which its narrating Sergeant is attached carries out interrogations, indulges in passing love affairs, pieces together the shattered stories of displaced persons and tries to weed out the truth about the Nazis. It is a novel that is surprising in the breadth of its sympathies, and psychologically acute, and because it must be in the circumstances, fanatically precise in its estimate and placing of people observed or encountered. As the allies push deeper into Germany, they find the conquered people compliant, almost welcoming, likely to deny Nazi involvement, and at all levels they help themselves to the spoils of victory, especially women, despite the non-fraternisation orders. MacInnes reflects on what it would have been like if the Germans had invaded Britain, and concludes that English women would have been equally eager to find German boyfriends. What is unique in the book is its directness and determination to get under the skin of a heroic view of war, and its eerie sense of the incoming English having conquered their own country, their own dark twin. Equally eerie is that, apart from a passing reference to the concentration camps, the book says nothing about what has happened to Germany's Jewish people—at this point it as though they have been simply excised forever, and the invaders don't even notice their absence.

It might be said that MacInnes' London novels carry the social and psychological mapping he began in *To the Victors the Spoils* onto new and different terrains, recording a society in flux with a detached eye that caught a great deal of sociological detail and took a great deal of psychology for granted. It is certainly true that MacInnes' point of view remained that of an intelligence officer and that it is not really, as some have written and as MacInnes himself intended, the subaltern classes who truly speak in his London novels; rather an observant commentator with a panoramic view who has already taken in the ruins of Europe. His second novel, *June in Her Spring* (1951), is a far more modest performance than his first, also autobiographically based, but in his Australian upbringing. Like *Absolute Beginners* it is about teenagers and shows what a very different experience coming of age was a few years earlier for middle-class Australians in the small outback town of Ballantyne (possibly named after R.M. Ballantyne, prolific Scottish writer of boy's tales of exploration and adventure). The young people at its centre live only a step away from the wilderness, but are hemmed in by the mores and morals of their parents and a community whose ways, although relatively recent, seem steeped in traditions and social anxieties that would not be out of place in the English home counties:

> 'He can damage himself. He can damage us if he likes, but I won't have him damaging the families in the district.'
> 'That's selfishness and snobbery.'
> 'It's not. It's pride if you like.'[2]

Thus June Westley's father on her delinquent brother Arthur as their parental misgivings concerning his unruly behaviour simmer gently in the run-up to the annual gymkhana, an event at which high and low rub shoulders on once-a-year equal-terms 'dreaming for the day that Ballantyne's a tented camp and all are met to defend it against bushrangers within a wood stockade.'[3] Ballantyne has a squirearchy and a firm sense of social place. June's best friend Cleopatra has formed an alliance with Ed, the son of a local bank manager who is studying accountancy but whom her parents consider unsuitable because his father is not a sheep-owner. June herself is keen on Ben, who has been brought up by a guardian, the former accompanist of his father, a successful opera singer who died when he was a young child. His guardian, the creepy Uncle Henry, is a paedophile. *June in her Spring* tells the story of June and Ben's summer romance under circumstances where sex is seen to lead to immediate marriage and marriage is fundamentally an economic and social alliance between families of equal standing. The young couple are ignorant both of sex and of what life has to offer them: they too are absolute beginners in a time and place where the condition of being a teenager has not yet quite been invented:

> Time stretching out before them all the summer would reveal these secrets if they had to be revealed. And life would be on their

side (as it is with youth when youth knows its real age: neither lagging behind not thinking ahead of its animal years)—life was on the side of those that loved it, as June did that summer.[4]

If the sense of social claustrophobia and constraint in the novel is reminiscent of Jane Austen and its picturing of encroaching terrifying wilderness and emptiness is uniquely Australian, MacInnes' prose is limpid, poetic and refined in a way that recalls the work of Irish novelist Elizabeth Bowen, its doomed romantic subject-matter concerning the loss of innocence of a sympathetic young girl quite similar to her novel *The Death of the Heart* (1938). In *June in Her Spring* both of the young lovers are rebellious spirits. Ben is a musician, the only child of an opera singer, brought up by a strange guardian to follow in his father's footsteps. He is more of a snob than June—both aloof and fiercely defensive of his sense of high culture and difference from the surrounding attitudes and familiar speech of the Australian working-classes, as in this conversation with a coachman:

> Passing them on the down journey, he waved and said, 'That was a dinkie-die do down at the Liquor Palace when Arthur stoushed you! By oath, it was. Too-a-rooster!'
>
> 'Now you can understand,' said Benny, in Uncle Henry's voice, 'why my uncle and I don't go much around the district.'
>
> 'What does that mean?'
>
> 'To hear conversation like that.'[5]

Unlike Benny Bond, June has no objection, real or pretended, to the coachman's conversation, which, to my ear, like much of the Australian speech in the book (as noted by MacInnes) has an almost Elizabethan flavour to it: a relish and inventive approach to slang that will stand him in good stead in his London novels. In *June in Her Spring* Ben and June's quarrel cements their growing love for one another as they ride out together into the bush to consummate it and we are offered a summation of the process of Australia's colonization by white settlers, a sort of speeded up version of the establishment of North American society. Virgin land is at first crossed by nomadic bushrangers and prospectors, grabbed by opportunists whose thefts are then backed up by a legal apparatus and a 'civilised machinery', and within two generations whole vast areas of former fertile wilderness have been tamed and are 'parcelled out like the main streets of a city'. The aboriginals whose land has been grabbed and whose ancestral dream-time has been apparently replaced with liquor and the white man's 'ticking clocks' retreat further and further into deep bush, 'fascinated and horrified', followed by whites who are unable to settle, still believing in the dream of unlimited vacant territory, and fetch up on the edges of the central desert at the salty margins of the white man's law. The rapidity, urgency and inevitability of this process of conquest, incorporation and modernisation to the marching time of those ticking clocks expresses the sense of urgency of an unfolding historical process of 'civilisation', in a moment that is always frangible, decaying and reforming, a wilderness that is to be incorporated and exploited and exhausted, a process MacInnes later applies to the march of fashion and the teenage culture in *Absolute Beginners*: 'Beep beep' say the goon squad in David Bowie's song 'Fashion', ordering any laggards out of their way and imposing their compulsory new order on an agog multitude.[6]

June and Ben soon encounter the Hacketts, a small patriarchal clan who have moved beyond the edges of the settlement of Ballantyne to found a timber industry, and pushed on as they uprooted the forests in their path:

> The further they got, the more timber cost to bring to Ballantyne. At present they earned about enough to keep alive. And after Old Mum's death, Old Dad had made over Daybreak to the boys and gone to live alone in a shack high up Mount Majestical, like a Moses waiting for a sign that never came.[7]

Old Dad has some portentously doom-laden advice to offer the young couple. Likely to come horribly true, we feel, as Ben shows off for June, kills an encroaching tiger snake and wrestles with Hackett's son. During this 'trip up bush' what might have been, and is, a small scale social novel about choosing a husband takes on a strongly allegorical dimension as they move through an untamed, threatening landscape whose overpowering quality is in its seductively beckoning uncertainty. Tracks peter out, ruined houses appear unexpectedly where none had been previously known, maps are only agreed hearsay, and horses may bolt in sudden fear: a supernatural, swallowing landscape of the kind that has been evoked in so many Australian films, particularly Peter Weir's *Picnic At Hanging Rock*, based on a much later novel about an incident in which a party of Edwardian schoolgirls mysteriously vanished without trace at Ayers Rock, the largest such boulder in Australia and an aboriginal sacred place.

> The plain was all in sun and the heights were in the shade, so that they saw the landscape from the darkness as if in a cinema. Up in the blue above was nothing except for two minute ineffectual clouds—why was the vapour in them not drunk up by so much heat?[8]

In such a trackless, deceptive environment it is easy, if one is not extremely careful, to become 'bushed'. Not only lost in the bush and therefore quite likely to die but also lost to oneself: to lose strength and hope and to experience then 'the deeper drop into a total loneliness; and then into worse—into a solitude that is not I without them, but I without I: a disintegration of the personality that bears a foretaste of the end of life.'[9] And indeed the lovers do manage to lose their horses and each other for a while, but everything blunders together again after a while and they make love desperately: 'Well, Benny, that's not how the film stars do it, I suppose,' June remarks, but her abandonment is accompanied by a sense of dread and powerlessness no less threatening to her identity than being 'bushed'; indeed, this sex may be another form of ambush, and she experiences a powerful feeling of fatality:

> June lay and looked at him in wiser silence, then all at once there rose up in her heart such anguish, such anguish now she was a prisoner of chance and time—now her youth was measured, now her joy was held in the hollow of another careless hand, and she flung her arms around him as though to hold him and the moment there forever.[10]

The newly bonded lovers desire nothing more or less than to begin their lives, their real lives together, to go somewhere together and start living from scratch. They are looking for a brand new start, as the song will put it a few years later, but in the traditional world they inhabit the exercise of such unfettered choice is sure to be denied them—as indeed it will be. As the book progresses we see the hierarchies of its small-town world as more and more fragile and that, if deeply felt they are forever coming apart at the seems, or seams. Ballantyne is replete with haunted, defeated, broken people—again reminiscent of William Faulkner's vision of the American South, complete with its carapace of gentility and dark family secrets and its overpowering sense of being haunted. Names hold a similar significance in *June in Her Spring* as they do in the novels of Faulkner, for their symbolizing zest and verbal extravagance: Addie Budren is burdened as sure as Old Dad Hackett chopped a path through the Australian outback. Clarissa Canterbury's name has a fine ring, combining Richardson's choosy, virginal, raped Clarissa and a certain classy horsiness, just as Faulkner's Temple Drake from *Sanctuary* is a dead cert for a virgin-oracle-whore who will be inevitably sacrificed by novel's end. The assertiveness and verbal showiness of these names is a reverse analogue of the insecurity and borrowed nature of the culture they represent. Benny's real surname (his Christian name is that of the simpleton in *The Sound and the Fury*) is that of his all-Australian singing father not his abusive guardian, Bond (to whom he is bound) and there is the implication that his talent has been stunted by the imposition of false-genteel cultural values: a victim of a poncified English-inflected elite's fear of the creativity and energy of the mob.

At this point MacInnes is producing a kind of Australian Southern Gothic: hereditary madness comes to a quick foaming head in *June in Her Spring*; June cannot contemplate having children due to her fear of inheriting her father's melancholy, her brother Arthur has already manifested it himself in his drunken excesses. Benny can be assumed to have inherited both his father's musical abilities and his turbulent nature and tendency to dissolution, which made him unfit for dealings with women. Uncle Henry's sexual interference with Benny hasn't inhibited his tendency to boisterous slap-happiness and horseplay, which we see is at the root of Australian masculinity, but he is determined to make it to the capital and hence to Europe, to England, where, as a Ballantyne barman in the Liquor Palace (where he is playing for tips) warns him: 'England!' the barman raised his eyebrows to the ochred ceiling. 'I knew a pommie once who tried to milk a sheep.'[11] Nevertheless, in flight from all this and from a homosexual taint that MacInnes names as openly as he dared in early fifties Australia, Benny is determined to make his escape from the world of Ballantyne with its gymkhanas, Fancy-dress balls and rowdy beer parlours.

June in her Spring is an uncertain but sometimes beautiful novel which makes moves in a number of directions, involving in parts but ultimately unsatisfactory. It is as though MacInnes is afraid of the small town Australian world he depicts: its meshes and snares have left unhealed wounds; he is unable to fully invest himself creatively in this painful story of broken love, incest, rape and madness and play it out to the hilt, to the end, but is already floating some way above self-romanticising Ballantyne in a kind of careless irony, which is after all the habitual tone in which its young characters address one another's pains. All Benny can do is leave June behind, and all June can do is accept a life of frustration and limitation—a somewhat heartless way of disposing of a young woman who gives her name to the book and offers it and her all to its male principal; only to find that everything is taken away from her, as she foresees early on in her affair with him: 'They waved as often as the light would let them, and then Benny rode off too, separated from her as lovers always are, always, always, always, if they are lovers.'[12]

But what does this slight, sensitive Australian novel with few great ambitions have to do with the brash London world of teenage fashion-victims? Colin MacInnes' characters in his most celebrated novel are absolute beginners because of their sense of starting from scratch without real precedent, of being in near the beginning of a new consumerist youth culture that had already slightly gone off for his narrator and also, despite his young friends' sense of sophistication, being naïve teenagers. MacInnes himself has an attitude to youth that is both besotted and cynical. Being observed by a sympathetic older gay man makes for a book not so dark as Anthony Burgess' over-symbolising *Clockwork Orange*, far closer to its youthful subjects and much better on the naïve joyousness of juvenile delinquency, androgynous dandyism, and the sense of being at the eye of one's glorious moment with a feeling of absolute confidence that you are it, it is now, and that is that. *Absolute Beginners* opens with a definition of its narrator's sense of centrality and the absolute perfection of his point of vantage:

> Looking North you don't see much, it's true, and westward the view's entirely blocked by the building you're inside. But twisting slowly on your barstool from the east to south, like Cinerama, you can see clean new concrete cloud-kissers, rising up like felixes from the Olde Englishe squares, and then those gorgeous parks, with trees like classical French salads, and then again the port life down along the Thames, that glorious river, reminding you we're on an estuary, a salt inlet, really, with crazy seagulls circling up from it and almost bashing their beaks against the circular plate glass, and then, before you know it, you're back again round a full circle in front of your iced coffee cup.[13]

The first thing to notice is that MacInnes' technique as a novelist has developed, and radically changed, between his first two novels and his fourth (it is the second of his London trilogy, sandwiched between *City of Spades* and *Mr. Love and Justice*); the second thing is that he is no longer explicitly writing out of his own experience; the third thing is that the London teenagers are far more confident and articulate than those depicted in *June in Her Spring*. In the earlier novel they are far more like real teenagers: full of self-doubt, ignorance, and desperate urges than the all-too-knowing denizens of the coffee-bar world of Blitz Baby and his cronies. Nor is it difficult to believe that hip London teenagers had a better time than middle-class Australian kids stuck in places like Ballantyne, but the loquacious eye of *Absolute Beginners* is obviously a mask for a middle-aged novelist. This is a far more ventriloqual book than *June in Her Spring* and the fourth thing to notice about it is that the colourful, inventive, intoxicating argot spouted by the narrator has an unmistakably Australian twang. Contemporary reviewers opined that MacInnes' London novels were 'worth more' than innumerable dry sociological tomes or papers on race or teenagers—as though they were indeed and nevertheless reports from the front lines of experience. But to read these books now is to notice how thoroughly they are enmeshed in sociological and newspaper accounts of the phenomena of teenage rebellion and immigration, sources on which they do continually draw and offer a comment on, often to good, amusing effect. MacInnes' unnamed teenage photographer should be a walking sixties sociology textbook of disaffected youth, a one boy folk devil and moral panic, but he is himself as moralising as his creator, much to the irritation of his socialist father and his sexually-active mother, who is something of a perpetual teenager herself, still having it off with her 'beefy Malt' lodgers. Everything about his style of dress is an affront to his 'oafo' brother:

> I had on my full teenage drag that I knew would enrage him—the grey pointed alligator casuals, the pink neon pair of ankle crepe nylon-stretch, my Cambridge-blue glove-fit jeans, a vertical-striped happy shirt revealing my lucky neck charm on its chain, and the Roman-cut short-arse jacket just referred to… not to mention my wrist identity jewel, and my Spartan warrior hair-do, which everyone thinks costs me 17/6d. in Gerrard Street, but which I, as a matter of fact, do myself with a pair of nail-clippers and a three-sided mirror that Suzette's got, when I visit her flatlet up in Bayswater, W.2.[14]

Their adolescent son sneers at adults as 'tax-payers' and has so much bought into the concept of being a teenager that he feels able to define a whole social experience and attitude simply by opening his mouth and engaging first gear on his Vespa scooter. MacInnes is writing about the unprecedented moment, admittedly a long one, in which young people could credibly believe they were having a radically different life to their parents, and living in a new world with quite different expectations and challenges: this is the important sense in which they are absolute beginners, and despite their naivety it is not altogether illusory. For MacInnes' archetypal teenager everything about the adult world is 'a drip-dry drag', including the Labour politics of his family:

> 'I dunno about the trouble with me,' my oafo brother finally declared, but your trouble is, you have no social conscience.'
> 'No what?'
> 'No social conscience.'
> He'd come up close, and I looked into narrow, meanie eyes. 'That sounds to me,' I said. 'like a parrot-cry pre-packaged for you by your fellow squalids of the Ernie Bevan club.'[15]

And the boy is quick to explain further:

> 'You poor old prehistoric monster,' I exclaimed. 'I do not reject the working-classes, nor do I belong to the upper-classes, for one and the same simple reason, namely, that neither of them interest me in the slightest, never have done, never will do, Do try to understand that, clobbo! I'm just not interested in the whole class crap that seems to needle you and all the tax-payers—needle you all, whichever side of the tracks you live on, or suppose you do.'[16]

MacInnes' penchant for extravagant naming runs riot in a style both eighteenth-century baroque and Beat-influenced: his narrator dubs everyone of his acquaintance with some sort of fanciful defining soubriquet. His brother Vernon is dubbed Jules, after the author of *Around the World in Eighty Days* (and the novel he is writing is just such a panoramic rapid round trip) but his truculent sibling appears to be alone in repudiating his name with threats of violence. Ed the Ted, the Wiz, Crepe Suzette, Mr Cool, Call-me-Cobber, Zesty-Boy Sift, Dickie Hodfodder, the ex-Deb-of-Last-Year, the Fabulous Hoplite, Dido Lament, Kid-from-Outer-Space, Big Jill, Two-Thumbs Tumbril, Dean Swift, the Misery Kid, Mickey Ponderoso and Laurie London are among the cast of characters named and narrated by Blitz Baby (his mother's name for him, since he was born during an air-raid), and such an ad hoc pantheon seems like a rehash of Steinbeck's *Cannery Row*, a rehearsal for Dylan's 'Desolation Row' and *Tarantula*, for John Lennon's *In his Own Write* (in which Greenod Bladder and Enig Blyter are variants of the famed children's author's name), for the Beatles' piling up of walruses and nowhere men, or for the Simpsons: Two-Thumbs Tumbril and Bleeding-Gums Murphy are both jazz musicians, Dean Swift is both Kerouac's Dean Moriarty and of course the author of *Gulliver's Travels*. *Absolute Beginners* may be a tour of Lilliput or of Brobdignag: size is relative and can change in MacInnes' London—at one moment you might be tied down by your hair by an army of toy soldiers; but only turn the corner and a giant child curiously lifts you up for inspection between his pudgy, inquisitive fingers.

The narrator is unnamed, but I will adopt his mother's nickname for convenience: Blitz Baby. His dysfunctional family live in Pimlico, and some of the book's best lyrical snapshots are taken around that area and on the nearby Thames embankment: 'Whoever thought up the Thames embankment was a genius. It lies firm and gentle round the river like a girl does with a girl, when it's over.'[17] On the far side are 'the big new high blocks of glass-built flats, like an X-ray of a stack of buildings with their skins peeled off'[18] but in Pimlico itself 'the old, old city raised her bashed grey head again, like she was ashamed of her modern daughter down by the river, and I went up streets of dark purple and vomit green, all set at angles like ham sandwiches.'[19] Eventually his father, a sensitive, put upon, sympathetic character for whom he has a grudging respect, leaves him the money stashed in a tin box under his bed along with the manuscript of his long worked on book, 'The History of Pimlico'—a reference to *Passport to Pimlico*, an Ealing comedy of a few years earlier in which bomb site subsidence reveals this South-west London area to be an independent duchy, prompting its plucky inhabitants to declare UDI as a protest against the privations of rationing.

Absolute Beginners is a brilliant, slick little book, a self-conscious fashion-statement brimming with new-minted cliché definitions of English society, the work of a returned native who feels he must simply reinvent or remap the mother country, much like J.G. Ballard returning from Shanghai. First time around it is an intoxicating read, but a cooler eye reveals it to be a made to measure bestseller about the London young which sees them principally as overdrawn types or sex objects. Perhaps it is the novel's very prototype quality that makes it so fascinating and irritating in equal measure, as well as its recording of micro-histories of consumerism that are elsewhere overlooked in English fiction of the time. Astride his dinky-toy Vespa, the unlikely gift of a South American muscleman, MacInnes' nameless mouthpiece is a confection, a slumming social tourist who lives in squalid accommodations out of choice because he finds them colourful and interesting. His co-tenants include Big Jill, a lesbian pimp, Mr Cool, a mixed race 'spade' and a number of other bohemians. The book's depiction of racial tension builds throughout, but although there are social tensions in operation: you have to dig for them: the deb, the hooray henrys, the media types, and working-class incomers like the narrator and his friends all happily rub shoulders and accept one another, orchestrated by Call-me-Cobber, an ersatz Australian media type who may be meant to resemble Colin MacInnes himself or may be a countryman of whom he disapproves. In an aptly named Soho club called The Dubious, Call-me-Cobber offers an instant take on the new celebrity culture that proves Andy Warhol wasn't the first to think of the idea of everyone being famous for fifteen minutes: 'Today,' he announced, 'each woman, man and child in the United Kingdom can be made into a personality, a star. Whoever you are—and I repeat, whoever—we can put you in front of the cameras and make you live for millions.'[20]

During its course we are shown two kinds of history in the making: pop history and real history, and in both cases Colin MacInnes tries to take us behind the scenes to see the painting of flats and the frenzied carpentry that goes into the making of youth crazes and pop moments; to witness the incidents that can really spark riots and observe what an on-hand media can instantly do with them: in both cases they are processed into myths and social punditry, but in the former these might be all they ever consisted of. Except that even the most transient fad needs a constituency to which it can be marketed, and which may in some cases play a part in shaping its own micro-history as consumers. Blitz Baby has a film idea of his own, just as crumby as everyone else's, in which a deb meets a working-class Prince Charming and they live happily ever after. Soho is the hub of his world and of the teenage pop moment, but as he explains to a more naïve youngster he is showing around:

> 'I tell you, Wolverine,' I explained to this simple trusting soul, as we started walking down the boulevard, dodging prowlers, dodging gropers, dodging layabouts and tarts, 'I tell you. All those these things—like telly witch-doctors, and advertising pimps, and show business pop pirates—they despise us—dig?—they sell us cut-price sequins when we think we're getting diamonds... no teenage nightingale ever was 'discovered' in that place until the telly cameras and the journalists moved in there for the massacre... I tell you, Tarzan, that fish-bowl over there is just as real as nothing.'[21]

Not all the cultural operators in *Absolute Beginners* are shallow: some are urgent and obviously sincere, like Rod Todd, the Marxist folksong promoter, a stand-in for Ewan MacColl, or the jazz musicians and their fans who haunt Soho nights, or the narrator's socialist father with his palimpsest history of Pimlico. The narrator himself moves between the fringes of the media world, which he documents and earns a living from with his photography and these other worlds, social and cultural. He is a half-ironic product of early teen culture but a critic of it too, and as narrator—and equally importantly namer—hopes to get under the surfaces he describes and records, and to arrive at a true definition both of himself and the transient London worlds he inhabits. Blitz Boy is distrustful of the ethos of the fold and blues people, it seems because he distrusts their politics. One of his golden rules is 'not to argue with Marxist kiddies, because they know. And not only do they know, they're not responsible—which is the exact opposite of what they think they are. I mean, this is their thing, if I dig it correctly. You're in history, yes, because you're budding here and now, but you're outside it, also, because you're living in the Marxist future.'[22]

In this view Marxists evade any sense of responsibility for the times or the countries in which they actually live, and having seen through the teen culture that defines him, he is drawn to the immediacy and social mix of the world of Soho jazz clubs:

> But the great thing about the jazz world, and all the kids that enter into it, is that no one, not a soul, cares what your class is, or what your race is, or what your income, or if you're boy, or girl, or bent, or versatile, or what you are—so long as you dig the scene and can behave yourself, and have left all that crap behind you, too, when you come in the jazz club door.[23]

But as MacInnes demonstrates in spades you can always pick up 'all that crap' again on your way out. Unrealistically there is little drug use in the book, except for one token junkie, and despite all the advertising, no good writing about jazz or rock and roll, just a superficial fashion take on everything. He makes Teds—early rock'n'roll fans who had triggered the teenage marketing moment by tearing up cinema seats in their enthusiasm for Bill Haley and His Comets—anti-American (which some of them may have been) when the broader picture suggests that the London working-class had been enthusiastically pro-Yank and intoxicated by American movies and styles since the thirties or even earlier: Ted style was a rock'n'roll style, based on American music. I'm stating the very obvious here, especially if you have any inherited memories of that moment in post-war youth culture, but if you didn't know you could easily read *Absolute Beginners* from cover to cover without realising just how questionable is its account of these things.

The cockneys—the real white working-class characters in the book—get a hard time from MacInnes, their speech is rendered phonetically to emphasise their stupidity in a way that would be totally unacceptable if he was depicting Asians (the narrator's smiling landlord, a brief portrait of notorious slumlord Peter Rachmann), Jews (his poet-friend Mannie and his wife Miriam) or 'Spades': African or West Indian characters (whose speech isn't represented at all, and would in reality have been fairly difficult for the narrator to understand). The Teds' speech very much resembles the 'Mokni' spoken by the inhabitants of the Isle of Ham and their amusing beasts of burden, the Motos, in Will Self's *The Book of Dave,* a novel I will be discussing further. Here he is talking to Ed the Ted, a character relentlessly portrayed as a Neanderthal and ridiculed to a vitriolic extent that should earn Blitz Baby a smack in the mouth, but somehow doesn't register as offensive to middle-class readers:

> I eyed the primitive.
>
> 'You mean,' I said, 'that bunch of tearaways have thrown you out?'
>
> 'Eh-y?' he cried.
>
> 'You heard, Ed. You've been expelled from the Ted college?'
>
> 'Naher! Me? Espel *me*? Wot? Lissen! Me, Ar lef *them*, see? You

fink I'm sof, or sumfink?'

I shook my head at the poor goof and his abracadabra. 'Do me a favour, Ed. You're scared of the boys, why not admit it? Old-style Teds like you are, wasted, anyway: they've all moved out of London to the provinces.'[24]

One problem with his approach to the locals is that it makes the behaviour and attitudes of the Teds towards immigrants all but incomprehensible except in terms of a white tribalism or perhaps their innate stupidity, and racism becomes a kind of mysterious taint of the blood which truly hip people have somehow transcended. Colin MacInnes appears to know this isn't true, but he also sentimentalises the bohemians and depicts the white working-class kids as unreasoning savages: no vileness is beneath them, and when the Wiz reveals himself to be on the wrong side during the Notting Hill riots his apostasy towards the hip Soho attitude to 'spades' is both unexpected (although it has been signalled earlier) and places him immediately beyond the pale, beyond reason: he ceases to be human. There is a displaced, ugly, inverted racism in his handling of the English working-class characters. The young aristocrats become allies and Crepe Suzette's sexual negrophilia puts her on the right side politically, for MacInnes, which, it strikes me, ain't necessarily so.

MacInnes was one of the first writers to turn the tables in this way on the English working-classes so radically or viciously (apart from someone like Waugh, or Kingsley Amis) although many have followed in his wake. However, there does seem to be an affinity between older people and the immigrants in *Absolute Beginners*: an elderly female greengrocer shelters an African boy fleeing from the racist mob; an old man protects another young man with his body. These last feel a sense of anger and shame at the behaviour of the racist mobs, a traditional working-class sense of decency is counterposed to the ugliness of the bad new degraded masses, and these characters show direct solidarity with the older West Indians who are defending their lives and businesses.

Blitz Baby is intoxicated by the multi-ethnicity of London (then as now) and usually supplies the ethnic history of his friends and acquaintances, his 'characters'. The area he lives in he calls Napoli—the Ladbroke Grove end of Notting Hill—because of its high population of Italians, Maltese and Cypriots, but he has an especially soft spot for the Jewish people. His friends Mannie and Miriam live in North London and Mannie is a respected poet, which gives MacInnes a good platform for attacking the hated Angry Young Men: 'Mannie wasn't in on the Angries kick, though he appeared in print about the same time that bunch of cottage journalists first caught the public nostril. Mannie's verse… is angry only about the grave.'[25] He wonders early on if all his attitudinizing really amounts to anything beyond its surfaces, but in the last thirty pages of the book the absolute beginner is forced to take sides with the blacks, and does so, but we see that he's enchanted by black people, whom he has a sentimental view of, that is no less dubious than the sexually predatory attitudes of the young woman he hopes is his girlfriend in waiting, Crepe Suzette. The Napoli riots kick off when two working-class mothers—one black, one white, collide on a pavement and their ensuing argument draws a participating crowd, and if the myth of hip young Londoners leaving all their prejudices at the jazz-club door and transcending racism is an appealing one, it is belied by Blitz Baby's account of the incident that sparks this sudden bushfire of interracial violence:

> Coming along, pushing a pram and wearing those really horrible clothes that Spade women do (not men)—I mean all colours of the spectrum and the wrong ones put together, and with shoes like Minnie Mouse—was a coloured mum with that self-satisfied expression that all mums have. Beside her was her husband, I imagine it was—anyway, he was talking at her all the time, and she wasn't listening. Then coming from the opposite direction (and there always seems to be an opposite direction), was a white mum, also with kiddie-car and hubby, and whose clothes were just as dreadful as the Spade mum's were—except that the Spade girl's looked worse, somehow, because you could see at any rate, that she was trying, and hadn't given up all hope of glamour.[26]

The spade chicks look terrible even compared to (none too stylish) white working-class women; it is only spade dudes who look cool, driving their cars as though they were wrangling some magnificent beast in the jungle: a cool version of racism and snobbery is never far beneath the surface of MacInnes' London, and it is still present today: they are one of the subjects of the novel, and that might be a fairly good excuse, but *Absolute Beginners* doesn't really have any satisfying purchase on English society, popular culture, or on our racism. MacInnes mixes memory and desire, insight with ignorance, intoxication with hangover, love with disdain. So English working-class racism finally comes to a pustulant head in the riots, but the narrator's unlikely response is to flee the benighted country in supposed shame at being English, only the arrival of yet more charmful African immigrants staying him from immediately boarding a plane for Sweden or Brazil with the stack of green pound notes his father has left him, which he has thoughtfully split with his nasty 'Bevanite' brother before walking away from his remaining family for good.

Absolute Beginners is sometimes claimed to be the best book ever about being a teenager, but this may just be a teenage opinion—it certainly glamourises and flatters them. In fact it has been rather overpraised in an understandably nostalgic way by people who were around at the time, but it is also a compendium of then current class attitudes as well as an analysis of the forces at play in the construction of youth culture. MacInnes writes like a more controlled Kerouac by now; his prose in this book has something of the ride and snap of a spontaneous bop prose adapted to commercial fiction—and as such it is just the sort of thing Jack himself would have probably disliked. MacInnes is more fashion-conscious, more ersatz. His biographer Tony Gould described him as an 'inside outsider'. His mother was an English novelist, his brother in television. He had good media contacts and was therefore well placed to 'do Kerouac' for the English market, and he produced something of an observant pop sociologist's view of an England for which he had a strong feeling for but no real affinity. He is a snob, an upper middle-class interloper, a flash-merchant who sold us to ourselves as hipper than we really were. He had a long love affair with a London which he saw in Cinerama, pre-produced, pre-packaged for all the sixties film directors who were to create swinging London in his wake. He is proud to show off 'the knowledge', which is a bit like a London cab driver's but without such depth, and makes use of it to undertake superficial social mapping based on postal districts—the worst sort of middle-class prattling snobbery—and to assemble a gallery of hip young urban types upon which subsequent London novels and pop music have often drawn.

Just as every spontaneous youth craze was predictably predated upon until they no longer sprang up afresh, every new sociological phenomenon was instantly processed into journalistic punditry and commercial fictions. *Absolute Beginners* manages adroitly to be both an example of this and an insightful commentary on the process of turning these well-publicised revolts into marketable styles. It is a somewhat cynical take on youth under its besotted surface, and to this reader it also seems that there has been something of a collapse, a loss of faith on MacInnes' part in the ultimate seriousness of the novel since his earlier work. But readers who wish to understand the origins of the yawning gap between British social realities and the media world of acceptable fictions and instantly recognisable types should start here and continue with MacInnes' other London novels, *City of Spades* and *Mr. Love and Justice*. *City of Spades* in particular gives the era's fullest account of London's African immigrants. He is surely amongst the most interesting commentators on the early postwar era and deserves to be looked at through later eyes.

Chapter Four

Samuel Selvon, V.S. Naipaul: Between the Ganges and the Nile

See how we movin', see how we groovin', see how we step in style
One nation under a groove, the Ganges has met the Nile
—David Rudder, 'The Ganges and the Nile'

'I wouldn't mind some of that jungle juice myself', remarks one of the South London women in Nell Dunn's *Up the Junction*, a sentiment shared by teenager Crepe Suzette in Colin MacInnes' *Absolute Beginners*. Samuel Selvon's stories of West Indians in London depict, amongst other things, the flipside of that sexual equation. Selvon's books are one of the first attempts to write what was to become the black British experience. His male characters are often in pursuit of, or pursued by, not remote but perfectly accessible blondes. Much humour is derived from this, and from the support of feckless black males by long-suffering white girlfriends. This may well be taken as negative stereotyping, and justly. The basis of such relationships may not stand up to close scrutiny but this is something yet to be found out either by the priapic men or by the 'native' women who enjoy them. Much of the time there's a spirit of innocence and humour about it all, like a calypso about Millicent playing the saxophone, although it was nothing new. C.L.R. James wrote amusingly in his account of his first visit to London in 1932:

> The girls, far from being prejudiced, are very much interested, but they are afraid of public opinion… any man of colour who is not repulsive in appearance is a great favourite with the girls… For the English native is so dull and glum and generally boorish in his manners, that the girls turn with relief from these dreadful Englishmen to the smiling and good-natured West Indians.[1]

James and Selvon were both writing before the ascendancy of Frantz Fanon's theories of the sexual psychology of imperialism, and this may be part of the explanation for their levity on this subject, also that for such theorists and their successors the books should tell a much sadder and more disturbed story than they do. But as well as experience there is a wishfulness and generosity about Selvon's point of view, as in his suggestion (pre-Notting Hill riots) that the indigenous working-class and the Caribbean arrivants are natural allies, and, as we shall see, Samuel Selvon does not fail to explore the questions raised by hungry blondes and their consorts.

The Lonely Londoners is a highly anecdotal book, forgoing the pleasures of closure for the blisses of going on and on—its manner is additive, digressive, like a bloated short story or an out of hand treatment for a film that will never be made. Stories are told, atmospheres—of London places and social situations—sampled, snapshots taken of characteristic dialogue and interactions. In this way Samuel Selvon slowly (in what is after all a short book) accumulates the experience of his lonely Londoners in a way that is exploratory, unforced, multivocal. He is being a kind of self-conscious folk-artist in this, moving on from the technique of his first novel, *A Brighter Sun*, with its conventional realist movement between macro-economic life and the micro-struggles of the impoverished young couple who are fending for themselves and learning how to be adults from the ground up. *The Lonely Londoners* is totally focused on the point of view of those ground-level livers. In a sense the lonely Londoners are like that young couple: they are coping with new situations on their wits. (Selvon is right as a child of necessity to work this way on the new territory he is mapping.) His characters have no overarching view or set of categories that will unlock their situation, their island manners don't quite play anymore. They can only watch to see what the others are doing. Some men are like this, some men are like that; some men make fools of women, others are made fools of—it is an ad hoc but traditional view of an unfolding experience.

The Lonely Londoners is articulated around the friendship between two Trinidadians, Moses and Galahad—an old hand and a new arrival—and their relationship provides a simple and natural way of containing a lot of explanatory talk and many many stories about West Indians in England, shared between them as Galahad shares with his mentor the plump pigeon he has caught in the park, garnished with rice and peas. Moses sees himself as a kind of liaison officer for new arrivals, a necessary role because newcomers have need of some bearer of the tablets of immigrant law, a reliable guide to these particular circles of hell:

> …this sort of thing was happening at a time when the English people starting to make a rab about how too much West Indians coming to the country: this was a time, when any corner you turn, is ten to one you bound to bounce up a spade.[2]

Like C.L.R. James before him Selvon's Moses has found the English to be a people ruled by newspapers and the media: it's not strictly necessary to be informed about what they are saying about immigrants, because it will be repeated to you in every corner shop. The papers are the English Bible, he explains. Galahad's Tanty Bessie arrives on the same train and we see her story unfold her voice a commentating chorus on the doings of the men. The sun seems to give no heat, just to hang in the sky like 'a force-ripe orange'. The colour of the sky is so desolately grey that it casts a melancholy aspect over everything for the West Indians and Galahad is afraid of everything: unfamiliar with the money, scared to talk to a policeman, and above all self-conscious, locked in the unwilling silence of a non-native speaker.

> 'The only thing,' Galahad say when they was in the tube going to the Water, 'is that I find when I talk smoke coming out my mouth.'
>
> 'Is so it is in this country,' Moses say, 'Some times the words freeze and you have to melt it to hear the talk.'[3]

Moses shows him around the Labour exchange:

> 'Is a kind of place where hate and disgust and avarice and malice and sympathy and sorrow and pity all mix up. Is a place where everyone is your enemy and your friend. Even when you go to draw a little |national assistance it don't be so bad, because when you reach that stage is because you touch bottom.'[4]

Although even in the mid-fifties there were some regulars who never seemed to find work:

> 'You see that fellar there?... He is one of the regulars. He does only draw dole. The last time I was here was last year, and he still in the queue.'[5]

And routine though signing-on and looking for work is, there are tell-tale signs to the West Indians that not all jobs will be open to them:

> 'Now, on all the records of the boys, you will see mark on the top in red ink. J—A, Col. That mean you from Jamaica and you black. So that put the clerks in the know right away, you see. Suppose a vacancy come up and they want to send a fellar, first they will find out if the firm want coloured fellars before they send you.'[6]

The ability to take things as they come is an important lesson all immigrants must learn, and it is part of Selvon's technique to show adaptation to a new place as a cumulative and exploratory process. Patience, stoicism and opportunism are all invaluable qualities, and Selvon is more likely to show—in his precise way—more or less how things are, how they in fact turned out, than to provide a template for his readers or point an explicit moral. 'Things have a way of fixing themselves, whether you worry or not. If you hustle, it will happen, if you don't hustle it will still happen. Everybody living to dead, no matter what they doing while they living, in the end everybody dead.'[7]

People are not always what they seem to be, a paradisial sexuality could be the route to madness, and somebody who appears slow, for example, turns out to have hidden resources. The thing to do is to hang in there and not make too many snap judgements. One character, Lewis is taken on in a factory where black workers are paid at a lower rate than whites would be, but the preponderance ofn West Indians makes it a relatively easy place to work despite the work itself being hard. 'Lewis is another character that does put your thinking out of gear. Though he has sense, you would think he stupid, because he always asking questions, and anything you tell he he would believe'[71] But this, of course, turns out not to be the case at all with Lewis, any more than the other stories Selvon tells are of familiar types. They are offered as exemplary tales, in a way, but the outcome must be at least slightly surprising to the imagined listener. However, there is one recurrent area in which the judgements of men are not always as sound as they might be:

> 'White girls,' Tanty grumble as she put the kettle on the fireplace fire, 'is that what sweeten up so many of you to come to London. Your own kind of girls not good enough now, is only white girls. I see Agnes bring a nice girl-friend from Jamaica to see us, but you didn't even blink on she. White girls! Go on! They will catch up on you in this country!'[8]

Londoners don't know what is happening in the room next to them, let alone in the next street, nor are they particularly well informed about how other people are living in general. London is divided up into little parallel worlds, a place where you stay in the world to which you belong and know as little or nothing about what is happening in the others except what you might happen to read in the papers. A delight of the book is its determination to break out of this segregation and tell you about these different worlds, not only the immigrant one, but the rest of London as it appears to the West Indian observers, social class as it appears to them. And it is particularly vivid and telling on the world of the post-war English working-classes whose areas and, to some degree, whose predicament is shared by the new immigrants:

> It have a kind of communal feeling with the Working-class and the spades, because when you poor things does level out, it don't

> have much up and down. A lot of men get killed in war and leave widow behind, and it have bags of these old geezers who does be pottering about the Harrow Road like if they lost, a look in their eye as if the war happen unexpected and they still can't realise what happen to the old Brit'n.[9]

One of the more harrowing sights and sounds of London is of these veterans begging at the windows of the rich:

> ...sometimes they walk up a street in a plush area with their cap in their hand, and sing in a high falsetto, looking up at the high windows where the high and mighty living and now and then a window would open and somebody would throw down a threepence or a tanner, and the old fellar have to watch it good else it roll in the road and get lost... No song or rhythm, just a musical noise so nobody could say he begging.[10]

Oftentimes the tossers of coins didn't even look down from their white eyries, and likewise the old men didn't look up: it was as if these sixpences and threepenny bits had fallen from heaven, and Moses opines that life is like that—we don't see the interconnections between things and people and therefore don't really understand the consequences of our own actions. 'People in this world don't know how other people does affect their lives.'[11] Selvon describes early West Indian shops which resemble those at home, where you could get saltfish, blackeyed peas, pepper sauce, Brasso and Blue for washing clothes and pitchoil from a big drum in the back and wicks for the cheap heaters with which they heat their draughty lodgings.

Another group with whom the West Indians interact are Jewish tailors, who appreciate their love of sharp clothes and eagerly cater for their tastes in checks and lapels and crombies and strides with razor sharp creases. A cockney Jewish tailor near Aldgate has photographs of black boxers plastered all over his walls, and hands out free cigars on Saturdays. 'Come again, my friend,' he say as he give you another hand for the road, and with the other hand he pull out a card from he top jacket pocket and hand you.'[11] Galahad, of course, settles in well, is soon a confident man of the world with a sharp suit, a job and 'battle royal' with a white girl to his credit. He shines his shoes with Cherry Blossom for a date and fancies he is in a wartime romantic film like *Waterloo Bridge*. Tanty Bessie remains a village person, not moving far from the Harrow Road, and treating her immediate area as her home as she did in Trinidad.

The Lonely Londoners is a kind of megamix of social history and folk-epic, it is formally perfect and highly unusual, a lyrical, poetic novel that fulfils Glasgow poet Tom Leonard's definition of poetry as 'the juiciest bits in the juiciest order.'[12] A folk-memory-poem indeed, its highly-tuned speech modulates and twists in and out of narrative in a sometimes dizzyingly beautiful way. After the careful counterpointing of the stories of various West Indian men, each narrated as by Virgil to Dante, or Moses to Galahad, *The Lonely Londoners* builds to a kind of ecstatic Joycean glossolalia in which the laughing denizens of Hell recount snatches of their particular universal stories, crimes and punishments, remembered from a thousand conversations in old-talk. This section also recalls Virginia Woolf's *Mrs Dalloway*. But the park has turned hellish, into a scene of relentless carnival-bacchanal with a needy ghost-woman lurking behind every tree; it is an attempt at a summation of the West Indian experience of London women and the recollections turn as ugly as the racism they sometimes casually reveal:

> ...the sexlife gone wild you would meet women who beg you to go with them one night a Jamaican with a woman in a smart flat in Chelsea with all sorts of surrealistic painting on the walls and contemporary furniture in the G-plan the poor fellar bewildered and asking questions to improve himself because the set-up look like the World of Art but the number not interested in passing on any knowledge she only interested in one thing and in the heat of emotion she call the Jamaican a black bastard though she didn't mean it as an insult but as a compliment under the circumstances but the Jamaican fellar get vex and he stop to say why the hell you call me a black bastard and he thump the woman and went away all these things happen in the blazing summer under the trees in the park on the grass with the daffodils and tulips in full bloom and a sky of blue oh it does really be beautiful then to hear the birds whistling and see the green leaves come back on the trees and in the night the world turn upside down...[13]

We cut away from this scene of degradation to the introduction of a man called Five Past Twelve (blacker than midnight) and a resumption of ordinary life, a discussion of politics: the West Indians are labour supporters although one or two apparently have Tory sympathies, driven by an admiration for Churchill and a lust for respectability. There is a period of lay-offs and the onset of another winter to contend with in a lonely, alien place where meetings with others in the same boat provide the only warmth. The novel unwinds, unravels into more comfortable, familial relationships and community social events controlled by West Indians themselves, a series of freewheeling conversations about the glories and hazards of weed and reflections on the experience of a London that has at least become familiar: there are yearnings for home, a sense of being trapped, but an overall acceptance that life in Brit'n isn't always so bad, provided you keep your eye open for opportunity—as Cap tries to repeat Galahad's earlier trick with the pigeon by catching seagulls for the cooking pot.

Moses' final epiphany is Selvon's own analysis of the status of the West Indians in London and conveys a sense of gathering storm beneath the easy-rolling surface of the migrants' take on life:

> Under the kiff-kiff laughter, behind the ballad and the episode, the what-happening, the summer-is-hearts, he could see a great aimlessness, a great restless, swaying movement that leaving you standing in the same spot. As if a forlorn shadow of doom fall on all the spades in the country. As if he could see the black faces bobbing up and down in the millions of white, strained faces, everybody hustling along the Strand, the spades jostling in the crowd, bewildered, hopeless.[14]

Before Victor Headley's *Yardie* rewrote *Little Caesar,* W.R. Burnett's 1930 novel of an immigrant gangster, there was the novel of the yard—a near-equivalent in West Indian literature to the Scottish ceilyard writers, who celebrated the lives of the lower classes in a kind of bucolic, folkloric comedy of manners for the amusement of colonial masters, depicting its people as incorrigible, irremediable low-life. In his guise as critic C.L.R. James self-disparagingly places his own thirties novel, *Minty Alley*, partially in that yard tradition: his autobiographical protagonist is torn—much as is torn—between a colonial educational system and a native culture that can appear to be no culture at all to the one who is fated to try and escape from it. C.L.R. James' young student teacher is torn between the blandishments of the men and women in the yard who would hold him back and the discipline he must find within to raise himself above their level, and, as a rite of passage into the administrative classes, escape island ways to go abroad to the 'mother country' and further his studies. Samuel Selvon's London writing could be placed in a 'yard' tradition—he certainly lapses easily into low knockabout comedy—except that he is not writing for the amusement of colonial masters but in order to place the ground-level experience of immigration at centre stage. He is conscious of having both white and black readers and, particularly in *The Housing Lark*, employs a doubleness of address calculated to disquiet but also to include both in a comfortable intimacy. His approach to racism is to pursue a kind of comedic détente.

The characters in *The Housing Lark* live in a cramped, endlessly subdivided house in Brixton and they are just the sort of ne'er do wells one might expect in a comic low-life novel: the women are all on the game, the men are a feckless bunch: some hold down day jobs, others are thieves or musicians, but none of the latter is successful except for a hopelessly untalented, tuneless and stupid Calypsonian who, for mysterious reasons, the white folks have decided to lionise as the authentic voice of the Caribbean. Selvon winks at his black readers by familiarly addressing his white readers as he introduces a pair of characters he distinguishes by their relative height, because he knows they all look the same to us. He is sharp but forgiving, garrulous but uncompromising, and when the novel disintegrates into comic mayhem a choice is being made about whose sensibilities he wishes to play to—those of his West Indian readers. There is a shocking lack of earnestness in his treatment of his characters, and a heedlessness of 'good taste'—they, and he, get along in this light-hearted book by refusing to take their housing problems too seriously.

There are so many London novels, all of them offering to define afresh an experience that has usually been defined a thousand times before. The London books of Samuel Selvon are in a class of their own, both in the experiences they tell of and in their ways of telling them: unsurpassable because of their moment and their subject-matter. In his work the city is a place of intense sociability, as, for example, in the newly arrived Trinidadian workers' first interactions with the world of English public transport. Small Change, the main speaker of 'Working the Transport', invents a new dance craze, 'the hip and hit', in order to impress a blonde from the Elephant and Castle, and subsequently develops it on the lower deck of a 196 with his friends Alipang, All Fours, Catch-as-Catch-Can, Jackfish 'and a set of other fellars'. This story—an outtake or precursor to *The Lonely Londoners*—briefly maps a shared culture that sustains them through bemused, hilarious misadventures in London. It is also a place of intense loneliness, isolation, emptied of everything but sustaining fantasy, the conjuring of lovers real and imaginary, and the consolations, for Selvon and his characters, of the words that momentarily fill that emptiness.

In 'My Girl and the City' he is brought to similar reflections on fiction's fictionality—telling stories is telling lies—as those of B.S. Johnson's irritating catch-all catchphrase, with the crucial difference that, for Selvon, such conjuring (whilst being recognised for what it is), is admitted and finally embraced as all that stands between his narrators and a nothingness of marooned social exclusion: a sense of being land-locked in an alien environment, a sense of cultural and sexual dispossession that is seen as the essence of London life—and not only for immigrants. Fabulation is a necessity as well as a pleasure for these West Indian immigrants, these marooned islanders:

> At last I think I know what it is all about. I move around in a world of words. Everything that happens is words. But pure

expression is nothing. One must build on the things that happen: it is insufficient to say I sat in the underground and the train hurtled through the darkness and someone isn't using Amplex. So what? So now I weave, I say there was an old man whose face wrinkles rivered, whose hands were shapeful with arthritis but when he spoke, oddly enough, his voice was young and gay.

But there was no old man, there was nothing, and there is never ever anything.

My girl, she is beautiful to look at. I have seen her in sunlight and in moonlight, and her face carves an exquisite shape in darkness.

These things we talk, I burst out, why mustn't I say them? If I love you, why shouldn't I tell you so?

I love London, she said.[15]

Walter Benjamin's celebrated essay 'The Storyteller: Reflections on the Work of Nicholai Leskov', begins by telling us that the art of storytelling is coming to an end.[16] Nobody knows how to tell a story anymore, and that he sees as a grave state of affairs, because to tell a story, as its most fundamental level, is simply to exchange experiences. The reasons for that ending, he says, were connected with the First World War. Men came back from the battlefields of Europe, not with astonishing experiences to share, but with nothing to say at all. It was as though the scale and horror of that war, the upheavals and shifting of men, machines and money that it entailed, had completely wiped out the moral categories, the possible human common ground, through or on which anything at all could be said about what had happened. Everything changed forever in the trenches, and no kind of secure or settled wisdom applied or made sense any longer.

All storytellers have drawn from experience passed from mouth to mouth. Storytelling is a kind of collective account, a distilled collective wisdom. And the greatest storytellers were those whose written accounts differ least from the numberless, nameless oral accounts that preceded them. What is a story? What, historically, is a story? That's the question he sets out to answer. And he comes up with a brilliantly all-encompassing answer. It consists of the reports of those who stay at home and the reports of those who travel far away. On the one hand stories are tales of distant lands and their customs; on the other the daily accounts and transactions of the settled, continuous life of a town or village: its regularities, its repeated patterns, its long accumulations of practice and custom, its proverbial wisdoms. Stories came from experience and were passed back into it—they were collective. The novel, by contrast, was the work of an isolated individual—the novelist. And because the novelist was isolated, he or she had no basis upon which to offer advice or good counsel. That's why, according to Benjamin, the hero of the first great novel, Cervantes' *Don Quixote*, is a man totally devoid of wisdom. He's noble, great, good and so on, but his goodness is useless. He tilts at windmills—that's the thing everyone knows about him. He's a hopeless case. We may come to admire him in a way, but he think he's a fool. We're certainly not going to accept any advice he has to offer at face value.

When we are reading a novel every event in the character's life is a kind of staging post on the way to their death. Through reading novels—or biographies, which closely resemble nineteenth century novels in their narrative structure—we follow the life path of another; we share their experience of death. More than that: we see that, for a character in a novel, everything that happens leads somewhere—to a particular resolution, a particular death at a particular time. How did it happen? That, says Benjamin, is what feeds our consuming interest in the novel's outcome. So the point of a novel isn't the moral it teaches, though it may or may not be a highly moral tale, and have one or several lessons to teach, but that it offers a clear sense of life's overall shape or order that we can only have from our own life at its end, if at all: 'What draws the reader to the novel is the hope of warming his shivering life with a death he reads about'. In other words we see a fictional life lit up, given meaning by its close.

In asking and attempting to answer these questions, Benjamin stands at the beginning of a line of thought that investigates the power and meaning of narrative for the reader. Where do you situate yourself in relation to what you read while you're reading? What is this stuff doing to, with and through you while you're consuming it? Why keep turning the pages? There don't even have to be pages. What happens to you when you watch a film? Where are you? Or when you watch another episode of your favourite soap. Soaps must be the only place left where traditional wisdom, in terms of knowing how a particular story will turn out, still obtains. The regularity with which death occurs in films, it could be argued, is equally to remind us of eternity, of the infinite, as do the figures of death that Benjamin describes appearing in the processions of wooden characters that proceed from medieval town clocks when they strike the hour.

If Samuel Selvon can be compared to Benjamin's storyteller reflecting upon experience, contemporary Black British writer Victor Headley, author of *Yardie*[19] might be his novelist: our flight through his books is headlong, we race towards the yardie's death (which doesn't come, as it happens). Selvon's London world is full of ways—byways, routes and customs to be passed on to the reader. Healey's yardie is subject only to one law: the law of the drug-dealing jungle—it's either kill or be killed as he flees down a one-way street towards his own full stop, to ask with the cornered immigrant hero-rat of W. R. Burnett's *Little Caesar*: 'Is this the end of Rico?'[20] And as readers we are drawn along by the promise of such an all-explanatory ending: we wait for the death that can be the only result of his actions. Selvon's characters are full of memories and his stories full of observations and colour, but the world of Victor Headley's *Yardie* is a stark, elemental one and there are few friendly faces, just at best a few crumbs and a brief hiding place from his pursuers—the drug barons hunt him like the hounds of heaven through dreary, flattened urban spaces that are leached of meaning or familiar atmosphere. His predicament is similar to that of Bigger in Richard Wright's *Native Son*: it appears that he has chosen his own death, but unlike Wright's driven avatar groping to make sense of his life and actions, he never realises or acknowledges this truth.[21] His death is chosen in a sense but is not a willed, existential choice. In fact, he doesn't die at all, but returns in a number of sequels. And so does Moses, the elusive narrator of Selvon's *The Lonely Londoners*, by popular demand. He is not exactly the same character (who could be, twenty-years later?) but his essence, his spirit, lives on in *Moses Ascending*.[22]

Another aspect of Walter Benjamin's thinking about narrative that seems relevant here is elaborated in another famous essay, 'Theses on the Philosophy of History'[23]. In that great, complex, short work, he begins to talk about history itself as narrative. He considers the different shapes, and overall meanings, that are given to the events of the past by different ways of telling them. He begins to lay these different narratives of history side by side and to compare them.

'Theses on the Philosophy of History' was written in 1940, shortly before his death, in the context of the defeat of everything he believed in and the triumph of Fascism. The first kind of historical narrative he considers is that written by the victors. In this story history is a triumphal procession in which the spoils of victory are carried forward over the bones of the dead, the defeated. The spoils of victory are culture, civilisation. 'Only for a redeemed humanity is the past citable in all its moments', Benjamin writes. How can the suffering of the countless victims of history ever be atoned for, ever be made okay? It can't be, not really. But only by imagining a history that fully honours them, Benjamin says. Only by attempting to write a narrative that doesn't distinguish between small and large events, in which everyone and everything is given equal weight—and this can only be envisaged at the end of history, when there is no longer conflict because it has been transcended or abolished by the coming of the messiah—can justice be envisaged. Writing in despair on the edge of a holocaust he appears to foresee, Benjamin makes as strongly, desperately urgent a case for the victims as he can muster; but in the light of our history, and as a precept to guide us in the present, there is something almost comfortable in its impossibility.

And, finally, there is a perspective that has no narrative shape, no beginning, middle or end, that isn't linear at all. This is the perspective of the Angel of History. The Angel of History was an image that Benjamin developed out of a small painting by Paul Klee called 'Angelus Novus'. This is also messianic in a way, in that the Angel stands aside from or above history, but differs because the Messiah is presumably in control and knows what will happen next, as Bigger Thomas struggles to in *Native Son*, eventually affirming himself by seeing his actions as a conscious being-towards-death. The Angel of History has his wings spread wide. They're caught in a wind, or storm, that's blowing from paradise, so that he can't turn to look ahead, only backwards, at the results of the storm. This storm, Benjamin says, is what we call progress. And what, in all these narratives of history, is linear, a succession of events, to the Angel of History isn't a story at all, but one continuous disaster that is piling up bodies and rubble at his feet.

Not wishing to overpower Samuel Selvon's particular sense of storytelling by drawing up one of the big guns of European philosophical-literary criticism to defend him—it does seem to me that in his version of folk-epic he is thinking along the same lines as Benjamin, and that there is something like the dolorous perspective of the Angel of History at the end of *The Lonely Londoners* when Moses has his vision of swimming black faces as so many dots lost in the London crowds and experiences intimations of a racial apocalypse in which the meaning of the immigrant journey will be lost. Moses fears that the tablets he has borne to his people are shortly to be broken, that the words, sounds and power of his mighty commandments and his belief in a meaning for that journey will be turned into such a heap of broken images. *The Lonely Londoners* is a book of the mid-fifties, a decade still strongly shadowed by the Jewish holocaust, and Selvon, writing like all writers of his generation in the shadow of the atomic bomb, is haunted by fears of another holocaust, perhaps nuclear, perhaps racial.

V.S. Naipaul is one of the thorniest of all writers on the legacy of imperialism, and particularly so on the subject of the typologies and hierarchies of race, as well as the 'race-snobberies' that are the enduring legacy of slavery in the West Indies, both British and French. He is also a fascinating and insightful writer on social class in England itself, where he has mostly lived since leaving his native Trinidad in the forties to go to

Oxford. Considered by some to be one of the great novelists in English of the twentieth century, he was awarded the Nobel Prize for literature in 2001, and thus (and by his innate talents) naturally outclasses many of the writers I am discussing in this study. But a full discussion of one of his books in this context will illustrate the extent to which he is a creature of the same culture, and grappling with the consequences of being from a subaltern strata of it, as are many of the Anglo-Saxon writers in this study.

For Naipaul to be a colonial subject is as fatal as being born a Negro in the work of William Faulkner. His sense of unshakeable colonial and racial hierarchies seems reminiscent of Graham Greene in *The Heart of the Matter*, perhaps only because both writers are exploring the same subject, but Naipaul's anatomy of the West Indies is often set firmly in the midst of narrow streets that Greene's characters only glance down in a momentary forbidden sexual interest. For many Naipaul's view seems overlain with a relentless snobbery or caste-consciousness, which is questionable because, even in his books, people do move between castes, and societies are more dynamic than he gives them credit for, even in the sluggish West Indies, whose volatility can throw up new parties and leaders, but may dispose of them even more rapidly.

Naipaul's first attempts at this theme, *Miguel Street* and *The Suffrage of Elvira* are also what James would have called novels of the yard, serving up comically dysfunctional characters in a richly imagined small social world of the Trinidadian working and lower-middle classes. The latter is an amusing, colourful but ultimately unsatisfying account of one of the first post-war elections: democracy comes late to Trinidad, although his characters seem to understand instantly that splashing money and bottles of rum around is the way to win. Meanwhile the 'negro' candidate, Preacher, by far the most popular at the start of the campaign, is destined to lose his deposit and shake everyone's hand. *A House for Mr Biswas* (1959) is Naipaul's first real masterpiece amongst his early Caribbean novels, telling what is essentially the story of his father's struggles out of rural poverty into sensationalist journalism: a loving portrait and a coruscatingly funny and acerbic book about Trinidadian society, middle-class Hindu families, and the struggle to escape from the island through education.

The Mimic Men (1967) begins and ends in London, where Ralph Singh, a disgraced minister from the imaginary Caribbean island of Isabella, returns to live out his exile at the age of forty. Singh begins by remembering his student days, in a boarding house owned by the imaginatively named Mr Shylock, with an empty attic room for the young girls he seduces there and a basement for Lieni, his Maltese housekeeper, and her illegitimate child. 'Between attic and basement, pleasure and its penalty, we boarders lived, narrowly.'[24] Ralph Singh reflects on the career of a colonial politician as one that is inevitably short and likely to end brutally, taking place in a power vacuum where no real power exists, involving conflicts in which more is apparently at stake than in the West, but which are personal in a way that Western politics usually isn't, offering no safety nets and no long term retirement plan for a defeated leader. 'There are no City houses or universities to refresh and absorb us after the heat of battle. For those who lose, and nearly everyone in the end loses, there is only one course: flight. Flight to the greater disorder of London and the home counties.' While their white neighbours dream of winning the football pools and take them for immigrants, political exiles do their shopping at Sainsbury's and relive the past days of their power and glory.

Naipaul's view of London is similar to everyone else's: it is a very cellular city, one that seems to promise order and connection but which throws individuals back upon themselves in isolation, with only the idea of a city's overarching coherence and its physical beauties of light and space to sustain them. Singh plays with famous names, but finds them empty and fraudulent, the physical world he inhabits less real than his memories of corrugated iron and rotting wooden fences. Attending lectures, a young English student attaches himself to the exile, an eager young man 'doomed to later nonentity' who nevertheless dreams of careers in literature or the church or politics and uses Singh as a sounding board for these ambitions because 'He was like me: he needed the guidance of other men's eyes.'[25] In his boarding house, briefly taken over by Lieni, the housekeeper's lover, a fellow Maltese who resents being bossed around by her because she is of a lower class, compensates by becoming a kleptomaniac, while an isolated Frenchman types continually and Singh goes off to the British council to try—successfully—to pick up women. He does well with Norwegians and Swedes, people to whom he is as exotic as they are to him, either there or on day trips to Oxford, and becomes something of a ladies' man, keeping an erotic diary and amassing souvenirs of his conquests. They are seemingly unimpressed that his family bottles Coca-Cola. In all of these activities there is a fanatical attention to order and to hierarchy, often racially conceived, but the young Singh is terrified of any closer involvement with women, anything real that will expose him to closer scrutiny or possible commitments. He avoids women who speak English. Lieni becomes a reader of his diary and another lover. It appears that he is as irresistible to white women as one of Samuel Selvon's bus conductors, but there is a sense in which his erotic adventures are playacting, and in them he may be a 'character' that Lieni has invented for him. Singh is deeply inauthentic, he fears, and much as the English student needs an audience to make his poses real, his own personality is a fabricated one, as compartmentalised and unintegrated as the myriad isolated individual lives of the city: in his sex life he acts out increasing cruelties and becomes an addict of prostitutes offering domination, a process leading to his breakdown.

It is these very qualities of inauthentic role-playing that define the essence of the politician. Singh himself is neither a maker nor an artist nor an engineer, but an unstable manipulator and a seizer of moments.

> Politicians are truly people who make something out of nothing. They have few concrete gifts to offer. They are manipulators; they offer themselves as manipulators. Having no gifts to offer they seldom know what they seek… the true politician finds his skill and his completeness only in success. His gifts suddenly come to him. He who in other days was mean, intemperate and infirm now reveals unexpected qualities of generosity, moderation and swift brutality. Power alone proves the politician; it is ingenuous to express surprise at an unexpected failure or an unexpected flowering.[26]

Naipaul's definition of the politician as a performer, an approval-seeking creature of his own ill-defined and often contradictory lusts and aspirations, is a powerful one. It and many other luminous passages in Naipaul suggest that for him ultimate power lies not here—in being shaped by others—but in the ability to define others. After a period of wandering across the postcodes of London and travelling in Europe, Singh meets and marries Sandra, an Englishwoman from an East End background, a working-class snob, culture vulture and rapacious social climber who has no family and no connections with her own community: 'Her very rapaciousness attracted me.' From her Ralph Singh learns, or deepens his knowledge, of the marvellous English class system: 'She hated the common—her own word—from which she nevertheless freely acknowledged herself to have sprung and about which she therefore claimed to speak with authority; no-one knew "them" as well as she. To the end she had a cruel eye for the common, and she passed on the word and the assessing skill.' Sandra paints the nipples of her breasts, her ambitiousness excites him, and her positive striving energy supplies an impetus to his own sense of aimlessness and drift. She brings the city to life for him once more as he ambivalently admires 'those close-set, myopic, impatient eyes, that jutting lower lip.'[27] Their mixed marriage in a Willesden registry office is exciting to them, relatively novel, but strongly disapproved of by some on both sides of the racial divide. We feel that she is not much of a catch for Singh; she is what an island snob of Creole French extraction calls 'whitey-pokey', and there is a dark irony in the fact that the apparently total mesh of their complimentary racisms and snobberies involves mutual judgements in which each finds the other lacking.

There is something miraculous in Naipaul's ability to make compelling fiction out of such unsympathetic characters; but if an easy explanation for his fascination as a writer is needed, it is his lightness of touch as he operates as a surgeon on our sick social body, disclosing layer after layer of skin, fatty tissue, veins and arteries, until the diseased vital organ—always the heart—is lain bare for our pitying, disgusted inspection. His writing offers a sense of cruel but necessary disclosure by intellectual scalpel, and carried along by its apparent objectivity we may not at first notice that it also bears powerful distortions, makes powerful assumptions that are part and parcel of the psychological damage inflicted on their subjects by colonial societies which were founded on slavery and therefore transmit a deeply internalised sense of racial inferiority to their citizens. Sandra is no less enmeshed in the class equivalent of these attitudes, and her presence as a character helps to reveal England as not only the ultimate source of these false and corrupting values, but itself no less riven by them as a society, by the sense of ineluctable misery, hopelessness and frustration that hangs over *The Mimic Men*. But Naipaul himself begins to emerge as an obsessive orderer, a hierarchy-maker, whose judgements, though laced with compassion, smack of unquestioned imperial attitudes it would probably have been culturally impossible for him to escape, especially if he wished to disclose psychological realities of that legacy to his readers.

Back on Isabella, Ralph Singh makes it as a property speculator, but his marriage begins to founder on his wife's loud-mouthed opinionated exhibitions in local society—here we begin to like her. She is no worse than him; Singh enjoys having court paid to him by the wealthy foreigners who form his social circle, but rather than exhibiting the noblesse oblige expected of such a role, he relishes and encourages outbursts that reflect her 'gift of the phrase, her North London tongue, battling where it should have succoured and consoled. I encouraged her, I am afraid, by being amused. She often spoke damaging words in public for my benefit.'[28] Sandra evolves a series of denigrating racial epithets—'common little Lapp'—'subkraut' for a Dutch woman married to a man from Surinam—'sub-Asiatic' for a Latvian—and the ubiquitous hated Swedes 'over here collecting Voodoo songs to play on the Swedish radio.' Under pressure of isolation and at Singh's insistence the tables between them are turned, and she herself is degraded: 'She became a girl from the East End of London, without breeding or education, who had been rescued by myself, besotted by the glamour of her race.'[29] Their marriage deteriorates while their absurdly elaborate Roman villa is under construction, the house that is to be the centre of Singh's political career, so reminiscent of a plantation house. Sandra is no housekeeper; both are sexually unfaithful. She is herself a displaced person and a misfit, and like many of Naipaul's characters someone who can only rise in the world by failing to fit in, by a sort of upward pressure created by a sense of crushing discomfort and of the inadequacy of the world they have inherited to their dreams and fantasies. What Singh appreciates as her 'avidity' is his own, as is her upward glance and her snobbery. Once having ditched his common, embarrassing little wife, who shortly leaves the island, Singh moves in on the French creoles.

But *The Mimic Men* proceeds by a kind of elegant temporal looping in which chunks of remembered time recur and unfold at will, in an explanatory order that leaves us in no doubt that we are reading a kind of fiction that regards its mission as being to unlock the orders of myth and history: whereby we are now transported back to Singh's childhood and adolescence on the island of Isabella, learn far more about it as a microcosmic society, and begin to understand another key reason why Naipaul's narrator is far more likely to mention his family connections to Coca-Cola than to his socialist schoolteacher father. Singh expresses incredulity at English politicians' claims to be from poor backgrounds, whether genuinely so or not. On Isabella it is a disgrace to be poor, and 'to be descended from generations of idlers and failures, an unbroken line of the unimaginative, unenterprising and oppresssed, had always seemed to me to be a cause for deep, silent shame.'[30] His ex-wife's contempt for her origins is laudable, although he cannot understand her failure to conceal them altogether. Singh's father, it transpires, had not always been content to be a humble, honest teacher, and, one day, following an altercation with his employers, found himself borne aloft as the leader of a lower-class political movement with its roots amongst striking dockworkers, made an instant leader when he begins to talk to them sympathetically on a street corner whilst he is angry—swept along, rather like Charlie Chaplin in *Modern Times*, because a crowd happens to surge around the corner and he happens to be waving a red flag. Singh's father becomes a short-lived political hero of the black masses, a religious figure, and shortly thereafter, a disgraced guru, Gurudeva, doubly disgraceful to his mother's family for being a rabble-rouser and for crossing the racial line and repudiating their Aryan heritage.

Singh's schooldays have been passed as a scholarship boy at Isabella Imperial, where bright boys are inculcated with the English and French literary canon, with Latin, and taught to be impersonators of a European high culture they must learn painfully and by rote, often mocked by the masters for their origins, given disparaging nicknames, and learning to be comedians of their own inherent inadequacies. Browne, Singh's eventual political ally, is a black boy of slightly comical appearance who is struggling out of an impoverished servile background in which his father has compelled him to become a black-face minstrel, whilst he dreams of leading a slave revolt that never happened, and, for Naipaul, never could have happened. There is something pitiable and destructive of personality about the cultural mish-mash and sense of inherent inferiority of which Browne is the inheritor, something which makes it impossible to develop properly except as a fantasist, despite his intelligence: his inherited cultural stories just don't work, they all end in death and despair, and Browne's noble political aspirations are doomed to be forever tainted and stymied by the lowly social place his race occupies in the West Indies. Here is Singh's reaction to Browne's father and his family's milieu:

> He wore a grimy flannel vest. A flannel vest is proletarian wear—flannel the favoured material of Negroes enfeebled by illness or old age—and I wished I had not seen it on Browne's father. Next to the house was a Negro barber-shop called the Kremlin—Negro barber-shops liked to attach such remote drama to themselves—with a caged parrot in the doorway.[31]

By contrast, Singh's schoolfriend Deschampneufs is a French creole: wealthy, arrogant, and confident of his future in banking despite modest intellectual attainments. He mixes freely with lower-class boys and cracks jokes about interbreeding for intelligence, but he too is a mimic man, and his family's sense of cultural grandeur is based the supposed fact that a female ancestor of theirs was mentioned by Stendal in *Le Rouge et le Noir*—a tale of a revolutionary peasant made good that can only be stripped of political meaning and fetishised as a cultural possession in the corrupt island culture, but also a book which really says the same thing as *The Mimic Men*: that political revolutions can never really happen, and that rebels will always be co-opted. For the creoles the Niger is a tributary of the Seine, a sentiment Deschampneuf's father expresses by having an alleged photograph of their ancestor turned into a bad oil painting and painted on a plate: they are defining artifacts which are no different in kind from those that adorn Browne's parents' modest lower middle-class home, and which Naipaul enumerates with a gimlet eye and a facetious wince in a passage reminiscent of Flaubert's descriptions of upper-class furnishings:

> The marble was covered with a white lacy material. On it was a brass ashtray with a stunted but still top-heavy palm in a tin wrapped around with crepe paper. At the top of the tin the crepe paper was finely fringed, almost minced, and fluffed out. On one

> wall, ochre-coloured with white facings, there were farmed picture of Joe Louis, Jesse Owens, Haile Selassie and Jesus. Against the opposite wall was a glass-doored cabinet with coloured tumblers, cherubs and pink-and-white ladies in glazed clay, three drunk top-hatted men in battered evening dress under a lamp standard, and a bouquet of paper flowers. Above this cabinet was a large photograph of a Negro man and woman, a girl, and a much bedecked boy whose tight chin with water-drop wart revealed him as Browne the comic singer, all standing before a painted backdrop of a ruined Greek temple.[32]

Eventually, and it is a surprise we have been well prepared for, Singh and Browne are swept to power at the head of a popular black-based movement whose credibility is based on Browne's race and Singh's father's credentials as a guru; but their true authority is largely derived from Singh's family's wealth and both its leaders are deeply unreliable as political champions of the masses: they are opportunists and political performers who share the colonial masters' basic contempt for black people and wish only to inherit their cultural possessions and a place in the Governor's mansion. They are laughably incompetent rulers and are soon disgraced as such, as well as having little credibility with the electorate as imitation white people. Singh is exiled and we are brought back to the condition of a solitary man in London, who is now writing his memoirs and hoping to become a colonial expert for the BBC. What is most distressing and hard to answer about Naipaul's view of colonialism is his assertion that third world revolutions are inherently impossible, and where they do apparently take place it is because they have been permitted to succeed by imperial masters so long as they do not threaten their economic interests. Politics is the sphere of clowns and imposters because politics does not finally matter very much: it can never deliver on its promises to the constituencies upon whose hopes and aspirations it always preys. He also appears to suggest, to the anger of generations of anti-imperialists, that such racial hierarchies are inevitable and therefore to some degree justified.

Naipaul produces a surgically precise anatomy of the psychology of being colonised, or that is his avowed aim, but it has left some of its Caribbean readers with a sense of queasy self-disgust and anger—it undermines the prospects of any revolt against colonial power. But it is also heroic in the way it ruthlessly examines (and rubbishes) cultural narratives: imperial racial myths and myths of revolt, myths glamourising violence and domination and myths of easy redemption. It is, in this sense, and quite explicitly, also an essay in the spirit of Benjamin's 'Theses on the Philosophy of History'. Singh is indeed a singer, not a wry calypsonian but a criminal who 'sings' about crimes in which he has taken part, and a melancholic, back-looking raveller of the political and racial histories of the Caribbean. We are told he is first drawn to the writing of history, but the disturbed and complex nature of the histories he is given to write seem to preclude a linear narrative of any kind and necessitate a disrupted, personal version of the history of slavery and its legacy, a story in which he himself is a driven actor. Narratives of progress and of violent, paroxysmic revolution are laid side by side and their origins in human greed and fantasy painfully revealed; Singh's is no redemption song, although it could be argued that it is written under the sign of redemption nevertheless: it shares in the buffering humour, often cruel jokes, by which oppressed people often reel away from intolerable pressures and situations; but more than this he gives a voice to the pitiable, supplicating hopes of justice which accost both imperialists and their stunted creations, their colonial proxies, with accusing eyes.

In a Free State (1971) is a novel constructed out of two short stories and a novella. Opening and closing autobiographical fragments tell stories of immigrants in transit and the predicament of the colonial artist; of the two short stories, the first concerns a humble Indian servant who emigrates to Washington D.C., struggles to throw off a sense of his ordained social place but loses with it his sense of belonging and identity; the second story is about a pair of West Indian brothers who have emigrated to England. The favoured brother, supposedly a student, in reality idles his time away picking up girls, whilst his diligent younger brother patiently works his way up through the English working-class until he has saved enough to open his own roadside curry shop. In the course of attempting to build up this business he suffers a great deal of racial abuse from drunken yobbos before his shop is destroyed in a violent racial attack. In retaliating he kills one of his assailants; and finally, in what seems to Naipaul an ultimate betrayal, the feckless older brother marries into the white working-class, his wedding a joyless foredoomed occasion which his brother is allowed to attend handcuffed to a prison guard. If the narrative of the brothers is a mordantly dark fable of the British immigrant experience, the novella itself is about the white experience of Africa at the moment of collapse of colonialism. A pair of rather unsavoury English misfits: a gay man who has escaped to Africa in order to express his sexuality with African boys, and the young wife of a surveyor whose consuming interest in botany and cloud formations says it all about her and her husband's concern for Africans. These two take a long road trip by sportscar through an unnamed country which is on the brink of revolution. Between the safety of the English compound and the flyblown resort—formerly a well-appointed imitation of a European seaside town—which is their destination, lies a long desert road patrolled by an insurgent army and hemmed by an impoverished population. Naipaul is excellent at describing the unspoken contempt and sense of entitlement which protects this odd couple from feeling too much fear at their predicament; but, if a psychological critique of imperial attitudes is intended, Naipaul seems rather to relish, even to love these characters, Bobby and Linda, with their tentative romance and respective bubbles of unfulfilment. To a large extent he seems to look at Africa through their eyes, and to see it—and smell it—their way. Or perhaps he is taunting his readers to admit that, really, this is how they see the third world. Comedy and repressed violence erupt into the novel during a stop for petrol at a service station in a dusty non-place Naipaul names Esher.

It has been said of Naipaul that he settled comfortably into a long period of anguished displacement in the Avon valley. Exile and estrangement are his themes, and he has explored them meticulously from beginning to end; but his existential approach arguably ties him more closely to his generation in European literature than to his inherited Britishness, that of his beloved West Indian school readers. His personae, wherever they are placed on the post-colonial Möbius strip, invariably share in the heightened, flattened intensities and disaffected anomie of Camus' Meurseult, returning us again and again to the same point: seeking moments of authenticity—not in acts of explicable racial violence against the other, but in ever stranger (and more perverse) acts of repudiation, of turning aside, from those who have in their turn grown impatient with him.

Chapter Five

Art and Documents: John Berger, B.S. Johnson

John Berger and B.S. Johnson were twins. Separated at birth, these two men nevertheless met in later life and became friends. Berger lent Johnson his flat in Geneva during a difficult period when the latter needed to get away from the ravages of London literary life, and much later spoke movingly to Johnson's biographer Jonathan Coe about 'all those cunts writing in those papers… I could begin to make a little list of the people who the literary establishment had in one way of another assassinated: and he was on that list.'[1] When I spoke to him briefly during a series of events his publisher put on in London to celebrate his life's work, he offered the opinion that B.S. Johnson was a far better writer than him. But twins? The claim seems ludicrous. But they do have a certain amount in common. Both are Marxists. Both have strong working-class sympathies—Johnson actually from a working-class background, Berger by political affiliation and by living the life of a bohemian art student in wartime London. Both are interested in documentary: Johnson helped compile a book of National Service memories and incorporated a strong element of verité in his novels; Berger wrote documentary books about the life of a country doctor in England and on the experience of migrant workers in Europe. Both are formal innovators and both are intensely dissatisfied with the realist novel: Johnson believed that 'telling stories is telling lies' and did everything he could to break down conventional narrative expectations in his novels; Berger wrote an early 'post-modern' novel, then moved to France and tried to tell the untold stories of a disintegrating peasant community. Both are realists in a sense despite their aesthetic objections—Johnson has a painfully literal idea of truth: his objection to the realist novel is that it cannot represent reality except by gross distortion; Berger began as a realist painter, became a socialist realist critic who was equally attracted and repelled by modernism, and one of his most celebrated essays, 'The Moment of Cubism', justifies the cubist painters by saying that the explosive experience of the twentieth century is unrepresentable by previous means. Cubism, like anything else he admires in art, is, for him, a superior kind of realism. Both are attracted by French literary culture—Berger by family background (he had a French father); Johnson by his sheer rebellious disaffection from everything England had to offer. John Berger and B.S. Johnson are twins. But Johnson is the dark twin.

John Berger is a perennial optimist with a tragic view of history, still recommending 'optimism of the will' (as well as of the intellect) long after everyone else has pulled the blinds down and dedicated themselves to taking pot shots at the television or the cat; Johnson could never stop himself from picking the scabs off old wounds, in what was his stock in trade: he can't stop noticing how shitty everything is despite what people say to the contrary. Berger is a rationalist who conceives of a project then completes it to the best of his ability; Johnson wrote by instinct, often unsure what exactly he was supposed to be doing. Berger has a clear, relentlessly pursued programme; Johnson is a radical doubter. Berger has a mystical side: he likes Jakob Boehme's idea that God has written his signature on the underside of every leaf; Johnson is haunted by nightmares: the horrifying figure of Sheela-na-gig, an incarnation of the White Goddess as the death mother, appears to him squatting obscenely in the middle of the road. Berger is somewhat respectful of popular religiosity; Johnson hates all forms of religious observance and finds them incomprehensible. Berger's dead reappear to him and offer encouragement; Johnson is spooked. Berger has the flaw of being somewhat po-faced; Johnson is dark but funny. Berger can be hectoring and dogmatic—so can Johnson; both of them tend to argue by assertion, but Johnson, unlike Berger, is never sweetly reasonable or particularly persuasive in argument. Both state their positions and retreat. Neither has much respect for the opinions of those they see as enemies.

Berger would have agreed with the title of Williams' posthumous essay collection, *Resources of Hope*—hope being what a good socialist writer ought to be offering, if possible, and even if impossible: something forward-looking and upbeat. More to the point in his own intellectual background would be the utopian thinking of the long-lived German Marxist critic Ernst Bloch, who saw even tragedy as a hopeful, utopian mode of writing that makes models of heroically-flawed characters so that we can improve on them in the future. For Berger our hopes are reborn instinctively as soon as the prospect of immediate death passes. Hope is as inevitable and as necessary as breathing, which is to say not to be questioned although often deluded.

A Painter of Our Time, his first novel, explored questions of aesthetics and politics through the diary of a young English artist who is friends with an exiled Hungarian communist painter and is sympathetically engaged by his dilemmas about how to make art that contributes to a revolutionary struggle for socialism, and earned its young author, art critic of the *New Statesman*, round condemnation as a Soviet propagandist and apologist for Stalinism. Berger was certainly a sympathiser of the Soviet Union, and definitely not shy of controversy, but he didn't really deserve to be placed in the company of Joseph Goebbels. One of the novel's social sins was its yearning to be far away from a London in which only the exiles are seen as interesting, so that when its painter leaves the young narrator and everyone else behind to return to Hungary following the workers' uprising of 1956, we left uncertain as to which side he is on, and with a sense that the novel's young narrator seems to have been left behind, marooned in a foreign country, powerless to act and far from the important action of history.

In *The Foot of Clive*, which followed a few years later, Berger tried to overcome this sense of alienation and engage with contemporary British life. Clive is a hospital ward named after Clive of India, a setting that he hopes will enable him to pose questions about whether new socialist institutions can be built on the foundations of a semi-defunct imperial legacy. The novel makes use of multiple viewpoints and concerns the lives and aspirations of various characters who are laid up in hospital in a post-colonial Britain depicted as being in a process of undecided change. It is also a crime novel of sorts, in which the murderer is hidden in plain sight in a hospital bed, a mute measurer and witness of their lives who is elevated into that position by his own impending execution for killing a policeman. In a way he resembles the Quare Fellow, the generic man whose execution is awaited in Mountjoy jail in Brendan Behan's play, and in the same way Berger's six patients are all recognisable human and social types: the naïve boy, the itinerant Welsh labourer, the profound if religiose shopkeeper, the Italian immigrant. Quoted, observed in a muted way, from a distance, his characters and their dilemmas feel a little staged. England might yet offer some of them reparations for historical injustices they have suffered as well as new and better ways of living, although the novel's political landscape is one in which socialist hopes have already been betrayed. Nevertheless, it is a socially optimistic work, concerned with its characters' inner lives, and worried over whether the common experience of being isolated by illness can really lead to insights into one's wider condition. People in hospital are certainly being brought up short against death and mortality, but these inmates also confess, antagonise and confront one another. They are all philosophers of particular social positions. What is most startling and engaging about *The Foot of Clive*, and represents a step forward in Berger's writing, is the way he reaches for a kind of dreamlike poetry of definitions through his characters' semi-delirious voices, pulls towards a kind of everyday aphoristic mode, and also begins to write interestingly about sex and women, as here in the multiplying images of a wife who is also a model, in a passage which slyly alludes to the Song of Songs:

KEN: Her whole family! That's what I live with. Her two legs are twin sisters. She has two breasts who are cousins on her father's side. Her back is a young, beautiful aunt. They all live with us and I wait on them all. There are photographs of them everywhere. And they all have to be dusted and fed and paid attention to. She always sides with them. They are inseparable. They eat together. They repeat what each other says. They sleep together. We have a huge bed and we all lie down in it. Her family on one side—all curling and cooing round each other—and I on the other. [2]

Contemporary with *The Foot of Clive* in pop culture were the Doctor films, starring Dirk Bogarde, hit television series like *Emergency Ward Ten* and *Dr Kildare*—and in choosing to write about patients experiencing the national health service, Berger could also be accused of producing a sort of Marxist equivalent of *Carry on Nurse*. What is has it common with the last of these two is a kind of portmanteau storytelling: we move from person to person, from case to case, a little like a doctor doing his daily rounds; and what seems to interest Berger is the differences between his immobilised characters, with what is inherently invisible about them, or what is rendered invisible by institutional life, rather than with contriving any overall narrative thread. Berger's third novel, *Corker's Freedom*, is set in a South London employment agency, and finds a similar way of approaching being a social novel about England: through an analysis of the lower-middle-class conceptions of freedom of the proprietor and the lives and speech of the firm's clients and staff. One of this book's problems, like his second, is a static quality resulting from the basic situation he is writing about and a resultant failure to develop momentum, but in *The Foot of Clive* Berger discovered a number of subjects that have continued to interest him deeply and to which he was later to return in a different kind of book, a documentary, this time with a dynamic romantic hero who is more than equal to television's Dr Kildare.

A Fortunate Man is a documentary photo-essay, a kind of television series manqué (this is what he and his collaborator, photographer Jean Mohr had hoped for) about the life of a country doctor and his relationship with his working-class patients in an isolated village in the New Forest. The book opens with a definition of landscape that suggests it might be an occluding curtain that the lives of its inhabitants are hidden behind, offers a few subtle grey and misty photos in support of that view, then proceeds to open that curtain to show a few snapshots of a doctor at work, his patients starkly revealed, surprised, half-undressed by the gaze of a pair of peeping toms, Berger and his long time collaborator, the photographer Jean Mohr. A man has been crushed by a fallen tree and the attending doctor must offer reassurance, cope with his workmates as well as taking the swift action that will hopefully save his legs. A moon-faced young woman is inexplicably depressed and listless. The doctor manages to intuit the cause of her problems—she has probably been raped—but is unable to alter her situation. Berger sets forth the scope of a doctor's caring responsibilities and proceeds to an essay on the man he calls Sassall's predicament as a general practitioner caring for mostly poor patients in a rural practice. The book is largely a meditation on the idea and ethics of doctoring based on a close friend of Berger's who allowed him complete access to his working life. Sassall, we are told, is motivated by an ideal of service he has derived not from Victorian philanthropists, but from his boyhood reading of Joseph Conrad and his idealised master mariners. Sassall's consulting room reminds Berger of a ship's officer's cabin, with its compact stowage of medical equipment and its narrow neat examination table resembling a bunk. Added to this is his education, his belief in the Enlightenment ideal of the universal man and his sense of himself as bringing enlightenment—applying what he knows as an educated, rational man—to the everyday lives of his isolated and uneducated patients.

Berger admires Sassall for the work he does in alleviating pain and sensitively dealing with social problems, but he is also a kind of existential hero, a philosophical figure who has made an ultimately meaningful choice about what to do with his energies. He makes use of passages from Jean-Paul Sartre's novel *Nausea* to explain the ideas of contingency and the idea of meaningful choice. Our society and historical moment is one in which meaningful choices aren't usually made because they aren't offered. If you were French after the German invasion you had to choose to join the French resistance or not; if you were English you may have fought the Nazis, but not as a result of such a personal choice or decision: the question of which side to be on had already been made for you. In the postwar world opportunities to make such meaningful choices were even more rare. Berger asks whether this privilege—not to have to make life or death choices—is really a luxury of prosperity or a denial of human potentiality and freedom. Sassall, he suggests, is a fortunate man because he has been able to make an ethical choice to do work and occupy a place in a community that makes a difference and is of a different order than the usual choices involving personal ambition, or climbing the ladder of career success. Sassall has chosen an obscure rural practice while continuing with the kind of research that might ordinarily only be expected of a more ambitious doctor or a hospital consultant.

Berger continues his meditation on choice by drawing on Piaget's child psychology: a child knows there are no second chances because every event, once over, retreats irrecoverably into the past, he tells us. Adults think they know another chance will come, they have the illusion of an infinity of second chances based to an extent on experience—but it is an illusion because any given moment is indeed lost, and they cannot allow themselves to experience the truth of a child's desolation at lost moments, events. A young child's appetite for the next thing, the next moment might appear to contradict this but each experienced thing is different and genuinely new to a young child, rather than a repeated act. Another part of Berger's argument built out of child psychology, and suggested by the child-like vulnerability and trust with which Sassall's patients approach him as a doctor, is his exploration of the experience of grief or anguish and the adult's apparent regression to childhood at such times. A child cries to protest, in hopes of someone coming to make it better. An adult cries alone without hope; adult crying represents the end of a hope, but there is also the comfort of a regression to childhood in it, the hope of a recovery, which isn't real. According to Berger, there is no such recovery from the causes of anguish in adults.

> Most unhappiness is like illness in that it too exacerbates a sense of uniqueness. All frustration magnifies its dissimilarity and so nourishes itself. Objectively speaking this is illogical since in our society frustration is far more usual than satisfaction, unhappiness far more common that contentment.[3]

Such are the conflicting pressures on a doctor who must be priest, psychologist and counsellor as well as physician. Jean Mohr's photographs of him show a small, whippet-like man who is a bundle of concentrated energy, rushing from one situation, one context to another in his Landrover, with his bag of equipment. In a poignant passage about halfway through the book, Berger tells us that Sassall suffers from depression and tries to explore this briefly. Are its causes physiological or due to some yet to be uncovered childhood trauma? Sassall and Berger are both Freudians. But neither Sassall's self-analysis nor Berger's concentrated attention on his work offer any clear insights into its causes or possible cures, and Sassall can only throw himself into more work, more responsibility for his patients. *A Fortunate Man* builds to a series of far reaching rhetorical questions about contemporary capitalist society that its account of Sassall's practice has helped to frame and to which it is meant to provide a counter example to. Is our society truly humane? What are its ideas of the human? Do Sassall's patients deserve a better life than the one they have? Berger and Sassall's answer to the last question is of course yes, but it is an answer that really can't be given, Berger says, by anyone who has accepted the structure of society as it is, who has taken on the enforced hypocrisy of a career within a society that takes inequality for granted as a necessity. How can we speak meaningfully of human potential in a context where individual human lives are not valued in any absolute way? An improvement in conditions since prewar days may encourage a belief in progress, but the young people of this economically depressed and culturally isolated rural area are still having to settle for fifth best. Perhaps this is the source of Sassall's depression. Berger says that medical students may well stop thinking about the individual human life in any 'humanist' or sacralised way after they start performing autopsies. On the other hand, it could be the frequency of failure and the doctor's discovery of patterns and repetitions in human behaviour, and a perception of physiological and social types that militates against maintaining such a humanist (arguably semi-religious) view of the patients. Or maybe the pain of getting too involved, which must inevitably pass as he or she carries on, in only as a condition of survival in the job.

The humanist core of the book is carried by Mohr's photographs which, as well as depicting the rituals of village life, record the light of hope and trust in patients' eyes, their vulnerability with the doctor—to whom they allow the intimate access only a lover (or parent) would otherwise be granted. The photographs try to give an overall sense of the rituals of village life: they record youth club discos, political meetings and private grief, women sobbing inconsolably, men sharing jokes. The meanings of these photographs are both fragile and permanent—existing only in the eye of the photographer and the viewer of his photographs: they are so everyday (despite the patina of 'the past' that now encloses and distances them as black and white photos of a certain style from the sixties) that for a doctor (or a photographer) their sheer multiplication must begin to rob them of individual meaning. How can a writer generalise about experience without robbing it of such particular, individual meanings, and continue to lend personal difficulties some of the weight they must always have for the individuals themselves? If they do indeed think of themselves as individuals. This is a further subtlety of *A Fortunate Man*: it is in the nature of the kind of settled, traditional community the villagers live in for them not to think of themselves particularly as unique persons with individual aspirations. They are more inclined to accept their place in an inherited order, and part of Sassall's elected mission is to help them where the pressure to conform and accept is clearly damaging, for example by suggesting to a girl that, given training, she could do secretarial work rather than accept her lot as a factory hand, arranging time off work so she can go to the labour exchange and investigate. How can we make social being more active and meaningful? Berger asks. What would a more 'human' society look like? It is our task to make one, and Sassall is a model citizen whose exemplary life prefigures such a utopia.

A Fortunate Man is shadowed by his subject's later suicide, unknowingly pointed to in the book by Berger's reflections on anguish and depression, and this inevitably colours a later reading of it, but also suggests the urgency and reality of the book's themes, and shows the extreme difficulty of actually being such a 'fortunate man' as he so admiringly describes. But Sassall remains no less an Enlightenment hero and a Conradian master mariner whatever the flaw was that broke what Brecht might have called 'the lovely fork' of his mind. Berger has admitted that he underestimated the extent to which Sassall was a driven man rather than a rationalist hero and it may also be that the exalted nature of his view of his vocation drove him beyond his own human limits; but although it is by now a book that speaks from another time and political context, this is one of the high points of sixties writing and of Berger's career. The complexity and sensitivity of his exploration of the doctor-patient relationship, woven together with reflections on the history of medicine and a tissue of particular cases and interactions has made it a classic that is still sometimes used in the training of doctors. I have mentioned it to a number of doctors over the years, and most claimed to have read it. It is also in its way a highly entertaining and dramatic book that draws on novelistic techniques and uses its formal adventurousness to reach beyond the usual province of fiction.

In reaching for a satisfactory conclusion Berger mulls over the problems of the novelist, the biographer, and the autobiographer. If he were in this instance a novelist he would only have to decide that Sassall was admirable and to try to make him appear so; if he were writing his own autobiography self-justification would perforce dictate the account he gave of his actions and inner workings. However selective and distorting his account, nobody would be able to reproach him, except for an unkind reviewer with a nose for blatant myth-making, and the autobiographer is a fortunate man in that events over which he had no control can now be brought to order. He feels he is not a biographer either, since his subject is neither famous nor infamous, and nor is he dead. Drawing on Benjamin's storyteller essay, he begins to reflect on the difference death makes to our sense of an individual's life, and this he believes is what makes his book about a person in process one that defies these genres. Death makes everything certain about a person and if Sassall were already dead, Berger would have written a less speculative essay about him: everything would be known and he would wish to preserve an accurate likeness of his friend. As he is still living and working, much about him remains mysterious, unfixed, unfinished, and Berger is 'anxious to see the maximum possible, but inevitably half-blind, like an owl in bright daylight.'[4]

§

Walter Benjamin's 'Thirteen Theses Against Snobs', in his early book, *One-Way Street*, is part of a series of aphorisms on writing and criticism. It is set out in two columns which contrast the qualities of art-works and documents: the column of white space between them is a spine from which these theses, or the spaces between them, project on either side like a set of ribs from a human body, or alternatively, like a series of perches arranged around a vertical stick for caged parrots to settle on, or snakes to twine around, or sloths to hang from in Berlin Zoo around 1920. They creak a little, these contrasting assertions, and one wonders if they will bear the weight of the thought-creatures which sometimes hop nimbly between them, sometimes heavily flop from branch to branch, and are sometimes throttled and eaten by the coiling pythons of platitude, no respecters of sides or levels or relationships. Art is made by artists, documents produced by primitives; art is incidentally a document, but no document as such is art. Art is masterpieces; documents are instructive. Art is something for artists to learn how to do; documents are somethings from which the public might learn; great art-works are individual, incomparable, masterpieces; documents are an interchangeable means for the communication of subject-matter. Art is a fusion of form and content to create meaning, documents merely informational. Such is his dialectical gist, but perhaps, once he has achieved lift off, we should let Benjamin speak for himself:

> VII Meaning is the outcome of experience. Subject-matter is the outcome of dreams.[5]

At this point art and documents seem to change places for a moment: art appears to be on the side of reality, to grant access to reality, to the meaning of our experience; documents are the expression something fantasised or wished for—often seen as the main province of art. Possibly he means that a narrowly political or propagandistic language is the outcome of dreams, or speaks to dreams: it is propaganda that speaks to certain aspirations, certain fears. Or he means that there is something dream-like, obsessive about the way a particular subject-matter can multiply and take you over: once we are obsessed we see the object of our obsession everywhere: it begins to exert power over us, it defines us in a way. We certainly don't have the impersonal power over neurotically proliferating subject-matter that an artist has over a work he or she is creating. But, we might think, what about the dream of the artist? Particularly the kinds of artists Benjamin most admired, the German romantics, for example, or the French surrealists. Benjamin inverts his terms to associate documents with the subjective effusion of dreams and art with the distillation of historical experience, of personal experience seen as an instance of historical experience.

After this suggestive moment he returns to exalting art-works over documents. It's difficult to see exactly what Benjamin is trying to do with this piece. He opens with a 'snob in the office of art criticism' comparing a Picasso, 'a fetish', to a child's drawing and saying that the latter proves the worthlessness of the former. But it's not really the sort of thing art-critics say, is it? They don't try to sell children's drawings as art: they favour and foster the 'aura' over the document, here of a child's early development, and they created Picasso's reputation. The art critic's comment is one more likely to have been made by an uninformed person ('my kid can do better than that') than an art salesman. Later, in his famous essay 'The Work of Art in the Age of Mechanical Reproduction' Benjamin will celebrate the death of the aura of the individual art-work and the resultant democratisation of culture; elsewhere in *One-Way Street* he seems to grope towards a similar position with extravagant praise of the giant advertising hoardings which abolish 'matter-of-factness' and 'where toothpaste and cosmetics lie handy for giants'—the giants whom he hopes will one day pick them up. He is writing at a period when photography was developing at a great pace as an art which challenged the relationship between art and documents, but in 'Thirteen Theses Against Snobs' all he seems able to do is to mechanically exalt art (formal, synthetic, an energy-centre, enduringly impactful, virile, conquering) over documents (shapeless, always pregnant, needful of analysis, of novelty value only, innocent, primitive).

'Thirteen Theses Against Snobs' shows Benjamin unable (in this piece, anyway) to produce a satisfying synthesis of art and document, all he can manage is to manufacture a sequence of woodenly opposed propositions, digging them in deeper and deeper, suggesting an interpenetration of masculine and feminine qualities, but making no particularly unorthodox statements and illuminating the status of neither of his terms: the best he can do is veer from one extreme to another. As an attempt at dialectical criticism it is reminiscent of Kierkegaard's image of the dialectic as a cat shaking a fish, so that first one side then the other flashes in the light: vivid but unclear, offering no synthesis. But having said this, Benjamin's praise of the ability of art-works to synthesise and integrate experience and to stand alone is a perfectly reasonable and so far as it goes a good definition of art. He is right that something which offers to absorb a lot of your ingenuity in producing a convincing, satisfying account of it may well by virtue of its complexity turn out to be no more than a prolix and obsessive document of its maker's ill-thought contradictions. Apparent highfalutin difficulty and a strident challenge to unravel it in a manifesto do not guarantee a satisfying work of art, and perhaps it is fair to point out that B.S. Johnson grapples with ideas from this period of the avant-garde and its politics but that his stridently programmatic mind inherits difficulties as well as an enabling way of thinking about art.

B.S. Johnson's combination of hostility to realist narrative (expressed in a slogan whose underpinnings as an aesthetic credo are elaborated in his essay 'Telling Stories Is Telling Lies' but which appears earlier, in his second novel, *Albert Angelo*) and his solution to what he sees as the deformations of realism—his attempts to marry experimental forms which 'bare the device' to a commitment to recording experience in accordance with a literal notion of 'truth'—makes him an interesting figure through whom to explore the impact of the European (especially French) novel in England. In his books European modernism and a native realist idiom are brought into a tense relationship, producing explosive fictions that test the limits of the novel. His first novel *Travelling People* had initiated a violent collision of Grand Guignol and the everyday that was to become his special territory: its medley of prose styles is intended to destabilise the reader's response and overcome the naturalisation of realism, but actually suggests an unresolved series of prose try-outs and investigations of how to get a haphazardly found narrative to 'go on' and resolve itself satisfyingly.

The first chapter of *Travelling People* finds a hitchhiking ex-student in company with the driver of a lorry load of dead dogs bound for the glue factory, and subsequently with a sportscar driving man in the import-export business ('you don't have to be in one place to run my business') on his way to take over management of an exclusive country club in Wales for the summer. This business, it transpires, is actually only a recreation for its rich owner. The second driver sees a potential use for Johnson as host, an educated person who can speak to the guests 'in their own language'; the lorry driver sees no use at all for his education; indeed, Johnson knows better than to reveal it. This raises uncomfortable questions about what uses the expanded, redefined access to higher education that Raymond Williams had advocated a few years earlier might be put to—by 'society' (there is no 'community' between the lorry driver and the country club manager) and by its recipient, who has been socially removed from the cultural spheres of either. The cargo of dead dogs is, for Johnson, though not its driver, pregnant with meaning, an ironised metaphor for used up working-class lives; for the sports-car driver, Trevor—whom the Johnson narrator uneasily suspects of being a homosexual—it is meaningless, literal, unpleasant and fails even to raise a smile.[6]

'Telling stories is telling lies' does sound a little like a precept arrived at by Arthur Seaton: we have been told too many stories, too many lies, and we won't get fooled again by the nonsense on the goggle-box and the blandishments of the incoming government. At the same time as it is stirringly defiant, it strikes a dully literal attitude to towards fiction and is seemingly incapable of seeing that some lies are both entertaining and can grant access to areas where wishes come true; or, at a higher stage, that stories need not be lies at all, just somebody's provisional attempt to make a shape out of experience. Johnson is operating at a higher level still in that he is attempting to make experiential maps which countermand official or literary fictions, yet also partakes of fiction's inventiveness by finding so many elaborate ways to point up the dubiousness of its dubious truths. In this incident near the beginning of his first novel it is Johnson's working-class narrator who is the fabulist, the word-spinner, and Trevor, the middle-class sports-car driver with whom he has hitched a ride, who is unable to find any moral in what the storytelling liar is saying and feigns deafness as they plunge on through the Welsh night.

Albert Angelo was likely written in reaction to realist fictions and films about teaching (*To Sir with Love* is an autobiographical study of a progressive East End school by a young West Indian teacher; *Violent Playground*, an earnest juvenile delinquent saga in which 'Johnny' (David McCallum) holes up in the school with an old service revolver and takes a few hostages in closing scenes that horribly prefigure later real-life school massacres[7]) but is just as likely to have risen out of Johnson's experience. His novel carries an implicit claim to be more real than these—a more honest account of teaching, especially the supply teaching in an inner city school that Johnson had done for a living. It is also, as the title suggests, a book about a working-class artist's dilemma. As an artist he is a maker of patterns; and the teaching job is a means to an end; as a socialist and teacher he is dissatisfied with going through the motions in the way that secondary teaching in London's schools often involves:

> 'If we go on half-educating these kids anymore,' he said suddenly to Terry, 'then the violence will out. I'm sure they know they're being cheated, that they're being treated as subhuman beings. And the school is a microcosm of society as a whole.'[8]

The book is famous for a long rectangular hole than is cut through some of its pages, so that you see, or think you see, the assassination of Christopher Marlowe coming up in the narrative's future, a suitable literary murder that is both arrived at and vaporises. This is followed by a series of assembled (but apparently genuine) pieces of writing in which his inner city pupils, at his invitation, tell him what they really think about this provoking, sometimes cruel supply teacher. A little later the novel's strained account of

Albert's personal angst and problems as an artist in the uncaring modern world is interrupted again by a scrawled 'FUCK ALL THIS LYING' and followed by a raw exposition of what Johnson is really trying to write about, not architecture but his own dilemma as a social writer who bases himself on his own experience, and more than this, is unafraid to document his personal unhappiness. But before this closing outburst, an attempted breakthrough which is an admission of failure that resolves nothing, and lying alongside his social anxieties, Johnson tries to define the (highly suspicious) aims of art:

> Albert thought: a block of wood, a plank of wood. When does a plank become a block. At what point do you see that a block had become a plank? at what stage a plank a block. Plank. Block. He thought bout them until the words became meaningless to him, then ludicrous to him, then nothing to him. And he was left with wood. Wood is wood is wood, he said to himself, pleased.[9]

Art arises out of a need to impose a pattern on life, he believes, and from a dubiously motivated desire to defeat its flux and disintegration, to arrest and master time. There is nothing particularly noble in this, he explains, it is no different from his father's preference for the fixity of the past and for objects that define it to the contemporary world of change and risk: it is essentially both conservative and egoistic. Again there is a tension between a notion of art (integrative, honed) and document (direct, proliferative)—art and the role of the artist (here a fictional architect as a figure for Johnson and his predicament) is countered by an appeal to the documentation of the real (the children as the indefinable body of the world) which questions that overarching role of the heroic artist, throwing it into sharp relief. But Johnson must still provoke and arrange the responses of his pupils, and close the book with a staged scene in which they kill him, rather as Marlowe's politically motivated assassins dispatched the Elizabethan dramatist. There is nothing to complain about in the interruption, either its intention or effect in undermining Albert's authority as artist or teacher, but it is Johnson the meticulously arranging artist who closes the book with a boy's account of his (fictional) funeral that again compares art to an undertaker's prettification of a corpse:

> ...it was a nastey sight to see she said that the bodey was all painted up gust like someone on the stage thay panted the lips more red and the face hes pink and yellow thaye sat it proseves it bus I think its Just plan stupid two spend and wast all that money on a thing like that...[10]

Johnson's next novel, *Trawl* (1966) returned to the idea of mapping a journey, but it is a far more unified book than *Travelling People*, tracing a synchronous literal and inner journey, with excursions into the land of memories: a delineating trawl around the British coastline, a trawl through the past. The opening pages of *Trawl*—before the main body of the book cuts to the shipboard life of a trawler on its way around the British coastline—subject sexual episodes from Johnson's earlier life to intense and withering scrutiny. The pained honesty of this writing—the expectations of the woman whose three children are in care, sex in one room shared with another couple, and the narrators retrospective estimate as lover and man, provide an intimate 'lived' sense of sexual 'structures of feeling' that would be unavailable in more public writing about sex—as fantasy, as media images, as brave faces put on misery by the respondents to oral history or sociological questionnaires.

> I was lying on the right of her, it was the one naturally to hand, her left breast, and she said, Try the other one, the children haven't made that one all soft, and I thought Christ!...
>
> And did not let myself think any further, but felt the right one, and it was much firmer, and the nipple stood already, all ready for me, and I thought, How is it the children suckled only one, unless for such an eventuality?[11]

A paradox of Johnson, and part of the richness of his books, is the directness and detail of the social encounters described in them, paradoxical because this aspect of his writing—which is its very stuff and sap—can be valued only in terms that a proponent of realism like Raymond Williams would recognise as a form of realism, as a writing that draws on the resources of naturalism; his modernist insistences are directed towards a better, fuller—and literal—account of the 'real', of a 'truth' that he finds in lacking in both popular and literary 'realist' novels—his is a directness, a literal sense of 'reality' and 'truth' that runs completely counter to the aesthetics of the French New Novelists themselves, and is socially directed, not only in that it uncovers tropisms or social meta-narratives, but in that it provides direct social evidence of working-class lives. Johnson is a recording angel. Such contradictions were highly fruitful for him but are probably what tore him apart—as writing he undertook in the name of 'honesty' revealed layers and layers of deep unhappiness, irremediable, irredeemable suffering that could only be faced with the thinnest of brittle cynicism, which provides his self-shredding narrators scant protection from the corrosive insights and implications he thereby generates or uncovers:

> I must think of it all, remember it all, it must be everything, otherwise I shall certainly not understand, shall have no chance of understanding, that I most desire, that I am here for… I sat up, did not look at her, went to the bath, discovered I had lost the rubber, turned to her, told her, panicking. Forget what she said, all I could do was turn back and try to wash in that awkward space… This is all very painful, painful… Then suddenly she said, I've found it, dismayed, and I pushed back the cupboard door (for I was modest) and she was standing by the bed and pulling out the sheath from between her legs and the emission was sliding down the inside of her left thigh, and I was relieved, and laughed, and she made a face but did not laugh.[12]

The Céline-like dots, which isolate nuggets of described or remembered experience, elevate these moments in a way but also flatten them further back into the past, lending a relentless evenness and inescapability to the consciousness recorded in *Trawl.* The faint disgust of the word 'emission', calling to mind 'nocturnal emission', and added to a retrospective ironic self-disgust in the bracketed '(for I was modest)' plays against the lack of modesty that is allowed to the woman, Joan, and her sense of the unfunniness of having been exposed to pregnancy by him. Johnson's autobiographical focus has been criticised as not fully social, but arguably it's more accurately social in its unwillingness to generalise its experience, or to construct an imaginary life for the people next door. In beginning—with obsessive, fanatical accuracy—from the particularity of his own experiences, their finiteness, and his interactions with others, he is apparently more detailed and accurate in his information about structures of feeling than most of the others.

There certainly is something more urgent, direct—and pained—about his observations than those of most novelists. His unremitting autobiographical focus makes him a little like a Kerouac who never had any fun, and some of their dilemmas are the same. How to grow into a writer on the thin soil of personal memory, and how to be a working-class person who has moved out of his class but who wishes to continue to draw on its experiences, to draw authority from them in a sense? Johnson examines his continued relationship with his class—in *Albert Angelo, Trawl, Travelling People* (and maybe all of them)—in a manner which attempts to avoid the trap Williams describes (and tried to overcome in his own *Border Country*) and a critic like Stanley Atherton finds Alan Sillitoe trying to overcome, of the negative influence of a *Sons and Lovers* model: a working-class novel ending with an act of renunciation of origins: a rupture in which one moves finally and irrevocably beyond the world that has nurtured or deformed, which is thereafter accorded significance only insofar as it has produced this 'sensitive' artist-type, as a foil to him and a measure of his self-transcendence. Johnson's autobiographical personae 'go on', but like Kerouac's Jack Duluoz they still continue to circle their defining origins in pain and unease.

To return to Raymond Williams' dismissal of the outsider as somebody who is ratifying their own failure: *Like A Fiery Elephant,* Jonathan Coe's excellent biography of Johnson, shows that he did indeed experience an extreme fear of failure to go along with his seemingly confident bluster. And does indeed see and experience *himself,* in whatever social role he finds himself, whether supply teacher, accounts clerk, hitchhiking philosophy student, lover, assistant trawlerman, and, above all, writer, as an extreme existential outsider. However, he doesn't take much overt pride in this, exhibits little or no 'jaunty hardness', although there is always a certain bravado, but rather appears to be agonized by his condition, his sense of separateness, of baffled love, and by his failures of compassion towards his fellows, which are in his case combined with a self-analytical turn of mind that is often drawn to the exploration of human weaknesses and failures.

House Mother Normal is one of Johnson's best, most integrated explorations of the conundrum of art and documents. It purports to be 'a geriatric comedy' set in an old people's home, each chapter of which is narrated by a different inmate, prefaced by their medical diagnoses and ratings on a chart for diagnosing senile dementia, and having all the appearance of being based on oral history interviews, which they weren't, but do resemble in many ways. These are bracketed by a pair of similar 'interviews' from which the questioner has been edited out with the House Mother, who is both a normal house mother (a bit like the sadistic Big Nurse in Ken Kesey's *One Flew Over the Cuckoo's Nest*, and conceivably modelled on her), a 'normal' woman and a person whose own diagnoses and readings show her to be 'normal': to have her wits about her and to be suffering from no serious impairments. It also manages to suggest perverted sexual power games, which are the subject of the novel. But in this remarkable lyrical book Johnson spins a highly-wrought poetry out of the stuff of supposed senile reminiscence, at the same time making a strong correlation between the elderly people's level of physical and mental deterioration and the language he offers them to define themselves: the more senile and deranged they are, the more exaltedly avant-garde their mode of expression: a satisfying reversal of social hierarchy on the level of language. Appearing a few years later than his previous novel, and well after Berger's *A Fortunate Man* and *The Foot of Clive* (it is very much on the same territory, although not necessarily influenced by them, examining the relationships between carers and patients, between an ideal of service and the real institutions which manage, confine, and define their 'clients'), *House Mother Normal* was around ten years in gestation, struggled to find a publisher (before finding two) and was not particularly warmly received when it did finally come out in 1971.

What is most noticeably different about *House Mother Normal* and its successor, *Christie Malry's Double-Entry*, from preceding novels, is that the books are scarcely written in prose at all, but in a poetic line derived from Ezra Pound, William Carlos Williams, Charles Olson and other post-war American poets: *House Mother Normal* is in effect a multi-voiced long modernist poem, or a even a stage play. Johnson was a good syllabic poet who had at one time thought poetry to be his main vocation as a writer; in his last books he produces a hybrid poetic mode that outdoes both his earlier prose and his previous poetic output. What the modernist poetic line gives him is a grater precision of language and higher and more subtle level of organisation than his earlier books—and a greater freedom to be inventive as a storyteller. It is as though he is freed from the bugaboo of realist narrative, forgets to trip himself up, and organises his books on the page and for the ear with a kind of gleeful pleasure in speech rhythms and ways of notating them. Sadly, this wasn't really appreciated or noticed very much except by a few hardcore fans and fellow practitioners, and what with the vagaries and general conservatism of poetic taste in Britain contributed to B.S. Johnson being an rather under-appreciated writer, a slow-burner whose books have survived due to the support of people who have studied such things in universities: that and the sheer disturbance generated by an attempt to wrest meaning and humanity from subject-matter like an old man's recollected sexual excitement and simultaneous guilt while suffering constant pain from inoperable rectal cancer:

> a f e w p i a s t r e s s e e m e d
> s o l i t t l e a t t h e t i m e, f o r w h a t
> i t   w a s
> y e a r s a f t e r, t h a t s m e l l
>
> City of galloping
> knobrot
>
> ooooh!
>
> oooooooaoah![13]

House Mother Normal expresses what might be taken for a diametrically opposite view of healthcare institutions to John Berger's in *The Foot of Clive* and *A Fortunate Man*. For Berger there are metaphors of national community and post-imperialism to be explored, but also the real human difference care can make, and the possibility that an honourable man can do something valuable within the contexts of the National Health Service. Johnson notices first and last the doubleness in the agendas of administrators and office holders who are more likely to use their positions to turn a personal profit and satisfy their perverse sexual desires than anything else. The doubleness comes in the House Mother's deadpan sincere justifications of using her charges as a free workforce of outworkers in schemes involving the packaging of Christmas crackers and other such light assembly work, the adulteration of drugs (shades of Harry Lime) and the recycling of waste food as pigswill. She understands them well, better than anyone else, so she claims, well enough to know that disciplining them with 'the twitcher' is something they come to expect and that they enjoy it as much as she relishes its application: it is what they are used to, what their lives have prepared them for. Whether harnessing them in pairs for a 'tourney' around the living room or shocking them by having her Borzoi dog perform cunnilingus on her, she is distracting them from the consciousness of decay and dissolution and physical pain, and as she puts them through her strange paces she (and Johnson) force our senses of what is cruelty and what is compassion to change places in this striking justification of cruelty and perversity:

> I disgust them in order that they may not be
> disgusted with themselves. I am disgusting to them
> in order to objectify their disgust, to direct it to
> something outside themselves, something harmless.[14]

Her charges are full of vivid memories—of fighting in the trenches, married and illicit sex, the humiliations of being a servant, the compensations of running a pub: a thousand cruelties and small pleasures, with Johnson's mordant emphases milking a bleak humour out of the downside of life at the bottom of the social heap. One happy childhood memory involves a competition as a village fete for 'grinning through a horse collar': a way of learning the chirpy attitude to life required of the English working-classes as well as preparing them for what is to come. The upside for Johnson is that all this is good, amusing material, and as much grist to his mill as to that of the House Mother herself, something he admits with characteristic candour on the last page of the novel. He himself is a House Mother in the republic of letters, and their shared boredom, cruelty and lust for self-gratification are perfectly normal human behaviour. Perhaps it should go without saying though that B.S. Johnson finds this a disturbing state of affairs. In *Christie Malry's Double-Entry*, a tour-de-force in which he carries forward this new dark poetic mode, the protagonist invents double-entry moral bookkeeping, taking revenge by acts of mass murder on those who have slighted him. Johnson has become his own diagnostician and appears to see the absurdity of his sense of personal grievance as a writer, but it would obviously be quite wrong to think he had thereby cured his own ills.

The two anthologies Johnson edited, *The Evacuees* and *All Bull: The National Servicemen* advertise themselves as social history, or even as oral history, but are made up of commissioned contributions from mostly well-known writers and personalities. They are well-edited books with good material in them, but this is essentially a publisher's idea of how history should be written—We Can Remember It For You Retail—a later version of which is a staple of television: a group of celebs is rounded up to discuss some topic of popular memory, and thereby substituted for the viewer's own memories or sense of the past, with the patronising assumption that you will need prompting to remember that coffee was made out of acorns in the war years and so on, or that flared loon pants or gelled hair and sparkly shirts looked funny. Johnson's contributors are more interesting than most such line-ups: one of the most arresting pieces in *All Bull* is his fellow experimentalist Jeff Nuttall's memoir, in which he speaks eloquently of being an art student in the early 1950s and how he was finally persuaded to take the army seriously when someone asks to use the toilet during parade is frog-marched away and later discovered with a shaven head, badly beaten up, and clipping the lawn between two armed guards. Later such cruelties became funny. As Nuttall writes:

> When the sergeant persuaded a naïve squaddie that he was to be shot for violation of he rifle range regulations, and stood him against a wall, and had him dictate a last letter to his mum and girlfriend, I laughed. When I tore all the skin off my stomach and arms and half my face trying to get over a wall on an assault course, I laughed. The silliness was extended by the violence and the cruelty, and the moors stretched off to the right and left all around.[15]

Nuttall's is a vivid, interesting piece, as are most of the others. All the same, such stories could be multiplied a million-fold and there is arguably something inherently unsatisfactory about approaching these experiences though an A team of professional rememberers: Johnson apologises that there are a lot of officers in the book, pointing out that a disproportionate number of national servicemen were given commissions. But the fact that so many people of the same generation experience the same kinds of things, and that being paid to remember them is a prized and privileged job, points to another basic problem writers share: that of not having much to write about from their own experience which could be seen as having public interest. It may sound ignoble, but that is the problem B.S. Johnson is confronted with—what seemed inexhaustible soon becomes obviously all too finite, and his solution, once he has elevated his inability to make up stories into a principle, is to become ever more introspective and more compensatingly formally inventive. But along the way he had finally admitted that making up stories about imaginary people was a necessary part of novel writing.

Bryan Johnson produced two more finished novels after *House Mother Normal*, each more fictional, more fragmentary and more artful than the last, but was dead by his own hand two years afterwards. His lifelong insecurity is both programmatic and exemplary, and appears to arise out of the ambivalent position of being a working-class artist, albeit in a moment when this was especially wanted by some: an articulate spokesman for the inarticulate, an enabler of voices from below, in a general culture determined to undermine such subversive articulacy. His dilemma comes of being both a subject and an object in his art—an overarching perceiver and organiser and an object of his own analyses: 'the working-class' is a social object, a symbolic construct, it is the masses, the people, Marx's proletariat, yet also for him simply people he knew and grew up with and the things they liked, his parents, and most importantly himself as exemplary agonised sufferer of irresolvable contradictions. The terms of his unstable subject-object division are slippery, almost impossible to get down, and yet he manages it (insofar as he does) by a combination of increasingly audacious formal games and an emotional directness highly unusual in novelists.

But these problems are also the product of a confusion about his predicament and what he was supposed to do with it: Alan Sillitoe, whom, Johnson was appalled to realise, just made most of it up, seems to have experienced no such qualms, and the same is obviously true of many other fiction writers. Who can say? There is very often such a mystery about suicides. The ready, sometimes glaringly obvious reasons for their deaths, don't altogether add up satisfactorily for those who are left behind. Why didn't they just pull themselves together? Were they more clear-sighted than others, or less? Perhaps other writers were more secure in their middle-class identities, and therefore writing from a further shore whether they were born on it or not, not disinterested exactly, but confident of their innate difference from those they were writing about or representing. Maybe, or maybe not. B.S. Johnson seems to have experienced a deep paralysing fear and shame about being a charlatan—that is what his writerly anxieties amount to—and few other novelists appear to share it.

Berger's version of Marxist humanism is an ethical position that takes as its core belief, its necessary angel, not the industrial proletariat and its historical agency, but the perspective of the poorest, the lowest in society: the displaced, the dispossessed. That is the religious essence of Bergerism. It is a secular Christianity, an inverted Nietszcheanism. Elements that were present, subsumed within Marxism, are now released as particles of dust, or carriers of dust-borne bacteria, and come to the fore sometimes, flowering once more in the petri-dish of post-modern culture. Rightly, because the socialism of the West, of the post-Enlightenment, is nowadays an ethical doctrine more than it is a scientific method of understanding or redirecting the course of history. Marxists of his generation seem to me to stand up well in the present because history is obviously not over, and although his is a tragic rather than an emptily progressivist view of history, he never quite gave way either to a sense of living in the last days or to a complete abandonment of his project. His Vico in *King: A Street Story* (1999) tells us that the ages of heroes and men are at an end, and that we are now living in the age of dogs. But, as he might seek to explain with an engaging smile, dogs may have a great deal to teach us of loyalty and of survival.[16]

John Berger can be an uncomfortable writer about the English working-classes, except when looking over the shoulder of his country doctor, but found a satisfying way forward in this respect in the balance of his relationships with his land-working neighbours in the Haut Savoie village community that is his home and the basis for his *Into Their Labours* trilogy: a place where he is both insider and outsider, listener and reporter, a local storyteller who is also connected to a wider world, and therefore in a position to be an integrator of art and document. John Berger and B.S. Johnson are twins, each in his different way exploring the limits of the novel and attempting to find new ways to directly address the reader. Johnson was the dark twin, perhaps better able to dramatise his predicament, but only slowly and painfully able to creatively integrate his contradictions. Berger is a dialectician. He had this to say to Jonathan Coe about B.S. Johnson's life and death:

> He lacked the sort of protective carapace that other people have, but one has to add hat his achievement wouldn't have been possible if he'd had that carapace. So that the lack of a carapace was intimately related—was the same thing, almost—as his talent and his vision and his originality. It's as though in the remorseless tide of life, as he saw it, there are moments of respite, when some small hope can be constructed, some exchange can take place and the poignancy of this also comes from this lack of protection.[17]

Chapter Six

Up to Our Necks in Spunk and Bullets: Leslie Thomas

After his father, a sailor, was lost at sea during the Second World War, Welsh-born Leslie Thomas spent the remainder of his childhood in a Barnardo's Home for orphans in Kingston-upon-Thames, a childhood and adolescence he wrote about lyrically and faithfully in his first book, *This Time Next Week.* Like most able young men of his time Thomas was called-up for a period of national service, in his case in the Army. After his relatively uneventful national service Thomas became a successful journalist, but his military experience over a decade earlier as a clerk in a safe garrison in Singapore provided much of the background for his first novel *The Virgin Soldiers* (1966). The novel was a bestseller. Thomas had taken advantage of the relaxation of his sixties moment to write frankly about soldiering and sex as well as to tell something of the story of British conscripts' experience of national military service in the far east in the fifties and early sixties.

Leslie Thomas' writing is sensuous and titillating and in it sexuality is milked for good humour: there is an unmoralising acceptance of sex as part of life and an agreeable feeling of honesty and enjoyment in his approach that was relatively new at the time and helped to get his first novel made into a successful film. Notable in his later writings is a traditional but fragile sense of family: glowing scenes of married love and the kind of family life that was early and tragically snatched away from Thomas abound in his stories and the experience of shattered families and personal grief is not the least expense of war in his accounts of it. His view of institutions like the Army, their hierarchies and dubious purposes is always an insubordinate one, from the ranks; but there is a deeper sense in which the idea of family, and of nationality as a kind of extended family is important in his novels. *The Virgin Soldiers* is set in what had been British Malaya, on the island of Singapore, and is about national servicemen fighting the Communist insurgency in that country. The action takes place mainly at their garrison at a post that dates from before the war, and during it was occupied by the invading Japanese, but is most of the time remote from the action of the guerilla war of independence. It particularly concerns the predicament of young, inexperienced conscripts who have little talent or appetite for soldiering, who fear for their lives and are extremely anxious to experience sex before they die, usually with local prostitutes. The independence war does of course erupt into their lives and eventually make real soldiers out of them, dead ones out of some. But what is most striking about the book, probably an indirect result of Thomas not having seen much action himself, is the way *The Virgin Soldiers* foregrounds language as well as sex and frequently has recourse to allegory in order to both tell the story of its hedonistic and incompetent conscripts, and make their experiences resonate with the real meaning of being an army of occupation in a land where they are largely unwelcome. The Malayan war as narrated by Thomas is a war of words, of definitions, in which both the soldierly badinage of army-talk and the luminous details of banality are continually circulated and throughout pressed into service as symbols of the wasteful and bankrupt fag-end of British imperialism and its underlying economic purpose: to protect the lucrative rubber plantations.

The novel is full of things that bounce and people who try to, although not always successfully. Brigg, through whose eyes we see most of the action, is bringing a pail of tea from the cookhouse to the barracks. The army slang for tea is 'rusty nails', but as he swings the bucket along the brown liquid bounces in the bucket, almost as if it is alive: 'Some of the tea panicked and jumped over the side, committing suicide in a dank monsoon ditch as he stepped over it.'[1] It seems that 'rusty nails' has the density and viscosity of liquid rubber direct from a tree, and this is also true of Thomas' language throughout *The Virgin Soldiers*. The Gurkhas, or 'bongos' as they are known (along with all the Malays, Chinese and Indians who make up the population) by the conscripts, have itchy *kukri* fingers, reputedly chopped up a bandit (communist guerilla) 'into little cubes the size of an Oxo'[2] and the Army cooks offer the pail of tea with 'the secret smile that says they know there is dead rat in it.'[3] The purpose of the soldiers' language is to domesticate the conflict, to make it familiar and harmless, and is thus, it could be argued, is just the opposite of literary language, which according to the Russian formalist critics, 'makes strange' the familiar world.

But since this language and descriptions couched in it are strange to us as readers, it performs the opposite function than for its users, continually suggesting a latent violence that is soon to rise to the surface. The soldiers are by no means deaf to these meanings: they are the source of most of them. One of them, a character called Fenwick, is trying to make himself literally deaf to language by swimming a great deal in the camp's chlorine-laden pool, and thus win an honourable repatriation to England. Another conscript, bespectacled, harmless Sinclair, is a dedicated train-spotter who evades all the human realities of where he actually is by absorbing himself in details of maps, timetables and the specifications of antiquated locomotives. The language of the book is a kind of decoy: drawing fire, pointing to underlying political realities whilst evading them, revealing the agendas of those who stand behind imperialism, but in American poet John Ashbery's striking line, 'At the same time keeping the door open to a tongue-in-cheek attitude on the part of the perpetrators.'[4]

The conscripts of the Panglin barracks have received no casualties from the conflict they are there to police, but one of their sergeants, Driscoll, who has a guilty secret in that he is tormented by having shot some of his own men in the heat of battle during the second world war, points out that the nothingness of their military experience will soon be given body when it is translated into more words back home in England, and Brigg recognises that this is the probable truth: 'They would go around like proud little fighters, armed to the teeth with lies. Their stories would be as good as the next man's, even if he had spent his National Service with swamps and fear and true death waiting every day and night.'[5]

Future national service bores or not, these unwilling conscripts are genuinely anxious to lose their virginity, and of the competitive games which punctuate the book, the barracks competition over who can produce the most outstanding erection is pursued with some urgency. The soldiers are uninhibited in this particular competition: it is only the two gay soldiers who wear regulation issue pyjamas and turn their noses up at such antics. The Japanese had murdered some Australians at Panglin during the war and when their bodies were dug up, in a rain storm falling in 'big, individual bullets', their skulls piled up 'like coconuts', Sergeant Wellbeloved (a hated bully) uses them to impress the realities of war on his young charges. Brigg remembers his girlfriend Joan (he writes to her throughout the novel) and meanwhile Phillipa Raskin, the daughter of the regimental sergeant major, lays around naked in her room, her unwilling virginal predicament identical to that of the young men.

Phillipa is 'a self-contained lunatic asylum, a young and lovely nut, a collection of quirks, paradoxes and agonies, a psychological fireworks display exploding mostly inward.'[6] Phillipa has been subjected to sado-sexual bullying by her father—forced to hold pennies between her legs to cure her bandy legs and accused of lesbianism—and her sexual awakening is to counterpoint that of Brigg in the novel. Lying around in her room, she picks up some flowers with 'small globules of red rain' still on their petals and shakes them out between her breasts:

> The scraps of rounded water sat there patiently like a small group of fat people waiting for something to happen. There were two major blobs which Phillipa decided were the Mummy and Daddy and three little ones which were the children (…) The five drops of water scampered down her body in single file; the two big ones and one of the minor ones finally and gratefully rolled into the

> hole of her navel; the other two children missed their target and tumbled in infant panic down her belly and her groin and were lost between her thighs. She told herself it was a good attempt for a beginner.[7]

Colonel Wilfred Bromley Pickering is the commanding officer of Panglin, and one of the few officers to appear in *The Virgin Soldiers*—which is notable for depicting the other ranks mainly on their own ground. He is a comic grotesque who has lost an eye at Normandy through being stung by a bee while looking at a weed 'in a fatherly way', a misadventure that is of a piece with Leslie Thomas' view of the impostures and meaningless accidents of war, and a further example of the echoic use of natural imagery Thomas uses to weave the rapidly succeeding incidents and chapters his first novel seamlessly together. Bromley Pickering is an ineffectual, kindly, fatherly figure who is horrified that his charges are to be sent on a training mission in harm's way, just as Brigg's clerical duties have confronted him with the death of a young soldier his age whose paybook arrives back at Panglin caked with blood. But the training mission brings Brigg and the others to The Liberty Club in Singapore, where we meet Phillipa's native counterpart and the most important female character in the novel, less innocent only in sexual experience, the young Chinese prostitute, Juicy Lucy:

> She was Chinese. Brigg could never understand why they were supposed to be yellow. The peasants were brown, like paper, and the office girls were cream white, like paper. This girl, in the lights that simmered through the smoke, was the palest of them. Her eyes were half closed, gentle and bored, and Brigg watched her work her red tongue along her teeth looking for lipstick pieces to clean.[8]

The Chinese had invented paper after all, as well as gunpowder and kites, and again we are reminded of the writtenness of this history, and of the women in The Liberty Club, pale invented creatures who have been created by administrative fiat for the benefit of the soldiers, working at their age-old trade in a venue whose name advertises its wares as surely as 'Pleasure Island' in Walt Disney's film *Pinocchio* tells us it is the perfect place for naughty boys, the place that will turn them into donkeys. Private Brigg has no Jiminy Cricket on his shoulder and is soon told Lucy's name by a more experienced soldier, immediately buying the booklet of five dance tickets he needs to scrape her further acquaintance. They dance a little and leave. Lucy has her hand down his trousers in the cab, but upon arrival at her flat he pays her fifteen dollars and tries to put a brake on her eagerness for long enough to have a look around. She is defined by her language, her Chinese Pidgin English, her wide-eyed naivety and directness, and by the array of objects she has assembled into a kind of makeshift shrine in her bedroom. Brigg is reminded of his first visit to Santa's cave in London's Selfridges:

> There were dolls, fans and three stuffed poodles. Boxes and trinkets, books and comics, gramophone records, lubricant jelly, three sizes of contraceptives, a picture of Mao Tse-tung and a beautifully embroidered plaque saying 'Happy New Year from the Gordon Highlanders.'[9]

'Nice place,' says Brigg. Lucy flings wide her legs and says, 'This nice place too.' But Brigg is embarrassed, a virgin after all, and when he reveals his ignorance his hostess immediately drops the price by five dollars, 'and after we have cocoa. Cadbury's.' She then inadvertently christens him with the name 'Bigg'. What follows, like all of the erotic writing in the novel, falls well short of pornography, even literary pornography. Far less explicit than Henry Miller or the Lawrence of *Lady Chatterley's Lover*, let alone John Cleland's *Fanny Hill*, despite one of the book's first reviewers claiming that Thomas' hero is a male version of Cleland's heroine. It is only just softcore porn—more like a contemporary copy of *Penthouse* or *Playboy*, 'tasteful' as they used to say, not even euphemistic, strategically out of focus, masked by palm fronds. Strangely, Thomas seems more comfortable when vividly personifying the Malaysian swamp which 'stirred and groaned like a man in sleep' or describing the antics of tea or rain drops than the conjoining of male and female flesh, although this seeming innocence is as deliberate and knowing as Juicy Lucy's loving smiles. Thomas is aiming at writerly respectability—which he had already achieved as a television journalist—and W.H. Smith bestsellerdom. Precisely judged inoffensive titillation. Lucy calls Brigg a 'virgin soldier' and appears to feel that deflowering him is a privilege. He cries like a virgin.

Despite this last minute shyness about it, a reticence that accentuates or exaggerates its importance, the sex act in *The Virgin Soldiers* is always a higher, more authentic reality, suggesting all that might be known of human beauty and relationship, even when this is clearly countermanded by its economic basis in the case of Lucy, and is regularly counterposed to the evasive cant of the British Army, surpassed only by death. In that sense it has to remain somewhat mysterious, 'the big secret', perhaps almost sacramental in a Lawrentian way. The loss of his unwanted virginity and the full inheritance of his own physicality produce an eloquent burst of insubordinate insight in Brigg. He discourses spiritedly about the British Thumb: the thumbs up sign of the good old British tommy, all enduring, ready for anything that might come up, only to remind his hearers, and Thomas' readers, that their officially required confidence is often misplaced:

> 'Why did they do it always? Off they went again in the next war, those proud, confident, mistaken digits. Thumbs up on the troopships, thumbs up in the tail turret of the bomber, thumbs up on the Arctic convoy. That's right, lads, just show we're not downhearted. Come on now, you on the stretchers, thumbs up all those who've still got 'em. Thumbs up! Thumbs up! (…) Out to sea, fishermen lived in stilted village houses that seemed to be wading in the bay. At low tide they threw their nets at fishes who ran in and out of the hulls of the dead battleships—Prince of Wales and Repulse—lying clearly in the sand of the ocean. They had been there since 1942 and they were full of dead thumbs.'[10]

Having set the mainsprings of his novel in motion, Thomas begins to explore what those mistaken digits have assented to in terms of the jungle war itself, sometimes through direct encounters with the enemy but often via the allegorical turning and weaving together of anecdote and suggestion that is most striking about his method. We learn more of the characters he has introduced, fresh ones appear only to explode—the fat man, Fred Organ, who jumps on a forgotten land-mine while chasing a football on the beach—and having established Brigg as a protagonist he lets him melt back into the parade for a while to develop the others. Sergeant Wellbeloved is shown up as 'a frigging Nazi' during a raid on a remote jungle village when he terrorises the villagers and salaciously forces a sick fourteen year old girl to strip in a hut search, held back from further interference with her only by the uninvited presence of two conscripts, Brigg and Tasker, covering his rear. Sinclair continues to daydream about the trains back home in England, and Sergeant Driscoll, like most of the sympathetic characters in the book, puts in a stint of closely observing the flow of spilt liquids:

> Driscoll poured a slim stream of beer from his glass and watched it slide down the table in a liquid arrow. He increased the amount, thickened the flow, and watched it on its oily journey with satisfaction and huge interest. The yellow advance wriggled around some knots in the wood, was dammed a moment by a cigarette butt, but then continued, eventually reaching the bare arms of Wellbeloved and trying to nose beneath them.[10]

This incident nearly sparks a fight between the two antagonistic sergeants, obviated by Fred Organ (not yet dead) who comes between them 'like bouncing, disorganised rubber.' Having economically established Driscoll as a decent bloke ready to give Wellbeloved a good hiding for his disgusting behaviour during the raid, and Fred as a good and brave man who sings a broken hearted sentimental song, Thomas blows him up in the next scene. Brigg worries that he may have caught the clap from Juicy Lucy. Sandy Jacobs, a Scottish Jew, tells a story of the anti-Semitism his father experienced in Airdrie, and right on cue the soldiers are sent to be circumcised for reasons of hygiene. Brigg gets a modicum of revenge on Wellbeloved by 'accidentally' shooting him with a giant homemade catapault: we are returned to the childish, game-playing world of the conscripts in barracks, an essentially boring world that Thomas sometimes struggles to keep interesting.

Running beneath the tissue of misadventures and cruel accidents out of which his narrative is woven, is an allegorist's feeling for symmetrical justice without which Thomas as a writer feels his narrative would be without satisfying meaning. Colonel Pickering's blindness in one eye is balanced by Sergeant Driscoll's inability to close one of his. He is unable to stop seeing, in other words, both the men under his command he inadvertently killed in Caen and the dear wife whom his dedication to the Army has stolen from him (a result of his sense of responsibility to the dead compels him to reenlist). Driscoll's all-seeing eye has made him face himself, made him track down his ex-wife and witness her happiness with another man, just as it takes in and tried to remedy Wellbeloved's abuse of power. Beneath the surface of the novel, and the apparent chaos and injustice of the accidental, God's all witnessing gaze and the author's (one is reminded of the all-seeing oculist's sign in *The Great Gatsby*) takes note of every falling sparrow and looks for the working out of a final justice.

At this point we begin to hear more about the bullying Phillipa has suffered at the hands of her father, his accusations that she is a lesbian, and thus, by a long, circuitous route, at the dead centre of the novel, the second sex scene of this notoriously racy book pulls in like one of silly Sinclair's puffing trains: Phillipa Raskin loses her virginity. But who is to be the lucky man who climbs on board? At first we think it might be Brigg, the first man she notices at the garrison dance her father has forced her to attend, and it might have been if he hadn't staggered away drunkenly, apparently satisfied by a goodnight kiss, and if Phillipa, dead drunk herself and determined to conclude to evening's business, hadn't happened to spot Sergeant Driscoll passing by her window. Driscoll cannot believe his luck; but no luck has really been involved. Phillipa, who has a diffident charm as well as a young body, has chosen the right man for the job. Driscoll knows his sins have at last been atoned for and that heaven has rewarded him: he has never seen anything like her.

But Phillipa also has her uses for Brigg, and whilst the Sergeant satisfies her sexually, the hapless Private is to be her chaste, adoring escort on picnics, swimming expeditions and walks along the raised pipeline that runs away from the camp above the jungle. This is a role the ever-randy conscript accepts as somehow appropriate to his rank. They kiss and she demurs: he is cover, companionship, her official boyfriend, visible proof she is not a lesbian and acceptable to her father. Brigg continues to dream guiltily of Lucy, to visit her occasionally and write copious letters to his waiting fiancé, Joan, and the decencies of rank and social class are preserved: Driscoll of the bulging ever-open eye is, she gasps, her Sergeant.

Allegory becomes an analytical tool for Thomas: the situations he presents allegorically are closed in a sense, they are games, testing grounds with fixed outcomes on the moral debit or credit side, but credit is gained in these allegories to the extent that one breaks out of the given shape of an event or situation itself and fully pushes into the envelope of real action in the real world: changes something, gains something. This is difficult for his characters. It is though they are contained in a world of illusion that continually wrong-foots them. 'There were only two cards and Phillipa, to whom nothing simple ever happened, had mis-shuffled.' Thomas tells us, but her behaviour works out fine for her. Brigg teaches Juicy Lucy, whom he believes sincerely loves him, a sentimental greetings card rhyme:

Oh, but this world's a funny place,
And yet it's hard to beat.
With every rose you get a thorn.
But ain't the roses sweet.[11]

Lucy thinks it beautiful and wise, but it is merely trite and true: her thorn, the invisible worm of her death, is winging its silent way towards her.

The most telling sequence of quick change allegorising scenes in *The Virgin Soldiers*, many or all of which involve fights or contests, quests or journeys, are those which now bring the Malay emergency and the British Army's role there into clearer focus. The first of these is the monthly dog-killing expedition, in which the truck-charioted Sergeants, Driscoll and Wellbeloved, compete to see how many fleeing canines they can hit on the run 'straight up the backside'. They are supposed to kill only the dogs without collars, 'the waif dogs... who fornicated and multiplied': but there simply aren't enough of these and so they shoot at every dog: 'If they found it to be wearing a collar when they went up to it after killing it, then they took the collar off and hid it somewhere.'[12] Civilian pooch or bandit hound? The conscripts' performance at dog-slaughter tests their killing abilities: Brigg swears off altogether, Lantry misses everything, others acquit themselves honourably, but Brook freezes on the trigger, unable to inflict the coup de grace on some quivering acorn-coloured puppy. Before the ambushing snipers open fire, and the dog patrol turn on their tails and run, back to the safety of Panglin.

Before the week is out the city has exploded in riots and a shooting war had begun, and it is clear that the test of facing fire has come in earnest, and it is also clear that under such conditions it is equally difficult to tell which of the native dogs are wearing dog collars and which are untamed and dangerous. For the population has years of grievance to redress and a secret scorn for the occupying army, remembering the war and 'how the invincible British were quashed into submission by a Japanese Army mounted on bicycles.' The Cathay cinema is showing *The Wicked City* and *Panic in the Streets*. The efficacy of quelling a population by means of commanding language is demonstrated when the unit tries to disperse rioters by unfurling a banner telling them to disperse quietly in Malay and Chinese. But the banner itself is quiet, having been unfurled wrong side to the mob, 'a blank stretch of white canvas', and the empty, reassuring words of the occupiers are thus revealed as emptier still of meaning. This emboldens the rioters, and in the fracas that follows, Private Brook, pushed into inappropriate action by Wellbeloved, as unable to disarm a civilian as to shoot a harmless dog, is killed in his turn, impaled on an improvised weapon, a fence rail.

There is some light Carry-On knockabout during a solicitous visit to Lucy. Brigg loses his trousers when she throws them out of the window in a fit of pique and they are carried off by a passing Sikh on a bicycle. Fitted out with a pair of Chinese silk pyjamas, Brigg gives chase and has no compunction in threatening the man at gunpoint for their return. The man, who feels he has done nothing wrong, insists on civility. 'I will return them,' says the Sikh. 'Don't lose them again.' And calls at his retreating back: 'God save the King.'[13]

Language itself runs riot, as the figurative and the literal change places and settled meanings are overturned in this revolutionary moment, particularly the phrase 'Rusty Nails': the euphemism for tea that opens the book recurs with increasing frequency, becoming a kind of mad catchphrase Sergeant Driscoll uses to refer to almost anything. We then learn the true identity of Rusty Nails, who was a real person, a soldier for whose death Sergeant Wellbeloved was responsible during the war. Far from being the heroic jungle fighter of his stories, Wellbeloved was already in prison for desertion when the Japanese arrived. He turned Brigadier William Nails over to the Japanese for stealing food when they were both prisoners and they executed him. Driscoll exacts revenge from Wellbeloved in a long, balletic fight scene, a kind of no holds barred wrestling match (what could be more theatrical or allegorical) in the sports arena, The Golden World, where they are billeted during the disturbances, and where Friday nights usually host similar matches between local fighters with names like Charlie Chan and The Dragon. They roll in the mud and oil the wrestlers use—more rusty nails—gladiators in the empty arena, watched only by the privates, until blood is spurting from Driscoll's wide-open eye and Wellbeloved is lying unconscious. The fight is a lengthy sequence in which Thomas pulls out all descriptive stops (perhaps with an eye on its future filmed version) and during its course the combatants turn into successively into circus clowns, seals and finally apes, until the adjutant arrives and military order is restored. As the fight extends it loses moral force and meaning, turns into a lavish spectacle milked for effects, and one of the weaknesses of Thomas' method is revealed. In this case he has failed to exact justice from his allegory and merely written an enjoyable cinematic fight scene. We are disappointed, feeling that Wellbeloved deserved to die for his crimes.

Back at Panglin it is Brigg's turn to try to be a hero when the rebels attack the garrison. He rescues Phillipa and her mother, and her angel fish from their house when an angry crowd of Chinese is attacking, in another long set-piece in which they escape to safety down the pipeline. Phillipa stalks ahead, Mrs Raskin falls off and Brigg looses bullets at the pursuing mob. At the end of it we feel that Brigg has truly proved himself a hero and a worthy consort to Phillipa, only to learn in the cold light of day that the angry mob was in reality a group of fleeing friendly Chinese, trying to warn them, and that Brigg has succeeded only in shooting two fingers off an elderly laundryman named Fuk Yoo. It is another misadventure, a Don Quixote-like tilting at a windmill by a deluded idealist who has read too many stories, believed too many heroic lies. Thomas' use of the allegorical mode in *The Virgin Soldiers* is inventive, highly unusual, and brilliantly adapted to its difficult material. He creates allegories without heroes, and has only to set one of these up to elegantly puncture it by the irruption of reality. One of the most telling of these is when Brigg hears that the young prostitute whom he has idealised and loved has been kicked to death during the disturbances—his fears for her had been well-founded—by a group of British soldiers who believed she was a carrier of venereal disease. Brigg refuses to believe this unstorybook intelligence, visits The Liberty Club to find no Juicy Lucy and is bluntly told the truth he still can't believe. Until he takes a cab to her lodgings to find her room inhabited by another woman.

Other comic allegories occur, are deployed, including a trishaw race that nobody wants to win, and Thomas' final such set piece is a bullfrog jumping race at Panglin on which the soldiers place extravagant bets. This last has a celebrated literary antecedent in the shape of the story that made Mark Twain's name as a teller of droll tales: 'The Notorious Jumping Frog of Calaveras County'. For W.D. Howells, the nineteenth-century American realist novelist and critic, to allegorise is to sentimentalise, and his explanation of the continued preponderance of this kind of inferior storytelling in his country is that:

> I can only whisper, in strict confidence, that by far the greatest number of people in the world, even the civilised world, are people of weak and childish imagination, pleased with gross fables, fond of prodigies, heroes, heroines, portents and improbabilities, without self-knowledge, and without the wish for it… and it is a great advance for them to prefer the half-lies they get in romanticistic novels.[14]

Mark Twain is Leslie Thomas' principal model as a writer of allegories without heroes. The dark humorist who would eventually produce bitter fairytales like *The Mysterious Stranger*, about a young Satan's visit to Earth, and his final misanthropic *Fables of Man,* was for most of his career a successful children's writer among other things, and one who found the role constricting; but 'The Notorious Jumping Frog' is just such a gross fable of an improbable prodigy as Howells describes. At least, so it appears, for even in this slight sketch—which is all timing and indirection—Twain is mocking frail humanity's absorption in futile contests and pointless wonders, if such an anecdote can truly be said to be a profound allegory of the human condition. Twain's frog is named Dan'l Webster after Daniel Webster, the pugnacious nineteenth-century champion debater of Congress, a Whig anti-abolitionist who angered many liberals by betraying their cause repeatedly. He opposed the annexation of Texas and the Mexican-American war that followed on the grounds that the addition of the Lone Star State to the union would upset the delicate balance of slave and non-slave states.[15] When a rival of the frog's proud owner, Smiley, surreptitiously pours quail shot down its throat so it can't jump at all, Twain is wondering how far the famous Webster would be able to hop with a gut full of shot.

Thomas' bullfrog story closely parallels Twain's in many of its details. He catches it in the swamp at Panglin and names it after the recently murdered Juicy Lucy, and there is something at last totally sickening in this naming in that it seems to cheapen her life and her death, to turn her into a creature of similarly great jumping abilities. Brigg is trying to get over her death by seeing her this way, as what she was, a whore, but he is seeing if he can engineer her victory in this allegorical retrial of life's unjust bounding race, which he does manage, only to see his Liverpudlian rival attempt to deal out the same death to his losing frog as the soldiers who had kicked Lucy to death; but in this utopia of frogs, the loser manages to bounce 'like a ball' out from beneath the heel of his boot and hop to freedom in the Malaysian swamp.

The novel begins to wind down and to tidy itself up, not least in a chance meeting between Brigg and Phillipa—who has gone off to train as a nurse—when they finally get to have sex, and Brigg manages to learn something else that he didn't wish to know: that she has been sleeping with Sergeant Driscoll all along. But the book's true climax, and the only way it could tidily atone for the death of Juicy Lucy, which hangs like a pall over the last fifty pages, arrives in the shape of a long battle scene in which the train carrying the conscripts to the boat homeward is attacked by Communist independence fighters. Many of the main characters die in this ambush, some acquit themselves well in the battle, as does Brigg, but faced with the supreme sacrifice he cunningly escapes to 'get help'. Half-coward, half-opportunist, like the protagonist of the Czech writer Jaroslav Hašek's *The Good Soldier Švejk* or any number of Carry-On anti-heroes he is an everyman constantly on the make, in Brigg's case with a permanent hard-on rather than an eye to the black market.

The Virgin Soldiers battles to tell the truth about army life and about British imperialism, but like a lot of novels written with cinema in mind it has a hard job to reconcile its various aims. The book is a sparking, inventive performance, and most of the time Thomas manages to make his mostly self-imposed limitations work for him. These are challenges he rises to, sexual interdictions and official fudges he overcomes with ease to tell a boring story of unheroic people in the wrong place on the wrong side that is hard-hitting, sexy and frequently funny. If Malaya was England's Vietnam (or Korea), Leslie Thomas' *The Virgin Soldiers* is its *MASH* or *Catch-22*. It is certainly true that the novel's relentless structural symmetries and laughs are achieved at the cost of a lack of reach into the dark absurdities and true horrors of the best writing about war. But also that many readers would prefer what W.D. Howells' calls 'the romanticistic half-lies' of popular fiction, will wish that Juicy Lucy had lived to be a grandmother, and that Phillipa had secretly loved Brigg all along. Perhaps they could have married at the end, or at least got engaged—and such sentimental hankerings after a world that never existed do seem to run under the surface of the book. They are after all the always to be frustrated expectations of people without self-knowledge, even if they do have a desire to know the truth. Thomas did a fine job in publishing a good anti-imperialist, anti-militarist novel about Britain's more unwilling conscripts, which appeared at the height of the American war in Vietnam, and was moreover genuinely popular, capturing a side of national service that has been largely absent from most of the post Christmas dinner anecdotes of his fellow conscripts.

Thomas' follow-up, *Orange Wednesday,* appeared the following year and opens promisingly with another allusion to classic American literature. Its hero, Brunel Hopkins, half-engineer, half-poet, all clerk, is holed up in the small German spa town of Fulsbad where he sports a monkish haircut and looks after the British Army's Moribund Documents Section, a situation that recalls the final job of Herman Melville's recalcitrant clerk in his story 'Bartleby': the Dead Letter Office in Washington, D.C. All those short-circuited communications gradually drive Bartleby even madder. He hangs himself, as has the previous incumbent of Brunel's job. But Brunel, although dressed as an innocent, knows he is onto a good thing as the custodian of these censored records of soldierly mendacity towards women and monstrous incompetence by the authorities. There are always gullible fish to be caught in the small lake. His pay arrives regularly and there's nothing much to do except nurse his anaemia with port and raw liver and consort with local café-owner Otto, who likes to dress up in his old SS postman's uniform, and Brunel gazes diffidently into the arrestingly delicate eyes of his fifteen year old daughter, Hilde: 'She had a small bright face, like a coin, and very delicate eyes. When she grew old, her eyes would probably remain the same, as the face faded. He thought that when she reached sixty or so she would really be worth looking at.'[16]

The book's cover tells much of the story. A teenage temptress in a large silk shirt and little else, her hair mussed, her eyes in shadow, sits coyly displaying her panties and holding a revolver vertically upright in front of her by the barrel: a sex pistol. On the floor are a leather satchel and a red and black Nazi armband. Clearly Thomas knew what he was driving at—a double whammy. *The Virgin Soldiers* had a naked female torso on the cover, poor Juicy Lucy's, with a colour projection of a British soldier in tropical fatigues making his way through malevolent greenery all but obliterating her ample charms. Both covers are poignant, the second for the innocence of the girl, but while the first cover is resonant: the verdant body of Malaya under occupation, the *Orange Wednesday* jacket is an ad-hoc orchestration of erotically appealing elements, as is the novel itself : a caper, pure hokum. Still, it is interesting enough hokum. The publishers might have given us Nazis dressed up in cowboy outfits, ancient military amputees sliding in and out of the waters of the Fulsbad Spa's steam bath like wounded manatees, or perhaps one of the gigantically fat elderly prostitutes Germans are said to prefer according to Thomas. Orange Wednesday is the code-name for an allied plan to sign a secret treaty to bring about the reunification of Germany, so-named presumably because it is the day after Ruby Tuesday, Brunel is to play his part as a menial servant to the Americans. This scenario doesn't seem either politically astute or realistically intended. The remaining Nazis, organised in a nationwide confederation of semi-clandestine cowboy clubs, are all for it, as might be expected.

Keenor, his new CO, fresh from Saigon, is a cynical US Army organisation man, a whoremaster for the Russians who is in charge of security for the treaty signing and couldn't give a monkey's about anything except ensuring that nothing goes wrong: he is the spirit of corporate capitalism incarnate. He mistrusts Brunel's sensitivity, telling him the story of a bar in Saigon where lifting a giant round stone wins you a free night with any girl you fancy. It seems that this scenario of a hedonistic myth of Sisyphus defines the aim of worldly success, and having lifted the giant stone of fame and literary notoriety, Thomas is looking for a way to live honourably in the world; Brunel's monkish pose is to be tested by various moral choices. Exploitative sexuality once more becomes an uneasy metaphor for the spirit of imperialism in this novel. Rounding up a few whores for the Russians is all in a day's work for joy-girl Prudence, but for Brunel such industrialised sex as they find on Hamburg's Reeperbahn is disgusting: 'How anyone can go into an arse-holing place like that, a human supermarket, and shrug and say 'that's life' knocks me flat. That's death, that is! Very serious death.'[17]

But sexuality is inescapably currency in the world as it is in the novel, and despite its half-serious political shenanigans *Orange Wednesday* is mainly about sex: it is far more sexually explicit than *The Virgin Soldiers*. The narrative is powered not by the reunification treaty or its satire of German nostalgia for Hitler and of American global power but by Brunel's deferred sexual romance with Hilde. Like most of the other men in the novel, Brunel has actually sex with Prudence, who prefers her physical recreation on a bare iron mattress. Hilde is innocent, idealised, to be protected, left for last, and although Brunel's monkishness is almost undone when they roll together in the forest while spying on her father, their union is always deferred by the responsible Brunel. Thomas shows some of his allegorical and descriptive flair in a savage Bavarian head-butting fight at a teenage party in the mountains between a young Panzer with a large *kannon* and a shifty communist-pacifist type, meant to illustrate the different forces struggling for the helm of the German psyche. At the end of the fight, the victorious young Panzer 'proceeded to rain head blows on the other youth, his head rising and falling like a hen pecking corn.'[18] Waking up from a drunken stupor after a Brunel finds Hilde asleep naked on the bed, and Thomas summons up all his Welsh eloquence to lyricise her naked body for several pages: 'Brunel had never seen a young girl's breasts before. He had never known they were like that: like dainty blancmanges tipped with fairy pink, but firm and set, waiting for the birthday.'[19]

But today is not to be young Hilde's birthday after all. This time they are interrupted by Keenor who bursts through the oaken door with a sub-machine gun, accuses Brunel of consorting with Nazis and Commies. The Communist is a forty-year-old American permanent student who shows up in town and tries to get him to sign an Anti-Reunification petition. Brunel is haunted by a fear of his sexuality, that he may be a paeodophile, which has been prompted by an obsessively remembered incident on a Welsh beach in his youth when a young child innocently asked him to help her put on her knickers and he fled in terror. Having told Hilde this story, the teenager subjects Brunel to the same test. Unknown to both of them Keenor is spying at the keyhole. As if in punishment for what he imagines they have done and for his own illicit desires Keenor subjects the couple to a lengthily described scene of bizarre sado-sexual torture in the freezing spa baths, pouring cold water on their love, their loyalties, and leaving them trussed up for dead, half-submerged, and bound with leather thongs.

Whatever the ostensible political subject of the novel, this forbidden love and its punishment via Keenor's acted out sado-sexual fantasy is really the nub of what Thomas wants to write about in *Orange Wednesday*. Sexuality in his world is innocent, as innocent as Hilde is, and Brunel for that matter, but the real world of power relations is far from innocent and adult sexuality is part of that world. This may be to state the obvious, but in this book—as in *The Virgin Soldiers*—Thomas' question is how can one keep hold of one's innocence, or at least a measure of decency, in a world where such things are likely to be seen as naïve, laughable, even pernicious. The bad guys conspire to make people like Brunel look as bad as they are themselves, and if they resist are likely to turn very nasty indeed. Thomas writes his final scenes of mayhem and revenge with great brio: a dissident faction from the Kremlin attacks the world leaders as they arrive by helicopter, Brunel manages to engineer Keenor's death by large calibre weapon, harmless cowboy-Nazi Otto is killed for sport by a sinister French virgin-fancier and wartime Vichy-supporter Lestrange, and Bone, the petition-waving student, turns out to be an undercover American Major. The disaster of an assassination and a third world war is averted (phew!), and German neo-Nazis generously left to fester for another decade or two. Everything is hushed up, Brunel leaves his Bavarian haven for England, promising the tearful, still virginal Hilde that he will return for her when she is sixteen.

The novel handles its dark materials lightly, its promise of political allegory turns into an over-egged episode of *The Avengers*, undermining its loftier claims to be about the cynicism of power and the cheapness of human life, and where schoolgirl sex is concerned *Orange Wednesday* has its cake and eats it with some relish: readers who bought it for the cover would not feel altogether cheated, but they are served up a homily instead of an orgy. The beauties of the father-daughter romance are preserved; innocence and decency are protected. But still the book is a disappointment that doesn't cohere, poised between a war-comic view of the Germans and an over-sympathetic indulgence of popular Nazism, and a preposterous view of international politics—although how preposterous is a moot question, since Keenor was also involved in the Bay of Pigs. Where eager young Hilde is concerned, Thomas remains *in loco parentis*: on one level he offers an indulgent male fantasy of teen sex, but on another the freedom of writing hokum allows Thomas to ruminate on the relationship between family and responsibility: it is a novel woven about approaching middle-age and being a father to girl-children, and what matters finally is not so much the fantasies and anxieties it explores but what Brunel decides to do about them. Nothing immoral. Nothing at all.

There are two kinds of novelistic trilogies: preplanned and fortuitous. Leslie Thomas' sequels to *The Virgin Soldiers*, like Lynn Reid Banks' follow-ups to *The L-Shaped Room,* were a result of the continuing success of their first novels, and the liking of publishers and readers for continuity, to know what happened next. There is nothing much wrong with this for a popular novelist: it shows your characters are attractive and interesting, but often leads to typecasting and redundant books. In Thomas' case the whole shape of his writing career seems to have been determined by his first choice of subject-matter. His approach has remained critical but unashamedly populist: a dedication to popular cultural memory, and a strong sense of audience, is always at the core of his work. There is something reassuringly familial in the way Leslie Thomas writes about war and about soldier's lives that persists throughout his work. The conscripts in the barracks at Panglin are a family of sorts, and the army itself is a sort of corrupt community of familiars with its own codes and myths, and its questionable, forever carped at authority figures. There is an idea of working-class brotherhood and of male brotherhood that shows up on nearly every page of his work. To reach for a psychological cliché, he was an orphan who made institutions his family before becoming a family man himself: and like a good father he is anxious that the right sort of helpful account of how things really are should be passed on to his extended family of public library readers.

Thomas mined suburban sex comedy in *Tropic of Ruislip*, developed further as a comic-crime-adventure novelist in his Dangerous Davies series, and became a prolific and successful popular novelist who has written about many aspects of the British soldier's experience of World War Two. One of his most striking later novels is *The Magic Army*, which is about the D-Day rehearsals on Slapton Sands, Devon, a fiasco in which many American servicemen lost their lives: a novel that strongly returns to his greatest theme of military incompetence and its deadly consequences for the common soldier. Just as a relatively short periods at sea provided James Hanley with enough inspiration for a lifetime's writing about shipboard life, Thomas has built a long career of writing irreverently about the military out of a short period of around two years as an Army clerk in Singapore. Thomas' novel *Waiting for the Day* (2003), one of his last fictions, weaves a long story about the lives of a number of British and American servicemen as D-Day approaches in 1944, and we see he is still at that for which he will always remain most famous:

> There was a short gasp from the girl. 'Ben… You put that gurt thing away this minute.'
>
> 'But baby, hold it for a while… Just touch it…'[20]

Chapter Seven

False Stars and Psychokillers: Colin Wilson, Alexander Trocchi, Harold Pinter, Paul Ableman

Colin Wilson's *The Outsider*, a book written in the British Museum while its young author was living in a tent on Hampstead Heath, was a study of the European novel that was the surprise critical success of 1956. It was written by someone who was an outsider himself and it helped to popularise existentialist ideas in 1950s Britain, although Wilson's version of existentialism is much his own, and is offered as a critique of its French models.[1] Perhaps it appeared too late to have a very decisive influence on many of the novelists I have been discussing, but the climate in which it was so successful was one they and their readers shared. The Angry Young Men and Movement writers later presented themselves as cultural nationalists who thought the English a marvellous race apart from the effete French and the brutal Germans, but Wilson's study more intelligently shows that a sense of alienation, purposelessness, Godlessness, and in particular a perception of absurdity had already been explored by French writers and Russian ones. He was a bold cultural importer and well as a very English outsider influenced by romanticism and the mystical tradition, an interest inherited from Aldous Huxley—and this timely book made its own strong contribution to an overwhelming feeling in the young that the past and its collective myths were a dead weight that shouldn't automatically command the loyalties of thinking individuals in the post-war, post-holocaust world.

Colin Wilson's odd philosophy is embodied in his own novels, a particularly cogent example being *The Glass Cage: An Unconventional Detective Story* (1966) a book that more than fulfils the bold promise of its title. A reclusive scholar of William Blake becomes involved in a murder investigation after a policeman visits his remote cottage to enquire about the Blake quotations which have been left at the scene of his grisly crimes by a psychopathic killer who has been rampaging along the banks of the river Thames. Damon Reade's existence is spartan, and although he is a Blake expert of world repute, he is something of an innocent, a thirty-five-year-old virgin but a man with decided opinions on sexuality and the likely motives of murderers and psychopaths, a shy Apollonian scholar with a peremptory view of his neighbours' intelligence but more than an inkling of the attractions of Dionysian frenzy.

One of his friends is an antiquarian bookshop-owner in nearby Keswick, a man named Urien Lewis, known as Uncle Humphrey to his fifteen year old ward, Sarah. Sarah is in love with Reade and is eager to consummate their relationship and marry him as she had hoped to as a younger girl, particularly as her uncle has begun to take a sexual interest in her. He is controlling, treats her like a child, and yet insists that Sarah shows off the new underclothes he has bought her. Sarah confides all this on a visit to his room late at night. They lie chastely together, Reade agrees to marry her when she is sixteen, and the fantasy of this union between two innocents hangs over the remainder of the novel, as Reade travels down to London, and in the manner of all good amateur detectives, successfully second-guesses the flat-footed police in their bumbling investigations into the Thames murders. But it is the police who have surmised, correctly as it transpires, that the killer, who murders men and women indiscriminately, might be related to one of the many cranks and amateur Blakeans who write to him about his own respected books on the poet. Reade rarely reads or replies to these letters, but a reading of them soon throws up a number of possibilities. He finds it difficult to believe that anyone who knows their Blake really well can be such a bad person as all that.

The twists and turns of plot involve Reade losing his virginity to an eager young Negro girl in his temporary London lodgings, the passing of runes in the British Museum reading room (an incident seemingly lifted from the classic British horror film *The Night of the Demon* of a few years earlier), and a lengthy night on the tiles with a suspect of gargantuan appetites—all these elements, handled tautly and crisply, make for a gripping yarn and a detective story that is indeed unconventional, and as loosely illogical as one of Poe's prototypes of the genre. Reade is a beguiling detective, as opinionated, all-wise and apparently naïve as his creator, and *The Glass Cage* is a charming period piece in which Wilson is able to utilize his gift for expounding ideas, especially his own, about that curiously fifties creation, 'modern man', and offers a neat encapsulation of his philosophy—an amalgam of existentialism, romanticism, and 'commonsense' mysticism that is by and large optimistic, or at least forgiving and forgetting, about all-too-human nature. You can easily see why he was later drawn to writing about the likes of Gilles de Ray, the Marquis de Sade and Aleister Crowley, but also that (although he finds them glamorous and is in a way attracted by evil) he has a strong enough belief system of his own to encompass and in a way neutralise their more monstrous acts. Psychopaths and Satanists and criminals in general are, for Wilson, mystics and artists manqué, who have thrown off some of the shackles of habitual bourgeois morality and the limitations of commonsense ways of looking at the world, albeit in a purely egoistic, destructive and appetitive manner.

> Again Reade watched with fascination as Sundheim began cutting huge slices of the steak and ramming them into his mouth. The act of eating and drinking seemed to arouse in Sundheim a machine-like energy; he chewed like a hungry tiger. Reade had the feeling that Sundheim probably allowed himself to make low growling noises when he ate alone. He did not speak when he ate; simply concentrated totally on the food.[2]

The glass cage of the novel's title contains a python belonging to the murderer, a crawling king snake in the room of death that is actually a harmless, unassuming creature, symbolising sexuality, obviously enough, but also other slow, instinctual, natural processes. Sound familiar? D.H. Lawrence's snake again, detained forever on its journey to the waterhole; it is simply what it is, often feared but supposedly more harmless than it appears; its cage is society, of course—a secure glasshouse in which every species of being is visible to the gaze of public and zooologist alike: a place where the murderer has finally been found out, studied, anatomised, and whose invisible bars (the doors of perception as much as a Weberian social cage, a functionalist closed system) both criminals and mystics try in their different ways, according to Wilson, to break out from, to penetrate into a perceived absolute freedom that lies beyond, outside society and its blinkered norms. Snakes lie dormant, strike and strangle their prey, shedding blood-stained skins to come up good as new, fresh as paint. It is in their nature, and in the nature of Wilson's philosophy to be asocial, or to see society only as a matter of constraints to his desires. The attraction of Blake is that, for Colin Wilson, he accepts evil, and contains all opposites—as in the 'Marriage of Heaven and Hell', but in Wilson's philosophy there is no progression, so far as I can make out, only an understanding of our own dual nature to be gleaned.

In *The Glass Cage* there is an agreeable, trusting relationship built up between detective and criminal—who represent Apollonian and Dionysian poles—and the crime's solution involves not so much the following of clues to crack a puzzle, but a gradual process of human understanding and accommodation of otherness (their relationship is a romance of sorts) until the killer finally delivers himself up to the detective almost out of friendship. He feels no guilt for his crimes: they are only expressions of his nature (he is a little bit like the homicidal circus ape in Poe's 'Murders in the Rue Morgue'). But Wilson's murderer is bipolar, his bouts of suicidal depression relating to guilt over his father's suicide—a religious man who Christianised Blake—and his own hypersexuality is inherited from the nymphomaniac mother. But these are mind-forged manacles, Wilson implies, and Damon Reade's understanding (derived from Blake) solves both the crime and the riddle of the murderer's personality. He returns to his Northern cottage with the python as a pet, to continue his studies and to await the maturation of his child-bride.

It is an oddly satisfying book on all sorts of levels for the fantasies it articulates—the fantasy of the naïve genius turned literary detective, the close understanding between scholars and criminals, and the availability of teenage mistresses and brides with whom to lie happily ever after. Like its creator's philosophy it makes a kind of naïve, wishful sense of the cans of worms it so deftly prises open. Does the cut worm forgive the plough? Are the tigers of wrath wiser than the horses of instruction? Is the lust of the goat the bounty of God? Colin Wilson would answer all these questions with a Blakean affirmative, but if so his reading is missing something about Blake's ambivalence in the Proverbs of Hell—that he is as much describing the processes of earthly (or demonic) power as exalting them: the innocence of the lambs and children is to be prized, and shows itself here in the disinterested helpfulness of Damon Reade's attitude to life. The symmetries of *The Glass Cage* mirror those of Blake's philosophy and well as those of Niezstche or Hermann Hesse, and the book exemplifies Wilson's qualities as a synthesiser and promotor of ideas. It has a neatness and concision and a sense of closure about it, a sense of an idea fully explored and tied up so tight it almost suggests the fanaticism of the psychotic or the paranoid who finds detailed coherences where a sense of mess and contradiction might express a situation more sanely: a sense of too tight a fit, too exact a match between the symbolic world and the world of reality, so that the world rears up as overbearing, all too compellingly, unavoidably composed of symbols.

The worlds of the outsider and the criminal are of course explored powerfully by Albert Camus in *L'Etranger*, whose English title Wilson borrowed, and whose author admitted he had found his novel's final form and its way of writing an alienated consciousness from inside through the first-person vernacular narration of American crime novelist James M. Cain. Cain's influence in England is first seen in the thirties: Julian Maclaren-Ross, James Curtis and other; but a kind of taut poetic naturalism reminiscent of American crime novels and Camus serves Edinburgh junkie novelist Alexander Trocchi well in his first published novel.[3] The first fifty pages of *Young Adam* are spooky, poetic, claustrophobic—and as readable as its anti-hero is unreadable. He is an escaping murderer, a little reminiscent of some of Graham Greene's principal characters from the thirties, in particular the scarred fugitive of *A Gun for Sale*. He shares with those early

Greene characters a withheld quality, an implied inwardness—very much in the outsider mould: a category which can't be pursued properly without reference to Camus' novel. Colin Wilson's existentialist-influenced study of European fiction in also likely to have been significant for Trocchi. But like Albert Camus he makes use of the format of the American crime novel to express his vision of the man outside.

Trocchi makes much of the undertow, the undercurrent of the canals that pulls away the body of the woman his protagonist has murdered, and whatever led to these events continues to pull beneath the surface of his narrative, the invisible subterranean currents of motive and consequence that continue to tug him along, invisibly to the canal boat couple who take him on as a deck hand: it is the radical schism between his world and theirs that gives the novel its drive and its power—this guessed at source of his separateness makes him a mesmerising figure for the woman and a vaguely sympathetic one—both needy and useful—to her husband. Nevertheless his hosts are innocents and this particular 'young adam', who recalls the hero of Goethe's *The Sorrows of Young Werther* as well as all the tormented figures who trod the dark and lonely riverside path of repudiating the educational authorities in the early novels of Hermann Hesse,[4] is a prototype of fallen humanity: this time he has buried his Eve (who committed the sin of becoming pregnant) and has gone on the lam. He sleepwalks through his responsibilities on the boat, has sex with the woman on the riverbank, but, as in all good crime novels, there is no escape from his deeds, and there is disappointment as the book resolves itself by tying up these loose ends. Albert Camus' Meursault remains enigmatic for longer; he is never really explained except in terms of his gratuitous act, and is thus hard and irreducible. Trocchi's Young Adam is an unstable enigma who begins to unravel badly the more we come to know about him.

Cain's Book is, I believe, a far weaker effort than this first, creepy near-masterpiece.[5] It is as though Trocchi accepted his limitations too readily. Having found a sort of notoriety as an apologist for the early drug culture and a personality on the cultural avant-garde, he became too much a personality writer and manifesto producer and was thereafter unable to disappear into his fictions. Too stoned to think straight, he was lionised by the alternative media as a promoter of consciousness-narrowing drugs and dissipated his talents in that fragile moment of Beat-related celebrity. In *Cain's Film* (1969), directed by Jamie Wadhaven, he comes across as a rather withdrawn and somewhat pompous figure, a would-be revolutionary without much of a programme except for doing some Burroughs-like cut-ups and getting wasted on camera.[6] He wrote some pornography for

Olympia Press,[7] books which have great passages, but at the same time there is something about him that doesn't quite fit the shallow hedonism of his moment: there is a sensitivity in his best writing and a deadly seriousness of intent that might have powered a better writer to great heights. A pompous hedonist? An ethical junkie? There is something deadly and po-faced about being a proselyte for heroin and dope as revolutionary liberators, just as there is a hectoring thinness to his propagandist writings on behalf of the Sigma group, a proto-Situationist internationale of literary anarchists[8], and yet it is these involvements that made him a posthumous cult figure for latter-day would-be cultural anarchists besotted with anything that smacked of the glorious counter-culture. I can't help thinking something potentially better got lost on the way, but I suppose this is probably wrong. He was who and what he was after all. There's a sort of devil-may-care joyousness in the best drug writers that survives in their writings, or the sense, as in William S. Burroughs, that they have uncovered some genuine insights that were useful to others. Trocchi seems a shifty, uneasy character amongst them. Something else is there, he manages to suggest, some higher intelligence is at work. Something more is promised… but never delivered. Only the false glamour of injecting heroin, being cool: a handsome man who found himself at the eye of a moment in British culture's engagement with the European avant-garde.

Harold Pinter was another breed of weasel altogether, and could seem oddly placed in the company of the other writers I am discussing here; but his psychological themes, his interest in the detail of power relationships, his preoccupation with social estrangement on an intimate level and his interest in the psychotic, the criminal and the otherwise marginalised, place him closer to these poets of alienation than to the social novelists of the fifties. He is different because he developed earlier and independently and in relation to a theatre tradition; but his themes are often those of existentialism, and French surrealism was also one of the first modern literary movements to attract him. Pinter defines himself strongly and distinctively as a writer through his early poetry, which is strongly marked by the influence of Dylan Thomas and W.S. Graham and suggests a quite different lineage to the poets of the Movement, despite his admiration for and friendships with Philip Larkin and others.

Most of these early poems employ a strongly modernist diction, with many Joycean neologisms, and are also, possibly through Graham, touched by the spirit of the American poet Wallace Stevens, particularly his earlier poems in *Harmonium*, and particularly those razor-sharp, highly compact pieces depicting titanic power struggles. It would be difficult to believe that Pinter didn't know Stevens' 'The Plot against the Giant':

> Oh, la … le pauvre!
> I shall run before him,
> With a curious puffing.
> He will bend his ear then.
> I shall whisper
> Heavenly labials in a world of gutturals.
> It will undo him.[9]

Pinter once said casually, to hold off a questioner, that his work was about 'the weasel under the cocktail cabinet'[10] and has since both repeated and repudiated his oft-quoted remark as meaning precisely nothing to him. But the weasel under the cocktail cabinet, if not quite the same species, might turn out to be a creature something like Colin Wilson's python in its glass cage. Is Pinter's weasel an intruder or a pet? Either way, both creatures are representations of an uncontrollable force that is abroad in ordinary living rooms. In Wilson's case the force is sexual libido; in Pinter's it might be naked aggression of any kind. If Wilson's python is the uncontainable natural force of sexuality, Pinter's weasel might well be something similar, burrowing, biting and dangerous. Weasel does suggest an instinctual force, but also connotes 'weasel words', cunningly and hypocritically self-interested arguments or protestations, and as such, however casually offered, has far more political connotations than Colin Wilson's python. A weasel might be a spy (a mole?), or some other kind of creature that has weaselled its way in: it is vicious but is also cunning. Pinter is, above all, a writer who beats a path between the instinctive and the political. His writing contains both elements—the intuitive, involuntary side of writing and its ordering principle, which is both deliberate and cerebral, and among other things political. Harold Pinter might be said to have had a 'rage for order' similar to that expressed by Stevens in his poem 'The Idea of Order at Key West'[10], but in his case there is a sense of something instinctive and involuntary that is barely contained, whether a cry of pain or a murderous impulse, wrestled into a form it is always threatening to violently burst out of, although as his writing progresses this violence is itself an ultimate kind of control, articulated in a maniacally measured and brutally meticulous fashion. His early poem 'The Anaesthetist's Pin' (1952) expresses something of this lifelong programme. Like many young poets he is mannered and self-dramatizing, drawn by the extreme and the heroic, as well as by the grotesque and the gothic.

The anaesthetist's pin
Binds up the bawl of pain.
The amputator's saw
Breaks the condition down.

In the division of blood
That stems the fractured bow,
The wrist attacking hound
Snipes out the stair below.

At that incision sound
The lout is at the throat
And the dislocated word
Becomes articulate.[11]

'The lout is at the throat.' What a pinpoint to arrive at so early in his writing, as an impetus to urgent truthful speech: language as a matter of life or death in a street fight. Pinter's only novel, *The Dwarfs*, dates from the same period as this flawed but powerful poem, but was greatly revised and published much later, long after its young author had been established as a playwright of importance. As such it provided a backward glance at his formation, a kind of revisiting of his younger self by a writer whose main body of work had been more or less accomplished. Once published *The Dwarfs* seemed to define Pinter's moorings in a way that strongly illuminates much of his later writing. The novel is about the relationships between three friends: Pete, Len and Mark, and Pete's girlfriend, Virginia. Dialogues between characters are interspersed with short scenes, apparently excepted from Len's writings, usually narrated in the first person and concerning a group of dwarfs. Are these dwarfs the characters themselves seen from another perspective? Are they an audience for the action in a way, a symbol of the public of a play? Are they the generic elements in a crowd scene, symbolising the masses, the servile or working-classes? If they are a comic element, they are supremely unfunny: never speaking, often only visible at all through the detritus they have left behind, yet continually spying on the narrator, who must appease them, it seems, and tidy up after them. They resemble a group of rats living on a piece of waste ground, on an empty lot, and little further is done to define them: mute, insistent witnesses, by and large threatening but by and large impassive. They could refer to Pinter's audiences when he was an actor in repertory theatre at the time of writing, and maybe the key to their shifting identity is in this passage:

> Our intellectuals and the masses? Pete was saying. They do one of four things. They either ignore them, pity them, recreate them to mean something else, or complain about them. If you do the first

you limit your scope and you're a fool. If you do the second you're not an intellectual. If you do the third you're wasting your time. And if you do the fourth you're just like me.

What is a mass? Mark asked.

Get out of it. Haven't you ever heard of the poor, downtrodden, hardpressed, chainganged, pulverised lot of Jesuses who tell us what to do?

They only go about in hired cars, Len said. I've never seen one of them.[12]

Pete's anatomy of intellectual views of 'the masses' humorously defines Pinter's view of what is to be his subject-matter. The first is the view of a removed aesthete, the second—pity—not an intellectual view at all, according to Pinter, the third is that of a Marxist, and the fourth, amusingly, is complaint. Moaning about other people is of course the common human lot, and might be close to the view of 'the masses' of themselves: only the withholding of sympathy defines it as an intellectual view. The passage also contains the Lawrentian fear that the democratic masses might be in charge nowadays, as well as Len the writer's idea that they might not exist at all except as celebrity representations of themselves. These conversations resolve themselves into a power struggle over the woman, as in many a later Pinter work; but in *The Dwarfs* all this is in the nature of convivial, competitive sparring, a pooling of knowledge by a group of young men as eager to impress one another as they are to disclose the way the world works.

I lack guts, Pete said.
I wouldn't say that.
Yes. I lack guts.
Do you?
You mustn't think, Pete said, that I don't know what you and Mark are. I do. I recognise you both.
Me? Mark? What do you mean? What are we?
I take it you are my friends.
Len grimaced and clipped his palm under his jaw.
Yes.
Why don't you ask me, Pete said, if I recognise Virginia?
Why should I ask you that?
If you want to know another thing, I'll tell you. Because I lack guts, I commit spite. I suffer under that bondage. I commit spite at all corners, and in the face of the image.
He drew on his cigarette.
Do you know what that makes me?
It makes you Shammes to the Pope of China, Len said.[13]

The Pope of China is like Wallace Stevens' Emperor of Ice Cream: he is the only God there is, maybe, but is nevertheless of highly questionable authority, and to be his Shammes (both the sexton of a synagogue and the narrow taper used to light the seven candles on a hannukah menorah) is truly to be on a sticky wicket. A servant to nobodaddy. The three friends, who are possibly also a version of 1940s comedy film favourites The Three Stooges, enjoyed by Pinter, linger in cafes, visit one another in Hackney rooms, and stroll along the banks of the river Lea, attempting to live out their relationships in the terms recommended by William Blake's great perplexing poem of friendship, 'A Poison Tree':

> I was angry with my friend
> I told my wrath, my wrath did end.
> I was angry with my foe
> I told it not, my wrath did grow.[14]

Pinter was at this point a working-class outsider, a political outsider, and, as a Jew, in part a cultural outsider; but although he is perfectly prepared to stand alone, the intensity, and even repetitiousness, with which he examines all kinds of human relationships—familial, sexual, friendly and political—sets him apart from the more asocial kind of literary outsider, and the sense of rage that boils and erupts in his plays reveals him to be a kind of disappointed utopian, attempting to rescue human decency in extremis by the meticulous anatomy of its constant failure. In all of his work there is a continual hunger for connection with others on some other terms than those he relentlessly anatomises. But without residual hopes that things might be otherwise, his political anger wouldn't really make sense: there could be no humanity in any higher or meaningful sense to call to account for the activities of the world's shabby politicians and murderous governments.

There is much claustrophobia, aimlessness, laceration and a great deal of sympathy too—and an opening out of these in a party scene late in *The Dwarfs* in which the whole social world of which his characters are part is revealed in drink-fuelled glimpses, in arrested motion, as if by a strobe light. But it is evident that hostilities can never quite be suspended, and that friendship in the sense that these three young men have hitherto conceived it is not to be countenanced amongst adults. In the book's final conversation, ostensibly between Mark and Pete, but really a kind of divided up inner dialogue, the latter remarks that 'you can't cook in anyone else's oven', and although effectively ended by the sexual betrayal involving Virginia, it is this honesty of encounter between friends that gives the book its special quality, and relative warmth, but it also spells the end of late adolescent relationships conducted on free and easy terms:

> I mean, what does concern you? Surely not your friends as they wish to be, but only in so far as they can fit your requirements. Where they fail to do so, contempt, by your own logic, is the only outcome. It's their epitaph. They become for you an academic exercise in failure. Not because they themselves have necessarily failed, but simply that in attempting to retain what is their own, they have failed you.[15]

Paul Ableman's outsider-hero is the schizophrenic, particularly the schizophrenic as artist, making a world out of the world in his head and investigating the orders of language in a way that sometimes seems close to what would become the most powerful ideas about mental illness of the sixties. Like Trocchi's *Young Adam*, *I Hear Voices* was first published in Paris by the Olympia Press, but it is a far more complex and sophisticated book than Trocchi's.

Ableman had one of the strangest careers of all postwar British writers. A poet among novelists, he was prolific and talented, his early novels and plays are distinctive, surrealist, probing explorations of consciousness by means of poetic language, or perhaps exemplifications of the sources of poetic language in the brain's archival memory, to adopt his later terms. He wrote four subsequent novels, *As Near As I Can Get* (1962), *The Twilight of the Vilp* (science-fiction, 1966), *Vac* (1971) and *Tornado Pratt* (1977), a number of plays, such as *Green Julia* (1965) and also wrote short experimental theatre pieces, which were collected in *Tests*. Never achieving the popular breakthrough he craved as a novelist or playwright, he reviewed a great deal and wrote TV novelisations for a living while pursuing independent intellectual work and keeping a giant journal of his daily preoccupations. In *Arthur Daley Straight Up: The Autobiography* and many other original novelisations based on shows like *Porridge*, *Shoestring* and *Hi de Hi*, Paul Ableman builds a makeshift bridge between a serious modernist writer and the popular culture such modernism often despises. That he was unable to completely integrate these twin bit-steams was not for want of trying. His Porridge novel is written in a stream of consciousness style that makes Fletcher sound a bit like Virginia Woolf. His website (Ableman died in 2006) consisted of a short exposition of his theories of consciousness. It may be that the literary community felt he had turned into a something of a crank or crackpot, that's if they remembered him at all, but his mind remained sharp and his interests various. He also published books on nudism, on oral sex, and a neglected volume of prose poems.

I Hear Voices is a novel about consciousness in that it has a first person narrator and most of the action takes place in his head. As readers we are never quite sure what is real and what is not in the world he presents to us, but at the same time the novel presents a clear and thorough picture of a recognisable society, our own, through its layers of shifting realities and ceaseless evasive word play. Penning is punning and word play is world play in this book, which is woven from a skein of such *ad hoc* false definitions: a kind of analysis of the situation of the schizophrenic in which he discloses the people and systems around him, seemingly manipulates them (or believes he does) and thus appears to be evading an understanding of his true predicament, but as the book progresses it becomes equally apparent that the schizophrenic narrator is a lapidary social analyst whose judgement is unassailable. The book has been compared to Beckett, Kafka and Joyce too, but Paul Ableman's world, if claustrophobic, has a gentleness and whimsy all its own and is also reminiscent of French surrealist writings—the book's theme is an extension of their explorations of the world of allegories, dream-narratives and the unconscious—which is perhaps why Ableman sometimes sounds arrestingly like the American poet John Ashbery, who drew on some of the same materials and lived in Paris at around the same time: *I Hear Voices'* mock-explanatory quality, its digressiveness and gentle irony can resemble Ashbery, especially if arranged into lines. One of Ableman's narrator's voices, his brother Arthur's manager, accosts him in the wry but exalted language of the great poet's middle period:

> There are holidays abroad—you can fly almost anywhere,
> Though not to the poles yet, no matter how you crave
> Illimitable ice, but to Bongalulu or Trepan or the more familiar splodges
> Of the famous land mass, Prance, Hermany or Slain. You can
> Runnel and turret amongst the quinitudes of these vinish fiefs,
> Each richly stored with slabs and carved treasures,
> Good hotels, petrol everywhere. Of course, those places are being
> Developed now too and everywhere you go,
> Rising from the historic landscape, you'll find our blocks
> And antennae. Weeds. Weeds of progress, flowering
> In the ancient beds of culture.[16]

John Ashbery also works with broken allegories, and a syntax of constant deferral, but Paul Ableman achieves an equivalent in this novel by offering a relentless seamless succession of half-told stories and new characters, which tease and sharpen the reader's concentration. *I Hear Voices* works by disorientation and deferment. Ableman's novel has its own highly recognisable inner landscape we soon get to know. The book begins with the narrator being woken up, as he will be throughout, to be offered his daily egg by one of his attendants, Maria or Cousin Susan. The novel is to represent a day in his life. 'Twenty-four of the best, round cheeses of time,' his brother taunts him. 'Eat them, my lad, devour them.'[17] But the recurrence of the morning egg throughout suggests only that each day is much the same: a never-ending chain of cheeses. He lives in the house of an interrogating and destructive brother, Arthur, a successful businessman. Cousin Susan and Maria, the nurses who bring him his daily boiled egg and ration of fantasy are gentler creatures who tolerate and mildly admonish him. He knows he is ineffectual but cannot stop spinning oblique yarns out of his mundane, infantilised world, so filled with invented characters and voices and their implications that he is effectively immobilised by having to deal with their constant queries.

Arthur has a baby daughter, Jane, and it seems that Susan and Maria must wait on her too while Arthur is out at work—apparently at the helm of a large self-built corporation. Other characters come and go: Mr and Mrs Groggins, a couple who live opposite and whom the narrator spies on, the mysterious Merew and Merkitt, and two psychologists who attend and question him at different times: the professor and Commissioner Brangwill, the latter an exalted figure who is at the centre of everything, and whose rebellious nephew Gore is also an important interlocutor of the narrator. But one thing that all the myriad characters conjured out of his brain have in common is that he tries to turn them into collaborators with the world he is weaving in his madness, and they in turn appear to be playing along with his forever reworked scenarios with fixed roles and properties—offering no way out of a sublime solipsism that would seem to suit him rather well if he weren't continually challenged and undermined by such living phantoms, even as they bend kindly over his bed:

> 'He is muffled this morning.'
> 'He is stony.'
> 'He is turning again.'
> 'Quite a villain.'
> 'Quite well off.'
> Why do they do that to me? Why do they misunderstand my condition? I can't be held responsible in this way. I can't be worried. I'm not a swollen thumb, nor rags.[18]

Ableman's narrator continually feels misunderstood, and also that he knows exactly what is wrong with him and wrong with the world. As he attempts to explain to Susan: 'My racer's broken… it's stuck Auntie May, it's stuck.' In other words he is unable to keep up with other people, who are continually changing and growing, but is doomed to constant repetition and is marooned in infancy in a speeding world that simply won't let him in. But, to himself, his predicament is a complex one, and an all-absorbing game:

> And now my own affairs take precedence. It's obvious, at this stage, that only the most meticulous, the most elaborate and detailed, organisation will suffice to accommodate them. They ramify so. They extend their meanings. Their significance ranges and ramifies and multiplies its implications. All interact, weaving like a wind-stirred mesh of boughs. All summon, all presume—I have to begin. I must work at my plumbing job. I must think some more.[19]

His 'plumbing job' is to plumb the depths of his condition and his own fractured consciousness: it gets him out of the house anyway, and this vertiginous downward penetration to new levels of reality punctuates the book as one scene dissolves into the next and several new sets of related characters appear to interrogate and torment him. The bus conductor is the boatman of the river Styx, his journey fraught with encounters with surly ditch boys and attended by a continual forgetfulness about its purposes, so that he can only beseech heaven with a question seemingly impossible to formulate, except perhaps as a simple 'Why?' Arthur is both demanding and sympathetic but the narrator is unable to tell how deeply he understands his problems; or rather he is able to tell a great deal about his brother's ambivalence towards him but unable to appease his dissatisfaction. Arthur is the breadwinner, the responsible man of the household, but his complex tasks appear only as errands to the narrator. Thus, in a way, master and servants have changed places in the household they inhabit, and he and Arthur also change places throughout. Arthur appears to be searching the room 'for something which the very intensity of his search makes it seem unlikely will be there,'[20] while the narrator is confronted by a plethora of seemingly solider presences that press themselves upon him willy-nilly:

> I visit Ermine, the sullen queen who rules a tongueless people. I visit Koko and Jabwort who fight an eternal duel with bladders. Each time they smite, they turn to the nearest attendant slave-girl and explain that but a few more blows and he long duel will be at an end. Then, they intimate, with rolling eye and angling tongue, what spot, what animation! I visit Martop, the recluse, who has retreated from the tumult to reside in some barren corner of a divan. The results of his scornful reflections are not to be had for less than a casual greeting or passing remark. I visit Cortex the Statue, full-fleshed and heavy-handed, who, having already been exalted by all those present, need do nothing but manifest

> a presence. I visit Finway, the fluent, the knowing, who lies back, educating, with a stream of sophisticated anecdote, Clearleaf, the enthusiastic and Bell-like, whose girlish tinkle indiscriminately accompanies, even to his occasional consternation, all that Finway says.[21]

He remembers an injection he once received and wonders if those who share his world are truly human. Books might be a way of finding out, finding out something anyway, but the narrator is unable to read them. He can find no 'point of application' and they can't be read instantaneously. Books take time to read and he has no way of measuring time or the relationship between what they contain and his own inner and outer worlds. He can only ask others or hold off his voices in a quest to find the elusive 'Central Focus', the organising principle of his world. But he is not short of reflections on the nature of the world in which he moves. It is, he sees, a political world, a constructed world of interest groups and alliances and impostures. The people are restless and yet imprisoned by a 'rigid bony structure' that recalls Wilhelm Reich's notion of character armour, and political representations are made problematic by this imprisoned would-be fluidity of the polity: 'Governments are powerless to control it. They have not enough delegates. To keep the situation really in hand you need one for every handful of people.'[22] That is what speeding means: the pace of social change and that required of individuals as actors in it. Ableman's schizophrenic outsider is unable to be such an actor; but he is in a perfect situation to be a commentating artist on the modern world. He is a modernist: pseudo-aristocratic in diction, irritatingly above it all, in effect living on a private income and without social responsibilities, and it is for this he is tolerated, even admired, but also disdained by his more worldly brother.

> First he mocks and jeers or at the very best adopts a patronizing attitude—and all this quite rightly as far as I can see—towards my helpless and often quite unpleasant ways and then suddenly he begins to rage and fume as if what I had been saying was not merely the feeble outpourings of a distracted brain but veritable holy writ.[23]

It appears to the narrator that his stories have a certain authority for his brother, but this could well be a delusion. Another aspect of his predicament, and what really lies behind his various encounters with women, is the impossibility of his achieving a relationship, apart from one of unwilling dependency, with any of these women. Women are seen through the deep lens of infantile and adolescent fantasy ('You see Clara had blue eyes, little concentric rings on the soles of her feet and through these she peered grotesquely at the answering blue of days. She had blue holes in her armpits and blue testicles.'[24]) and their men are glimpsed through the green eyes of envy. Cousin Susan is motherly; Maria is invested with sexuality and therefore showered with gifts. Clara is a gazelle-like young girl over whom he and his brother are in jealous conflict. Arthur has never met her, we are told, and the narrator has created her for him: an unearthly creature woven out of the cloth of fantasy and memory. The girls in Arthur's office all flirt with his eccentric brother, but none of them can really hold a candle to Clara. The narrator imagines that Arthur has claimed her for his own, stolen her from his mind. Arthur's is a counter-poetry of possession and he feels he can withdraw her at will from his brother: if the narrator is a poet who utters his world into being, he is not otherwise powerful: managers have their poetry too, especially when drunk, and, as we have seen, some of the most lyrical writing in *I Hear Voices* is given to the expression of their desires and fantasies and to give body to their projects of conquest and modernisation.

An unravelling of these mysteries is only to be attempted by the professor, a pleasant, bespectacled man whose dogged literal-mindedness and patience is almost a match for the kind of evasive game-playing at which Ableman's schizophrenic narrator is an adept. They discuss eggs. They discuss mothers. They discuss ooze. They discuss words. The discuss memory. The professor seeks to persuade him that an egg is merely 'an ovoid of shell, calcium and so forth' and that he didn't hatch from one; that he had a mother, in fact, and that she wasn't a hen. He proceeds to attach a meter to the patient's throat while assuring him that even if words are 'long filaments and streamers' the basis of his problems is not purely verbal, but that he is 'the sport of misconceptions'. As the interview draws to a close they munch biscuits and Susan hovers solicitously. The professor points out that neither he not the patient is omnipotent and his profession can only offer 'Relative aid, limited assistance—we can heal the eye but not what it sees. We can mend the limb, but not what it does.'[25] His appears to be a realist view of schizophrenia that locates its causes as social, its symptoms as reflections of a wider social malaise, but leaves without having told him anything, dismissed as 'a professor of fish'. But the sonorous voice that interrupts puts the final kybosh on this social scientism, or illustrates why it is unable to penetrate to the heart of schizophrenia: the social world, even the mineral world of the stars, can only be grist to the mill of the schizophrenic artist's associative egoistic thinking, which domesticates as it makes strange:

> Look up at the stars. Are they up? Are you down? Do you see that bright star? We call that Sparkler. And that one Spitter. Spitter is a midgy star. Fit for Maria's finger. Sparkler is a blazer. Fit for a winter hearth. Switch on Spitter. Switch on Sparkler. But don't get too close to either. Bad tempered stars, they lick and splutter. They're on fire, you know, burning madly. Hiss, hiss, hiss they burn and have done, you know, for a long time (...) They are a family of stars, too far apart, poor things, for birthday greeting cards. But I've only been joking with you. They don't really have feelings at all. They're simply vortices of primal energy—and they will rage in empty space forever.[26]

Stars, in other words, are anything but what they actually are: 'black velvet has been stuffed between', and they are, as in poet J.H. Prynne's reading of the nursery poem 'Twinkle, Twinkle Little Star', both impossibly far away, allegorical, and reassuringly domestic 'sparklers' pinned to a woman's breast (or finger).[27] But whereas this universally known Victorian child's poem written by an Essex teenager begins in the potential disquiet or horror of not knowing 'what you are' and ends with the reassuring and helpful role of stars in guiding the Magi to the cradle of the infant Jesus, Ableman's stars remain menacingly alien, accusatory, and finally indifferent. Thus what seems to be a hiding from reality in the schizophrenic is, for Ableman the visceral and unbearably intense experience of a greater reality. In this condition merely banal truths always appear to him in their most troubling aspect, most painful as they most seem to confirm his infantile ego world. Nevertheless, his schizophrenic narrator decides to follow the professor's advice and try to overcome his misconceptions. This involves, among other things, further visits to Arthur's office and commentary on what takes place there. A lengthy interview with one of the secretarial girls involves trying to ground his fantasy of her in reality (although he cannot stomach the thought of taking her to a Monster film) and concludes with the narrator pleading: 'At the very least, don't call me metaphor.'[28]Arthur describes the directors of the company—one of them, Sir George, has risen from the shop floor and likes to go through the shops and greet the workers informally—while Arthur himself is close to being a director himself, and shows great familiarity with the ways of power and ease in his dealings with secretaries. He has risen far from his original station as a fellow plumber. Mr Groggins interrupts with a vision of the apocalypse when 'Finally the rats would come up against pumice stone and be appalled by the acrid smell. They would picture the earth's surface as so many smoking cones. Then they might sip delicately.'[29]

Italians play a shadowy but significant role in the world of the narrator. Maria has been affianced to one, a woman he later meets in a park invites him to her home to meet her typically dark and corpulent husband. I wondered if this racial association is not another symbolic displacement: if the Italians are not really black, or if all dark people are probably Italians, or if the narrator of *I Hear Voices* associates Italians with sexuality and any sexually attractive women with Italy, just as all men who have not attained the social station of plumber are automatically ditch boys. The professor reappears and advises him: 'You must start again… You must begin by "living in a picture" and then there's a next step. You must think about your mother.'[30] Advised to seek advice, to which he is always open, he finds himself seated opposite Commissioner Brangwill, who following the usual shrink's rigmarole about childhood advises him that his putative cure is dependent upon the erection of suitable screens:

> I use strong screens and I sit behind them and suck rind. Sometimes I whimper a little but this sound is effectively screened and no-one hears. I whimper because I see someone in need. I never see one person in need but millions. Then I stretch out my hand, still sticky from the sweet rind but I only touch the screens. That is how my screening works.[31]

Perhaps it is the narrator who is being screened, or maybe his visions and memories are themselves screens for some yet to be excavated sexual trauma—possibly involving his rejection by Maria. He certainly associates sexuality with death, as is indicated by the naming of Miss Casket, a desirable young woman whom Gore, Commissioner Brangwill's rebellious nephew, can't stop himself from desiring in inappropriate settings and circumstances. They are transported to her apartment, where she turns out to be part of the nucleus. Fellow guests Piner and Cup-Wash are hatching a plot there. He also meets Gore, who tells him of his uncontrollable desire, and they are soon embarked on a conversation about poetry. Poetry is both intoxicating and deceptive, loved and hated, but at any rate inescapable for both of them. Gore (the narrator) is a counter-poet, a disintoxicator who analyses through his associative language and reveals the structures of the world as well as fleeing from them. But Gore disappears, as do all his interlocutors, the therapy session is over and the narrator makes his way back to his domestic egg through a city populated by African giraffes and English squirrels, to be greeted by Susan and Maria, the latter soon skipping from his room: 'I can't stay,' she informs me, 'in this arcade. You live in the shadow of the world-spider.'[32]

I Hear Voices is a visionary novel whose protagonist is unable to tell the wood from the trees, but its basic structure is a fairly traditional one, that of a journey, not only the repeated non journey of the narrator's diurnal perambulations through an imaginary landscape, but a traditional circular quest narrative—it has the structure of the Odyssey, of Joyce's *Ulysses* or any number of other mythic narratives as described by French philosopher Paul Ricoeur in his study *Temps et récit*.[33] For Paul Ricoeur the journey of the hero in such epic stories, whether an ancient mythical quest or a modern autobiography, is fundamentally a journey of individuation. Odysseus is confronted by various tests on the way as the Gods hurl a hundred shape-shifting creatures and trials at him, returning at last having understood the world and proved his mettle to the weaving Penelope and her suitors. Ableman's novel fits well into this narrative scheme—despite the frustrations of its shifting cast and its narrator's apparent inability to make progress we see that he is trying to, and that his hopes include the notion that on his journey successive layers of illusion are to be peeled away and the truth of his predicament finally revealed. The imaginary people he projects onto his inner screen are certainly forthcoming with revelations, but the world he discovers is a perverse one: 'It's a law, an immutable law,' he is told. 'Pinnacles are pinnacles of idiocy.'[34]

His schizophrenic journey continues, transforming as it goes into a Judeo-Christian quest for God, a being whom he has implored early on in the novel to no avail, and finally into a pilgrimage of repentance. Ableman's schizophrenic narrator hopes to turn into St Augustine, the philosopher re-examining his youthful follies and enthusiasms through the prism of a revealed divine truth. 'I have come to repent, not to practice philosophy,' he tells the Italian woman he has met in the park, and following a conversation with her husband, Lewis, over whether he can achieve a lively Italian repentance or must content himself with a more Anglo-Saxon style expiation 'by sneaking', he begins his recantation of evil ways:

> 'I repent this and that,' I begin. 'I repent the demands I have made, the whips I lay to bowed backs at every step. I repent the sun into whose heat I have propelled my servants. I repent the service I have rendered them. I repent the motion and the deadly little vortex I stirred one afternoon near the shoe shop. I repent the drainage of other vortices. What may not have drained away? I repent my ability and my inability and my thoughts of either—'[35]

Impressed though his listeners appear to be, it is clear that his repentance has as little meaning for them as it does for him, and that his journey of repentance is just another attempt on the part of both character and author to achieve a teleological narrative, or any kind of redeeming closure. What has he to repent? Where can he go next? He may be guilty, as guilty as Joseph K, who is at least guilty of being a bachelor. The idea of forward movement is alien to him and can only be mocked by his afflicted consciousness, his permanent Augustinian *distensio*, suspended as he is in an agonising void between past and present with only regret and anticipation for company. Nostalgia or remorse, hope or fear: these irresolvable tugging options torment him as greatly as any pilgrim on the path to the Heavenly City, and he describes the firmament and his uncertain existence in terms that recall the penultimate chapter of Augustine's *Confessions*:

> It is airy atoms all floating together. It is unthinkable. It is the deceitful portal of the dreadful chasm of never-ending incompletion. It is here, here in my hands and far beyond the furthest grasp of the most tireless pilgrim. It is my heart, the red muscle has congealed from it. It is my brain which it has secreted and which, a ghastly progeny, turns back to devour it.[36]

But unlike St Augustine in the *Confessions* he has attained no further shore on which he is certain of God's love, and from which to contemplate or analyse his current predicament. Arthur has no interest in heavenly palaces, merely a bigger house with a drive, and another visit to his office reveals only 'extremely brilliant planes of coloured substance all about and three or four people trying to devise means of exploiting them.' Arthur dismisses these products in favour of a prong, a mysterious electronic device, possibly a weapon, possibly a communicator, or maybe just the ultimate plumbers tool, 'a prong for manipulating various modulors' whose purpose is to emit 'a clear, bell-like tone.' Arthur explains that his decision to reject the coloured planes in favour of the prongs is based on powerful intuitive abilities of judgement he possesses and that his brother does not, and we see that his sensibility is both the ultimate measure of value and the secret of his worldly power. Is Arthur truly at 'the centre of affairs'? This unbearable thought renews his quest for an elusive interview with God, or the Pope.

Commissioner Brangwill and his rebellious nephew are called into play, but they prove to be compromised in different ways: Gore as a pleasure seeker and Brangwill as a mere hireling of Arthur, and the narrator repudiates their false-authority as he has again and again rejected his brother's. In the end they share his epistemological problems and Gore's hatred of the uncle is 'really converted admiration'. The narrator curses his hateful demonic voices for failing to tell him anything he doesn't know, and makes a last attempt to attain the ear of God by means of the intercession of Radcliffe, 'the last of my molecules'. He asks Radcliffe to show him a model of a world, and inspecting its surface sees that it is inhabited by a single bad boy 'Who runs rapidly all about, imagining he is trying to escape from an angry parent or master.' However, the boy eventually notices that he is rushing about on the surface of a model and that, to his chagrin, there is no-one pursuing him, and he wishes there was such a punishing authority. Radcliffe, it transpires, has spoken to the Holy Father on his behalf, but he has no specific words for him: 'No words—I have no message for your master.' But like all his voices, Radcliffe is insinuating and speaks further when prompted. The Holy Father did indeed have more to say: 'He spoke of the destruction and distortion of many things. He spoke of straight lines incredibly warped by the stresses of expediency and desire. He spoke of continuity and lingered on its father memory,' but in concluding his vague ruminations on the connectedness of all things and the importance of his own office, he only repeats his refusal to offer a redeeming word.

The Holy Father might as well be the dead Emperor in Kafka's 'A Message from the Emperor'. Ableman's narrator is certainly the least of his emperor's subjects, and his words have no meaning specific to him. The Holy Father is even worse than Kafka's Emperor, who at least tries to be helpful before dying, in that this stand in for the deity specifically and categorically refuses to help the schizophrenic. 'There is nothing, not even a star,' he complains. The hearer of voices can only enjoy a brief period of quiet release as his voices abate and he looks out of the window into the grey suburban dawn to see a woman who might be Mrs Groggins in her nightgown but isn't after all, and to notice, on the other side of the street, 'a man and a small parcel pass rhythmically down towards the railings.' He lies down quietly on his bed, but before long the tormenting voices begin again to address him: the patient reader, having come this far, is cured of any tendency he or she may have had to believe in the insights of schizophrenia.

Paul Ableman would probably have agreed with R.D. Laing's advice in *The Politics of Experience*[37] that schizophrenics should be encouraged to listen to and contest with their voices rather than that they should be suppressed by drugs or electric shock treatments; more than this he was a proponent of a surrealist view of dreams and the unconscious as revolutionary agents, a sixties libertarian who also believed that sexuality was such a socially subversive force for good. But by my own reading *I Hear Voices* subverts the notion of the wisdom of the mad that it would like to entertain: as well as offering poetry and lacerating insights, it serves up dysfunction and circularity in equal measure, and that makes it a bleaker and truer book than it might otherwise have been, which is one possible explanation for Ableman's failure as a popular writer in his times, and why his first novel is still so resonant and good in our own disabused moment. There is very little optimism in it: all of the narratives of progress, redemption, cure, whether individual or social, are shown to be the empty self-justifying fictions of the powerful. Ableman's failed rebellious world-maker has little choice but to live with his family and miserably suffer their interrogations.

Ableman's is a literary version of schizophrenia rather than a schizophrenic text, although *I Hear Voices* owes something to psychoanalytic classics. He precedes Laing by a few years—we have no way of knowing if the mental illness he describes has been induced by his family. If so he never stops striking back and certainly gives them more of a run for their money than the helpless victims of Laing's case studies, condemned to a lifetime's incarceration and electro-shock for wearing coloured stockings and wanting to go to jazz clubs, or harmlessly believing you are a nun or married to Cliff Richard.[38] Like Jacques Lacan, whose famous 'The Rome Discourse' and his reading of Poe's story 'The Purloined Letter' appeared at about the same time, Ableman's view of the unconscious is influenced by the surrealists.[39] Lacan's emphasis on the centrality of language in structuring the unconscious might make a comparison worthwhile. For Lacan, psychosis or schizophrenia, and particularly the phenomenon of auditory hallucinations or hearing voices, arises from a distorted relationship between the Imaginary and Symbolic orders, which are roughly speaking the worlds of dream or fantasy and that of structuring language, and an elusive but pressing order of the Real—the world of sex, death and work. This makes sense of Ableman's vision in that the whole thrust of his narrator's yarn spinning is precisely to incorporate his hallucinatory and dream materials in the symbolic order of language and thus attempt to construct a viable self. A reality principle certainly also intrudes throughout, but is continually vanquished by the narrator, even when it disguises itself as fantasy or antic language: word play and world play. In most genuine case studies I have read the besieging voices reported to analysts tend mainly to make indecent sexual suggestions or mutter nasty criticisms that may well have a basis in reality. Paul Ableman's voices supply his narrator with a whole panoply of diverting characters and situations: a world far more interesting than the mundane order of the real, in which if the auditor isn't genuinely powerful and is unable to alter his situation, at least he consistently has his say. Lacan would say that the schizophrenic's voices constitute him, and Ableman's novel seems to bear this out, but the French analyst's reading of Poe's story 'The Purloined Letter' also provides an interesting parallel to *I Hear Voices*.

In 'The Purloined Letter' a compromising love letter, whose precise content remains unknown, is hidden in plain sight on a mantelpiece, is missed by the bumbling police, then retrieved and substituted by the brilliant detective Dupin, who then uses it to blackmail the blackmailer who had tried to use it to impugn the virtue of the Queen. The King thanks him. Lacan says the letter is a 'pure signifier', ie, important not for what it says (we never know) but for what people think it might say, and as such reconfigures the relationships, alliances of the people it supposedly concerns. It circulates, its meaning changes, and in doing so it constitutes (metaphorically) the unstable, illusory subjectivity, or inter-subjectivity of those implicated by its mysterious lost message, finally forged by Dupin for his own purposes. This calls to mind the many missed messages and interrupted circuits of communication in *I Hear Voices*, and also the mysterious package that is being delivered to a house over the road as the novel closes. What does it contain?

On the face of it this doesn't matter, it's just an early morning postal delivery; but the package seems as though it might contain the answer to the false-riddle of the narrator's predicament: one more parcel to open or layer to strip off and all will be revealed, except that we know it it is another false trail, another false clue on an endless circular investigation. And yet the narrator is reassured by it, wrongly so: now he can at last go to bed (where the voices soon begin again). The narrator is something of a parody of Edgar Allen Poe's scientific detective—Dupin's method is something of an absurd parody of science at the beginning of the genre of detective fiction. He may be right every time, and much cleverer than the police, just like Sherlock Holmes, but in Ableman's case at least, his brilliance counts for nothing since the mysterious package contains nothing significant. Ableman's mysterious package, delivered at dawn, is like Poe's letter: a pure signifier of his psychotic condition and the impossibility of its self-unravelment, of the inability of a consciousness that is in effect a processing plant of the twin bit-streams of the perceptual present and conceptions it has inherited to truly escape its own condition as broken mirror of a world that is far from innocent. Madness in this case is a sort of retreat into innocence, but one from which the cossetted schizophrenic is licenced to speak the truth about what he perceives; however, this licence to speak is bought at the cost of being completely ignored. Ableman's career is a chilling example of how a culture can completely ignore one of its most powerful and brilliant voices—and his gamely productive production of novelisations of popular TV programmes (although some would think it a waste of his abilities) shows he possessed the tenacity required to survive as an artist in such a culture. Ableman himself was an outsider hero, but one who continually tried to relate himself to a wider culture, and also one who left a substantial body of work behind him which will hopefully some day be properly reconsidered. Since this writing, Faber Finds have reissued several of his novels: an excellent start.

Ableman's humanist view of mental illness resolved itself into a mechanical theory of consciousness all his own. What he called 'the twin bit-stream theory of consciousness', expounded in a later book, *The Secret of Consciousness: How the Brain Tells the Story of Me* (1999), proposed that the double structure of the mind was as a kind of warehouse containing a vast archival memory, continually drawn upon, but as well as this a processing plant for incoming sensory information. Consciousness, which he sees traditionally as a big brain effect, exclusive to humans, consists simply of the mingling of these two independent data-streams. This process is best observed in dreams, when one of the data-streams has effectively been turned off and the free play of the archival memory can be observed in full operation. Ableman's theory, admittedly expressed in a highly personal way, predictably was ignored by all, but he had become obsessed by it, convinced that he had made an important breakthrough in the understanding of consciousness which vested professional interests had conspired to silence.

Chapter Eight

New Worlds, Old Hierarchies: Michael Moorcock, Angela Carter, Brian Aldiss, J.G. Ballard

Science-fiction and fantasy writers have often been seen, most especially by themselves, as the principal allegorists and novelists of ideas of popular fiction in the twentieth century; they have shadowed, sometimes foreshadowed, commentated upon and made their own bizarre social and intellectual maps of all the big ideas, technological advances and social paroxysms of much of the nineteenth and twentieth centuries; and the SF writers of the sixties in Britain, like their American and Eastern-bloc cousins, were a particularly innovative bunch, amongst the most genuinely radical writers of the post-war decades and the carriers of the cultural meta-narratives, or mega-narratives of that era. Science fiction's involvement with ideas of utopia, dystopia, progress, apocalypse, and last but not least, the implications of scientific progress itself, made it an ideal medium to refract and reflect upon the preoccupations, hopes and anxieties of an era of revolutionary hopes and more complex political realities. Shelley, a science fiction poet himself in early works like his feminist epic 'Queen Mab' and later poems like 'The Witch of Atlas' famously wrote that poets are the unacknowledged legislators of the world; in another part of his argument he says that poetry consists of 'shadows cast by futurity upon the present.'[1] It is a phrase that makes the poet or SF writer more mediumistic than legislative, more seismograph or electrometer than prophetic lightning conductor. But in all these senses British SF writers of the sixties felt they had more or less unlimited scope for invention and speculation.

In Michael Moorcock's Jerry Cornelius novels the recent ruins of British Imperialism are transposed and parodied in a new context—a simultaneous 'multiverse' in which all historical times and places as well as an infinity of alternative time-streams are present, possible, congruent and liable to overlap:

> Around them the air was jewelled and faceted, glistening and live with myriad colours, flashing, scintillating, swirling and beautiful. She clung to him. 'What is it?'
> 'The multiverse. All layers of existence seen at once. Get it?'
> 'Philosophy isn't my bent.'
> 'This is physics, dear.'[2]

The Cornelius Quartet, with its affectless prose, its channel hopping plotlessness in which characters change costume from scene to scene, strap on dildos, peel off identities, takes to heart Marshall McLuhan's axiom: 'the electronic information environment allows for no fixed positions or goals'. Like McLuhan's *The Medium is the Massage* (1966) or the novels of William S. Burroughs, Moorcock collages and juxtaposes materials from all over the place—history, aesthetics, travel writing, memoirs, pop music, advertising leaflets and other ephemera—in the hope that this brocolage will give body and purport to his long amiable spree of jokey sex and mock-class-terrorism. Cornelius devastates the polite middle-class ladies on Derry and Toms' roof garden by playing them George Formby songs from a Westland Whirlwind helicopter and gleefully torches London libraries in aid of cultural revolution; Karen von Krupp straps on a dildo and buggers Bishop Beesley. Working-class Jerry sips his pint of bitter, has a cup of tea with his cockney muvver, and hops into his waiting Rolls Royce Phantom VI. The soundtrack is Hendrix and Charles Ives, the landscape is sixties London and wherever else happens to pop up. The clothes are always spectacular:

> Jerry's skin, as black as a Biafran's, glistened… A man in his late twenties, with a healthy, muscular body, a large Liberty's neo-Art Nouveau wrist-watch like a bangle on either wrist; his skin was ebony and his hair not blond but milk white. Jerry Cornelius was a Revolutionary of the old school, though his stated objectives were different (…) He pulled on his lavender shirt, his red underpants, his red socks, his midnight blue Cardin trousers with the flared bottoms, the matching double-breasted high-waisted jacket, smoothed his long white hair, took a mirror from his pocket and adjusted his wide purple tie, looking at his face as an afterthought. A very negative appearance, he thought, pursing his lips and smiling.[3]

This time Cornelius is black, symbolically black: a pimp from a Blax-ploitation movie, with Hendrix's 'Foxy Lady' on the headphones: he is intended as a photographic negative of bourgeois morality, a clotheshorse (he is depicted on the cover of *The Condition of Muzak* as a cardboard doll, caucasian again, onto which cut-out military or harlequin outfits can be folded) with big ideas, whose cure for cancer is polymorphous perversity and the destruction of all stratifications of the symbolic order. If the cancer he is trying to cure is racism in all its forms, what better way to subvert those forms than to turn them all into dressing-up clothes? In the process of imagining his ridiculous protagonist, Moorcock invents the first English version of post-modernism, and in the final novel of the series, *The Condition of Muzak,* he offers an explanation of what he is trying to do by means of a quotation from George Dangerfield's *The Strange Death of Liberal England:*

> Important writing, strange to say, rarely gives the exact flavour of its period; if it is successful it presents you with the soul of man, undated. Very minor literature, on the other hand, is the Baedecker of the soul, and will guide you through the curious relics, the tumbledown buildings, the flimsy palaces, the false pagodas, the distorted nad fantastical faery vistas which have cluttered the imagination of mankind at this or that brief period of its history.[4]

Whether right or wrong, this is an agreeably modest and approachable way of justifying the melding of popular and high art, and makes an interesting claim for popular fiction as history. In a way it could stand as an entire justification for the study I am writing, and for looking again at novels of the fifties and sixties in order to make sense of their times—they themselves have certainly been pillaged often enough. There are of course those who would object that such an enterprise amounts to a cobbling together of a false past out of totally corrupt and questionable materials, and that, as such, the picture I am making of postwar Britain is an inherently factitious one with no true claim to historicity. Perhaps for Moorcock the orthodox hierarchies of evidence in historical writing are invalid, or perhaps he would say that he is writing a more subjective kind of history. Perhaps he would say neither of these things. What he is actually doing is justifying himself as a fiction writer attempting to get down the resonances of his times. He often builds these novels out of the ruins of Victorian adventure fiction, particularly the works of H. Rider Haggard, reproducing, anatomising through parody their racial typologies and their notions of femininity, including titillating lesbian and interracial sex scenes that can be accused of prurience and exploitation, and humour, but which are also a means of anatomising imperial fantasy and the power relations that lie behind it.

Perhaps the most historically rich and resonant of the novels is *The English Assassin*, in which Moorcock's love of name-checking from the histories of design and military hardware is given its head and the historical phantasmagoria suggested by the notion of the multiverse leads to some startling passages of alternative history and speculation; in *A Cure for Cancer* the Israelis have merely annexed Albania in order to guarantee the integrity of their borders; in its successor some surprising new alliances have emerged to redraw the map of Europe:

> 'Poverty,' said Auchinek to Lyons, the Israeli colonel, 'increased markedly in Europe last year. This, in itself, would not have threatened the status quo had not a group of liberal politicians persistently offered the people hope without, of course, any immediate prospect of improving their lot. Naturally they moved swiftly from apathy to anger. Without their anger I doubt if I should have been anything like as successful.' He smiled. 'I owe at least some of my success to the human condition.'
>
> 'You're modest.' The colonel stared approvingly at his troops as they joined with their Arab allies and began, systematically, to lay dynamite charges throughout what was left of the city of Athens. 'Besides, wasn't the collapse to some extent cultural?'
>
> 'It was a culture without flexibility, I agree. I must admit that I share the view that Western civilisation—European civilisation, if you like—was out of tempo with the rest of the world. It imposed itself for a shirt time—largely because of the vitality, stupidity nad priggishness of those who supported it. We shall never be entirely free of its influence, I'm afraid.'
>
> 'Basically—emotionally—I do think that. I know the question's arguable.'
>
> 'I detect a strong whiff of anti-aryanism. You support the pogroms?'
>
> 'Of course not, I am not a racialist. I speak only of education. I would like to see a vast re-education programme started throughout Europe. Within a couple of generations we could completely eradicate their portentous and witless philosophies.'
>
> 'But haven't our own thoughts been irrevocably influenced by them? I can't echo your idealism, personally, General Auchinek. Moreover, I think our destiny is with Africa…'
>
> 'The chimera of vitality appears again,' Auchinek sighed. 'I wish we could stop moving altogether.'[5]

Another strong element in the stew of cultural materials in *The Condition of Muzak* is the *commedia dell'arte* tradition, with Cornelius and his associates as time-travelling Ladbroke Grove equivalents of Pierrot, Columbine, The Captain, The Lover, The Doctor, Mezzetino, Harlequin and the rest, reappearing here in different guises as characters of a universal, transhistorical low-life comedy. A theatrical, dressing up kind of androgeny continues throughout the sequence there is. incest between Catherine and Jerry Cornelius is celebrated along with most other vaguely agreeable perversions, enjoyed and normalised as epitomising the glorious ways of the immortals, or at least as forming part of the likely mental landscape of most adolescents. Una Perrson and the other women are like Emma Peel, Charlie's Angels, or Bond girls—Jerry's Angels. Moorcock wants to liberate his readers, amuse them and turn them on to big, important ideas. Look around you, he is saying. There is more going on in the multifarious world than you think or have been taught about or have previously dreamed of in your sad little philosophies. Well, anyway, something like that is on offer in abundance.

Moorcock's Jerry Cornelius Quartet is almost textbook postmodernism in its mixture of periods and styles, of high and low culture, its sense of previous conceptions of history being exhausted, its lack of teleological narrative shape and its attempt to find a new one, non-linear, non sequential, open-ended, its mixture of erudition and pop, its resemblance to an over-populated episode of *The Avengers* or *The Prisoner*, its attempt to blast open the continuum of history with new insights, like an episode of *The Time Tunnel*, by having the Palestinians attack London in a flotilla of 1920s flying boats, its refusal to be serious about social class, its indulgence in stereotypes of all kinds, its non-belief in progress or the Enlightenment, its sense of its own multiple worlds as a virtual playground (before virtual reality was invented) for childish games whose outcome is crucial for the future of humanity, its total disloyalty to science whilst feeling free to avail itself of any useful items of impressive sounding terminology, its fixation on surface (though not the surface of its prose) and its denial of the depths which it is trying to plumb, its prolixity, its lack of focus, its lack of a sense of cultural possession, its pilfering of the citadels of culture, its air of knowing everything about the modern world, its failure to back anything up, its triviality, its fashion-consciousness, its apocalyptic strain, its boredom with the truth of anything, its boredom with boredom.

Jerry Cornelius may be a new kind of hero, but he is a hero still, and his mission is still a sort of redemptive quest in the ancient mould. Were he simply an intergalactic Harry Palmer he would be less interesting. He differs from both of these in that he doesn't have a boss, is working for no government, not even one he distrusts, as in Palmer's case. He is both self-defining and a shape-shifter, and for those reasons he tends to lose focus without unifying heroic plots to lend coherence to his actions. He is a trickster. Indeed, most of the time he is little more than a figment of the author's and reader' imagination. But Cornelius is after all only one of Moorcock's protagonists, only one of the incarnations of these masters of the time streams who are his eternal champions, his immortals. John Dakar in *The Eternal Champion*[6] wonders as he hurtles towards his next incarnation what will be demanded of him on his next planet, in his next heroic identity (he is Joseph Campbell's Hero with a Thousand Faces,[7] with memories of being Cornelius, the pale slayer Elric of Melniboné, and many others[8]): Daker becomes a character named Erekose, and before his brief adventure as the Champion of the Humans of the city of Mernidon is done he will have laid waste to an entire planet, fought and slain the Halfling Armies of the Eldren, so called because they are ghosts who can double and reappear behind the army they are fighting, before he must turn around on his heel and begin slaying his own treacherous, rapacious kind, in a futile attempt to stem their genocide of an older, wiser race.

John Dakar ends by marrying the beautiful but barren Eldren princess: the last of both their lines, but they rule over a wasteland. It is a lonely business being an Eternal Champion, not altogether a chosen role but one thrust upon us by history or by birth. Moving between exotic identities, occupying eternal roles in a virtual world: Moorcock appears to have conceived the now commonplace concept of designed avatars in fantasy role-playing games. In *Behold the Man* (1971) he attempts the ultimate occupation of a heroic persona and to square the circle of his moral ambivalence by retelling the Christian story from a Nietzschean point of view. South London misfit Karl Glogauer is bullied at school and might have been simply a loser, a suicide, but drawn to other marginal people he falls in with some occultists, one of whom has invented a time-machine. Transported to the shores of Lake Galilee, Glogauer makes contact with Essene sects, goes to Nazareth to discover that Mary is the town prostitute, Joseph a laughable cuckold, and Jesus himself a simpleton who is not of sufficient intelligence to carry on his father's trade. Karl realises that the Christian story will not happen unless he himself takes the place of Jesus, becomes Christ, preaches, performs miracles and shortly allows himself to be crucified. This role he accepts as his fate, and *Behold the Man*, a powerfully imagined novel, is a blasphemous work that both affirms and mocks Christianity.[9] Glogauer, unlike Elric, unlike Dakar, unlike Cornelius, all of whom have something of the the indifference of the hired killer—is terrified by the fate that has been thrust upon him, but realises that it is his duty to die on the cross, that he is, in fact, Jesus of Nazareth. A strong part of the attraction of most of Moorcock's stories is physical adventure, battle, and the worship of dexterity, strength and courage for their own sake—but his heroic characters also have the duality of the mercenary who knows very well that the world is unjust, but must place himself on the winning side in order to survive in it. There is in all of this a vast appeal to adolescent boys, who are wondering how they will be able to test themselves and how they will fare in the worlds beyond the apparently circumscribed arena into which they have been born, but also a kind of working-class Messianism—you too can be a hero, and use your strength and resourcefulness for the protection of the weak and the redemption of mankind. Karl Glogauer's case suggests that even losers can win a heroic destiny.

Michael Moorcock was one of the most spirited combatants in the culture wars of the sixties and after, offering this account in a later redux of the moment in which *New Worlds* was at the forefront of 'speculative fiction' in England:

> The majority of us round the so-called underground movement of the sixties were not pie-in-the-sky hippie dreamers or sharp operators in Regency-cut jackets. The publications and the bands I associated with at least were moved not by dope smoke but by the awful inheritance of the fifties, the oppressive smugness of the previous generation, the grey choice of lamb or mutton, tweed or flannel, Amis or Braine (…) Having, by the mid-sixties, at last escaped the bar-room philosophies, the unremarkable ambitions of the Angry Young Men, we became a little euphoric I suppose and thought our choices would naturally continue to expand.[10]

Much has been written of the figure of the male dandy in sixties culture, partly because he is so memorably incarnated by the pop singers of that era, by Mick Jagger, Ray Davies, Steve Marriott and dozens of others. In fiction he seems to begin earlier, in Colin MacInnes' *Absolute Beginners*, finds final full expression in the Jerry Cornelius novels of Moorcock—and also in the glamorous but unpleasant male character around whom the girls dance in Angela Carter's first novel, *Shadow Dance*.[11] This figure, sexually desirable, androgynous but not necessarily homosexual, can be viewed as an index of, and an important focus for the mapping of changes in 'the relationship' between men and women, of gender bending and the apparent breakdown or reformulation of traditional sex roles—which appears more strongly at first in the male characters in British fiction. Angela Carter works with an array of female types in this first book. They are both old and 'new', but can be reduced to innocent and vamp, doormat and sex goddess. An atmosphere of bogus junkshop pre-Raphaelitism hangs over the book, a bohemian young Bristolian world she is half-celebrating, half testing to destruction. The enjoyment of sexual cruelty towards her female characters first emerges here, in her first book. When the irritatingly vacant Guislayne's disfiguring scar appears across her beautiful face there's an almost gloating sense of justice in it; the destruction of her beauty isn't tragic at all but a handy piece of cultural terrorism against the kind of femininity she represents, or would be if she didn't seem to enjoy it herself; and, of course, Angel, the book's working-class South London girl is the only one of her female characters who doesn't quite succumb to the charms of the womanising dandy—she's both traditional (down to earth, in contact with reality) and new, an uninvolved, child-like figure—but she too is symbolically crucified and is finally left on her own pick up the broken pieces of her life.

Angela Carter's characters in *Shadow Dance* have been written about as recyclers, interested in the mutability of categories and values surrounding the reuse of discarded things; but it is the characters themselves who are mutable, uncertain in values and anxiously likely to be discarded by each other without a by your leave.[12] Do they care? What do they care about? They are merely would-be aesthetes whose preoccupations with objects, and with looking and sounding right, is cover for their carelessness and triviality. We are soon bored by their splits and recombinations and despise them for their heartlessness. Carter can be interestingly related to British new wave SF of the sixties, an important part of her original context and the one that gave her the confidence to be bold and inventive: it was also the means by which the forms of popular fiction entered her work. Guislayne's scar is not dissimilar to the one inflicted on the prim Miss Mavis Ming during her encounter with the Devil in Moorcock's satirical anti-feminist novel a decade later.[13] Angela Carter's women are seldom flesh and blood creatures, often literary concoctions. Her New Eve is a Monroe-like film icon, 'Black Venus'—in one of her best stories—is a version of Charles Baudelaire's Creole mistress, Jeanne Duval. In her explorations of such fantasy women and what male fantasy has made of real women she is poised between criticism and enjoyment of her own fantastic versions of them. Frozen into the positions of a mannikin in a crystal world, Angela Carter's New Eve enjoys the sense of erotic removal and position of icy observation while being an object of attention. But seeing in all these things a potential source of female power, Carter enjoys making up these weird stories about her mannikins, her dolls.[14]

If her first novel shows real socially observed characters playing in a shadow-show world of tried on roles and representations, her second, *The Magic Toyshop*, continues with this theme but turns the world of representations itself into a kind of inescapable dolls house, a more or less malevolent maze of violent sexualised images out of which her adolescent heroine Melanie must try and find her way As a country child in a large middle-class house, she and her two siblings, Victoria and Jonathon, find themselves living in a kind of historical phantasmagoria of ships in bottles, Biggles books, fairy tales and dressing up clothes, looked after by a gothically old, fat and ugly serving woman, Mrs Rundle, a refugee from Mervyn Peake, while their parents, a successful writer and his wife, tour America. Melanie cups her breasts, which are 'tipped as pinkly as the twitching noses of rabbits'[15] and stares out at the apple tree and the red, swollen moon. She has never been kissed, but will find her way out of the charged narcissism of girlhood into a world of puppets and power-relationships—to find that the world of adult representations is literally just another doll's house.

When her parents are killed in a mysterious air-crash, Melanie believes she killed her mother, dresses up in her wedding dress, and following her breakdown the children become the reluctant wards of Uncle Philip and his extended family in London. Uncle Philip is the bitter genius behind a scarcely visited exotic toyshop, a man who once sent his niece a jack-in-the-box with a caricature of herself to pop out and frighten her. Uncle Philip proves to be a power-obsessed and cruel surrogate father, an artist who spends his time making giant puppets for his puppet theatre and attempting to manipulate his family as though they are the same. Model-making is the family's main activity. They live in a world without television and radio and with precious few outside contacts, a world which refuses public cultural representations: the mad toymaker is too egotistical even to co-operate with the Sunday-supplement journalist who wishes to publicise his work as a 'unique fusion of folk and pop art'.[16] Melanie makes friends with Finn, a young Irishman of musical ability and twinkling eye who works at making toys for the shop, but Uncle Philip, obsessed with the spectacles he obsessively creates, attempts to destroy their innocent relationship by pushing Finn to deflower her.

> This crazy world whirled about her, men and women dwarfed by toys, where even the birds were mechanical and the few human figures were masked and played musical instruments in the small and terrible hours of the night into which she had been thrust. She was in the night again, and the doll was herself.[17]

Melanie avoids Finn's embraces, although she is attracted to him, and the novel proceeds with dream-like Ovidian Metamorphoses of raped swans and toppling statues of Queen Victoria and fantasies in which they are romantically fused; but Melanie cannot escape from the self-consciousness of being observed, an object of the male gaze—a pretty young girl in someone else's fantasy of her:

> She thought vaguely that they must look very striking, like a shot from a new-wave British film, locked in an embrace beside the broken statue in this dead fun palace, with the November dusk swirling around them and Finn's hair so ginger, hers so black, spun together by the soft little hands of a tiny wind, yellow and black hairs tangled together. She wished someone was watching them, to appreciate them, or that she herself was watching them, Finn kissing this black-haired young girl, from a bush a hundred yards away. Then it would seem romantic.[18]

Tristan and Isolde references surround them like a dark wood: Finn is Irish, they are of different tribes, she middle-class and he a dirty beatnik, they must sleep with a sword or a bolster between them, their love is cruelly encouraged but forbidden by patriarchal authority. Uncle Philip's destructiveness towards Melanie is said to be a kind of class revenge on her family, particularly on his dead brother. Finn explains: 'You represent the enemy to him, who use toilet paper and fish knives.'[19] His brother was more successful than him, and the toymaker is a working-class genius who shuns even the limited success that would put him in his place: only absolute power over others satisfies him. But, of course, he cannot have it. His wife, Auntie Margaret, betrays him, and the toyshop and all his works are destroyed in a night-time conflagration: Finn and Melanie, alone in the garden at night, free of his power but not of one more literary allusion, 'faced one another in a wild surmise' like Cortez' men in Keats' sonnet 'On First Looking into Chapman's Homer'. Now they can get down to some freely chosen sex. It's a nice, romantic ending: the young lovers are united and ready to remake their own world.

But I personally find it disappointing that in a novel about constraining representations, patriarchal erotic repression and frustrated sexual awakening, Carter's characters never seem to escape except into another paper landscape of lurid, half-familiar inventions: a fairy-tale world she continually adapts to make her fictions about female eroticism and power. It has been argued that Carter's is always a version of female erotic power designed around a male pleasure, a male gaze with which it colludes. These are clichés of Angela Carter, a writer who has been talked to death, but there is always something second hand about her inventions: she herself is a recycler. It remains to be seen whether her books will continue to resonate for the women readers of the future; I suspect their burnished old-fashioned charm will rescue them from reserve stock, that and her posthumous, A-level syllabus canonisation. As a writer on social class she is always, it seems to me, working with fixed and received categories—cheeky cockney trapeze artists and dandified bad guys. Perhaps George Dangerfield's idea about popular fiction isn't exactly right: although the realist novelists of their period aren't in any sense higher artists, they also offer a window into the soul of their times. The brilliantly realised worlds of Moorcock and Carter have multiplied and migrated into other mass media, but the retrospect they offer is of a history yet to be written: wild projections and fantasies concerning all-defining myths that are no longer so resonant, or if they are seem to lead further and further into a hall of mirrors.

Brian Aldiss' *Barefoot in the Head* is set in a post-apocalyptic world in which the youth are being led towards Chartres cathedral by a boy messiah as though on a pilgrimage to the ultimate free festival: he is probably the true source of David Bowie's leper messiah Ziggy Stardust ('he was the Naz'—i.e. Jesus of Nazareth in a hipster monologue by New York comedian Lord Buckley) and of his post-apocalyptic science-fiction vision in general on later albums like *Aladdin Sane* and *Diamond Dogs*.[20] Aldiss is not exactly a neglected figure, but tends to be largely unknown outside the world of British science-fiction, particularly of the sixties, in which he was an important figure who, like J.G. Ballard and Angela Carter, was published in Michael Moorcock's influential magazine *New Worlds*. Both Ballard and Aldiss wrote generational starship stories. Aldiss' *Non-Stop* has a classic SF plot involving escape from the tribe and its puerile synthetic apostiori religion to run hard up against the steel wall of absolute truth as a defiant young hero and heroine set to put humanity right on the forgotten purpose of its long journey to the stars. Ballard's treatment of the same theme is more mundane, more deadpan, and more menacing: he offers, for example, a brief poetic evocation of a maintenance crew deprived of any sense of time and motion who have therefore regressed to a primitive, fearful state and are inching forward, barely able to perform their function.

But it is Aldiss' brilliantly lyrical *Hothouse* that, although it is hard to locate in relation to any particular sixties anxiety, whose premise is strange and wonderful enough to immediately draw this reader into its layered allegories of human devolution and seems to have the most to say about the hopes and fears of its decade. In this novel humanity has evolved—or devolved—into small green-skinned creatures which live in the upper branches of a giant tree and spend much of their time avoiding giant poisonous insects. Intelligence has had its day on this far-future earth, which is ruled by strangely evolved insects and ambulant vegetable life-forms, wonderfully imagined and named by Aldiss. It is a grim warning that evolution can work in unexpected ways, like backwards, and that the present arrogant rulers of the earth might not always be so cocky; therefore it is a reaction against the over-confident scientism of fifties American SF. There is an early Philip K. Dick short story, his only venture into fantasy, in which sentient ants stealthily take over the earth,[21] but Aldiss' novel is a far more fully realised and more disturbing fairy world, one that might almost have been inspired by the child-like imaginings of John Clare's poem 'Insects':

> No kin they bear to labour's drudgery,
> Smoothing the velvet of the pale hedge-rose;
> And where they fly for dinner no-one knows—

The dew drops feed them not—they love the shine
Of noon, whose suns may bring them golden wine
All day they're playing in their Sunday dress—
When night reposes, for they can do no less;
Then, to the heath-bell's purple hood they fly,
And like to princes in their slumbers lie,
Secure from rain, and dropping dews, and all
In silken beds and roomy painted hall.[22]

But the life of humans who share the worlds of the insects and mutated plants in *Hothouse* is far from idle or idyllic: they have definitively fallen from grace and are now the prey of the vegetable kingdom. More intelligent than most of the other creatures of their world, they are nevertheless forced to use all of their resources for survival, and as a consequence their lives are as fragile and usually as short as those of any mayfly. Life is nasty, brutish and short for the tribes of small humans who live in the branches of the Banyan tree, and intelligence itself may no be a survival factor in a world where evolution is running backwards. It is a world in which, like the tropical rainforest Brian Aldiss saw on active service in Burma during the second world war, every form of life is a predator. It is a novel that has a complex view of evolution and of the relationships between instinctual, natural selection and ratiocination, and as the book progresses we meet a wide variety of rudimentary human types, from the matriarchal warrior bands who live in the treetops, to the flymen who gain their wings as a response to radiation on a hazardous journey to the moon aboard a traverser—a mile-long drifting vegetable creature that regularly floats between the earth (the heavy world) and its satellite (the true world), to the tribe of singing herders who live in the shadow of the Black Mouth, to the silly tummy-belly men, the Fishers, who are harnessed to giant plant-trees by their long green tails and lack all independent volition, to the dog-like Sharp-furs, the Arablers and the all-wise Sodal Ye, part-man, part-fish, who knows all and has cunningly enslaved them all.

Aldiss' starting point and inspiration may have been Alexander Pope's *Essay on Man*, a poem of the English Enlightenment which seeks to vindicate the ways of God to Man, expounding Creation as the Great Chain of Being, with humanity at its summit: Pope's hierarchy of beings is basically medieval Christian, but also humanist as it seeks to rationalise endless struggles in Nature and the human world, along with the seeming infinity of gradations and types of being, to express a duly optimistic vision of natural hierarchies and dynamic progress under the guidance of a Divinely provided Reason:

Far as creation's ample range extends,
The scale of sensual, mental powers ascends:
Mark how it mounts, to man's imperial race,
From the green myriads in the peopl'd grass:
What modes of sight betwixt each wide extreme,
The mole's dim curtain and the lynx's beam:
Of smell, the headlong lioness between,
And hound sagacious on the tainted green:
Of hearing, from the life that fills the flood,
To that which warbles through the vernal wood:
The spider's touch, how exquisitely fine!
Feels at each thread and lives along the line:
In the nice bee, what sense so subtly true
From poisonous herbs extracts the healing dew:
How instinct varies in the groveling swine,
Compared, half-reasoning Elephant, with thine![23]

Pope's vision of Nature is so excessive, so detailed and full of gusto in expression that it threatens to overturn the hierarchy it composes; certainly it is more to the glory of man than God, and is in particular a hymn to the cleverness of he who composed it, and never altogether without the irony that an unlovely hunchback, a poet-spider with a fine touch, should find himself the crown of creation—he celebrates the particularity of the beings he enumerates, and their super-human faculties. Aldiss' sense of the sheer proliferativeness of Nature is touched by Pope's 'All matter quick, and bursting into birth', but his attempt to describe and overturn all his creaturely hierarchies begins by replacing them with semi-sentient vegetables. The bug-like humans who live in the upper branches of the forest are matriarchal: women customarily lead and are more numerous; men are prized for their strength and for sexual reproduction. But it is the emergence of one man, Gren, who is both adventurous and unable to take wrong orders, that leads to his expulsion from the group and to most of the exploration and adventures in *Hothouse.* In this sense it is an heroic fantasy, a little like one of Moorcock's early books, full of fighting and slaying and journeying and led by a strong male protagonist. But Aldiss has a more complex and nuanced view of the relations between men and women, if ultimately a biologistic one. The women of the forest certainly get to do their fair share of slaying: Lily-yo and Toy lead by virtue of their physical bravery and astuteness and are shown to be generally more flexible and intelligent too; but amongst the herders more traditional sex roles seem to be in place. It is here that Gren picks up his final mate, Yattmur, and their arguments provide much of the dramatic tension in the remainder of the novel. He also picks up something else—an intelligent parasitic fungus, the morel, which is able to burrow deep into his species memory, extract the history of humanity and its sudden drastic curtailment, and which thereafter harries Gren onwards from place to place on a new but ill-defined quest, a new ascent of man to his former glory.[24]

Richard Dawkins' *The Selfish Gene* suggests that evolutionary mutations are not directed by instincts of species survival, as more communitarian proponents of Darwinism suggest, seeking to put a social-democratic gloss on the survival of the fittest, but by the short term selfish goals of personal survival of individual specimens, so that competitive individualism and the Hobbesian war of every man against every man are indeed Nature's way.[25] *Hothouse* appears to agree with this to some degree, but Aldiss recognises the necessity of intelligence and the higher plan in evolution, in the crippled Captives on the moon who direct the flymen's raids on the heavy world—to steal human young for transportation to their moon colony, and in the parasitic morel fungus which is acting out of short term self-interest but is able to drag humanity's history out of Gen's unconscious, inadvertently teaches it to him, and supplies a rhetoric of collective aspiration to motivate his host and drive humanity on in its long slow ascent to regain the stars. Thus he finds a way to make social-evolutionism or ideas of progress both the self-interested fictions of interested would-be leaders and a genuine motor of evolutionary change. What it clear is that both co-operation and initiative are necessary. Neither the witless mumminess of the tummy-belly men, nor the sniggering yaps and rending teeth of the Sharp-furs will lead anywhere, except to the elimination of the former by the latter. The beauty of this book is that in trying to tell the story of evolution in a childish adventure story, it manages to suggest some of the complexity of humanity's destiny and to convey the idea that there is always something to pull for: and if it's between you and a bug or a giant stick of celery, you should kill them without a moment's hesitation.

Aldiss' idea that intelligence itself might be parasitic, not strictly necessary, alien, with its own agenda that is not in the direct interests of its bearers, is a darkly amusing twist on evolutionary theory, and he extracts from it as much comedy as horror, its human types all too recognisable from everyday experience. Gren is a little white bull of the far future who is being used and consumed by his parasitic fungus of intelligence, but at least the cancerous morel, speaking in his mind with its characteristic twang, gets him out into the arena of bravery and tells him where and when to strike most effectively. Brian Aldiss is good at describing such savagery, and brilliant at realising new sports and variations on vegetable life that have taken the place and the functions of animals in his endlessly proliferative backward evolution. Thus have the oak trees invented gun powder by sucking up charcoal and sulphur from underground, forming it into giant acorns with which to bombard the creatures that scuttle beneath their boughs, and letting down cages to imprison prey they will later feed on as it rots. The humans are armed only with sharpened thorns, but become skilled at slicing through the green snaking tendons and sucker-pods of the thousand other species that would entrap them and drain their life-force, so that they 'fall to the green'.

J.G. Ballard's early novels *The Drowned World, The Drought* and *The Crystal World* are extensions of a kind of apocalyptic popular fiction and film that had become current again in the previous decade, but in Ballard's versions these reifications of apocalyptic fears offer an emptied world as a kind of surrealist-influenced dreamscape, on the one hand desertified, on the other inundated, tropical, and in his most extreme case frozen into a kind of crystalline mineral perfection by a leak from a research institute that turns everything into art, like 'Europe After the Rain', the Max Ernst painting that seems to suggest this particular vision. Nothing can live in this world, everything is frozen into three-dimensional tableaux and thus, he would have us believe, they are to become one with God. Except that, of course, Ballard does not believe in God, so his stories, tangentially commenting on the human uses of religion and myth, must more accurately be said to concerned with the perversity of the human imagination and the persistence of dark forces and impulses beneath the surfaces of technological and social progress.

His early story 'The Garden of Time' addresses hopes of infinite human progress through genetic manipulation when scientists working at a research institute find a way of activating the two 'silent genes' in various organisms, leading to various extreme mutations: walking orchids, giant lead-filled bugs, and oddly visionary humans. But extraterrestrials, communicating by means of a countdown on tickertape, suggest that what is on the cards for humanity isn't a giant leap forward but galloping entropy: the silent genes turn out to be a kind of auto-destruct button that leads not to the stars but to species immolation.[26] 'The Flowers of Time' introduces the image of crystallisation in Ballard's work in a tellingly reactionary comment on the advance of 'the masses'. It is influenced by Edmund Wilson's powerful study of modernism, *Axel's Castle*, in which the American critic defines the social outlook of the aesthetic movement by writing about the aristocratic leading character of a late nineteenth century French prose work by Villiers de L'Isle-Adam, one Axel, who contracts a suicide pact with his wife, famously declaring: 'Live? Our servants will do that for us.'[27] In Ballard's version of the story Axel and his beautiful doll-like wife pluck the last of the exquisite crystal orchids in their garden as the ravening masses of advancing revolutionary democracy overwhelm their world; all beautiful, useless things are certain to be destroyed forever, and only a pair of ravishing frozen statues are left, unnoticed before a ruined castle. Edmund Wilson's book, and this essay in particular, which also treats of Rimbaud, seems to have had a profound effect on him.

The most poetic of Ballard's early novels and the one which most definitively breaks with the conventional science fiction disaster excursion to become something else entirely, is set in Africa and narrated by Sanders (Sanders of the River from the imperial adventure fictions of Edgar Wallace). *The Crystal World* queasily imagines, well, a crystallised jungle, is closer to the prose poetry of Saint-John Perse or earlier French symbolist poets than to the swashbuckling quest-romances of H. Rider Haggard's *King Solomon's Mines* or *She*, and the main pleasure to be had from the book lies in Ballard's descriptions of the jewelled dark continent and its human and animal inhabitants. The point is that the Africa that Baudelaire imagined in Jeanne Duval's hair—in 'A Hemisphere in a Head of Hair'[28]—of which Arthur Rimbaud fantasised in his boyhood poems and eventually, disappointingly, emigrated to, has been literally taken over by the European imagination, and therefore can no longer grow, develop, and be a real place in which people live, only a fantasy landscape of crunchy things and heraldic crocodiles.

Crystallisation is a metaphor for imperialism, a subtle and highly seductive one in that we can't help but be entranced by the beauty of the crystal jungle, or the beauty of the Africans who threaten to appear in it as exotic sex show performers, but thankfully never quite do: a chapter heading, 'the mulatto on the catwalks', speaks of fashion, and prostitution; its content serves only to move the story along. There are no explicitly sexualised bodies in *The Crystal World*, only the transmogrified body of Africa itself; but nevertheless it is a novel that broods about the European objectification of Africa and Africans, and luxuriates in it at length in exquisite prose poetry. Crystallisation sacralises, reveals the hand of God in the creation, the signature on the underside of every leaf: its beauty impossible to refuse but bearing a terrible cost for those who are crucified by it. In Rimbaud's 'Après le déluge' 'dream flowers tinkle, burst, illuminate' and the Hotel Splendide opens up for business in the ruins of Europe.[29] Ballard began to explore the meaning of such dream flowers in slightly earlier stories like 'The Garden of Time'; *The Crystal World* is also about a timeless, frozen world—in which the real problems of Africa: underdevelopment and deprivation, leprosy and starvation—are frozen into grotesque aesthetic tableaux. There is also a simpler, non-literary associative chain underlying its central images—from crystallised fruit to 'Strange Fruit' (the Billie Holiday song about lynchings in the American South)—and its crystallisations and time distortions obviously have their origin in early experiences of LSD. It is also rewrite of Conrad's *Heart of Darkness* (as was his later novel, *The Day of Creation*) and is set amongst African independence struggles in which 'the horror' becomes more fully visible as that of the rapaciously exploitative European imagination:

> ...but what most surprised me, Paul, was the extent to which I as prepared for the crystallization of the forest—the crystalline trees hanging like icons in those luminous caverns, the jewelled casements of the leaves overhead, fused into a lattice of prisms, through which the sun shone in a thousand rainbows, the birds and crocodiles frozen into grotesque postures like heraldic beasts carved from jade and quartz—what was really remarkable was the extent to which I accepted all these wonders as part of the natural order of things, part of the inward pattern of the universe.[30]

Like much of J.G. Ballard's work, *The Crystal World* retains the ghostly structure of an old-fashioned detective or adventure fiction. *The Atrocity Exhibition*, a densely-woven novel of linked stories broken down into captioned paragraphs, draws closer to the work of Willian Burroughs in its sense of disorientation and non-linearity, but also comments more directly on its times with chapters entitled 'Why I Want to Fuck Ronald Reagan' and 'The Assassination of John F. Kennedy Considered As A Downhill Car Race'. It also crystallises Ballard's interest in medicine and psychopathology and first throws up the themes that will come to fruition in his much celebrated novel about sexuality and automobiles. His technique in *Crash* as elsewhere is to take a cultural theme and to realise it literally—here a club is dedicated to car crashes and sex—producing in this and most other cases a series of scenarios so preposterously absurd as to be merely laughable to some readers. It is as though he is testing his ability to make such preposterous scenarios stick, to make his readers take these ridiculous overblown allegories seriously, which he does by means of a kind of earnest deadpan narration that is also reminiscent of William Burroughs. Are we really expected to take the theories about addiction of Dr Dent in *Naked Lunch* seriously? Perhaps not. But the author himself seems to take them seriously, and if we don't at least entertain them we are just as unlikely to get the ramifications of Burroughs' metaphors of addiction, language and control that proliferate through his later books: so it often is with Ballard's mock theorising.

Concrete Island is a 'state of the nation' novel that attempts to analyse British society in microcosm by means of an allegory based on Defoe's *Robinson Crusoe*. How far does he succeed and what is his diagnosis? Defoe's novel is another early example of the English Enlightenment; like Pope's *Essay on Man* it combines an enthusiasm for reason with a sense of the naturalness and inevitability of class (and racial) hierarchies and, in this particular case, an unshakeable belief in the ultimate superiority of the enterprising English middle-classes. 'The will is the strong blind man who carries on his shoulders the lame man who can see,' Schopenhauer wrote in *The World as Will and Representation*[31]—and at the novel's climax the 'working-class' circus strong man carries the relatively sharp-witted dwarf who represents the lower middle class (or is it the crippled labour movement?) to enable the stranded white middle-class male hero to escape from the island and reassume power in the real world. The woman has subordinated both in the first place, but ultimately they become the tool of the alpha middle-class male whom they help to overcome her and to escape from the traffic island on which his car accident has deposited him. In the midst of all this broken modernity we find ourselves in a marginal social space in the company of an author whose sense of social place is an inflexibly feudal as any eighteenth of nineteenth century writer, with the possible exception of his 'new' woman' character: she is really the 'old-young-woman' who manipulates and subordinates all men by means of her mysterious sexual power; this presiding female spirit of the abandoned cinema somehow connected to the outside world turns out to be a modern version of Rider Haggard's *She*. 'Er indoors, as *Minder*'s Arthur Daley jocularly christened this most powerful and enduring of female archetypes. The little woman. The angel of the household. She who must be obeyed. Ballard's powerful little woman character is both modern—an urban hippie or early punk—and highly traditional in the sources of her power over the men in her world. But to her withheld, intriguing sexuality Ballard adds a devious—and eternal—female mind; and a detachment we are constrained to find chilling.[32]

Ballard is wildly inaccurate as a prophet of the early twenty-first century: 'Vietnam, the first TV war, had given the viewers all the excitement of live transmissions from the battlefield, but wars in general, not to mention newsworthy activity of any kind, had died out as the world's population devoted itself almost exclusively to watching television.'[33] Later he developed into an English version of the deadpan Yankee comedian, but the development of this slight story with a theological twist shows this was always an element in his fiction. War didn't die out and he makes no interesting political prediction, but we did get global satellite saturation and the world's media companies indeed coagulated into a few conglomerates offering standard substandard fare, so he was a little bit right. No wars, but the desire to watch carnage survives, demonstrated by global mass audiences for shows revisiting great battles of the past following the discovery of time travel. Ballard has fun with this; it's a light piece with none of the crystalline poetry and genuine nightmarish urgency of his best early work, but this makes his basic attitude to modernity and progress plain. In Ballard's writing technological advance and the social possibilities it throws up are always stymied by good old bad old unchanging humanity and its motives. Deadpan is frequently deployed in that strain of jovial mock-utopianism in Ballard, when he wants us to believe he is a wide-eyed enthusiast of modernity. He is a dystopian of Swiftian tendency, pretending to find the suburbanisation of the world and a resultant affectless removal from any face to face experience a highly exciting prospect, full of possibilities and enjoyable anxieties. His novels and stories show that it isn't so wonderful: in their attempts to find new ways of connecting, of being social, his often cardboard characters reveal their affectlessness, their anomie, their perversity and their relentless drive for individual self-gratification and destructive power over others. Ballard is an orthodox Freudian, ahistorical and biologistic, with a Nietzchean streak and an strong accent on Thanatos and polymorphous perversity. Sublimation didn't really work as far as he is concerned. He often likes to draw on Enlightenment thinkers, but it is usually only to mock and negate their ideals. However, without their intellectual backbone his fictions would be so much wibbly-wobbly jelly; but this thoroughgoing questioning of the Enlightenment strongly links him both to surrealism and to later, post-modernist thinkers.

Did Ballard have a decisive influence on Jean Baudrillard, the once-fashionable French philosophical exponent of simulacra and virtual wars and the Disneyfication of the world?[34] It would appear so, and may be why the most celebrated cultural critic of the last decade of the twentieth century often seems to be exaggerating for rhetorical effect: he is another deadpan comic pretending that reality no longer exists. Both could be described as conservative cultural critics in disguise, even as radical conservatives, but that usually entails a nostalgia for feudalism which Ballard is well able to draw into his manic dystopian visions. But I think we can discount Ballard's seriousness on this or most of his points. After all, he hasn't embraced militant Islam, but in his old age has produced a series of mordant satires on the kinds of gated communities he might like to retire to and spy on his neighbours. These have moats and drawbridges, uniformed guards, rigid social hierarchies, and within their controlled confines lords and ladies are allowed to indulge their polymorphous perversity to the hilt. The strongest of them, *Cocaine Nights* and, especially, *Super-Cannes*, are amusingly cynical books exploring utopianism and the meaning of the social contract, quite as good, or to my mind better, than most of his earlier, younger work, and more youthful in spirit. Like other science fiction and fantasy writers of the sixties, he seemed to be the first of something, but may have been amongst the last, and dystopian ideas that once seemed startlingly prophetic haven't escaped the impress of the times which called them forth. They influenced the styles of the future, but at the cost of soon looking as quaint as a sparking robot in the window of an antique toyshop.

Ballard didn't often show an interest in working-class people; it was mainly the diseased middle-class psyche that appealed to him. *Crash*'s spliff-toking stock-car driver suckles his children on his man-boobs, but his final novel *Kingdom Come* weaves another pretty tale of a bad new working-class nationalism about to spew forth from the shopping malls of Surrey, one in particular near the site of the old Brooklands racetrack of the 1920s, which he models on the 'giant' Bentalls mall in Kingston-upon-Thames.[35] I often used to visit Bentalls with my parents when it was a department store; a many-levelled magnet to us and many others. A generation before wide-shouldered spivs traded nylons and off-ration butter in the milk bar, and posher ladies had bought hats or lampshades or bloomers or had their fortunes told in its intriguingly subdivided arcadian emporia since Edwardian times. I well remember annually visiting Father Christmas in his grotto there, but for Ballard its expansion into a mall suggested a sinister night-time rendezvous for a shadowy Fascist group troubled by the invasion of their suburban living space by Moslem families. Fair enough, you might say, and indeed such racist attitudes are fairly commonplace in the home counties: but this is comedy that offers nothing of genuine import about the interstices of what George Orwell once called 'the sleekest countryside in the world'; and opportunist writers who offer any more of this on the basis that they are plumbing the depths of British realities will unwittingly be contributing to a phony and unaccountable kind of journalism: derivative, paper thin, shallow dross that will blow away, eventually, like a swatch of discarded roadside rubbish glimpsed once as a youthful passenger on a summer's car journey down the Portsmouth Road. Or maybe not.

After reading *Kingdom Come* with these misgivings, I wrote to J.G. Ballard, enclosing a copy of my own small book, *Cyclomotors*, which is set in the same area, and asking if he thought we were really all that bad. And soon enough the following gracious postcard arrived:

22/9/06

Dear John Muckle,

Many thanks for *Cyclomotors*, which I look forward to reading. Are we that bad? Probably not, but who knows? There's something about English shopping malls—in particular the Bentalls Centre at Kingston—which worries me—I hope I'm wrong.

Best wishes
J.G. Ballard[36]

Chapter Nine

Tally Boys and Media Tarts: Jack Trevor Story

Jack Trevor Story's *Live Now, Pay Later*, like Joyce's *Ulysses* before it, opens with a scene of shaving and some reflections on the dispensability of women. Like Stephen Dedalas and Buck Mulligan before him, and like Bill Naughton's Alfie, there is something repellently self-satisfied about tally-boy Albert as he completes his toilet in his cramped bachelor bedsit and prepares to hit the street in search of the things that make him happy and provide his reason for existing: money and girls, girls and money. Oh, and girls. '"There are two sorts of people in the world," he used to tell his mother; "slaves and masters." His mother, by the time he was fifteen, was already aware of this fact.' His racism shows up on the second page in a bit of unlikely bantering repartee on his way out with the head of the black family who have moved in downstairs. Or maybe it isn't so unlikely and is accurate to its time and place—how do we ever know in novels? What we do know is what motivates Albert is being perennially broke due to his self-employment. His boss, Mr Callendar, likes to keep the boys feeling hungry and insecure so that they try harder to 'git the goods in the 'ouse':

> The good tally-boy was the man who enjoyed the sharp suit and the van and a pocketful of other people's money, the handling of new shiny goods and the vicarious pleasure—not always vicarious—of chatting up other people's wives while the children were at school. The good tally-boy possessed elements of delinquency, amorality and furtive adventure; showmanship, self-delusion, and self-aggrandizement. The good tally-boy was perennially and incurably improvident; when he bullied a woman for her arrears he really needed the money.[1]

Albert Argyle's calculated smarm and the imagined power it gives him over other people, is, like Alfie's more famous charm, chiefly directed towards women: but unlike Bill Naughton's Alfie Elkins his motives are directly economic. Story is matchless on the mentality of the tally-boy; Alfie is a class act compared to Albert and his colleagues, partly because their storyteller is far more cynical about his characters, possibly he is even as cynical as they are. *Live Now, Pay Later* presents a world in which everyone is cynical about everyone else, particularly if they are men. Mr Callendar despises both his employees and his customers; the tally-boys look down on the women they smarm and insinuate and manipulate into surrendering their housekeeping—and everything else—and these customers, as well as despising the neighbours with whom they are trying to keep up, tend to look down on the vulgarity of the tally-boys. However, many of the women are easily hypnotised. Mr Callendar's golf partner, Reginald Corby, independent candidate for the local council maps out the political lie of the land as they tee off on the Labour-Council golf course:

> 'Second-hand aristocracy, old boy, that's what they are. Biggest snobs in the country today, the working-class. They don't want that "living wage for the working man" stuff any more. Call anybody a working man today and he's insulted. He surrounds himself with the left-offs of his betters—second-hand Jaguars made for somebody else, big houses made for gentlemen, refrigerators, washing machines—well, you know better than I do. Half the riding schools are full of snotty-nosed gorblimey kids from the council houses—you don't know where you are these days. No quality anymore, Cally.'[2]

The old labour allegiances are breaking down, local politics is no more than an insider carve-up of lucrative building contracts anyway, and the real concerns of the community—that their town be kept white—are impossible to address on a public platform by any politician who doesn't wish to be labelled a fascist. What can these greedy, stupid newly affluent working-class snobs be promised that they don't already own? The trick is to appeal to their pretended sentiments. Callendar suggests drinking troughs for dogs on every corner, and Reggie regards this as an imaginative campaigning idea that will position him nicely as an 'idealist' for the electorate. Forty-years after it was written *Live Now, Pay Later* might have been a template for many a political novel about the Essex contingent of the bad new working-class, but has had few sequels, combining as it does the unsayable with the unsaleable, and offering the point of view of an Essex working-class novelist who appears to enjoy a sour, cheery contempt for the people about whom he is writing.

Story's third-person, expository style withholds sympathy from his characters; his aim is to anatomise rather than empathise; they are insinuating but unable to insinuate themselves into our affections. Many sexually ambitious young men have modelled themselves on Alfie; Albert and his colleagues Jeff and Arnold (a former car salesman whom Callendar admires for having narrowly escaped imprisonment) can have inspired few to follow in their doorstepping footsteps. An earlier English novel to explore the world of the salesman was Julian MacLaren-Ross' *Of Love and Hunger,* published in the late forties but dealing with a thirties seaside boarding house world. Its salesman is a down-at-heel charmer who sells vacuum cleaners and who, like Albert, has a romantic weakness for women, and like another of Story's tally-boys, a patina of assumed poshness. With its undercurrent of hopeless romantic longing Maclaren Ross' novel bears certain resemblances to George Orwell's *Keep the Aspidistra Flying*, dropped down a notch of two on the social scale (Gordon Comstock is a copywriter, a salesman in print rather than on the doorstep), and it somewhat unconvincingly pitches English social realities and a new culture of consumerism again socialist values.

What is so melancholy about the life of a salesman or an adman are the home truths it reveals about what seems to make human beings tick. For all its brash cynicism, Story's novel therefore harks back to the political and literary context of the thirties, like so many novels of its era, a context which it reviews and updates. What is new is its sheer knowing disparagement of the new working-class consumers who are at its centre: selling is lying, and you don't habitually lie to people for whom you have any great respect. And yet these novels, and Story's is a vivid, unsparing, sharp piece of comic writing, unique in its focus on the early phase of post-war working-class consumerism, do manage to tell us a large part of what keeps the wheels of commerce turning: they tell us what really makes the world go round and the uses to which the information gathered by mass observers and focus groups alike is normally put. The cynicism of the salesman is hard to defeat except by slamming the door in his face, an act of renunciation which few manage—and why should they if they want the goods and the air of generalised sexual promise that can make ordinary life float above the mundane?

Albert is sufficiently cynical to know that sincerity pays off but remains susceptible enough to believe his own lines: he is as overburdened with hire-purchase debt as any of his customers. What has made Albert into Callendar's best salesman are the very qualities which guarantee that his boss and his colleagues will never take him seriously: he is empathetic and a believer, even a poet of working-class consumerism. Contrasting him to an older salesman, Jeff, a moustachioed monster who has endured from the pre-war days of salesmanship, Jack Trevor Story compares them in terms of masculine and feminine qualities:

> Albert could fall in love several times a week, twice in a day; but Jeff Jeffries didn't know what it was. On the interpolated line between masculine and feminine Jeff Jeffries was masculine; he had no woman in him; he had never felt the thrill of a touch of hands or a gaze of eyes, never sensed the woman's need for tenderness or fulfilment or protection. Love as he understood it was soppy, un-English and embarrassing—as any decent, full-

blooded, rugger-playing boy knew. Jeff Jeffries could cut into one of Albert's many soliloquies about a pretty girl he had seen walking in the sun with: 'But did you get there old chappy, that's the point!'

But it wasn't the point and there was the difference between them.[3]

For Albert, or for Alfie—who may have been modelled on Jack Trevor Story's character but definitely stands on exactly the same ground as a male type—there is always a further point, a purpose hard to pin down and elusive, meanings piled up in the future like a warehouse full of explanatory goods, ill-grasped and forever deferred, as nebulously defined as the exact extent of his hire-purchase debts. Story's suggestion that Albert is not quite a man (although Jeff Jefffries is scarcely an inspiring role model) may be quite simply explained by pointing out that he is still a boy: a quite clever boy who has been spoiled by his mother and allowed to get away with loafing and dreaming. Unlike Alfie he is apt to be taken in by women, to be taken for an expensive ride as surely as he believes he is conning his housewives and to spend twenty pounds on attempting (and failing) to seduce a girl in a striking green coat he has seen getting on a bus and followed around for a day in the firm's Morris Minor van.

For many of the women, of course, it's often all a bit of a lark, especially if, like Mrs Gallety, 'her deceptively sleepy eyes were headlamps on an intelligent brain and a cynical sense of humour. She was a unilateralist from way back and had sat down tenaciously with the best of them in all sorts of uncomfortable places.' Mrs Gallety turns seductress, entraps Jeff Jeffries in a close clinch, immediately accuses him of assault, backed up by her neighbour, and the two of them con a demonstration Wondersew machine out of him for nothing. 'It would be something to laugh about at the next pacifist demonstration.' This amusing scene turns Mrs Gallety and her friend Daisy into somewhat unlikely proto-feminist CNDers: subversives through and through, they will stop at nothing to get their way. If they can outwit Callendar's second best salesman's hands-on technique for 'gittin' the goods in the 'ouse' what chance do naive governments have of insinuating all those shiny new Polaris missiles across their thresholds?

For elderly female subversives death can be another handy way of evading the salesman, or else they might subvert his techniques by preferring a noisy vacuum cleaner to one that's 'as silent as a kiss' because the racket it makes is 'like fighting back' against the pneumatic drills and concrete mixers of the developers who are chopping down ancient trees, knocking down old cottages and throwing up new housing around them. Jack Trevor Story's sense of what is at play in the bored suburbs is broad, observant but played for laughs. Whether it is the woman whose entire house is furnished with goods she has acquired part-exchange for sex with willing tally-boys, the philandering Callendar and his naïve hero-worshipping wife, the vulnerability and sense of social inferiority of posh local council candidate Reginald Corby's working-class wife, Story's is a reliably low estimate of the denizens of the human fishpond. One can either be a slave or a master—it's shag or be shagged, and dog eat dog in the world of the cockroach. It is sometimes difficult to say which sex Jack Trevor Story has the lower estimate of—although women are generally sympathised with—but class war of a kind is always working its none too subtle way through this novel:

> 'Of course, they're all phoney as arse-oles,' Albert said, 'if you'll forgive le mot juste. I mean, they're as lady-like as hell on sherry, but you get a few vintage ciders into them when the old man's not around and see 'em get their finger-nails into your back.'[4]

Everybody on the council estates and golf courses of this small suburban town is class-obsessed and cruel things are done in the name of small social increments and distinctions that would be meaningless to those a few rungs further up Raymond Williams' ladder. On the other hand, everyone covets the same consumer goods and buys from the same catalogue, a point which Williams approaches in a different way when he declares that working-class people don't aspire to be middle-class as some sort of social or cultural possession, they simply want what middle-class people have in the way of material goods and income levels. In *Live Now, Pay Later* everybody wants the same things and 'class' attitudes, snobberies, are social markers of how many of these things you have managed to obtain. Believers in the reality of 'class' values can include people who are as much victims of them as those tally-boys and their customers who have been taken in by the aura surrounding new consumer goods. The women who believe in their husbands, the women who believe their competition with the neighbours is meaningful, and the men who believe what women tell them. A fool in this world is anyone who believes in love in any form; to be wise is to be a disenchanted manipulator, an imposter in a fallen world that doesn't appear to know it's fallen, and in which imposition is so commonplace as to be strictly speaking unnecessary.

Albert reaches for *le mot juste* as others might reach for the Brylcreem: 'When people started behaving like human beings he ran out of patter.'[5] But his kindness towards Joyce Corby allays her sense of inferiority as an 11-plus failure with the thought that she is both in the right and in the majority, and that, chosen as a beauty queen by her politically ambitious saloon bar snob of a husband, she is more than justified to think herself good enough as she is and that her 'inter-marriage was wrong'.[6] Albert's sense of women, and of what he needs from them, is defined above all in his relationships with Grace, a friend's wife one of whose children he has fathered, and Treasure, a girlfriend whom he has acrimoniously split with before the novel begins. There is a milkiness and cleanness and underneath nakedness about Grace that, in their scenes together, shows how the combined roles of mother, lover and intimate friend appeal to him, and in a sense define him. He is a familiar of the world of women, chooses their clothes, fixes their hair, sometimes fathers their children, but is not ultimately marriageable—partly because he doesn't want to be—partly because they perceive him as too selfish: 'he got all he wanted and went.' But, on the other hand, there is a quality in him as a lover that women recognise and want, accepting his blithe lack of responsibility and what passes for his honesty without too much pain: 'Take care of yourself was a polite cliché to all except those who loved and then it was a sacred responsibility.'

Live Now, Pay Later reads somewhat like a novelised film script in the rapid way it introduces, defines and suspends characters for later plot use. Its storytelling has the efficiency and symmetry of a film and a certain resulting shallowness of characterisation make for a reading experience that often offers little more than cynical laughs. Jack Trevor Story's Albert Argyle series began as a script-adaptation of prolific Australian writer Jack Lindsay's *All on the Never-Never* (1961). Lindsay published 170 books in his long writing life; Story didn't quite match his level of output, but there's an irony in the fact that the best known character of this most singular British novelist was poached from another man's book. If Albert inspired Alfie, and half-Australian Colin MacInnes 'defined' both African immigrant experience and the Soho scene behind early British pop music, and Sid James was really South African, whole vistas of imposition and theft begin to unfold in British definitions of working-experience. It's a toe-curlingly patronising area—all about as authentic as Ed Miliband's accent.

The film that was made of it is little known; but it's subject matter and central character so closely resemble the blockbusting and definitive *Alfie* a couple of years later that it is unsurprising it should have completely disappeared from sight. Casting may not have been successful, and the novel's biting tone is hard to reconcile with a light-hearted sex comedy. It may well have been a model for Alfie, a test run, a noisier demonstration model quickly superseded by Michael Caine's star performance, with its perfect and smooth as a kiss delivery. Story's novel is a kaleidoscopic one that manages to block in an entire sense of small town society, the sex war, consumerism, and social class, in a little over 150 pages.

An example of this kind of plotting is seen when the narrative steps away for a moment from the world of the tally-boys and their boss into an arena where it is women who are fully in charge. The local secretarial agency is a paper thin cover for a call-girl operation run almost inadvertently by the respectable Miss Alcott, a perennially innocent Victorian lady whose card index of temps is a bulging portfolio of young women who are in higher demand for their sexual services than their typing skills, and it is through this business that many raise the extra cash to keep up their hire purchase payments to the tally-boys. Miss Alcott has stumbled into prostitution after her naivety led her into trouble with the police over a manuscript of pornographic poems she typed and duplicated while remaining in the dark as to their meaning: their author turns out to have been none other than that poet among tally-boys, Albert. Everyone is at it, but there is little that is joyous in sexuality. The novel's sense of a class war comes to a head in the police investigation that follows Joyce Corby's accidental death. Albert is vindictively determined to lay her death at the feet of her husband at a coroner's inquest, but Callendar attempts to bribe him out of this in solidarity with his grammar school golf course chum Reginald. The local police, however, eleven-plus failures to a man, automatically side with Albert against the snotty grammar school types who run the town and whose attitudes are so graphically represented throughout:

> 'And another thing that gives them away is their windows,' said Mrs Wisbech. 'You don't have to meet the people just look at their bedroom windows. The working-class, no matter what kind of mansion they may be in, always block out their windows with the ugly back of a dressing table… they prefer themselves to the view or the daylight,' the woman said. 'Complete lack of aesthetic feeling, you see—no amount of money will ever give them that.'
> 'And they always vote Conservative,' said Mr. Wisbech, 'It's a kind of defence, I suppose. Not that class bothers me, mind you—it's a completely classless society nowadays.'[7]

Albert's would-be nemesis and one of the few women in the book to consistently fight back against the male-dominated small-town society is his vindictively vengeful ex-girlfriend,Treasure, whom he has exploited and forced to miscarry their child. However, she is Albert's Achilles' heel because in his way he is still in love with her. Her ways of seeking revenge aren't as subtle as the manoeuvres of the women who entrap Jeff Jeffries and threaten him with an assault charge. Treasure smashes up Callendar's warehouse, approaches the police with accusations that Albert is a murderer—he pushed Mrs Corby out of the window—but the untruth of this aside, the police are full of male solidarity for Albert. It's clear that a woman has no chance of being believed or taken seriously by them. Treasure's berserk behaviour is her only outlet and as good a way of seeking justice as any other. The novel ends with Albert attempting a reconciliation with Treasure, and her evasion of this in at a drunkenly priapic 'jazz party' where she offers herself up as a more or less willing rape victim in an attempt to hurt him.

We see that his romantic feelings towards Treasure are as self-deluding as the rest of his outlook and that his selfishness and gift of the gab are conditions of his survival. But there is nevertheless a certain poignancy in the emotional high-pitch at which Treasure and Albert conduct their dealings: real things are at stake, and we wish it could have been different for them. Their relationship has a ring of truth, Treasure's pain and confusion show through as human consequences of the tally boy lifestyle and the values it represents. But it is the grammar school types who come out on top, as ever, when the tally-boys' communitarian act of collecting signatures for the old people's petition against the uprooting of the sycamore tree is adopted by future councillor Reginald Corby as a more effective vote gaining council election ploy than installing all those dog-troughs.

Live Now, Pay Later is one of the few novels written about the home counties working-classes, and it is a sympathetic and clear-sighted one, funny but with a simmering anger against the injustices of social class and the corrupt king carp who continue to rule all such small ponds. It is a kind of defence of the salesman and the women who use his catalogues to get the things they want, and it offers a knockabout political critique of what George Orwell had seen coming as the consumerist 'world of shoddy' in *Coming Up For Air* thirty years earlier; but it remains a sympathetic chronicle of lives lived on the never-never and as such it is an unjustly overlooked gem of a defining period in post-war English social history. Story's cynicism, his mixed loyalties, and his refusal to sentimentalise (no-one is flattered in this book except the author) are part of what have made his work unacceptable to our later (but not much later) day: the novel speaks of continuing realities but in no acceptable political language, and beneath its cynical rapid-fire surface, it is a painful book, not one that offers much in the way of healing balms or nostrums, unless acceptance of life as it is. We end where we began. After one more screw, with his first non-paying customer of the day, Albert is late for work again.

Two more volumes of Albert Argyle's adventures followed hard on the heels of *Live Now, Pay Late*r: *Something for Nothing* and *The Urban District Lover*, novels in which Albert gets older but fails to grow up, although he acquires a wife and continues to philander. Early reviewers of Jack Trevor

Story in *The Guardian* and the *New Statesman* compared him to Sterne, Fielding and the early Evelyn Waugh. The last comparison is particularly apposite: he has Waugh's razorish disdain for most of his characters and a similar fiendish compulsion to anatomise the minutiae of social class; but Story has none of Waugh's real fury, and not much of his hungry identification with the landed aristocracy, although Story's later liking for living in caravans, a circumstance of his later autobiographical character Horace Spurgeon Fenton, might suggest something of an affinity here too. Those early reviewers praise Story for his intimate knowledge of the fringes of the lower middle class ('couldn't be more different') which says more about the Marxist inflection of the book pages of *The Guardian* and the *New Statesman* in the early sixties than the real milieu of his early books, which have small town working-class life at their centre. The trappings and pretensions of middle-class life are aspired to in the milieu of these novels, but they are only trappings, and most of Story's characters could as well be understood as gradations in the working-class: the left-liberal London art-journos couldn't countenance that such venality and loose-living existed in truly proletarian circles.

Jack Trevor Story is a more amiable writer than the Waugh of *Vile Bodies* and rather than developing towards piety he reveals himself to have more in common with his Alberts than anyone else: sex becomes his stock-in-trade, polygamous relationships with younger and younger women, and an autobiographical narrator who finances these happy, chaotic ménages by writing for film and television. His manner resembles the freewheeling storytelling of American writers like William Saroyan, whose *My Name is Aram* depicts a small town world with sympathy and gusto, and in later books, Henry Miller. Miller's retailing of his sexual adventures and his egoistic way of forcing the reader and his characters to give him permission to 'be himself' and to be adoring accomplices in his latest exploit are also stocks-in-trade for Story: there is a growing sense of compulsive loquacity and compelled listeners as his work wears on.

By suggesting that he himself is a character not at all unlike Albert Argyle—endlessly obsessed with sex and bedding women—Story undermines the social authority of his earlier books and loses his critical edge. Did every woman who bought goods on the never-never or collected green shield stamps really pay the bearer of these benefits with sexual favours? It doesn't really matter: enough probably did for a convincing comic novel. Story moves at a level of culture that always seems to be about sex, that is always prurient and looking for such an angle: it is what sells English newspapers, traditional comedy and much else. I'm reminded again of C.L.R. James' horror at the overwhelmingly sexual contents of the English popular press in the thirties and the alacrity with which they are consumed:

'When you stand before a newsagent's and see all these papers, advertising, each as boldly as it can, what it has provided for millions and millions of readers, you are amazed. Far better the *Port of Spain Gazette* than any of these products of a great civilisation.'[8] Story's turns out to be a shallow outlook, really, and an unappealing world, peopled with unreflective and heartless 'characters'. He enjoys 'the jaunty hardness of the outsider' a little bit too much and disappears into his own beautiful legend: a braggart.

'If she's too old for me, dad,' one of his narrator's sons remarks of a twenty-year-old girlfriend in *I Sit in Hangar Lane*, 'she's too old for you.' Gloriously unapologetic for his fantasy way of life, more fluent, and a bit chunkier, Story's later novels give him more room to stretch out his own personality but less room for the reader to sit back and judge his characters as he gleefully assumes our identification with his reprobate persona and working-class attitudes: he is larger than life in these later books with the consequence that there tends to be a bit too much of him. *I Sit in Hangar Lane, One Last Mad Embrace, Little Dog's Day* and later books tell, or embroider on, his and his family's adventures, but there's nothing in them to provide a foil for his central sexually arrogant persona. It is a matter of approval and disapproval. We can disapprove of Albert Argyle, indeed we are invited to somewhat look down our noses at him; we are not permitted any such distance from Horace Spurgeon Fenton.

But there are those—and Story is amongst them—who would think that his own story is more interesting than anything he could tell us about Albert Argyle and his ilk. In *I Sit in Hangar Lane* Horace Spurgeon Fenton's foil is another Albert (the same one), a milkman who enlists his support in a scheme to establish a brothel in the local vicarage staffed by penniless young Irish girls he will import fresh from Dublin. But by the end of the novel Fenton and his amanuensis-cum-chauffeur have changed places—it is the milkman who is in the film business while Horace plugs away with his milk round, trying to think of another good plot. The solitary mindlessness of the job makes it good for scheming escapes, which is obviously what Albert has done at Horace's expense: working-class camaraderie is just as likely to nourish a viper in one's bosom as a friend for life. Story's stories are absolutely contemporary, or timeless if you wish, but the laughter can ring a little hollow, as perhaps it sometimes did even at the time they were written:

> I saw him first on a cinema screen, in the newsreel. Arturo Conti with some of the beauties of the Cannes Film Festival. I was an engineer going to pieces between the factory, night classes, washing napkins and writing all night. I hated the plump Italian in the white suit with the beautiful bikini girls on the sunlit beach.

> 'I used to be a bastard, Horace,' Arturo informed me later. 'I had every girl there was. Every girl I met I had—my God I had girls, Horace! Not any more. Finished. I love my wife.' This sadly, miserably, then again alight with joy: 'By God I was the biggest bastard on God's earth!'[9]

One Last Mad Embrace is a farewell to the sixties and to youth that finds a fifty-odd-year-old Horace involved with a sixteen-year-old girlfriend and with yet another Albert who has been killed off and somehow come back to life. There is a strange, compulsive quality in Story's detailing of hard-to-follow family relationships and recurring characters. We need to be reminded, he needs to be reminded, just who everyone is, and if individuals become generic, there is a strong need to assert the contrary. The world of writing for television is a backdrop, and Hampstead, where Horace shares a house with a bevy of nurses and more or less happily shags his way through to the end of the love decade. If reality and fantasy are hard to distinguish in 'real' life, Story's take on the TV social realism genre is typically and cynically undermining of its claims to be anything more than a series of career opportunities for those involved in making these programmes:

> The UM series was going to be about a pretty Unmarried Mother fighting the good fight in present-day London. Dinah Thing (this is not her real name) had been cleverly chosen to star on the strength of her long-standing Wayward Girl image and the fact that she was a well known self-publicised unmarried mother.[10]

Jack Trevor Story is eager to offer the inside dirt on such corridors of power as he has trodden, and we soon hear that this ostensibly worthy project is in effect a loss-leader, or a way of losing a disliked executive, he confides, changing names to protect his future career: 'Apparently the UM series, far from being the fulfilment of a long-needed want, was no more than a way of getting a disliked executive to waste a hundred thousand of the corporation's money and get himself the chop.' You could probably learn a lot about the inner workings of television from reading Story, which has become more self-consuming and its multiple ins and outs more ubiquitously visible than in his day. He also offers an interesting sidelight on the contrasting corridor cultures of the BBC and ITV:

> Everybody was laughing as he went out of the room and I thought this was good: it was more like an ITV party. In a strange and yet understandable way the extra prudishness you meet in writing for the commercial channels, because of the authority censorship, gets reversed in their private off-screen happenings. One company in Golden Square had a back lift permanently labelled 'Out of

> Order' for use as a staff love-in. With the BBC it's the other way round; anything goes on the screen but the corridors are like monastic orders.[11]

All this is fair enough, although ploughing through it forty years later it has congealed into something of a stale picaresque pie and the precise basis for its kind of humour no longer seems to exist, because characters like Jack Trevor Story no longer quite exist. Upwardly mobile working-class writers who are employed and tolerated because they are characters and seem to know all about 'what it's really like' down there have been quite thin on the ground for some time, or perhaps they are just keeping quiet about it. Whether they ever did exist or are really what is claimed for them is questionable: reviewed old TV footage, where it hasn't been judiciously wiped, gives an uneasy impression that many of these people were about as working-class as music hall's Mother Kelly was Irish. In fact, the tenor of Story's social observations and somewhat harsh tone reminds me a little of Sam Mayo's 'I've Only Come Down For the Day', a music hall song in which 'the immobile one' tells the tale of a day trip to Hastings in a stolen Eton cap, a song narrated by a schoolboy whose deadpan captures all the callousness of the slumming-toff's point of view, as the boy who is aping his betters airily declines to help a begging old soldier find his 'lost' leg and proceeds to take sexual advantage of a deranged young woman who has detached herself from 'a party of lunatics' who happen to be passing on the seafront.

Overdrawn attitudes, lived stereotypes, personalities rejigged for corporate and living room consumption: whatever the excuse, we might be prepared to nod and half go along with it all and cheer the latter-day inheritors of the mantle of media-created working-class culture from our firesides. But Jack Trevor Story has a unique way with him and a penchant for letting it all hang out that sometimes threw up passages like this:

> I called in the off-licence at Temple Fortune and bought a bottle of Pernod for me (for her) and lemonade for (for me). Then I went into one of those tatty little wog-shops, the only one open, for some groceries. The black man running it frightened me to death. It always seems to me they're wearing one of those black Guy Fawkes masks with their eyes shining through at you. I want to walk round the back of it to see who's there. You feel embarrassed for them. Besides all the curry-smelling rubbish and tins of chopped fingers and Caribbean debris and rotting prawns they have these shelves of real food, though it all looks like it's been dried out after being ruined by flood-water.
>
> 'No corn flowers, sir, only corn pads,' he said.

> 'Cornflour. It's a kind of powder,' I explained for ten minutes.
> Do you think sometimes they're taking the mickey?[12]

On the face on it this is just unpleasantly racist, and yet it's honest enough in its way, and Story is obviously trying to get under the skin of racism: the relative unfamiliarity of black faces, the curious glimpsed possibility that someone else, someone real is lurking behind their apparent mask-like implacability, and what seems the 'alien' atmosphere of immigrant run shops: these are perceptions of a passing moment, a snapshot taken on the run, and reveal a mixture of condescension and unease on Story's part: a world he has known well is being encroached upon, he doesn't like it much, and produces the hope that there is a white person behind the black face. In a way he shows his grudging acceptance of black people through this. But this scene reveals other things too. That things have changed in London, for one, also that the point of view of the bad new working-class, or white working-class as they would soon begin to be called sometime in the later seventies, has been largely censored out of existence in mainstream culture. Attitudes that were once commonplace, and remain so behind the masks, have been banished to the fascist fringes where they no doubt belong politically, but will there continue to fester and grow—as many white British people feel they have become strangers in their own land: an official multi-culturalism and a subterranean polarisation wasn't inevitable but is increasingly likely with the decline of working-class socialism and trades unionism, educational provision that is drastically unequal yet highly policed—and sadly the denial of real cultural expression to the white working-classes is unlikely to rebound on the body politic. White riots, whether predicted or not, are a relative rarity and soon spun out of existence.

It might be objected to this line of argument, of which I am playing devil's advocate, that whatever happened to the British working-class has happened by now and was therefore inevitable, or even that any justifiers of a white working-class case are pandering to racism. The phoniness of a literary and media world of representations, representatives, cultural impositions and impostures finds a high-spirited commentator in the later books of Jack Trevor Story, a keen exposer of its contradictions and hypocrisies as he spins his own version of a working-class poetry of spiralling memory and mad conspiracy theories:

> Driving down from Scotland I kept thinking of my independence and the novels I would write. I planned to write *Hitler Needs You* at last, about me and my friends and my family and the radio factory in the thirties, all happily pursuing our lives and oblivious of what was happening in Germany—the people Hitler needed

> most. And I planned *The Wind in the Snotty-gobble Tree*, which was a fantasy about an underground state, a sinister story of a plot to kidnap the Pope and replace him with a stooge. I thought of the great twist of the Pope turning out to be Lucky Luciano—that the mafia had got in first. You can only indulge in the luxury of writing these things on spec if you've got money and don't have to waste your time on the UM series.[13]

However, his published works are neither conspiracy thrillers nor conventionally sentimental compendiums of working-class family memories. Story was a *Guardian* columnist for some years, writing in a self-referential, self-amused style that is still highly characteristic of newspaper columnists, except that Story's version—like Ray Gosling's—is self-consciously working-class. With both writers there is a sense of barely marshalled chaos honed to a sort of provisional stream of consciousness perfection which the reader must track carefully to get the point. Story's writings in this vein often have an oblique, surreal and dark humour that is totally his own, which makes them strong, heady but best sampled in small doses. For a while in the late seventies he even had his own TV series, *Jack on the Box*, in which he said a melancholy and extended farewell to a departing partner whom he had written about at novel length in *Dwarf Goes to Oxford.* Another late performance was a book about his difficult experiences as an NHS patient, pointing up the yawning differences in quality of healthcare and treatment for those who are unable to pay for private medicine: recording another aspect of the failure of the postwar social democratic dream of equality.

Story is irascible, funny, and increasingly paranoid, a professional writer who wrote innumerable scripts and treatments, threw off rejected ideas for *Dr Who* and lived out his own glorious self-made myth. His instinct is always to undermine what he sees as middle-class impositions and views of the working-classes, to play them to the hilt where necessary, and hold the world of the phonies up to ridicule where possible (and it invariably is). In retrospect he sometimes sounds like the sort of person who has been indulged to bite the hand that feeds him, or appear to, but I expect it would seem a different story if you walked a mile in his shoes. In his own eyes he remains ever true to his working-class roots, unapologetic. Those who do not sympathise will not find him terribly sympathetic, and even those who do will sometimes be exasperated. He is unique in postwar English fiction: a disturbingly solitary achievement for somebody whose point of view is so typical of his place: a brilliant satirist of Essex small town life as well as an eloquent exponent and exposer of its hysterias and extravagant fantasies. His later work turns into a kind of defiant celebration of his difficulties and supposed dysfunctionality and of getting on with fucked-up life.

Chapter Ten

Keith Waterhouse and the Land of Lost Content

Iona and Peter Opie's *The Lore and Language of Schoolchildren* (1959) is a classic study of children's folk-lore, the summation of ten years work on the subject of playground rhymes, jingles, repartee and rituals collected from 5000 schools across the British Isles. The Opies compared variants of rhymes, some of which went back to the eighteenth century, others of which were fresh-minted irreverences featuring the names of current film and music stars. There were rhymes for skipping, bouncing, taunting, folded paper devices for fortune telling, riddles, squibs and Lear-like darkly surreal nonsense verse based on impossibilities, like 'I went to the pictures tomorrow/and took a front seat at the back'[1], as well as many names for the simple game of annoying the neighbours, like Knock down Ginger, Rip Rap, and Nicky Nocky Nino. According to a late article by Iona Opie the universal coverage attained by their work ('They're All Little Savages'[2]) took the authors of this meticulous, highly readable—and appealingly nostalgic—scholarly study by surprise, and the book remained a favourite with working-class watchers for many decades, long after verses like 'Diana Dors lost her drawers/In the British Home Stores' (which doesn't appear in the Opie opus, although a number of similar items do) had ceased to have any great contemporary resonance. Apparently, it's all been replaced with video games nowadays.

Keith Waterhouse's first novel, *There is A Happy Land*, appeared two years before 'Lore and Language', but to read it is to be assaulted by hundreds of items that seem to have been culled from its pages: an impossibility, but evidence if any were needed that this kind of popular folk-lore was extremely popular in the early post-war period, and that the study of the culture of working-class childhood was seen as important evidence of the creativity, intelligence and potential of many children who had hitherto been overlooked by the education system. It was the unsupervised street play of working-class kids which led them to express themselves in this way, and to the popular notion of childhood culture as autonomous and subversive:

> Good King Wenceslas
> Knocked a bobby senseless
> Right in the middle of Marks and Spencers[3]

Waterhouse's Yorkshire kids reel out a stream of puns and rhymes, and converse in a form of what the Opies call 'tangletalk' which is known as Argy Pargy ('Carjan yarjou sparjeak Arjy Parjy as warjell as margee?'), but the land they live in is far from happy—they may have subverted the words of the popular hymn, but the juvenile world is an extremely cruel one, full of bullying and vicious hierarchies of physical strength, and hung over with a sense of aching sadness and nostalgia. Many of their sayings come from the *Wizard* and the *Rover*, and their tastes are serviced by newsagents who operate a money-system based on Licorice Chew wrappers—twelve of these, smoothed out, buys a Shirley Temple lollipop, and a mysterious adult who ingratiates himself with children by uttering the word 'Grr-quack' is instantly identified as Charlie Peace, the uncatchable London criminal who was still a hero of British comics when I was growing up in the sixties. But children are seen as making up their own world, creating their own jigsaws out of old pictures, telling their fortunes by adding up the numbers on tram tickets, and, in the case of Waterhouse's scrawny boy narrator, making a poppy garden of half-bricks with his sweetheart Marion Longbottom at the end of their garden. He also produces his own newspaper and is preparing a film star book for Marion.

The boy's mother is dead; in his dreams she is 'beckoning me from the other side of a field', which mades him feel 'sad like you get back from church on Sunday nights and the house is all quiet with reading.'[4] He is in the care of his Auntie Betty; but the details of this family story remain hazy, accentuating a sense of the boy's isolation and dependency on whatever fellowship he can extract from his fellows. Thin gruel indeed. Waterhouse records their shifting alliances, evasiveness and downright nastiness, especially of the girls:

> Barbara Monoghan and Kathleen Fawcett started whispering again.
>
> 'How old are you, Marion?' said Barbara.
>
> 'As old as my tongue and a bit older than my teeth,' chanted Marion.
>
> 'She's the same age as me, cos she's in our class,' said Kathleen Fawcett. 'Aren't you, Marion?'
>
> 'What if I am?'
>
> 'Oo, what if I am?' mimicked Barbara Monoghan, baring her teeth.[5]

'As old as my tongue and a bit older than my teeth,' is another line recorded by the Opies. But in *There is a Happy Land* it is clear that the purpose of most of these children's language games is to exclude, to torment and to enforce a sense of hierarchy. They are a way of acting clever without being particularly clever, deliberately unanswerable answering backs and rebuffs, formulaic taunts likely to be most admired when most ill-spirited. And like much of the rhyme and fable that was taken as evidence of the native genius of children, this one is clearly of adult origin. The girls having taken care of Marion, the boys start on her consort, with a more physical form of bullying, and it is clear that their friendship is some skin off the noses of their friends and that they are determined to humiliate the pair and split them up. Finally one of the boys, Big Raynor, beats him up in a fight, and Marion, as the price of her acceptance by the other girls, turns her nose up at his homemade film star book. One problem with the novel, which is more of an effective piece of apprentice work than a fully realised novel, is its lack of narrative drive or dramatic tension. Having detailed the children's world and outlook, the young Waterhouse is unable to generate a story from it or much real sympathy for the children. Little savages indeed. His narrator isn't an attractive character but something of a coward, no better than his fellows, just weaker, and without the intelligence to produce the definition of his world that he does. The novel ends with the violent death of one of the children, but it feels rather forced, gratuitous, unconvincingly abrupt, and arouses little interest or sympathy in any of the characters.

There is a Happy Land has been described as a classic and in a way it is: Barry Hines' *A Kestrel for a Knave*, written ten years later, appears to follow very closely in its footsteps, and is a much stronger performance than the book upon which it is probably based. A couple of years later Keith Waterhouse and Willis Hall scripted *Whistle Down the Wind* (1961)[6], a film about a group of Northern children, one played fetchingly and with glowing innocence and piety by Hayley Mills, who find an escaped convict hiding in a barn and mistake him for Jesus. Based on a novel by its young star's mother, Mary Hayley Bell, this defined a minor British film genre of films about children of which Ken Loach's *Kes* is often taken as the summation. Waterhouse played a significant role in the development of the British naturalist cinema that continues to define the early sixties in popular memory. The filmed version of Shelagh Delaney's play *A Taste of Honey* opens with a group of girls singing 'The big ship sails on the alley-alley oh', a beautiful Newcastle skipping rhyme that evades inclusion in the Opie's book, but which seems to sum up the whole period of hopes for working-class children, as Delaney's play and Rita Tushingham's wonderful performance in it say all there was to say about the brevity of love and aspiration for those fortune-telling, dancing working-class girls.[7]

And yet, as the Opies pointed out, much of the rhyme and fable that they themselves took as evidence of the native genius of working-class children is of adult origin: antique or modern, conventionally pious or insolent, the creative produce of teachers, Northern comic writers, Music

Hall and vaudeville and scout leaders were taken up into oral tradition and remembered and adapted for generations; but someone had to do the remembering, and that person was more likely to be an adult. Nevertheless, much of the poetic quality of early sixties naturalism is taken over from folk-rhyme and working-class children's speech, and the conventional piety of remembered hymns from 'Onward Christian Soldiers' to 'God Is Working His Purpose Out' is converted into an automatic inversion or rote nay-saying that appears to the collector or user of it to express a native intelligence and a healthy agnosticism; but the religious air of it all comes from the hymns, and the conversion of the redemptive hopes they express to secular and social democratic uses. Keith Waterhouse understood this cocktail of wishes and cruelties from the inside and constructed a strong version of working-class aspiration and potential out of it—one that he himself was promptly to subvert in his most famous book, which continues to strongly draw upon vaudeville and comics and variety.

There is a Happy Land both draws on and undermines a conventional notion of a 'land of lost content'. Drawn from A.E. Housman's late Victorian poem *A Shropshire Lad*, the phrase, along with 'blue remembered hills' evokes both nostalgia for childhood and an English dream-time of unfettered rural freedom and good old ways—although Housman's poem is a good deal more complex and powerful than this suggests—but like the hymn, reworded Opie-style, which Waterhouse's boy overhears, his novel subverts conventional pieties about childhood and the beautiful village life of the good old days:

> There is a happy land, far far away
> Where they have jam and bread three times a day.
> Just one big fam-i-lee,
> Eggs and bacon they don't see,
> Get no sugar in their tea
> Three times a day [8]

The passing lad who concludes this ditty 'with a strange lilt' passes onwards and out of sight without speaking, limping off down Coronation Grove like some latter-day informant of the Wordsworths; but there is an adult's humour in the notion that the rural past was even worse than compulsory eggs and bacon and sugar in your tea. Waterhouse is not really that sentimental a writer, as we shall see, at least before his epic performance as a newspaper columnist modelled on 'Man O' the Dales', his own comic creation in *Billy Liar*, began—and he slowly transmogrified into a rememberer of the good old ways of working-class community, discipline and respect for the dubious benefit of the never-had-it-so-good generation of the sixties and seventies. But throughout his career he is still, to some extent, and when appropriate, with Housman, remembering the lost lads who never lived to see the world beyond the village fair, 'The lads that will die in their glory and never be old.'[9] Amongst these are those who fell in the wars of empire, the lads of the Severn who lie beside the Nile, and will never grow, to experience change and life in all its aspects:

It dawns in Asia, tombstones show
    And Shropshire names are read;
And the Nile spills his overflow
    Beside the Severn's dead.[10]

A.E. Housman's lad stands behind a number of the novels I have discussed in this study: he also loses his sweetheart to a boy who has bested him with his fists; his is one of the dead thumbs in a troop ship sunk off the coast of Malaysia. There is an element of quiet subversion in this lyrical celebration of the hearts of oak: the men of the village of Ludlow sing God Save the Queen, but it is their courage that has saved her again and again; it is a soldier's poem, written in a strain of mournful remembrance shadowed by the acute consciousness of failure, dissolution and death—and this is a powerful undertow too in Keith Waterhouse's first novel.

Raymond Williams' writing about television has to do with the sources of information thus brought into the living room; also with who controls what he calls that 'total flow' of information and entertainment, who shapes it, and to what purposes. As always he is interested in media as tools for democracy: in focusing on their output critically and in trying to teach about them he hopes to create more critical viewers.[11] Keith Waterhouse's *Billy Liar*—also a stage-play co-written with Willis Hall, a film with Tom Courtney and Julie Christie, and much later a television series—suggests on the contrary (in common with most novelists and cultural commentators) that television creates and feeds fantasists. Billy Fisher, his central character, is a young clerk in an undertaker's office, who lives with his parents and chafes against the hierarchies of the small Northern town he has grown up in, and together with his best friend, is a mocker of everything they believe in. His mockery is childish in a way, certainly adolescent, but is also of a sophistication that would have been impossible a generation earlier. He draws freely from the world's television—and films—have shown him, but however critical they have made him of the small world of his origins, his response can only be to wish to climb into the world behind the screen, to join in the apparent and real fantasies it depicts, which he does in his own dreams and fantasies, gradually becoming a more and more alienated and dysfunctional liar.

Lying, consciously or not, is Billy's way of bringing things to a head. It's impossible for anyone to give advice to someone like Billy Liar, especially if the advice is to 'be realistic'. For one thing he has no respect for their opinions, for another he despises reality. All he can do with the imagery he draws from television is to dramatise his own situation, his sense of separateness, but his dramatisations—fine as a safety valve of self-entertainment—can never resolve his problems only multiply them. And the saddest thing about this book is that Billy never escapes. All he can do is accept his lot and disappear into the small world that has produced him and will continue to accept him. Not such a bad fate, you might think, but he has been offered an escape route he is unable to take. It's not such a sad ending either, just a little wistful. After all, Billy is just another small town liar or fantasist, and in accepting himself as such he has resolved his brief moment of rebellion in a way likely to prove 'right for him', or at least, it is the only possible way he can go.

Billy Liar is a comedy of the kind of aspirational fantasy commonly thought of as wishful thinking, but it's central character is someone who is genuinely too big not only for his boots but also for the small Yorkshire town in which he lives with his parents. Perhaps because he is, inevitably, the creation of a person who did escape to London; someone who knew his character's predicaments as his own and was able to turn them to his advantage, at least from the further shore of success. Waterhouse looks back at his younger self not in anger but with a comic shudder, availing himself of an opportunity to thoroughly satirise the mores of local community and politics as well as exploiting and discarding the persona who offers him these insights. These are the kinds of tensions and motives that lift a novel out of the ordinary, and the main reason why Billy Fisher is a more engaging and convincing character than the narrator of *There is a Happy Land* and Waterhouse's second novel a deeper and truer book than his first. Billy is in many ways in the same world as the children in his first novel—the world of fable, rhyme and schoolboy fantasy, but this late adolescent has turned these materials into an art-form as part of that most fatal of ambitions: to be a writer.

Billy works for local undertakers Shadrack and Duxbury's as an incompetent clerk, but spends much of his time in a fantastic country he has invented, called Ambrosia. Ambrosia has its own armed forces, its own national anthem and its own liberator-cum-president: Billy Fisher. He also has three more or less compliant girlfriends, an unwritten but closely planned public-school novel, *The Two Schools of Gripminster* ('I say, weed. Aren't you a new bug?'), a local career as a stand-up comedian and songwriter and a letter from TV comedian Danny Boon saying he likes his material and inviting him to come to London. He is the boy most likely to leave the stifling Yorkshire town of Stradhoughton, but he is also a fantasist and a petty thief, with a stack of the firm's calenders he had stolen for the postage in the Guilt Chest under his bed and a sheaf of unposted letters he has written to various people in the voice of his mother. Like many people who are too clever by half he has enemies as well as friends, but a sparring partner in the shape of his friend and co-clerk Arthur. The two of them work out comedy material, much of it about local characters, including a local newspaper columnist called Man O'the Dales, proponent of a sentimentally nostalgic Yorkshireism the friends particularly enjoy parodying: 'I want progress, but I want a Yorkshire tradition of progress' with dialogues full of invented dialect words and plenty of high-spirited youthful bombast:

> Stradhoughton was littered with objects for our derision. We would make fascist speeches from the steps of the rates office, and we had been in trouble more than once for doing out Tommy Atkins routine under the war memorial in Town Square. Sometimes we would walk down Market Street shouting 'Apples a pound pears' to confuse the costermongers with their leather jackets and their Max Miller patter.
>
> The memorial vase to Josiah Olroyd in Shadrack's window always triggered off a trouble at t'mill routine, a kind of serial with Arthur taking the part of Olroyd and I the wayward son.[12]

These routines provide Billy—and Waterhouse—with an ever-varying tissue of jokes and patter that keep the surface of Billy Liar lively and interesting, and distract the reader (especially the fourteen-year-old me who first read it) from its somewhat paucity of plot. We join Billy in the last week before his supposed move to London, as he attempts to dispose of the stolen calenders by stuffing them up his jumper and down his trousers, and persuade his girlfriends one by one finally to have sex with him. Billy marshals his plans and his thoughts by means of Number One and Number Two thinking. Number One thinking is positive, fantastic (or ludicrous) and satisfying; number two thinking is negative, paranoid (or realistic) and likely to get you through the day. Underlying all this fantasy and role play is a sense of corrosive rage and frustration, particularly towards the women in his life. Here he is on 'The Witch' as he tries to figure out a way to slip her a passion pill:

> What I most disliked her for were the sugar-mouse kisses and the wrinkling-nose endearments which she seemed to think symbolised some sort of grand passion. I had already cured her of calling me 'pet lamb' by going 'Jesus H. Christ!' explosively when she said it. The witch had said sententiously: 'Thou shalt not take the name of the Lord thy God in vain. I disliked her for her sententiousness, too.[13]

I can remember taking *Billy Liar* out of the school library, one of the first 'adult' novels I had read. I remember looking at it in the back row of a maths lesson, and the colourful graphic cover with its engaging hand-done lettering. But when, in the film version, Tom Courtney was unable to jump on the train to London with Julie Christie—despite my urging—and had to return to having cups of tea made for him by his mother and clocking on at the undertakers, I found it a deeply unsatisfying cheat. Who would pass up a chance of Julie Christie for his mum? Someone who deserved all they got. But I was in no doubt as to what decision I would have made, no doubt at all. I would have crawled out of that place on my hands and knees, Julie Christie or no Julie Christie. And yet people do made such decisions all the time. Something tells them they have limitations—usually someone, but they accept these freely-offered opinions, usually because they have no choice. They go on being Billy Liar, refighting every battle with themselves as hero and victor, making excuses for not grabbing Julie and reassuring themselves that it will all be different next time. The whole story gives me the creeps. It points a mocking if truthful finger at hopes and aspirations insufficiently grounded in reality—it is a story of the aspirational early sixties, which commits the cardinal sin of not having a happy ending. It also seems to side with those who mock at having ideas above your station—you might find yourself on the platform, have purchased a ticket, but be unable to get on board. As far as I am concerned it is a particularly nasty horror story. Nobody fails to get on a train to London with Julie Christie. Unless they already know how it will turn out, in which case Billy Liar's defeat is really a victory of commonsense, and he has won. But his dilemma recalls the alternating straplines of William Empson's poem 'Aubade' in which 'It seemed the best thing to be up and go' of one of the earthquake-avoiding, parting aliens is always followed by the miserably chiming descant of 'The heart of standing is you cannot fly.'[14]

Billy's problem in the novel is that he can never quite convince himself that his dreams are real, that he can be what he wants to be, anymore than he can really believe his emotions are real: he has none, only a talent for play-acting and a desire for sex with girls whom he has to tell that he loves (except for Rita the waitress, whom he snobbishly looks down on) and it seems that he has second-guessed out of existence everything that might be of value to him. But if Billy were a real person it might have to be said that his main problem is his parents utter lack of belief in him, their complete disregard of his feelings and incomprehension of his ambitions. Billy's parents are stupid, ignorant and brutal—comically so—but it is they who have turned Billy into a comic character, someone who is only able to laugh at himself and submit to being a small-town person… or so we might be tempted to believe. But there are two sides to every question, and we are forced to accept they were right all along: merely impatiently long-suffering of their son's delusions of grandeur. At the novel's close they continue to offer him shelter for another day, and Billy, who crucially has not actually submitted his letter of resignation, prepares to re-enter the daily routines he has failed to break. His friends will not be surprised that he hasn't departed from their midst. Waterhouse has delivered the requisite kick up the arse to the procrastinating young reader who might be able to make the break that Billy didn't manage. Billy Liar is about the moment of transcendence, the requisite leap of faith in which an identity, a false-self, is defined and becomes first an anti-self and then a mask through which to operate in a work of fiction, or of life.

Maggie Muggins is a later novel in which Waterhouse takes as his central focus the life of a working-class London woman. Maggie is in her forties, living on her own, and at the beginning of the novel has already suffered a devastating loss: her gay friend, the keystone of her precarious support system and sense of identity, has recently committed suicide by jumping under a tube train on Earl's Court station. Billy Liar might have ended up a bit like either of them if he hadn't been sensible enough to stay at home and accept his limitations. But Maggie's was an adventurous spirit, although her life, to an outsider's eye, looks like a series of squalid misadventures with men met in pubs and in rooms inhabited briefly and not very happily. Tony, her friend, was similar, and in an attempt to unravel the puzzle that a suicide always is, even when of someone who was always, like her, a depressive, as a last service to her friend, Maggie trails around the houses that Tony lived in, to collect his largely non-existent mail. These are the last obliterated traces of an unimportant city dweller, and like Walter Benjamin's detective, Maggie attempts to gather them all. Billy Liar, Maggie Muggins: their names define them, like the characters in an eighteenth century novel. Billy is of course a liar. Maggie is a muggins—a fool, a mug, somebody who has been easily taken in and taken advantage of, and left with nothing but a child and an addiction to alcohol—but in Waterhouse's unexpectedly tender novel about her Maggie also discovers that she is something her friend was not: a survivor, for the moment anyway.

Muggins is a word often bestowed on themselves by women who believe they have been cheated by marriage. Maggie is a muggins who continued to sentimentalise men and to believe in romantic love a long way beyond its and her own sell-by-date. But she turns out to have hidden resources. One of the sources of her strength lies in her determination not to be defined as a victim, to accept the consequences of her life as her own doing without whinging. She knows that the world cares as little for her as it did for Tony, but she manages to accept this and decides to try and survive on her own terms. Another things she has going for her is that she knows the ways of social services, the hated 'nanny state' that Keith Waterhouse, by this time a right-wing columnist and a supporter of Margaret Thatcher, had always felt to be degrading to those it purported to help. Maggie, like her creator, hates the liberal state and hates handouts—she is a cleaner by trade—and, although plainly damaged, is determined to avoid becoming 'one of the walking wounded by the Portakabins': those who have surrendered their dignity to the 'victim culture'. Part of the interest of the novel is in its political contortions. It is difficult to imagine that a real Tory novelist would choose to celebrate the life of someone like Maggie Muggins, or be as forgiving of her failings as is Waterhouse. On the contrary, they would regard her as a piece of worthless flotsam and her predicament as not worth considering. Waterhouse is an apparent believer in 'tough love', which in this case would—and has—resulted in no love at all. But his refusal to take a social worker's view of Maggie results in a novel that grants her autonomy and dignity.

Unfortunately she remains the creature of a novelist with a political agenda that neither fits her problems nor provides any answers to them. If Keith Waterhouse is saying that there are no political solutions to the problems of people like Maggie Muggins—that hers are simply the life problems people like her will always have to cope with and always more or less alone—he may well be right, but as a political novelist who has produced dozens of books about changing British society, one wonders how such a position can make any overall sense of the lives of its people. Like so many successful people from working-class backgrounds Waterhouse remained a self-made and somewhat self-satisfied individualist who distrusted the Welfare State and the standard social democratic account of what people's problems are. Human nature is Billy's nature, and Maggie is admired for biting her own bullets and facing up to things.[15]

Before moving to the Tory right he was a moderate trades union supporter who wrote for the *Daily Mirror* and also wrote its style manual. His forthright, funnily nostalgic columns enlivened my mid-teens, and in them he seemed to still be a bit of a Billy Liar, playfully mocking the remembered details of a working-class childhood. He was a proponent of the good old working-class, and a funny, irreverent one, but also a kind of Man O' the Dales. Like all working writers he revisited the scenes of his childhood and his youthful language games and mined them until the seam ran out. The political dimension of all this was that, according to Waterhouse, today's greedy trades unionists didn't know they were born; they had never suffered the real poverty he had seen in his youth as the son of a Leed's costermonger. He furiously denounced flying pickets and industrial militants whenever they popped up (quite frequently in those years) and generally recommended to striking groups of workers that they settle immediately, thanking their lucky stars. But, to be fair to Waterhouse, there are probably few who now remember those days of serious industrial strife with any great nostalgia, largely because the strikers were usually defeated, and because the other Maggie, Mrs Thatcher, came along to beat the trades unions with a big stick until they were afraid to go on strike, which a great many people in England, like Keith Waterhouse, think was definitely a good and necessary thing.

It seems that even the most irreverent and spirited comedian of youthful rebellion, the most unstinting documenter of stifling working-class communities and the greatest sympathiser of those who are stuck in them, is likely one day to succumb to the deeper cynicism of political nostalgia, conservatism and newspaper family values; and, as our moment slips away, we all become a little more like Orwell's George Bowling, the overweight nostalgic salesman of *Coming up for Air*, making our fruitless journeys back into the land of lost content to find our first girlfriends, to walk the fields we think we once played in: only to discover that the pool with the giant Pike in has been drained and the stream that fed it diverted long ago, and that sandal-wearing middle-class socialists have taken up residence in the new ticky-tacky houses, and that even our most watertight cases have turned into colanders, our ideas and conceptions easily summed up by songwriters. Keith Waterhouse's journey to the political right wasn't too surprising given his own struggles to achieve and his right-wing populism, but he also helped to articulate a sense of prelapsarian working-class innocence and stunted potential that inspired the more hopeful elements of the post-war left.

Chapter Eleven

The Bubble of Consciousness: Barry Hines

Billy Casper, the scrawny bird-lover at the centre of *A Kestrel for a Knave*, is always being interrogated by those around him. His brother, schoolfriends, teachers, none of them will ever stop asking him questions. His immediate world is one of sparring, testing, assertion, and a conviction that he is very likely being told a pack of lies. No lies are acceptable, but they are omnipresent, even necessary. The boy back-pedalling on a bicycle parked in the bike sheds isn't going anywhere, but needs to feel he is. On his paper round Billy spies through a rolled up newspaper furled into a telescope, looking at the small world of his village from afar, trying to sight it more clearly. Delivering the morning papers to a large stone house he notices that the tyres of a Bentley parked in the drive have 'imprinted two patterned bands, reminiscent of markings on a snake's back.'[1] This is the first time in the novel that the natural world maps itself onto the social one, and this is to be a trope that recurs throughout the book. Billy's observation is, of course, for him merely something he has noticed; for us it is a metaphor: in other words, it is another find of fiction.

Billy's only conduit into the world of fiction as such is through absorption of the pages of *The Dandy*, where he reads the adventures of Desperate Dan. Dan, we may remember, is a dirty old man who washes his face in a frying pan and combs his hair with the leg of a chair. This time he is looking for a handsome new hat to wear to a wedding, but none of those on offer are big enough for his head. Having destroyed some of the miniature stock of a gentlemen's outfitters, Dan clears the street by setting off a fire hydrant and steals the hat off a stone statue of the mayor of Cactusville, which fits him fine, although it proves too heavy for the cloakroom assistant at the wedding. It is a story about how to get what one wants. Desperate Dan isn't a malicious character, although he is gloriously, insouciantly selfish. Billy, a small boy rather than a powerful giant, will have to improvise to get what he wants; he will have to break the rules laid down in his small community and for boys like him and behave like a stubbly giant in a battered cowboy hat, a man who can usually get what he wants—sometimes he is vexed and lines surrounding his head like a halo of spikes show his anger and frustration—merely by reaching for it. Billy will need both cunning and resourcefulness: qualities he displays early on by stealing groceries from the milkman and giving his boss—the miserable owner of the paper shop—a fright by apparently shaking his ladder as he passes. Or has Mr Porter merely lost balance for a moment, magnetised by the proximity of a boy who is more powerful than he seems? He doesn't seem to know. He remarks that it is not his job to teach Billy anything (only to exploit him), but by now we should know that it is Billy's job to teach us something important about truth and fiction, reality and fantasy, intelligence and resourcefulness.

But Billy's familiar world is a world shaped by fictions, clichés and rote behaviour: teachers' clichés, mothers' clichés, older brother clichés, librarian and shopkeeper clichés, youth employment officer clichés, and children's' clichés. So many clichés in fact that *A Kestrel for a Knave*, and especially Ken Loach's film *Kes* can be seen, and has been parodied as a compendium of Northern and social realist clichés. Harry Enfield's well-known TV sketch *It's Rough up North* was a parody of *Kes*. And it is like that, both difficult and easy to read: distillations of school experience so perfect and so familiar that it's hard not to skate over them in impatience. But they are telling clichés all the same. Consciously clichés perhaps, but that they seem so may well be in part a symptom of the book's popularity and success in defining working-class childhood and experience of the education system. All the same they are clichés of teachers: the unctuous headmaster, the sadistic sports master, the sensitive English teacher, and the clichés they spout bring the adult world to the children.

By 1968, the year *A Kestrel for a Knave* appeared, Barry Hines was writing in a well-established genre and his approach to writing working-class life was a dominant literary idiom that had been formed by some of the other writers in this study—he had read Sillitoe as well as Lawrence. Richard Hoggart's views on the good old working-class and the bad new class were attitudes frequently espoused by headmasters and teachers everywhere, and perhaps they always had been. The boys are no more than fodder for the mass media, the headmaster tells them as he lines them up for the stick in his study. 'Why is it always the same old faces week after week?' How hopeless is his task of instilling any respect for authority into them. In the thirties times were hard but they bred people with good values and self-respect, boys who knew how to take a thrashing and thanked you for it later. Now there's only abuse flung from a car window by well-heeled yobbos listening to their music. They never had it so good and this has led to a breakdown of communal values.

As he runs through his tape of headmaster clichés, so familiar to the boys that they are scarcely listening, we see the hollowness and hypocrisy of this view of the working-classes as well as its punitive outcome. But the regular miscreants, who are proud of their wrong-goings, know how to hold their hands, slightly curled, to absorb the blow from his swishing cane, while the innocent messenger he is also unjustly punishing holds his hand out straight as a board and so feels the full painful impact of his stroke: a useful lesson in the result of not withholding respect from this arbitrarily punishing authority and 'taking it like a man'. Underlining this negative view of school authority, the sports master is on the side of the most bullying boys, a stupid, uncomprehending man who courts cheap popularity, promoting the thuggish hierarchies of the football field, punishing Billy for his poor performance by cornering him in the showers with a goon squad of boys as confederates in a lengthy scene with strong elements of sexual sadism. In another cliché meant to underline his oppression, Hines describes the skinny, naked Billy, entering the changing room showers, looking for a moment like an emaciated Jewish child 'hurrying towards the final solution'[2] in a Nazi concentration camp. The youth employment officer brandishes a form, which asks about 'aptitudes and abilities' and tells Billy that conditions have greatly improved in the mines.

Billy stands out from, and over, and against, this world of clichés, but also standing out against cliché is the children's language: some of it is dialect words that find their way into the narrating voice much of it, like many dialect words—'miniter' is the Devonian word for 'spick and span', 'bling' an African-American term for flashy, glittery style—is onomatopoeic language. 'Jonked' is a word for the sound a bicycle makes coming off a kerb: it is a sensory, immediate language, full of inventions made out of mistakes, dialect words, rhythmical and bouncy. It is a rich brew compared with the officialese of teachers and the dead language of adults in general, but starkly impoverished too; another world of linguistic clichés, it might be argued, and it is true that the children do not really possess their language in a self-conscious way, nor do they use it to construct an overall sense of things that is their own: their language reflects vividly at times, but is unreflective. In the book it is often elicited by the English teacher, who is something of a cliché himself, and framing this language are the English teacher's clichés: a sympathetic teacher who tries to engage his pupils and get them to express themselves, he is slightly sceptical about the authorities, at a oblique angle to them anyway, and it is he who describes the kestrel, in the language of Lawrence's animal poems, as a creature self-defining in its pride: the hawk is a celebration of pure, fierce being and Billy seems to recognise in this his own view of the bird and what it is for him.[3] 'If men were as much men as lizards are lizards, they'd be worth looking at,' quotes Mr Farthing. Framing this, at the highest level of language in the book, is the author's descriptive language—a lyrical, immediate nature writing reminiscent of Lawrence's descriptive prose, as are lyrical passages embodying Billy's immediate sensory world, as when he is blowing solitary soap bubbles in the school toilets:

> Then out it came, a jewel, hanging heavy in the air, He reached out to catch it. It bounced off the buff of the air, then wavered in the suction as he withdrew his hand. He followed it, and as it fell, he placed his hand below it, allowing his hand to fall more slightly than the bubble, slowly, very slowly, the bubble fell closer to his hand.[4]

This shows the precision with which Billy is able to match his responses to natural phenomena, but it is also an image of the fragile bubble of his consciousness, as well as his sense of self-worth. He is always sighting things with a hawk-like, beady eye, whether practicing a perceptual distortion that turns his schoolmates into midgets or toys, sighting an air-rifle, crashing through the undergrowth or above all training Kes: a language that appears to offer a pure immediacy but is actually highly conceptual, containing Lawrence's—and the Romantic poets'—ways of writing about Nature and, in that it comes to represent Billy's highest level of consciousness, defining him as 'a pure electrometer', as Coleridge described Dorothy Wordsworth: he is a highly sensitive recording and registering instrument; a way of conceptualising his subjectivity which effectively excludes him from the world of conceptualisation and rational argument. On one of his bird-watching tramps, Shelley's skylark makes an appearance, with its vertiginous vertical flight and glorious, unfettered song, 'like an unbodied joy whose race is just begun':

> Better than all measures
> Of delightful sound,
> Better than all treasures
> That in books are found,
> Thy skill to poet were, thou scorner of the ground![5]

Billy Casper himself is a version of this well known blithe spirit with its famously unpremeditated art; he is a creature whose own full-throated ease is only found in his appreciation of Nature, in his communion with animals and in his soft musical calling to Kes as he swings his lure. Like the skylark's his singing of the song of the falconer is all but illegal in its joyousness, subversive, and gravity-defying, because knaves aren't allowed to soar. Shelley contrasts the unearthly purity of the skylark's song with human existence. The bird appears to sing out of love for its own kind and in a blissful ignorance of mortality, whereas for human beings: 'Our sincerest laughter/With some pain is fraught.' We fear that Billy is destined to sing his heart out and drop into the corner of a field to walk around in unknowing dull feathers and obscurity for the rest of its life. What he has is just too good not to attract the destructive attention of the human world in which he must live, a world that with a few exceptions—including his English teacher and the butcher who gives him free meat for Kes—seems to have little understanding of him. Billy has apparently learned no conceptual language at school and has seemingly little understanding of the world around him, but his actions show him to be capable of grasping situations immediately through asking the right questions, as well as being someone who is more than capable of fighting back against injustice and seeking his own advantage. It is his perfectly reasonable calculation of the unlikelihood of Jud's horses—the ominously named Crackpot and Tell Him He's Dead—actually winning their races which leads to his downfall: the innocent bird-brain Kes is punished for his master's sins of craftiness.

Barry Hines has written in a recent paperback afterword to the novel that he regrets writing the children's dialogue in dialect. He feels the voice doesn't really come across on the page and suggests that Northern contractions like 't'stick' (for the headmaster's cane) might make the book less universally accessible than he'd like. He is thinking of the difficulties some young people might have with a regional speech that is not their own, now that the book is a widely known set-text that must reach thousands of young people from similar backgrounds to Billy; but possibly he is forgetting the importance of regional and onomatopoeic language in the structuring of the novel's world and the defining social hierarchies in the midst of which Billy finds himself: for the most part it stands for the spontaneous mind of the children and their resistance to authority. It's a slim book about an unhappy teenage misfit, but as Hines says: 'somehow the chemistry works.' Apparently a teacher once asked him if he had written the book 'on purpose or by accident', seemingly unable to believe that such a novel had been the product of deliberation, planning and craft. Hines managed to avoid this question, although his response to the teacher's incomprehension of what it takes to write a novel is plain enough: he too can barely believe it is not on purpose.

But there must always be an element of surprise, of happy accident, when a book by a first-time novelist works as well as does *A Kestrel for a Knave*. It is one of a number of novels in this study to have been optioned for the screen immediately upon publication and filmed the following year. In this case film and book have been regarded as classics ever since, although there were lean decades when anything which dealt in such a close-focus way with working-class subject-matter was regarded as innately rubbishy and 'boring'. One strong reason why the chemistry works is that Hines was from the community he is describing. His father was a coal miner, and but for having passed his 11-plus might have been a Billy Casper—a sensitive misfit but with no way of proving his intelligence of deriving benefit from it. There is no element of personation in the book: Hines is who he says he is and therefore can be said to speak with a special mandated authority on his subject. Hines says that many of his friends failed the 11-plus and that the secondary modern schools in the area were notoriously violent and educationally poor. Worst of all, having been classified as stupid at eleven, many of these people went on believing it for the rest of their lives. Barry Hines thus made his book a passionate argument for the intelligence and potential of working-class children, all the more keenly felt because he feels that he himself only just escaped a similar fate.

But I think there is also something a little disingenuous about Hines' remark about chemistry. He seems to deliberately underplay the sophistication of his book, and his own cleverness in writing just such a book in such a way at exactly the moment he did: all of which are a large part of the secret of success on the scale he enjoyed. Looking at it with the benefit of hindsight there were some very cleverly plotted moves in *A Kestrel for a Knave* which make it seem unlikely that the book was just a happy accident. Of course it may be unusual for a coal miner to have a son as clever as Barry Hines, a genetic fluke. But it can't have escaped anyone's notice that D.H. Lawrence was from a near identical background. Hines avoided writing about his own family, at least so far as we know, which is what is still expected of first time novelists of working-class parentage, although it's perfectly possible that, as someone who stood out as clever (and knew it), he might well have experienced the jealous antagonism of his siblings, the incomprehension of his parents and the sneers of those very friends and contemporaries whose lives he is writing about in his novel. We can only hope that he was loved and admired by them, especially when he turned up with a film crew.

What I mean about plotting is the almost formal perfection of *A Kestrel for a Knave*, the beauty and knowingness of its articulation of different levels of language, the literary sophistication of its ways of presenting Billy's world and its precise awareness of the moment in which he is writing: a moment in which there was much to draw upon in the novels and stories of his immediate predecessors. There had been successful films starring Hayley Mills, *Tiger Bay* and *Whistle Down the Wind*, which explored the world of working-class children, the latter featuring a lovable small boy who may well have been a prototype of Billy Casper. Almost everything in the book had been done before—the world of rough schools, for example, in E.R. Braithwaite's *To Sir, With Love* and B.S. Johnson's *Albert Angelo*—except to write about the world of a self-defining working-class child in precisely the way he does. And once Hines had written *A Kestrel for a Knave*, at the end of the sixties, the moment of working-class experience as a fashionable thing to write about was all but over, and having been so defined it plunged out of apparently real existence and into the realm of cliché. This is one reason why the book is so slick and so full of clichés: it is hyper-aware of what has come before it, it is making moves that have been made before, and is aware of exactly what is required, of the standard it must reach, in a way that Alan Sillitoe, for example, probably couldn't have been in the early fifties. It is one of the last books of its kind, not one of the first. It may also be one of the best, a clever grammar school boy's book, seeking an approval which it immediately won.

All of which makes Barry Hines sound more a calculating schemer than an enthusiastic dreamer, like Billy, and I could be taken to be trying to take something away from such a brilliant writer of working-class childhood. But that is not my intention at all. Hines' career moves may well have been just as instinctive, and in a way automatic, as Billy Casper's response to animals and nature, and the keenness with which he immerses himself in books about falconry and training his hawk: he simply has a feeling for it. His will to power in taking the career opportunities offered to him and making capital out of his experience in his first novel, is no more reprehensible and may be understood to have the same sources as Kes' proud, fierce, independent being, her uncaring attitude to everything except her own feeding and flight. Literary politics may indeed be no more than this, and I expect D.H. Lawrence may well have agreed.

To return to the teacher's question: perhaps what made him ask if it was written by accident had something to do with the sense of inevitability it has, not that accidents are necessarily inevitable, but some of them do seem to have been just waiting to happen. Perhaps he thought that Barry Hines seemed too stupid to have planned anything, or perhaps he was unable to appreciate the way his novel so carefully places itself in a literary tradition. On the other hand, he may have been highly aware of these things and wondered, like me, how consciously such career masterstrokes are arrived at, in hopes of making one himself. After reading *A Kestrel for a Knave* we are unlikely to expect much of teachers. We will never know what this one meant, but the sense of the book being enmeshed in a world of clichés, and of having being cut from this cloth—everyday life and real problems are clichés—remains, as does the sense that it is an artful triumph over them. Barry Hines is the left-wing working-class poetic naturalist, if there is one, par excellence.

In the final pages of the book, after Jud has killed the kestrel, all the styles and tricks and modes that have gone into the making of it are played through and orchestrated to a climax as Billy responds to the knowledge of death and its cause in his world. As he runs through the estate its architecture and house lights are reduced to a series of abstract repeating patterns, pleasing or not; and it is as though this municipal housing has been built over and supplanted nature, which has been reintroduced within it as twig-like trees planted in iron cages: the residents use them as waste bins, echoing Billy's headmaster's view of the bad new working-class as degraded specimens, and when he finally reaches home it is to walk in on an artfully composed domestic scene encapsulating Barry Hines' withheld way of showing working-class life as itself withheld, emotionally stunted, withholding of people's full potential, crushing Billy's spirit. As ever he presents the meaning of this world by means of a seemingly accidental aesthetic arrangement, a tableau of precisely placed objects. Jud is sitting at the table mechanically eating biscuits in a miniature desolate industrial landscape:

> Jud took no notice of him. Directly before him, equidistant between the edge of the cloth and the comic was a pot of tea. At the side of the pot stood a cylinder of biscuits, taller and thinner than the pot. Wisps of steam rose from the tea, and every few seconds Jud's exhalations blew the wisps over the slopes of the comic. The whole effect was reminiscent of a model for a new industrial plant.[6]

And it is in these pages we learn more fully what has already been implied about this family, why he is fatherless, and why it is a violent, dysfunctional family in which the youngest boy has turned to thieving and the eldest has turned into a brutal, selfish bully. The clue and key to it all is in his mother's inability to respond to Jud's murdering of Kes. He sees this as a legitimate response to Billy's failure to place his winning bet and his pocketing of the two half-crowns that would have turned into a ten pound note, and their mother, despite Billy's taunting and rage, refuses to challenge Jud's sense of justification. In this climactic, heart-rending scene, Billy himself turns interrogator, asking his brother and mother again and again: Why? Why? Why did Jud kill Kes? Why is he never punished for his cruelties? But Billy's mother just doesn't care about it, and we see that she has no feeling for justice, nor any motherly values or sense of proportion. Anything for a quiet life. She refuses to either punish Jud or comfort Billy but simply turns the pages of her magazine. Billy's outrage at this and his attempt to confront them with what they have done by smashing the tableau, hurling himself upon his brother's back, fishing the hawk's body from the dustbin and flying it at them is frightening and pitiful, but even this fails to ruffle their feathers very much. They have no sense and no feeling.

Unable to produce any family catharsis, to have any impact on their selfishness and cruel indifference, Billy makes his way to an abandoned cinema he has visited with his father where he imagines he is watching a film in which he is the heroic falconer and a giant Kes exacts her revenge on Jud in glorious technicolour. This final scene was left out of the film, I'd say because it would have broken the spell of Ken Loach's studied naturalistic style, and in truth it is rather an unconvincing and unsatisfying conclusion, partly because Billy has shown no previous desire to find solace or compensation by immersing himself in the symbolic world of fiction. It doesn't ring true somehow. Billy is the hero on the big screen, as he is to become in the film adaptation of Hines' novel. This is meant to suggest that the only justice Billy Casper is likely to receive is in his own fantasies or in an imaginary world where ordinary people are heroes. Afterwards he carefully buries the kestrel and returns to the house to sleep and we feel he has been forced to accept his family's grim version of reality: the only reality he is ever likely to know.

Interpellation and Disclosure

Barry Hines has rightly said that comprehensive education was only ever introduced in 'a half-hearted way' in Britain. There is in effect streaming in comprehensive schools: many of the smaller ones are indistinguishable from the old secondary-moderns; they are the same local schools and LEAs in effect practice a several-tier system to sort young people in terms of their abilities and social class of origin. Governmental measures—or more often teacher pressure—that are intended to equalize educational provision will, it seems, always and inevitably be subverted by the greedy, pushy middle-classes or those who can afford to send their precious children to private schools. But Billy is in the lowest stream, the 'C' stream of his school, so would, it could be fairly argued, be unlikely to benefit much from being at a school labelled Comprehensive. Hines himself had no direct experience of being a pupil at a secondary modern, although he had been a teacher in one by the time he wrote *A Kestrel for a Knave*. Still, the school scenes in his novel are made out of the distilled memories of others, myths, hearsay: a real community's overall account of what its local school was like.

Like many readers of *A Kestrel for a Knave* (of my age) I first encountered it as a film on television when I was about the same age of Billy Casper. Like Billy I was the child of a manual worker, although my family life was nothing like as violent or loveless as his. My parents stayed together and I had a younger brother to torment; but we lived in a council flat on an estate and like Billy I shared a bedroom with my brother. I attended a small secondary-modern school, a village school, and the clichés of teachers were all highly familiar to me, as was the stereotypical behaviour of some of them: I had kind teachers, indifferent sanctimonious ones, and one who might well be suspected of sexual sadism. The headmaster was rather a kind man, but like the headmaster in Hines' novel kept order by means of the ultimate sanction of corporal punishment. To his credit he abandoned the practice, refused to use the cane, sometime before it was legally outlawed. I remember being 'given the ruler' as school, but only at primary school, for laughing when I got some spellings wrong. Like Billy I hated football and the whole process of being picked for teams (like him I never was and was therefore likely to end up in goal) as well as being judged on sporting prowess. The school could be quite a violent place and had its share of bullies. On the other hand I was encouraged at school, considered to be fairly clever and destined for further things. Unlike Billy I was pretty articulate, but like him I was a misfit, physically not that strong, and tended to view myself as an outsider. Like Billy I tended to escape into worlds of my own. At first it was the world of making model aeroplanes out of balsa wood and tissue paper. I remember a dramatic Kes-like scene when my angry father smashed one of them to matchwood, and experienced a similar feeling that there was no justice in the adult world, no court of appeal. A bit later I was absorbed by the worlds of drawing and painting, music, poetry and novels. Unlike Billy I had no particular feeling or animals, although I did like the family dog.

I mention such details only in order to try and talk about what happens to us when we respond to fiction. The film seemed to disclose my own world to me in a powerful way, to make it present, to reveal it in its true colours, but at the same time it cast a certain light on those familiar elements of school and home that, possibly, reshaped my view of them in a somewhat hopeless and negative direction. The French Marxist philosopher Louis Althusser called this process 'interpellation', a word that comes from the Latin 'interpellare': to interrupt, to thrust between, and often means to formally question, to interrogate. Ideologies interrupt us, call us to into question or to account: in a sense they interrupt our previous conceptions, call out to us, or hail us. According to his view *Kes* called out to me, much as if it were hailing a cab, then hopped inside and started giving me directions. Or perhaps Kes was the cab I found myself in, and like some autonomic device envisaged by Philip K. Dick, it started bending my ear and my mind about what it was to be working-class.

This is an over-simplistic way of describing a complex process, but according to Althusser it is how ideologies, or the bearers of them, works of art, construct our sense of our own autonomy and centrality, explain the world to us within certain parameters and insert us into it. In the case of novels this is usually through placing us in the position of a central character with whom we identify and through whose eyes we are shown the world. Billy Casper is such a character, even though the novel is written in the third person and we are never invited to directly share his thoughts. *A Kestrel for a Knave* is written in a way that is already filmic: it tells its story exclusively by means of visual description, dialogue and action. We are following Billy as he crashes through the bracken, but Billy himself doesn't articulate his view of things, even to himself. Hines' presentation of him leaves him as something of a blank space in the novel, a space that induces us to fill him up with our own thoughts, to make him in our image and ourselves in his. Since being taken over and defined in this way is a passive process that runs counter to our sense of self-importance, it is, for Althusser largely an unconscious one, likely to be forgotten or denied. We don't like to admit to being influenced by others, even the teachers who have plainly imparted our conceptions, it is injurious to our vanity. Perhaps this is another reason why, rereading the book about Billy Casper, his world and his story seemed so overwhelmingly familiar, and so clichéd.

But for Althusser works of art aren't purely retailers of ideologies: they work by placing ideologies on display, by presenting beliefs in such a way that we can see them more clearly, as they are experienced, how they work and interact. *A Kestrel for a Knave*, or any good book, does disclose, show, and make us see something: it enables us to see the formation of ideologies, their interplay and how they are passed on. We could say that Billy is being interpellated by Mr Farthing when he tried to get him to see his falconry through the prism of D.H. Lawrence's ideas about the superiority of instinctive being to educated self-consciousness. But although Billy says 'Yes sir' and seems to agree with what he says, it is more that he is confirmed and pleased by his teacher's interest and sympathy than that he is convinced of anything. Like his hawk, Billy appears to exist in an instinctive world beyond that of teacher or author. Hines' shows us how this works for him, in a way, at the same time as he convinces us that Billy's 'aptitudes and abilities' are far greater than what school has seen in him, and passes on his own view of the untapped potentialities of working-class children. Althusser writes as follows:

> I believe that the peculiarity of art is to 'make us see', 'make us perceive', 'make us feel' something which alludes to reality… what art makes us see… is the ideology from which it is born, in

> which it bathes, from which it detaches itself as art, and to which it alludes… Balzac or Solzhenitsyn give us a view of the ideology to which their work alludes and by which it is constantly fed, a view which presupposes a retreat, an internal distanciation from the very ideology from which their novels emerge. They make us 'perceive' (but not know) in some sense from the inside, the very ideology in which they are held.[7]

In his classic *Criticism and Ideology*, Marxist critic Terry Eagleton, whose criticism took some of its original bearings from Althusser, criticises him for vagueness on these ('see', 'perceive', 'feel') points and for suggesting such a process can only occur with 'real' or 'authentic' works of art (novels by Balzac and Solzhenitsyn) but never with more mediocre literary works. He suggests that Althusser is trying to rescue art from the realm of the purely ideological, whereas as he goes on to show, novels in particular are effectively 'ideology shows' in which different levels of authorial, aesthetic, class and general ideologies interact: there is, he argues, no space in them which ideology fails to occupy, not even the interstices of prose style.[8] But so far as the reader is concerned, I would suggest that this 'interpellation' by fictional characters is a far from universal response to reading about them, and occurs mainly with characters already close in situation to the reader, particularly with characters who are left vacant or blank for the reader to occupy, as Billy is, characters who, to misquote the American poet Frank O'Hara, have a space behind the eyes into which existence can stuff its wounded limbs: characters with whom one 'identifies' by projection.

All of which suggests to me that 'interpellation' in this sense is not as involuntary or unconscious as Althusser and Eagleton appear to suggest: just the outcome of a technique of fiction, suspension of disbelief, and a conscious, active response to a character who echoes or articulates preoccupations and conceptions the reader has already formulated. Subjectivity is not an illusion, nor is it created by language in the ways they say. Their whole model seems to allow little agency to the person who is being interpellated by an ideology, beyond an instant of recognition and acceptance, although Althusser's rescue operation on art does seem also to suggest distanciation or a perception of difference on the part of the reader and an alert, active response on his or her part. Vague or not, for Louis Althusser as a realist philosopher, art does in an important sense disclose the reality it represents.

Did *Kes* and a number of other works I have discussed help to form my own view of what it was to be working-class? Did they condition my responses to educational and familial authorities, suggesting to me—for example—that poetry was an act best performed in secret, or at least privately? That my real self and my preoccupations were likely to be trampled upon by anyone who found out about them? *I already knew that, I already knew*: a common refrain of people who don't like to be told anything, especially if they happen to be insecure or indeed already know what you are trying to tell them. But there can be a powerful feeling of relief when your problems, sense of isolation, of being bullied and misunderstood (experiences I myself remember strongly from primary school) are expressed on television. On the face of it this seems quite likely to have affected me deeply and immediately, but it is also clear to me that another suggestive blank space in the text of *Kes* was one I readily tried to occupy: that of the working-class writer as defined by Barry Hines, which may be a desired response of working-class children to his book; it offers itself and is still sometimes offered by the national school curriculum as a literary style-manual on how to do working-class writing, but is more likely to satisfy a young teacher wondering about the sixties than a child in the early twenty-first-century classroom, or so it seems to me, as I write this in the shadow of a nearby London secondary school.

Chapter Twelve

Gillian Freeman, Iris Murdoch and the Undergrowth of Class

Gillian Freeman's novel *The Leather Boys* (1961) is best known through the film that was immediately made of it and appeared in cinemas a couple of years later, but the novel has also led an afterlife of its own as a 'classic' of gay literature. First published under the name Eliot George, the film and subsequent editions of the book revealed the author of this working-class gay novel to be, somewhat unsurprisingly given her pseudonym: a woman. The edition I own, republished by New English Library as part of their pulp biker series of the late sixties/early seventies, sports a photographic cover that suggests it tells of the adventures of an unzipped Hell's Angel biker chick—and the blurb duly says it is about 'Britain's Wild Ones—the motorcycle cowboys who live for fast machines and faster girls… it is also the story of Dick and Reggie and the strange, twisted love that sprang up between them.' In fact, is it a bleaky naturalistic story of a failing working-class marriage and petty criminality: the love that dare not speak its name is the least twisted element in a book that withholds sympathy from everything else. Gillian Freeman was a middle-class, middle-brow novelist whose early credits had included a biography of Einstein in a 'famous Jews' series, and whose later work includes a path-breaking study of pornography in literature as well as, most recently, a novel about the home life of the Bloomsbury group. *The Leather Boys* remains by far her most successful book. She had been writing novels about working-class life since the early fifties.

Freeman also wrote the script for the film, which was directed by Sidney J. Furie, a young American who had directed Cliff Richard's *The Young Ones* and brought his own love for bikers and a greater understanding of their culture to the project; but its storyline differs significantly from her Brixton-set novel.[1] In the book the two young men enjoy a physical gay relationship from early on, although it is never described; in the film their 'strange, twisted love' is not realised and is only felt by one of them. In the film Pete is a gay man who conceals his sexuality to get close to the bikers and specifically the younger Dick, whom he tries to gently gently cajole into being his lover, never explicitly, which makes it a story about male friendship; in the novel neither Dick nor Reggie are self-defined as queer: they find one another spontaneously and on an equal footing, although Dick is still a virgin. In the novel Reggie is married; in the film it is poor

Dick who is striped up with the unlovely, scheming Dot. The film is a romantic triangle between the three of them, with Pete as the interloper; in the novel Reggie's and Dot's relationship has already all but broken down. Dot is a more sympathetic character in the film—her pregnancy (which is an invention) is her mother's idea and she only half-heartedly attempts to deceive Dick with it, in order to win him back. In the novel she is a stupid, cold-hearted and calculating liar and it is clear that neither of them ever had any really deep feeling for each another.

One writer on the film has strongly criticised its misogyny[2]; but the novel is even more unsympathetic to women: the mothers are particularly horrible, and only Dick's gran, with her all too knowing cussedness towards her uncaring manipulative daughter, wins our reluctant approval. Dot does not hesitate to betray Reggie to the rest of the gang in a plot strand altogether missing from the film: Dick and Reggie's life of crime as burglars, through which Reggie hopes to pay for Dot's abortion. In the film Dick and Pete share a love of bikes—and its documentary footage of the Ace café and loving recreations of bike runs to the coast and to Scotland are part of its charm and credibility. The novel mentions bikes far less than the film; only Reggie actually rides one, and it is clear that Freeman is a bit at sea about their details: Reggie spends part of the proceeds of his first burglary on 'new lights', he has attached a fake radio aerial to make him look like the police, but that's it as far as motorcycling lore goes. In the film Pete has already been a sailor, which makes his scheme to run away to sea with Dick more credible; in the novel it is a romantic dream that apparently springs out of nowhere.

Pete, the experienced gay man, with his reticence, intelligence and his hopeless longing for his somewhat dopey and confused mate, and Dot, an ill-educated but well-meaning girl who genuinely wants to make her marriage work, are in the film sympathetic characters; but a flaw of the book is that despite a sensitivity of observation and a kind of sympathy, it contains no truly sympathetic characters. The working-class world she depicts is a largely loveless one, and Freeman, try as she does, can muster little love for it—and even less it seems for her own sex. The emotional drama in both versions is all in the relationship between the male lovers, who try to stand aside from the world they have inherited and yearn for something else. The affecting final shots of the film where Dick trudges dismally away from the sailors' pub having belatedly realised what shipboard life is likely to consist of and that, for him at least, there is no escape from the world of women or from being a man, and Pete looks after his hunched, retreating form with a melancholy gaze that reveals both his genuine love and his own marooned predicament attain a focus that is never quite achieved in the novel. Pete's melancholy gaze at Dick's retreating form stands in for our own as we pull away from the lost working-class world of the film, with its helpless innocence, madcap enthusiasms and emotional turmoil.

But the novel is worth talking about in its own right. If a comparison appears to reveal its flaws, one can see why the film-makers leapt at it as a subject, and also that, as author of both novel and script, Gillian Freeman writes well in a spare idiom that fits her subject matter like a leather gauntlet. Some will prefer the film for its vivid documentary footage and its atmospheres; both film and novel are ahead of their time in depicting working-class homosexuality, although the novel goes much further in this, as I suppose would have been impossible for the film. Freeman's novel is more revealing of its time in the obtruding chunks of pop sociology and journalistic stabs at 'what working-class people think' which pepper it liberally, apparently compulsory at the time: preconceptions attending the fictional study of this particular lost tribe which are now all that remain of it. Many of her characters seem to have walked straight off the pages of the *New Statesman*. Their dislike for vicars, judges and the police are given full rein, as well as their delinquency, despite her dedication of the book to a friend in the legal profession. An interesting aspect of the novel is its attempt to depict what authority consists of for these confused and sometimes desperate members of the bad new working-classes—disdained, flouted or misunderstood, it still exists for them, making its presence and pressure felt in a strangling, coercive feeling of guilt for the women, a guilt seemingly, strangely absent for the two gay lovers: it is a negative quasi-emotion that leads to tears and sometimes briefly inhibits her characters from expressing what is seen as an innate selfish indifference, cruel motives—love is as unreal as the buckets of tears shed by Dot, who is depicted as straightforwardly stupid and manipulative. Gillian Freeman appears to identify with her characters' sense of life's brevity and urgency and she withholds judgement in her final court scene where everyone except poor dead Reggie gets off relatively lightly: Reggie's killers escape being sentenced for murder; Dot enjoys her brief newspaper notoriety and new freedom; Dick inherits Reggie's spirit, accepts his sexuality and disappears to find a new dicing partner on his dead friend's motorcycle.

The Leather Boys is a clumsy novel judged by some standards and yet it has qualities that lift it way above the average effort. Written with brevity and force in a cool, stark manner, it is unsparingly unsentimental and efficiently delivers a story with a punch. Freeman has an excellent ear for London working-class speech for one thing, and even better than that she has an understanding of the way family members, young husbands and wives, uneasy friends and gang members, talk or avoid talking to each other. What is most striking is the way she radically questions sex roles; and if the language she offers her characters is impoverished this contributes to the novel's unvarnished view of human relationships, and, especially unusual in a book written by a woman, to the way it withholds any particular sympathy from most characters, especially the women, whom she often tries to look at through the eyes of a sexually indifferent or otherwise contemptuous man:

> He felt an intense repugnance at the warmth and tickling sensations of Brenda's body. Dot was enough for him. Why had he picked up this tart, out on her Sunday routine? Why get tied up with a couple of stupid birds when he and Dick could have spent a pleasant day on their own? It was an effort to be with girls. You had to talk and flirt and neck, even if you didn't feel like it. He had thought that after all these months of not making love to Dot, he would be all ready to do it with someone else. Well, he wasn't.[3]

Taking her cue from the Angries, Gillian Freeman's earliest theme is hypergamy between the working and middle-classes. Her early novel *The Liberty Man* (1955) is about a cross-class romance between a sailor on leave and a young middle-class schoolteacher in her first job, and the yawning cultural and intellectual gulf it reveals between the unlikely lovers. Her subsequent effort, *Jack Would Be A Gentleman* (1959), is about a football pools winner, Jack Prosser, and his struggle to adjust to winning a £50,000 jackpot; like *The Leather Boys* to come, its strongest sense of working-class life is of lovelessness, incompetence, sexual repression and the downright stupidity of working-class people. Clearly she and her publishers thought she was being sensitive and sympathetic—and in some ways she is both—but this must have been an excruciating book for working-class readers, although I see from my reserve stock library copy that it was extremely and enduringly popular in local libraries, having been taken out by readers in North London nearly every month of the 1980s. However, as nearly every character in this book is repellent, unlovable and also apparently irredeemable, it is difficult to see why, unless it's that working-class people like being told the truth about themselves, or that winning the pools was a common fantasy in that decade; Freeman's aim is clearly to resoundingly disprove her socially optimistic early seventeenth century epigraph: 'Jack would be a gentleman if he had money.—CLARKE, Paroemiologia, 1639.' No way, or 'I think not', is her response in this novel whose beautiful cover shows overlapping irregular rectangles in delicate pinks and greys, like a fifties place mat or some other domestic or kitchen design, enclosing a scrubby pen and ink drawing of a street scene with Jack emerging from his terraced house in overalls, pipe and hat, and pasted in a reproduction of an old 2d treble chance pools coupon, its forty lines filled in with his winning draws. The book itself is also such a window into a vanished, murky world, but the view it offers is not such a comfortingly nostalgic one as the library-friendly cover artwork suggests.[4]

Jack Prosser is a middle-aged housepainter with a nagging wife, his Beatrice, and two almost grown children: Barry, who is an apprentice car mechanic and Moyra, a slightly cleverer girl who has been to grammar school and is currently attending a secretarial course at college. We meet the Prosser family before their pools win changes their fortune if not their fortunes. Beatrice is ironing shirts on her broken board in the small house she hates, Jack watching her with his metal collar stud loose, expanding metal bands holding up his shirtsleeves—once common items of male working-class attire that have vanished, and like all such details (Freeman is pretty good at them) they lift the prose, and we hope this is going to be a strange, evocative glimpse into the world that contained such objects, as least as it exists in memory. Even the odd approximations of the dialogue and all those flying apostrophes and the familiarity of her characterisations and plotting, a sort of disembodied woodenness produced by a peculiar archaic belief system and structures of feeling that were probably true of most British life in the fifties, and in her early pages this somehow conspires to make her version of that world seem as radically strange and obviously made-up as the small town world of Philip K. Dick's *Time Out of Joint*, invented to reassure Ragle Gumm that he is living in a reassuring fifties America when he is in reality predicting missile strikes by doing the local paper's spot the ball competition, in a world where solid objects can dematerialise in front of your very eyes. But not really, not this time, not in England: everything is all too solid, all relationships and class characteristics apparently set in stone.

In *Jack Would Be a Gentleman* the Prossers are struggling along in a conflictual relationship, imprisoned by false beliefs and in a marital transaction with a built-in antagonism factor that will continue till doomsday. Beatrice vents her many dissatisfactions with their middling station in life by nagging in a penetrating descant that continues for the length of the novel, until Jack invariably, inevitably heads off down to The Crown for a pint or two of mild, and we wish we could join him. Beatrice's immediate reason for unhappiness is that they have a twelve inch 'tee-vee' which receives only BBC programmes when their neighbours, the Wards, possess a larger model that gets ITV: a vastly superior set as Elsie Ward is continually pointing out. Jack is unambitious and long-suffering. Reasonably happy to work as a painter and decorator, he stubbornly refuses to make the effort to set up his own business as Beatrice thinks he should. He is happy in his job, with his pre-war Ford Popular, which he has recently painted maroon (a colour that recurs later when Freeman wants an example of the tasteless hideousness of working-class taste) and his pub friends. Beatrice dreams of mushroom carpets throughout and thinks lots of walnut veneer would give light to a room. She doesn't work outside the home, but spends her ironing downtime preparing vegetables for the evening meal and watching jugglers, excerpts from *Swan Lake* and *Farming Today* on her flickering twelve-inch tee-vee. But, unfortunately, in Gillian Freeman's created world things are actually what they seem, this is the real world not a government sham designed to induce a captured communist spy to commit suicide and once the strangeness has worn off *Jack Would Be a Gentleman* pursues its relentless way down memory lane to invent the worst story it can think of for the most miserably predictable family on earth.

The effect of a predictable, inevitable unfolding is further accentuated by the novel's division into ten chapters of approximately equal length, each creeping along at the same petty pace, so that even the most dramatic happenings lose impact and our response to them blunted; the middle-class characters, principally their daughter's public school boyfriend and then husband and his semi aristocratic milieu (whom he is sure to keep far away from the Prossers) and their son Barry's car racing friends, plus a few snooty neighbours. One highly predictable aspect of the Prossers is that they are always telling everyone their business, luckily for eavesdropping novelists like Freeman but not so luckily for themselves. These stupid ignorant braggarts are quite unable to hold their tongues about anything, let alone having won the pools, and throughout the novel they alternate between being insecurely over-trusting and deferential to people who plainly despise them and subject to outbursts of defensive, bullying rage when frustrated by their stupidity or by the seeming snootiness of waiters and other flunkeys.

They, of course, are snobs themselves, particularly Beatrice who has already told the butcher of their good fortune before she even knows the precise amount of Jack's pay-out, but whose housewifely canniness protects her from accepting the none too fresh chicken he tries immediately to palm off on her, in favour of her usual pound of traditional sausages. They are snobs who don't quite know what to be snobbish about, locked in painful conflict and unable to resolve their differences, weak-willed and full of attitudes that are likely to bring them and their children to harm, and do. Theirs is a heartbreakingly dispiriting story told without real sympathy or understanding. *Jack Would Be a Gentleman* is a withering look at the English working-classes at their worst, imagined and concentrated into an unappetising smoothie of ideologically motivated sludge by the most condescending writer ever to make the proletariat her own special project. One exceptional quality they do have is a religiosity, a conventional piety, that is highly unusual in the English working-class nowadays. Moyra is a regular churchgoer and is at first reassured by her boyfriend James' attendance of services with her, later to be disgusted by his advocacy of abortion (as well as premarital sexual intercourse) and plagued by never to be allayed suspicions that he is marrying her for her money. Well, we come to realise, it can't have been for sex. Jack invests in a record shop, is soon ripped off by the pub friend he has installed as a manager, who invests the takings in a few extravagant and disastrous dead certs on the horses. Over-confident, vainglorious and none too bright dreamer Barry is killed in his first race in the Lotus that Jack has bought him as his horrified mother watches him in pride on tee-vee. Trying to overtake a toff is impossible, however much money you have won. James doesn't bother to attend the funeral and the Prossers weep alone. But not for too long. Jack is soon off down to The Crown to drink with his cronies. Beatrice returns to the great and only solace of her life, her tee-vee set. It is a story that only Hubert Selby Jr. could have told convincingly or well.

The real working-class writers of the fifties and sixties tended to give more scope to their characters, ascribe more feelings and intelligence to them than Freeman does—basically their own feelings and intelligence. There are middle-class writers who do this too—as well as those who, like Kingsley Amis and John Braine and others, feel a compulsion to lash out again and again at the benighted masses for poor service, spottiness and generally being to blame for everything wrong with the filthy modern age. Gillian Freeman isn't notable for her animus towards the working-classes, only for the thoroughness with which she sees it through in her fifties and sixties books. There's something a little disturbed about it, and this disturbance can make her fictions interesting to read, especially when they concentrate emotions to a point in slanging matches; but there is also a suspicion that such problems and painful experiences weren't really hers to appropriate, and that it is mere insensitivity rather than any special insight into her subject that makes her so insouciantly lacerating. On the other hand the unlicensed observations of novelists may offer more insights into class attitudes than the fictions of a liberal politics of politeness towards subaltern social groups. Freeman is writing on the periphery of her own social awareness, about something that is moving in the undergrowth, and thereby mapping a territory of common assumptions about the working-classes of her time, revealing what women like her thought about people like us.

The Prossers are a traditional working-class family, but the storyline of *Jack Would Be a Gentleman* could be from yesterday's newspapers, and exemplifies the qualities ascribed to the bad new working-classes of the fifties: they are just like today's 'chavs' who win a fortune on the lottery and spend it all on helicopters, whores and cocaine, and contemporary readers of what used to be called the yellow press are just as delighted to hear how they have come unstuck on the sharp bends; their new neighbours are no more friendly than the snobs Beatrice Prosser finds next door, and the habits and attitudes of a lifetime are apparently no easier to leave behind than they ever were. Maybe all pools winners should be presented with a copy of this novel, or better still a ten part tee-vee adaptation might cure lottery addicts of wanting money and a life of ease they are obviously ill-equipped to enjoy responsibly. But we shouldn't be too tempted to shoot the messenger. Gillian Freeman has her insights and may well have had it all right, and the merciless attitudes of the middle-class woman may have turned out to be what we didn't want to hear but had to be told for our own good: that we are no good. It is useless to protest that the fifties were a period of unparalleled opportunity in which many working-class families moved into the middle class and the children of the working-class moved up through education (unlikely) and entrepreneurial flair (quite probably). It was a generation that seemed to adapt to changed circumstances and demands with apparent ease. It is equally true that some people really are immutable, don't adapt and appear to derive no benefit from prosperity or governmental initiatives to turn them into a different class: they are manual workers, 'allus will be', and they are likely to be proud of it.

Gillian Freeman continued to ply her trade with working-class themes during the sixties, perhaps because by then she had been typecast as a female Angry Young Man. She wrote two half-interesting but hard to find novels about British fascist groups and their constituencies, one of which looked at a how a ruthless bully preys on the racist sentiments of a rag-tag bunch of no-hopers. *The Undergrowth of Literature,* her study of pornography, takes a libertarian approach to the subject that is of its time but might now seem a defence of the indefensible to some in the light of the internet porn explosion. In this respect she became part of the post Lady Chatterley trial moment which gave birth to the British underground press, made possible books like Thomas' *The Virgin Soldiers*, and cemented the popularity of European sex and politics films like *I Am Curious Yellow*, led quickly to mainstream porn films like *Deep Throat* and to what was soon to become the over-celebrated *OZ* trial.

A later novel, *The Marriage Machine*, is about hypergamy of a different sort: a middle-class English girl who marries an American. The machine of the title is located in a New York bar and dispenses instant marriage licences, but the marriages thus sealed are real ones if renegotiated during the course of her story and Freeman seems more at ease and truer in the register of this book—with few if any working-class characters to worry about she can be as eloquent as she likes: there's no-one to feel sorry for or to pity on account of their inadequacies, although it is clear that the English class system always grated on her when she writes a little about evacuees arriving in an English village. A pair of East End boys are sent packing by the vicar for being rude and dirty and never pulling the plug, while a better turned out girl is allowed into the local fee-paying school (the vicar pays her fees) but she turns out to be not too classy after all and not particularly bright compared with the regular fee-paying pupils, a year behind them. If there is a natural social level in fiction that people can write in comfortably and without strain, and it's not simply all a matter of technique, then this is the one that seems to suit Freeman best: she has sometimes been said to have improved as she went on, but this is untrue: there is nothing much to distinguish her once she has left her working-class themes behind. Her latest novel, *But* Nobody *Lives in Bloomsbury* (2006), shows her to be as besotted by the Bloomsbury group as any undergraduate, particularly interested in the Woolfs as a Jewish family of their time.

Gillian Freeman is part of the undergrowth of class in fifties and sixties British writing—firstly because she was a writer who picked up on fashionable themes and made a career out of them; but secondly and more interestingly in that she was drawn to areas which few novelists of her time tackled or even seemed to know existed: she has a more realistic version of the romance between working-class men and middle-class women than D.H. Lawrence, she also seems somehow to intuitively grasp the travails of working-class homosexuality in a masculinist culture that might well also give rise to it; to grasp both the lure of winning the football pools and the difficulties of starting your own business when you are a manual worker with no head for figures, and, as a Jewish writer, she is understandably concerned about the influence of the far right. Her view of working-class women and of family life is her own—unsparing and unforgiving, unpalatable to many, but without doubt highly recognisable to many more. For all these things she deserves to be remembered.

Iris Murdoch—sophisticated, a writer of real intellectual reach, and middle-class to a fault, may seem to some an odd pairing with Gillian Freeman: a novelist who can't match her abilities in any respect; not in delineation of complex, driven characters and their moral dilemmas; not in descriptive powers; not in plotting; not in dark humour; not in any kind of philosophical richness or achieved subtlety: but nevertheless they do have certain things in common. Murdoch's *The Bell* (1958) also deals with male homosexuality in a sympathetic way, albeit at the opposite end of the spectrum of English class society, and Murdoch is likewise is a justifier and elaborator rather than a questioner and critic of dominant middle-class assumptions surrounding English social hierarchies: a writer who, try as she might, is unable to quite grant full humanity to her working-class characters, although she does write quite tellingly about their feelings of inferiority.

Under the Net (1954), is the starting point of Iris Murdoch's journey as a novelist, a book which slightly anticipates and shares much with the writers of the Angry Young Man era. It is, as the original blurb tells us 'set in the intellectual *demi-monde* of London, where struggling writers may rub shoulders with successful bookies, and film starlets with frantic philosophers.' Dedicated to French novelist and poet Raymond Queneau, and told in the first person by a translator of French novels, Jake Donaghue, this serio-comic picaresque owes much in mood to Ealing comedies of the time, but also mentions Queneau's *Pierrot Mon Ami* (1943), a beautiful novel about Parisian fairground folk published during the Nazi occupation of France, in its opening pages, and it is clear that Queneau's lightness of touch and ability to combine it with philosophical interests without losing narrative impetus is important to her. One thing she does not share with Queneau or the Angry Young Men here is any pressing social concern. *Under the Net* salutes the birth of a new post-war era of liberation and possibility, but without any corresponding sense of anguish or feeling that there is anything particularly painful from the past to be let go of. Murdoch's posh down-at-heel bohemians, her charismatic entrepreneur of fireworks and films, her actresses and affluent bookies, are at this stage, people untouched by any pressing emotional needs. Carefree bed-hopping, gleeful arguments about Marxism, staged riots and madcap adventure are the order of the day. At one point Jake encounters Lefty Todd, leader of the New Independent Socialist Party; a wide-ranging discussion ensues:

> 'Come, come,' said Lefty, 'we've confessed to the illness, haven't we? Let's get on towards the cure.'
>
> 'All right,' I said, 'it's this. English socialism is perfectly worthy, but it's not socialism. It's welfare capitalism. It doesn't touch the real curse of capitalism, which is that work is deadly.'

Lefty is soon forced to admit that his new party has no long-term strategic goal, certainly not to make its leader a Prime Minister, but somehow his critics just don't see the point:

> 'People accuse us of being irresponsible. But those people just don't understand our role. Our role is to explore the socialist consciousness of England. To increase its sense of responsibility, New social forms will be forced on us soon enough. But why should we sit waiting with nothing better to keep us company that social ideas drawn from the old one?'[5]

This is Murdoch's angry young man statement, and a fine one, if lightly tossed off in a pub debate. Her poetic and descriptive abilities, her skill in turning an aphorism and flair for philosophical dialogue are very much in evidence, and carry what might have been an average first novel into the realms of masterpieces. It is moreish. Reading it feels like an adventure in itself, an adventure in language in which credibility of plot doesn't matter, most of the concerns of realism are mocked or shrugged off, and whole ridiculous scenarios unfold with nothing much to support them but a pure pleasure in narration. It's a book in which we feel the author discovering her nascent powers (her narrator is in the way of waking up to the realisation that he is a serious artist), an imaginative tour-de-force of stand-up comedy, of a restless, playful intelligence, and, compared to her later books, although elegant, slangy and broad in diction.

Under the Net might also do as a further example of a marvellously explanatory fifties book cover. A pen and ink drawing in an old-fashioned book illustration style, it depicts, printed on pink, a small feminine-looking man with loosened tie blissfully asleep in a giant brown bear costume, his arms in its paws, his head nestling within the canopy of its open jaws. Bear and man are resting on a rug, against a half-open theatrical trunk from which a few clothes are spilling; above him, on a net hanging from an invisible wall, three masks smile down: a balding laughing bookie, a classical-looking woman with arched eyebrows and bow lips, and a fleshy man with long hair who seems to be speaking to the sleeper. This must be Hugo, the charismatic enchanter who has elicited Jake's philosophical dialogue. On the floor surrounding the latter there's a French horn, a rocking horse wearing a crown, two large feathered hats, and a serpent rearing from a snakes-and-ladders board, or it may be a washboard, its mouth open, tongue flicking: a viper perhaps. It expresses the book perfectly. Jake's blissful dreaming smile is as Irish as his helpful alcoholic sidekick Finn. It is a whimsical comic masterpiece which, if amusingly cynical about most people's motives, is also comfortingly optimistic that good will always triumph, and that evil is just a lot of straw men. Iris Murdoch announces herself as a richly gifted novelist with a paper thin philosophy, albeit one she is brilliant at expounding.

Michael Meade, the charismatic if withheld leader of a lay Anglican community in *The Bell* [6] is not a homosexual character who would seem sympathetic to many contemporary readers. His hopes of the priesthood have been dashed by an emotional involvement with a young boy in his first teaching job, and now, years later, that boy, Nick Fawley, a grown-up and possibly vengeful dissolute, shows up at the gates of Imber, a precariously established community in the grounds of an ancient Abbey, involved in market gardening and daily prayers. He is tempted by another young boy, who has arrived for the summer, and tried by the errant wife, Dora, of another member, Paul Greenfield. Paul is there to do historical research, but his haughtiness and bullying behaviour towards his wife, make her spirited flirtatiousness and triviality of outlook seem attractive qualities. She is a woman out of her social and spiritual depth, largely identical for Murdoch, but this magnificent novelist makes her—with Meade—the moral centre of this deeply probing, insightful and, characteristically, preposterously plotted novel. The preposterousness of her plotting is an element of her playfulness as a writer and surely leavens her themes, which would otherwise lay there an inert, bland and unappetising flatbread of High Anglicanism and Platonist moral philosophy. Her daft plots provide the buoyancy of sex in her novels, their improvisatory quality of a piece with the fluidity and changeability of her characters—a protean quality which makes them compelling and believable, however securely they may be anchored in an ironclad grid of social types that may be questioned at peril in the presence of many of her readers. Iris Murdoch's neo-Kantianism—she is a believer in transcendental moral absolutes though not in God (or in the divinity of Christ)—serves her well as an overarching moral format for her characters' actions and development. Poor lower-middle-class Dora may well be inherently 'a bitch' whose intellectual limitations lead her to substitute all kinds of other things for virtue, but it is her playfulness and inability to submit to her husband that draw us. Michael Meade's unspeakable passions for young boys may be unsavoury, but to him they are as pure as any love, and Murdoch's belief that 'all love is good' and therefore induces goodness allow him to achieve redemption of a kind while others may perish through his soul searchings and his absolute compulsion to behave correctly.

In *Bruno's Dream* (1969), a confused, unsuccessful novel that tries to deal with ageing and death, her elderly title character's son, Danby, a prosperous printer and one of those disintegrating middle-aged lotharios with whom Murdoch is so fascinated and sympathetic, continually introduces his long-term bed-mate Adelaide de Crecy (a Huguenot name that sounds much too grand for her) as 'Adelaide the Maid'. Murdoch has him cut her and betray her again and again, until she physically attacks him and cries out:

> 'You despise me,' she said. 'You regard me as a servant. You treat me as a slave. You wouldn't dream of marrying me, oh no. I'm cheap trash. I'm just good to go to bed with for a while. I'm convenient, easy. You don't really care about me at all. I hate you, I hate you, I hate you.[7]

But although Adelaide is allowed to express her pain it is, one feels, of a slightly lower spiritual quality: she is never going to be the star of a novel, she is a born stop gap lover and purloiner of items from the book's McGuffin, the old man's valuable stamp collection, and is finally shuffled into the realms of a sort of miserable low comedy, married off to her turbulent, unstable cousin before being tidied away into a preposterously bright future. Murdoch's novelistic sense of social place and therefore of the uses of working-class characters is always rigidly Shakespearean.

The Sea, the Sea (1978)[8] is a far stranger and stronger book, whose charismatic older man, Charles Arrowby, is a retired actor/director who harbours an obsession with his adolescent love, Hartley, touchingly named after Samuel Taylor Coleridge's troubled son, which eventually drives the poor woman and her violent ex-soldier husband to emigrate to Australia. In 'Frost at Midnight' (1798) much is expected by Coleridge of his infant boy, in whose glittering eyes the poet had seen the whole reflected sky in his opiated notebook scribblings, and much is made by Murdoch of this great poem, out of which she builds many of the haunted alarms of her tormented protagonist:

> Sea, hill and wood,
> With all the numberless goings-on of life,
> Inaudible as dreams! the thin blue flame
> Lies on my low-burnt fire, and quivers not;
> Only that film, which fluttered on the grate
> Still flutters there, the sole unquiet thing.
> Methinks its motion in this hush of nature
> Gives it dim sympathies with me who live,
> Making it a companionable form,
> Whose puny flaps and freaks the idling Spirit
> By its own mood interprets, everywhere
> Echo or mirror seeking of itself,
> And makes a toy of Thought.[9]

Hartley Coleridge was a prolific sonneteer who struggled in his father's shadow. His own poems, 'Long time a child, and still a child' and 'To a Deaf and Dumb Little Girl' also seem to be important inspirations for Iris Murdoch's Hartley, the usually silent and mostly abused middle-aged woman whom Arrowby discovers by chance to be living nearby the secluded seaside house he has bought in order to write his memoirs and evade the many women in his life. Hartley Coleridge writes of himself that he has never grown up—'And I am still a child, tho' I be old'—and of the mute girl that she is 'Like a loose island on the wide expanse,/ Unconscious floating on the fickle sea... And yet methinks she looks so calm and good.'[10] Out of these poignant materials Iris Murdoch weaves a masterpiece of obsessive, misplaced love, and out of Harley's steadfast refusal of Arrowby's Gatsby-like machinations, his determination to repeat the past at any cost, she creates her most dignified and touching working-class character: a woman who expects to be bullied but whose mysterious autonomy and apparent self-knowledge remain miraculously intact. It's the little we come to know of her that produces this effect, whilst to Arrowby she may finally amount to no more than his fancy toying with a piece of filmy soot caught in a draft in the grate.

There is much more than this in *The Sea, the Sea*, from the comedy of her narrator's eccentric meals, to his own fickleness, to explorations of the supernatural, and the absurd magnetism he appears to exert over all other women. Love is central to Murdoch's philosophy of goodness, and Arrowby's enactment of his love for Hartley is a compendium of wilful, egotistical errors. 'Love is the general name of the quality of attachments and it is capable of infinite degradation,' she writes in an essay, 'but when it is even partially refined it is the energy and passion of the soul in its search for Good.'[11] She also believes that the inner life is central to morality, which cannot therefore be judged purely on the basis of public acts, which may well be dissembling, or simply a wilful imposition of good intentions; rather it is a quality of loving attention to the real. This is a lesson that Charles Arrowby slowly and painfully begins to learn, but Hartley's inwardness remains hidden from him, although her intentions may be inferred by us. She is a lost continent of done decisions and accommodations to the real. But since the reality of her life comprises absolute submission to another in the shape of her marriage to a violent man, we are entitled to wonder if Murdoch hasn't acquired a level of irony in respect of her early philosophy.

Gillian Freeman showed *The Liberty Man*'s star-crossed lovers to be capable of little more than a pretence of mutual understanding. Try as he might, her hapless sailor is never going to get European films or sipping glasses of wine, and his hopeless deference and helpless devotion to the young lady teacher cannot for long mitigate his stultifyingly boring company. Murdoch would doubtless concur, but like Freeman she does sometimes give her working-class characters ridiculously lucky breaks—Adelaide the Maid in *Bruno's Dream* marries her feckless cousin Will and ends up a millionairess—but also their moments of being in the right, of truthful plain-speaking. Finn, who is Jake Donaghue's stooge in *Under the Net*, also has the wit to quit while he is ahead, decamping to Ireland with his share of the proceeds of one of their scams. It is precisely at this level of fantasy that Murdoch occasionally tries to award them some measure of justice.

Chapter Thirteen

Bill Naughton and David Storey: What's It All About ?

Irish-born and Lancashire-raised, Bill Naughton created the most remembered South Londoner in literary and film history: Alfie. He first appeared in a 1963 radio play, *My Funny Little Life by Alfie Elkins*, as a film in 1965, and as a novel in the following year. Alfie was a character waiting to be written, he already had been written by the novelists of the eighteenth century, but more recently by Jack Trevor Story in his *Live Now, Pay Later*, which had already been written and filmed by the time Naughton's play hit the airwaves. Story is no less sympathetic to his Albert Argyle than is Naughton to Alfie, but the latter is a more soft-centred creation, and once he had been portrayed on-screen by the charming Michael Caine, was pretty much guaranteed to be remembered as the definitive working-class ladies' man of his era. Jack Trevor Story's protagonist was played by an insinuating Ian Hendry who brought to life a far more unsympathetic character as smarmy tally boy Albert Argyle in the film version of *Live Now, Pay Later*.

Naughton has been praised for depicting the underlying decency of the working-classes, and his most famous character is a lovable rogue, but his stories are often more accurately about people who think they're decent and whose desire to think well of themselves compels them to behave half-decently.[1] 'The Little Welsh Girl', one of a number of stories in his collection *Late Night on Watling Street* that offer prototypes of Alfie—who is actually indecent by many standards but self-justifyingly thinks himself a fine fellow—concerns a couple of petty criminals who share a room (they may be homosexuals since at one point the narrator refers to an underground public convenience as a 'cottage', unless this is a wider working-class usage that has become part of gay language) and befriend a young Welsh girl, freshly arrived in London and homeless, in a caff in the Elephant and Castle.

Half-reluctantly they put her up for a while in their room; neither makes any sexual moves on her—they are trying to outdo one another in gallantry—and they suffer her cleaning and general feminising of their living space much as Alfie would, in a language soon to be taken over by Naughton's most famous character: everything is too pongified (constructions like 'pongified', 'poncified' stretch back at least to the dark ages in London speech: the latter appears in James Curtis' 1938 thriller *They Drive By Night*[2])—and after showing her some kindness they finally kick her out amid complaints that she is using too much soap. The men are cowards, and unable to tell her to her face she is no longer wanted, they arrange for a friend to break the news. There is nothing to distinguish their attitudes, but they appear to operate as a check or conscience on each other, so that when the girl, met again a couple of years down the line in a chance encounter, now a prosperous Soho prostitute, acclaims them as the two decentest men she has met in London, they are somewhat put out. They have bought her make-up and the accoutrements of womanhood—and she has put them to use. If they'd known she was going to turn to brass couldn't they have sent her out on the bash themselves?

There is much that is hidden in this story, as well as much in the motivations of its two men that appears to be hidden from themselves, including the sexuality they withhold from the girl: the selfless love and kindness they show her is shown to be more of a manifestation of the good opinion they have of each other—and although this is entirely unstated ('cottage' is my only tenuous evidence for it) they may be a couple of gangland queens who are unable to admit to it. Naughton is good at depicting relationships between men in competition for women, and in his work friendships are more often forged than spoiled by this—it may be that his deeper point is that the two men do not wish to spoil their friendship by competing for this worthless girl, who turns out to have been worthless only because she was still innocent and childlike at the stage they met her.

Another case of a woman trying to come between male friends is described in 'The Half-Nelson Touch', a tale about a pair of wrestlers, their role-playing routine in the ring and their precarious life on the road. Sharing digs and billing as part of a travelling show, The Cosh, Feline Fred and the narrator, Billy the Kid, get along fine and always obey their own rules about how bouts are to turn out, until The Cosh picks up Katie and she joins them in their digs. The problem for Billy is that she keeps borrowing his Edgar Wallace books, which he like to keep close to his side even when he is not reading them. This comic genre piece about wrestlers is particularly reminiscent of 1920s American short story writer, Damon Runyon: funny, colourful, and slight. It's a charmingly told little tale, once again stressing the primacy of male friendship, but despite its 'authentic' working-class setting and tone, it is very reminiscent of stories by W. Somerset Maugham (whose first novel was a working-class genre piece, *Liza of Lambeth*), such as 'Gigolo and Gigolette' or 'Three Fat Women of Antibes' both in the arm's length at which it keeps its characters and the unsensational sense of 'human nature' or 'justice' that is seen inexorably to triumph. There is a moral to the story in a blatant way that leaves little to the imagination and is not terribly satisfying. Bill Naughton is working with an idea of what a short story is, derived from de Maupassant but without a fraction of his subtlety, or his ruthlessness.

'Late Night on Watling Street' offers the scenario of a lorry drivers' café where everyone fancies the proprietor's young wife. She is friendly and a little flirtatious (a bit like Cora in *The Postman Always Rings Twice*) and Lew, her husband, middle-aged and unlikely to best anyone in a fight over her honour, handles the situation with considerable aplomb. However, this is not a comic story: it has death in it, as one driver, Jackson, who hopes that Ethel will run away with him, becomes involved in a testosterone-driven duel with the policeman who is forever trying to make life difficult for the drivers. He manages to kill the copper who has been dogging him, but the innate working-class sense of decency and fair play of the café's other customers ensures that, although they do not shop him to the law for murder, he is no longer welcome as a driver on Watling Street, leaving the coast clear for the story's narrator to become Ethel's next suitor. This story's manner is very reminiscent of an early work by James M. Cain, 'The Baby in the Icebox' or *The Postman Always Rings Twice*, its lorry-driving milieu handled in a way similar to that of James Curtis' *They Drive By Night*. Sex is the driving force of Naughton's story, although it is never quite given its head. Naughton is held back at this stage of his writing career, it seems, by his sense of the mundane realities of working-class life: the sense of its inhibitions and codes, of fantasies being often entertained but not fully acted out, true or not, and of people rubbing along with their dissatisfactions. Apart from Jackson's fatal dice with the police, the only other violence in the story is sparked by his insistence that 'The Tennessee Waltz'—Lew and Ethel's song—should not be played on the jukebox. Jackson's transgression of the code about not acting out, even his murder, results not in a descent into sexual madness, pursuit by vengeful furies of an absolute morality, nor to eventual confession and self-immolation of an early James M. Cain novel, but is punished only by a sneer and a cold shoulder.

'Weaver's Knot' is an evocative piece, one of a number set in the Lancashire of Naughton's boyhood, and is again about a competitive situation between two men. A young boy grows besotted by the thirty year old unmarried woman who works beside him on the looms, and Naughton finely captures the sense of erotic play between them as she befriends him and teaches him the job. After a time it turns out that she has become pregnant by the overseer, whom the boy loathes, but when she collapses at her loom and miscarries her child, the triangular situation leads not to irremediable enmity but to a cross-generational understanding as the boy grasps for the first time what motivates the adults around him and that they are playing for keeps. A beautiful little story, this, that ends with the boy leaving the mill to live the rest o f his life, realising his love for Hetty is trivial compared to her relationship with Harry Ackers, now a disappointed old man with only his invalid wife to care for, all his hopes lost with Hetty's baby, and the boy wishes he could take the formerly hated overseer with him. In 'The Bees Have Stopped Working', Miss Trotter, an abruptly departing neighbour, makes a pair of small boys the gift of a bottle full of white bees—'like slimy overboiled rice'—that will make wine for nothing if properly fuelled with water and sugar, kept happy, not subjected to bad language or other ill-treatment, so long as the wine is kept in a cool place and left to ferment for the right amount of time, 21 days. Careless disregard of these instructions quickly leads to the end of the bees as an active wine-making community, and the moral of this story seems to be that you should follow instructions or you will kill the goose that lays the golden eggs—the vices that lead to the death of the bees are greed, an attempt to deceive and a failure to follow Miss Trotter's instructions, despite the fact that the bees have already made perfectly good wine. Her simple rules turn out to have been a morality as absolute as the punishing categorical imperatives that hunt James M. Cain's characters to their deaths once they have committed their murders, and in refusing to take them seriously they have shown themselves unworthy of the gift of the bees or the limitless supplies of delicious free wine which would otherwise have been theirs.

Naughton's first novel, *One Small Boy*, is an autobiographical book about growing up in Lancashire. Some of these stories are contemporary with it, others show Naughton's attempts to get under the skin of a wider variety of characters, to find something that fits and will enable him to tell a deeper, more critical story. It is not unfair to see his struggle to do this as one in which he has—in part anyway—to overcome his own working-class allegiances, his inherited good opinion of working-class people and his desire to do right by them. I could happily retell every story in the collection: they are a highly engaging set. Naughton's is a traditional view of human character but a generous one: there is a warmth, and sentiment, on the surface of all his writing. What makes his characters attractive is that they tend to find themselves attractive and this, especially in the case of Alfie, appears to make them attractive to others. It's the gulf between Alfie's good opinion of himself and the consequences of his actions that makes him more compelling than any other of Naughton's creations. Alfie has legs, as they say, and is still ambling in the direction of his next woman. His core of relentless selfishness and self-justification is the grit around which this particular pearl has formed, and it doesn't only apply to his treatment of women. The ideal of male friendship in the stories is absent. I'm tempted to think that Naughton has his reasons for no longer believing in it and that *Alfie* may be in part his revenge on his own sex. For Alfie they are only competitors: he lies to and deceives them all realising that this is without consequences. He gets his comeuppance again and again, but it makes little difference. We know he will bounce back as soon as there is someone else to be taken in by him, which there always will be. Alfie's kind of craftiness and relentlessness is as unstoppable in real life as in fiction and we feel unwillingly dragged into celebrating it. He is a kind of working-class victor, a survivor, and those people are attractive to us: many have wrecked their own lives and those of others in attempting to emulate him.

Bill Naughton knew South London well through being a Civil Defence driver during the war, which probably accounts for his infallible ear, his intimate knowledge of London working-class attitudes and mores and his sympathy for the people he had known in adversity. He easily convinces us he is as much south London as he is a Lancashire lad or a son of Ireland. Alfie's deadpan narrative voice, all-knowing but unaware, trying to be funny but not sure why you are laughing, is thus the creation of a reader who knew the territory but was an outsider to it, a reader of American vernacular short stories by Damon Runyon and Ring Lardner (the latter's *You Know Me Al* is a ringer for *Alfie*'s style). Alfie has honed his abilities as a comedian on the best audience of all—people who will laugh at anything:

> I find with women it's not what you say, it's the way you say it. And if I get one of my comical strokes I can make most women laugh. The fact is, most women don't expect you to be funny—all they want to know is, do you want them to laugh. They'll bleeding laugh. You've only got to look at these Palladium comedians to know that. Then I take her bikini briefs out of my pocket and throw them to her. 'Mind you don't catch cold!' I shout.[3]

We first meet Alfie *en famille* with his 'regular Thursday night bint', Siddie, and hear of his view of women's clothing (clothes maketh the woman):

> I mean they can say what they like about the female form divine and all that sort of caper, but if you ask me I reckon three parts of the charm of a woman is her clothes. Silk petticoats, suspenders being fastened over a nice thigh, nice black lacy bra's, and things like that interest me much more than a great big woman would, stretched out naked on a bed. I know this might sound kinky, but I believe it's dead normal.[4]

This sounds quaint now, not exactly kinkily fetishistic but, as he says, dead normal—for the tastes of men of a certain generation. It sounds more like wartime eroticism than the sixties, more like the sentiments of a reader of the *Daily Mirror*'s cartoon strip 'Jane' or an admirer of Betty Grable (or Jayne Mansfield) than of Twiggy or Jean Shrimpton or Julie Christie. We can expect working-class men to be old-fashioned as well as frank in some respects; but there is something else about Alfie and his duplicitous ways that is redolent of the second world war and particularly the period of rationing that continued well after it. He is a practised fiddler. His first job on leaving school was as an errand boy for an East End clothing sweatshop, where he used to steal suits for resale in the pub by his step-mother by putting them on under his clothes, but when caught out by his boss (for looking a bit too bulky for a fourteen year old) although he is sacked, we feel that his employer both admired and respected his enterprising spirit. He lectures one of his shop-girl girlfriends for not having her hand in the till, offers advice on a few till fiddles and recommends having an 'interest' in your work, but not looking too suspiciously happy in it. He himself is highly suspicious, especially of the wiles of female entrapment, saying of Gilda:

> She always let me do what I want, have what I want and be as I am. Of course that might be another way a woman has of putting the block on a bloke. She's a very contented little gal. She's a standby and she knows it, and any bird that knows its place in this life can be quite content.[5]

Another good old London working-class attitude—and not only for women—is knowing your place, so redolent of the glorious prewar and wartime cockney. A fiddler who knows what's what and who knows his place, and is not (he believes) too greedy (only three women on tap): this is an ideal of manhood all should be pleased to aspire to. A conversation with Lofty and Sharpey, a couple of mates in the pub, reveals the political dimensions of all this vis a vis industrial unrest, the parlous state of once Great Britain and the greedy affluent worker—of whom, like everyone else, all three disapprove. But it is Alfie who cuts to the root of the problem of working-class arrogance and disaffection: people aren't scared enough.

> 'There's only one answer to all today's trouble,' I said, 'and you know it as well as I do. It's human bloody nature. If you got a bloke with five kids and you scared the life out of him, like they did in the old days, that he don't get a bite for them kids or himself and his missis unless he works all the hours God sends—you'll get him working.'[6]

To Lofty and Sharpey's half-hearted objections, Alfie retorts: 'If you can't scare 'em, and you can't kid 'em—you need some bloody big incentives to keep 'em working.' This is a key to Alfie; it is a story about people who aren't scared enough, and as such it stands clear of most of the working-class novels of the fifties. It celebrates working-class affluence and confidence in an unashamed way, and suggests that a cockney know-all like Alfie might well be onto something good. Of course there are consequences: women (and men) who are hurt by Alfie's philandering, an abortion, a health-scare—but by and large these are reverses that people are able to cope with, and if Alfie floats free of his responsibilities, it is implied that the women know what they are doing and very much please themselves too. At the bottom of all this is an acceptance of 'human nature', a positive view of working-class resilience and community and an appeal to experience of what is going on under the official accounts of them, and the doomy nostrums of pundits of all political stripes.

> Funny, ain't it, you pick up the papers and read 'em and you'd think there was nothing else went on in this world but raping and coshing and robbing, but once you move out amongst the people with women having kids and one thing and another, you'll find people are quite kind. It surprised me, it did.[7]

Alfie Darling, Naughton's sequel, finds a still at it Alfie on something of a spiritual journey, as befits the later sixties, and offering us his reflections on what is to be human in a lengthy acid-like dream-sequence in which he encounters a lot of seal-like giant foetuses, wanders over some Downs repeating a mantra passed on by his young Catholic girlfriend Abby ('I am the bread of life' in German) and discovers with her that we are all lonely spasms of eternity. However, Alfie's reflections on the sexual division of labour, or the division of labour in sex, remain familiar and deploy a more reassuringly mechanical metaphor:

> After all, when all's said and done, and you get down to essentials, screwing all boils down to a bit of an engineering job. Say the man's the mechanic, and the woman is the engine, and she's not sparking, so that maybe her distributor needs touching up, or her plugs need cleaning, or a the worst she might even need a rebore, but whatever it is, it's the man has got to do the job.[8]

Sentiments which might have come straight out of Delta blues singer Robert Johnson's 'Terraplane Blues': 'Gonna get deep down in this connection/ Keep on tangling with your wires/And when I mash down on your little starter/ Then your spark plugs will give me fire'[9]. But are somehow not as profound without an anguished delivery and a chiming, descending guitar part. Finally, Alfie reveals the real secret of why he is so attractive to women, doesn't really have to try hard to attract them, and can generally take female company for granted. Nature has endowed him generously. There's an incident surprisingly late in the novel where Alfie is abandoned by a lover after she has 'caught sight of my person' and promptly runs out of the door—and no further explanation is needed for the laziness, effortlessness, and in general non-assertiveness with which Alfie conquers women. He has an almost feminine quality they find attractive, we might think, but it is his mighty member that really attracts his endless succession of willing new skins.

This would be a charming element in sex comedy and have enough truth in it to satisfy those who need to have everything fully explained if it weren't for the relentless grating misogyny of its prideful possessor. But this doesn't play quite as it once did. It could be that there is no longer a public space in which 'what men really think' can appear, and that men would be fools to own up to many of Alfie's thoughts: he's no longer so amusing, his attitudes are hard to take page after page, and if he battened onto you in a pub you would soon run out of the door. But if common-or-garden masculinity needs defending in our feminised culture and ever finds a voice it's unlikely to be one that sounds anything like this thorny, horny avatar of male desire. Alfie's picaresque adventures don't completely escape being a nasty laugh at the expense of women—he doesn't really love them as Don Juan is said to—and his inwardness, reflectiveness, inventiveness and pitiful beseeching of the Almighty don't do much to mitigate him. He will always cajole us into accepting the unacceptable, we are charmed into submission and left gasping for air.

The remake of *Alfie* starring the irritating Jude Law takes the precaution of making him middle-class, in diction, anyway, still a chauffeur but with a business plan and social aspirations, and duly Americanised: 'couples should never split up between thanksgiving and January 2nd'. He is a social climber who only seems to go out with Americans. Alfie II is just too goddamned caring and preoccupied with calibre—not of his member but his women. Alfie II is not the seducer anymore but the seducee, and he's looking for 'the one'. In Bill Naughton's original only women believe in that sort of nonsense, and Alfie I is definitely in control of the situation, at least most of the time: when he isn't, when he's in jeopardy, he becomes 'human'. Alfie II is just a good-looking guy in a suit, a guy who can't 'commit': Jude Law anachronistically (illegally) rides a scooter without a crash helmet—so his carefully mussed hair doesn't get mussed in the wrong way. Alfie II hides his feelings, but they have a quiet way of sneaking up on him when he least expects it. However, the comeuppance is the same. He's always saying sorry, but he seems to do most of the suffering in this remake. Maybe he's just the same old geezer in a slightly different set-up.

Is Alfie just another back door man or is he trying to achieve social mobility by screwing out of his class and constantly playing away from home? In a way the tales of Alfie's misadventures with women in all his incarnations repeat as knockabout farce what had already been told as tragedy by earlier writers of the Angry Young Man moment. David Storey, the third son of a coal-miner, was another Northern working-class writer in search of success in the South in the early sixties. His first book, *This Sporting Life*, had covered the territory of aspiring working-class fortunes through the story of Arthur Machin[10], a man who achieves distinction by playing Rugby League Football but is at the end of his professional career. An unusual story about a working-class hero who, like Arthur Seaton, remains in the working-class, it was turned into a successful film with Richard Harris.[11] But Storey's second novel, *Flight into Camden* is a better, if somewhat incongruous, comparison to *Alfie*, as well as an unusual instance in this paroxysm of writings about the travails of working-class men, in that it is a pained relationship novel that is told through the eyes of a woman, Margaret Thorpe, the daughter of a miner, and charts the troubled course of her love affair with a married lecturer in Industrial Design named Howarth (is he Rochester, Heathcliff or Branwell Brontë?), a disaffected failed artist figure who is from a less secure and respectable background than her own traditional working-class family. Its mournful tone is closer to Robert Johnson's 'Come on in my Kitchen' ('it's bound to be raining outdoors') than the jaunty 'Terraplane Blues'.[11]

If social mobility is one of the main subjects of the Angry Young Men and the legacy of D.H. Lawrence one of their principal resources for exploring it, David Storey's *Flight into Camden* is one of the most sensitive and anguished novels of that moment, in which the post-war dream of social equality unravels and the ideal of freely-chosen relationships between men and women proves more difficult to sustain than had been expected. As Alfie observes his women at their domestic chores and chafes under their possessiveness, commenting for us out of the side of his mouth, Margaret observes her man around the house, dealing with his divorce and separation from his children, his hated teaching job and the collapse of his dreams, and tries to understand what makes him tick. It is a novel supposedly about passion, but although it is full of descriptions of physical love, these have a curiously withheld and analytical quality that makes them all too convincing. Like Alfie's ruminations about his procession of women, Margaret's observations show she has understanding but not very much sympathy for Howarth's problems—she makes him sound rather a repellent character, and somewhat loses the sympathy of the reader herself with her refusal to take the predicament of his wife and children seriously. Her consciousness is scalpel-like, and under her incisive gaze, in the seedy rooms they share in Camden, Howarth is as dehumanised as any of Alfie's girlfriends:

> I had a habit when I was lying on the bed and Howarth was across the room, of twisting my head, of twisting my head into the sheets so that I could see him upside down. His face then appeared like a piece of apparatus, mechanical and amusingly inhuman. His big toyishness was emphasised by the silent shutting of his eyes and the clamp-like openings of his mouth… Once, when he caught me looking at him in this way, he laughed: the horrible mechanics of it, the great split of his mouth and the huge cogs that were his teeth, the shutter of his eye, convulsed me. The nostrils opened and quivered, the cheeks creased back in thick folds, flushing with the effort of his laughter. The sound itself was transformed into a vibrant mechanical sobbing; the flanges of a great machine rasping together under a heavy load.[12]

Margaret feels guilty about seeing her lover this way, especially as he has abandoned his wife and two children for her, but she cannot help wondering what it is of him that is human, what indeed is human about any human beings as they scurry past her on the London streets: these characters are Lawrentian creations, written at the height of his post-war influence: disgusted by the half-aliveness exhibited by most of God's two-legged creatures and supposedly determined to be fully-awake, fully-sensual, fully-alive. But one notable thing about this claustrophobic novel is its vision of London as an empty, rotting place of flight and isolation, an ultimate stark reality where the last moves are to be played out and the limits of fantasy reached once and for all: a place of truth and consequences. Lawrence also has a hand in its view of society in general, of love and family relationships in particular, and on Margaret's odd mixture of qualities as a female narrator: her apparent lack of self-knowledge, her intermittent sexual passion, and her alienation. Howarth is an intriguing character: morbidly sensitive, ruthless, but finally unable either to deliver on his ambitions or simply to be happy. He is a sort of anti-Alfie—arrogant enough, but self-importantly brooding, and completely devoid of charm. He is a naturally isolated and inward person and seems to be roundly hated by nearly everyone he encounters.

Albert Camus' celebrated essays *The Rebel* and *The Myth of Sisyphus* ask a central question of the immediate post-war world. How can a person live authentically and meaningfully without the consolations of a belief in God or a triumphalist humanism? Absurdism is his version of St Augustine's state of *distensio*, Søren Kierkegaard's fear and trembling, or Martin Heidegger's philosophy of temporality—in which individual consciousness is marooned in a perpetual present without access to past or future, except as futile regret or specious hopes, the latter always played against an awareness of impending death. Camus, however, continues to ask how one can resist the impulse to lose oneself in suicide or empty hedonism and achieve a kind of clear-sighted moral agency towards others. His outsiders can't really be said to be trying 'to ratify a personal failure in unconcern', and nor can David Storey's working-class rebels in *Flight into Camden.*

The novel opens at her grandfather's funeral, at which she and her brother Michael are the only non-labouring members of the family. An introspective and apparently friendless girl who has been to the local Grammar school and now works for the National Coal Board, she is overshadowed and overawed by her brother Michael, a successful young university lecturer whom she regards as something of a bully. Michael takes her to a Christmas party at the university, and it is here that she meets and dances with Howarth, and immediately agrees to meet him again, much to her brother's anger and disgust and the foreboding of her family. Howarth takes her to a local literary circle whose attendees read out and discuss the poetry of the great, and their own, and she sees that he is a frustrated outsider and something of an intellectual snob, wincing with facetiousness towards those with whom he associates, feeling that the efforts of these people make a mockery of the ideals of education and self-improvement in which he no longer believes. He himself has repudiated art for industrial design, in which he is frustrated but in a way secure: in common with many people who have decided they are not good enough to be artists, he enjoys deriding the pretensions of others. This quality fails to put Margaret off and before long they have embarked on a love affair. In the spring they lounge by a hidden woodland pool and once Howarth has his shirt off, she notices he has two deep scars on his back, which he tells her are from shrapnel wounds. Like many heroes of early postwar novels, including Joe Lampton, he has been tested in combat and is the bearer of wounds from the war: scars that will never properly fade, disappointed hopes and the sense that the progressive rhetoric of post-war reconstruction is a sham and a lie—a soured romanticism of which he is unable to quite let go. Margaret's commentary on Howarth's opinions and responses suggests that she experiences most things through him, including the landscape around their town:

> I sat on the fence while he cleaned his shoes. He stared down at the track, as though dazed by the seclusion, by the emptiness and the lack of use. The single line cut cleanly through the untidiness of the wood and the mine, its curve disappearing slowly and neatly round the shoulders of the cutting. It was the uselessness that excited him, like the wet and disintegrating darkness of the mine. He gazed through the fence at the cutting while he bent down scraping his shoes.[13]

The main source of Margaret's sense of the insufficiency of her own perceptions, of her modesty and her buried resentments is revealed when her mother tells her that one of the reasons she hadn't been allowed to go on to college was that her brother thought 'it'd be a waste of time and money educating a woman. At least beyond the Grammar School. And your Dad agreed with him.'[14] She brushes aside her mother's revelations and tries to be a dutiful daughter, to perform her housework in her mother's 'domestic mannerisms' so as not to upset her sense of authority in the house, and she listens meekly to her father's miserable, guilt-inducing insistence that 'She'll be in her grave afore you do ought about it.'

Michael and Howarth seem to be agreed on one point: the notion that people can be improved though education is 'the big fallacy of our times' and that therefore Michael and Margaret's father's reluctant 'sacrifices' in that direction have been futile and misguided. Working-class people just aren't made 'different and better' by education, and even the successful ones, like them, will only be employed in buttressing these pernicious myths. Michael loathes Howarth as a self-important creep still attached to the bogus notion of art, while Margaret's lover describes her brother as 'an intellectual gangster', a condition he ascribes to his being working-class: 'Your brother always shows he's working-class. He has a habit of taking advantage of the disinterested nature of his work to make *personal* claims for it—and other things. It's a workman's habit.' If outsiders ratify a personal failure by unconcern, the aspiring working-classes bring everything they learn about their class condition to their personal interests, they draw their new knowledge into a consideration of themselves in a kind of advantage-seeking special pleading. I myself have heard it argued that to deploy such arguments is in itself a sign of intellectual inferiority, but in defence of those who do it might be said that every disadvantaged group has done exactly the same thing in contexts where a dominant group appears to define the parameters of knowledge in a social way: women, racial and religious minorities and homosexuals have been equally unable to accept that knowledge of them *is* 'disinterested', and have advanced themselves by challenging its truth-claims, but may only do so in contexts where to do so is regarded as semi-legit.

On the other hand, as a grammar-school girl, Margaret finds Howarth's liking for football matches and much else about him helplessly 'crude', especially when he is unguarded and acting by instinct, and thinks that that is what defines him (pejoratively) as an artist for her brother Michael. Howarth in turn accuses her of being afraid of feelings and of expressing herself physically and emotionally, while Margaret claims that to be 'a person, not just a selfish lout', order and discipline are necessary. He tries to challenge her conventional responses to the demands the world makes on her, she claims to love her family and accuses him of wanting to destroy everything around her so that she is forced to turn to him for support:

> 'You're not as weak as all that,' I said. 'It pleases you to think you're helpless. The poor orphan. You're always talking in that sick way about the working-class and your awful parents. I can see the implication all right.'
>
> 'It was you who told me I was helpless.'
>
> 'Yes, and you are. But my God, you know how to take advantage of it. Don't ever tell me you don't.'
>
> 'I don't know… I must seem very artful to you.'
>
> 'There's nothing babyish about you, Howarth. You're clever and smart, I can tell. And you know how to destroy.'
>
> 'How am I helpless and crude, then?' he said, knowing now that he had triumphed.
>
> 'Because other people make you helpless. They're prepared to deny themselves so that you can be as you are. It's really them who've given everything to you. You're like a lost person to other people, but you irritate them by insisting that you know exactly where you are. It's so obvious you're wrong.'
>
> He laughed at his incomprehension. We walked up the avenue between the rows of houses without speaking. He glanced up occasionally at the blank fronts as if they vaguely amused him.[15]

This is the matter of their relationship, its mutual approach and the main areas of conflict, but it is the sex which flares up between them that cements them as a closely-bonded but somewhat contradictory couple. Margaret finds Howarth to be 'shut in' a lonely world of his own private opinions, whereas 'You could have shared opinions, like other people's.'[16] If there is a bleak irony in Margaret's recommendation that Howarth should share in the kinds of opinions that have defined her social parameters as a woman, there is an even bleaker irony in Howarth's definition of

Michael's inescapable working-class quality as being his inability to take a disinterested view of knowledge, whilst he himself is alienated to the point of contempt from art, education and people in general. However, *Flight into Camden* isn't an ironic or witty novel, rather it is one that grapples painfully with the definitions of its time and the possibilities, or lack of them, that they offer its characters. What is clear is that both of these lovers are 'shut in' and that possible escape routes are also highly problematic, requiring also an act of absolute faith in one another of which neither seems likely to be capable.

Margaret and Howarth's affair soon leads to some ill-spirited gossip her mother is unable to bear, and rejected by her family, at the book's mid-point, the couple flee to Camden, Howarth deciding to leave his wife and children and make a new start in the city. Like much of what occurs in *Flight into Camden* there is something abrupt and mysterious about all this, despite the fact that Margaret has plenty to flee from. The final rift with her father is particularly painful for her to bear, and is a good example of Margaret's estranged middle-class tone towards her family. It might seem implausible but powerfully suggests an imprisoned intelligence; it also describes her father's way of punishing her (supposedly for hurting her mother, but really for betraying him) in terms of a kind of theatre of suffering or martyrdom:

> He had a miner's uncouthness about him, and a miner's silence in pain, retributive, embracing all those who watched it. He had a miner's indifference to the physical, a savage complacency, that turned his silent reproach on me with a long association of childhood meanings. He had nothing to say or advise; his helplessness sustained his desire to hurt me. Yet if I didn't respond to him he would think I despised him, that not only had I betrayed him by bringing someone to the house in his absence, but was unrepentant about it.[17]

We learn a little of Howarth's relationship with his wife and children, something of his feelings for Margaret, but not very much of what motivates her, apart from an understandable desire to escape from the constraints of living at home. In their arguments Margaret insists that she loves her family. It is as though her lover has taken her over in a way, but Margaret's consciousness filters everything, imparting a disquieting sense that this highly intelligent, sensitive but passive woman is unable to be anything but a toy of circumstances and conceptions that have been supplied to her largely by men. The novel is an essay in frustration that creates its novelistic resonance out of the lack of fit between its characters' self-conceptions, the expectations of their families and communities, and what they allow themselves to hope for but are unable to grasp. Howarth (his first name is Gordon, but tellingly he never uses it for fear of ridicule, and Margaret calls him by his surname) is similarly constrained by a hostile community that has destroyed his ambitions to be an artist but continues to antagonistically define him as one. Margaret and Howarth's affair seems to be intensified by her brother's sudden conventional marriage to the bubbly, vacuous Gwen. Margaret wonders if Howarth is simply using her as a way of getting away from his wife, Howarth tries to convince her of his love—he is undeniably preoccupied with what he is leaving behind and his own attempt to start again seems ill-grounded, desperate. Margaret seems to offer a second chance at happiness, Howarth a possibility of escape, although not much of one, but for a man excited by uselessness and a young woman with nothing to lose, Camden is an inevitable destination.

> I tried to ignore the scene, just as he ignored me: I had a vague impression of streets narrower and buildings dirtier that I had ever expected; of row after row of sordid houses, filthier than anything I had seen at home. The area we went through was one of disintegration and decay, infected with a parasitic disease that fed on the buildings, the brick and the stone. It was its desolaiton and the persistence of its life that wearied me: the streets were full of eager, rushing people.[18]

Nothing could be further from the swinging London which is Alfie's backdrop and the ultimately trivial attitude Alfie has to his women—his cheery vision, not of a later serial monogamy but of unofficial confluent polygamy—than David Storey's dark vision of an encroaching community and a city of refuge which offers anonymity but no real respite from the problems his characters carry with them and the crushing sense of isolation both continue to feel. Alfie exploits the sense of subservient devotion that some of his women appear to exhibit towards him, and feels hurt when others exploit him as a recreational vehicle as he regularly does them. What's sauce for the goose is ultimately sauce for the gander in Bill Naughton's city, which is a place of hedonism, rapid turnaround and a seeming lack of consequences for sexual misdemeanour. David Storey's lovers are devoted to one another if pained, and their sex is treated as a kind of exploratory sacrament, truly terrible when it falls short of this ideal:

> 'Aren't you satisfied with me?' I asked, complacent.
> 'Yes. If this is what you mean.' He felt my breasts, almost derisively arousing me. 'Yet you and your body… they're miles apart.'[19]

The lovers are dogged at every step by family ghosts and obligations on streets thronging with blind hurrying Eliotic masses inhabiting ancient subdivided buildings whose very brick-work is diseased: infested by a strange corrosive blight which will soon put paid to any inoculating hopes its inhabitants may once have harboured. A flu jab would perhaps be in order, but even this would be unlikely to hold off the viral despair that nags at Howarth and Margaret as they try to make their fragile new relationship work in the city they have fled to. Earlier in the book Margaret can find 'no underlying pattern, no reason' behind Howarth's sudden changes of mood, 'unless it was a deep and virtually implacable pessimism.'[20] But the same might be said of Margaret's withering intellect. Thrown on one another's company, isolated Northerners in North London, their relationship is close but strained. Howarth's hopes of finding work as a commercial artist fail to materialise and he is forced back into teaching in a secondary school where the pupils seem to hate him, and his contempt for education and its dedication to 'mediocrity' is further deepened. Margaret finds secretarial work at the BBC, and is treated far better there than her saturnine lover, but comes to feel she is little more than a machine. It appears there is only the life of their physical relationship to sustain them and that Howarth's flight was a falling down, an acceptance of defeat and rejection by the community he has left behind. His divorce fails to materialise, he misses his children, but Margaret is unable to face the part of his life he has left behind: she is unwilling to look at pictures of them and is uninterested and completely cynical where his abandoned wife is concerned. Their sex finally hits the rocks when Margaret refuses to use contraception ('artificial') when, so far as he is concerned, it is quite impossible for them to have a child. Howarth's overwhelming experience of the city is one of floating, robbed of reality:

> 'You know, I always used to think I was a 'real' person, But recently, now… I'm beginning to feel I'm only a figment of my own imagination. Isn't that odd? I've always charged myself with being down-to-earth, with being one of the unfeeling poor But now, though… it's as if I'm floating in the air, that, that I've never once had my feet on the ground. (…) I was a joke, I know, in the university common room because I took some things seriously. Anyone who does that nowadays is suspect straight away.'[21]

The end of their affair arrives suddenly when her brother materialises and attacks her in the street, insisting that she should come home because her mother is ill. Margaret at first refuses, believing rightly that this is a ploy to force her to return. But Howarth insists that she should go back with her brother, and she does, unwillingly, only to receive a letter from her lover a day later terminating their affair. Once more Margaret is imprisoned by her family. She and Howarth are never to meet again, and at the end of the book we discover that Howarth has dutifully returned to his wife and children. Michael—happy in his own new marriage—has triumphed as ever over his sister's independent will, and comments that Howarth 'might be human after all.' *Flight into Camden* is built around Lawrence's conceptions of love between men and women, his pessimistic views on education and mass society, his oppositions between the mechanical and the human, but it ends in the defeat of his ideas as embodied in Howarth and Margaret. You can't leave home. You can't escape from society or from what Lawrence calls 'the work prison'. Furthermore, there are no second chances. It is a novel that is as implacably pessimistic as Howarth is—their relationship has foundered on his lack of courage rather than Margaret's—but it can certainly be read as a critique of the Lawrentianism in which it is inscribed, it is an ideology which in practice offers them no real solutions, and is ultimately despairing since a pair of rebellious lovers can't defeat the stultifying social mores of their community, although there are no acceptable terms of reference outside of the terms of Howarth's attempted revolt and Margaret's brave repudiation of her family's expectations. Michael's final crushing remark about Howarth's humanity is the bleakest irony of all, and we know that Margaret's wings have been clipped forever: she will not fly free again.

But how to account for the drastic differences between *Alfie* and *Flight into Camden* as working-class novels of approximately the same moment? Is any such account needed? Why compare them at all? After all, why shouldn't they be different? They are by different writers of course: a comedy in which people die and a tragedy in which nobody does. The simple explanations of their differences turn out to be not so simple as you'd think, but as a preliminary how about the notion Naughton was a writer who'd grown up in and experienced a variety of working-class life, hadn't been to university, and doesn't really accommodate middle-class views of his subjects? Both he and Storey were miner's sons, but Storey is of the generation who progressed through education in the post-war world, and thus takes on the dominant ideas about the working-class in the post-war world—those of Lawrence and Leavis—and shares with the other Angry Young Men a turbulence borne of this collision of values: the experience of moving up into a context which is ostensibly sympathetic but has an underlyingly negative, pitying view of you and your experience, or at any rate a radically different view than you are used to. On the other hand

Storey was a professional footballer and wrote eloquently about people who stayed in the working-class. Storey's characters are real people with problems; Naughton's are sentimentalised comic creations. Naughton's characters are real working-class people with authentic attitudes; Storey's are middle-class people in disguise, preoccupied with middle-class ideas about class, and especially with negating the assumptions of socialism and social democracy, questions which occupy Naughton hardly at all in Alfie, although his autobiographical writings show him to have vivid memories of the twenties miners' strikes and lock-outs and the General Strike of 1926, detailed family accounts of which he offers in his marvellous late memory books, *On the Pig's Back* and *Saintly Billy*.[22] In fact he is probably more of a socialist writer than David Storey, and certainly more of a populist. The upwardly mobile characters of Storey and the Angries certainly make no bones about feeling superior to the class they have come from, and, as we have seen, Storey, who spent most of his working life in education, is concerned to show it is not really the solution to working-class problems. Naughton has no particular interest in these questions. Naughton is an Irish writer. Storey is English. Naughton is an accepting Catholic; Storey is in an argument with Christian morality and the very idea of a congregation. Naughton views communities as nurturing, supportive and people (especially women) as essentially trusting: it is these qualities Alfie is able to exploit to his advantage. Storey views communities as stultifying and families as uncomprehending, full of antagonism and ultimately destructive of individual freedom: they and the values they represent are the rock and the values of the middle class as found in education and the wider world are the hard place between which Margaret and Howarth are finally caught in the man-trap out of which they cannot walk.

Alfie has found a perfect way of walking out of such social traps: he sees them coming a mile off. The films do their best to make him abject at the end, or at least rueful about his womanising, but in the books he romps home free and his old girlfriends are always glad to see him again. Once again film closes down a set of liberatory insights into a moralising allegory, and with no particular social accuracy either—in real life it is not all that unusual for men or women to hop from partner to partner until they can hop no more, and to suffer no particular ill-consequences of this, so long as they are determined, well-heeled and endlessly self-justifying, whatever their hopped over partners may come to feel about them. *Alfie* is about a repeating pattern of restlessness in many relationships, but it is really about working-class self-conceptions: it is important for Alfie's presentation of his outlook, his sense of having something to impart and his resultant self-importance about his funny little life, that what he is telling us is the word from below, perfectly reasonable and honest but untramelled by the tramlines of any educated or middle-class thinking; he thinks he is already educated and is apparently taken as an authority by others. *Flight into Camden* explores the pains and consequences of a single love affair, but its not very subterranean subject is conceptions of the working-class current in education and their impact on working-class people struggling to redefine themselves in transition from one class to another.

There is a difference too of course in who is being addressed in these fictions: *Alfie* was a radio play before and a film simultaneously with its appearance as a novel, aimed at a working-class audience as well as a middle-class one: it is an a entertainment. David Storey might have hoped that *Flight into Camden* would be turned into a film as brooding as that Lindsay Anderson made with Richard Harris in *This Sporting Life*. But that anguished novel and brooding film was about a sportsman at the end of his days. *Flight into Camden* might just about have made it as an arthouse film, more if the sex angle was played up; the grimy locations, the atmosphere of psychological lower depths, sexual repression and unbreakable class allegiances might have brought it to the screen; but *A Kind of Loving* was made instead. David Storey's second novel, lacking in dramatic action or much romantic pathos (its leads are fairly unattractive people, unsympathetic to a popular audience whoever might have played them) had merely to be read—its truths were too hard, its treatment of sex and class too thorny, its preoccupations too literary, and as a novel is too concerned with unravelling myths and exposing the limits of love and art, and the fudges involved in official views of social progress through mass education to really have done anything much at the Odeon box office. How does Tony Hancock's celebrated film *The Rebel*, which came out in the same year, compare to *Flight into Camden*? Galton and Simpson's protagonist is a corpulent poseur in a cosy version of bedsit land; Storey's characters have real things to rebel against and pay a hard price for their attempt to take the difficult path of leaving their community and families behind to start anew. *The Rebel* is a fable about the pretentiousness amd crookedness of the art world. Hancock hasn't the talent to make it as an artist, but has all the qualities hew needs as a crook, stealing his talented studio-mate's paintings with familiar upbeat results. Storey's lovers are defeated by the reality of London life, and the reality of love.

A recent report suggests that social mobility through education, rising significantly from 1958 until the end of the sixties, the approximate frame of this study and the preoccupations of many of the key novels I have discussed, stalled in around 1970 and that social progress via this particular ladder has not recovered since. According to Dr Jo Blanden of the Sutton

Trust, an educational charity set up by Sir Peter Lampl, a three-year-old child from a poor home who shines in early testing is likely to be overtaken by a low-performing child from a rich background by the age of seven, and the expansion of higher education between the early 1990s and 2002 has been achieved almost entirely by an increase in the numbers of low-performing children from middle-class and rich backgrounds taking up new university places. Although social mobility had risen considerably to reach 1970 levels, Britain was at that time bottom of an international league table of social mobility. Children born today face 'stark inequalities' with 44% of young people from the richest fifth of the population going on to university, with only 10% of children from the poorest fifth of households. As Sir Peter Lampl says, 'It is appalling that young people's life chances are still so tied to the fortunes of their parents and that this situation has not improved over the last three decades.'[23]

It is interesting that the sudden disappearance of this theme from British fiction should coincide with the moment at which social mobility stalled, as well as that the orgy of painful socio-cultural navel-gazing that accompanied Britain's short post-war period of rising social mobility so closely reflected the agenda of labour politics and education in this period. Writers like Naughton and Jack Trevor Story, who never ventured into universities, could be articulate spokespeople for a kind of recidivist working-classism, while those, like Storey, who ventured into the rapids of middle-class culture found that even the most distinguished writers from the pre-war working-class, like D.H. Lawrence, had by a process of mysterious osmosis, turned into anti-democratic ideologues of an aristocratic view of culture and a timeless sense of social place in which the dark instinctual consciousness of the lower classes might be accorded an honoured, invisible position. Interesting too that the United States comes joint bottom in these studies of social mobility. How could it be that the countries which shout loudest about social equality and meritocracy are the poorest performers in realising its actuality? How could it be that poor children who are brighter than rich children at the age of three are stupider by the age of seven? Could it be that the working-classes are consuming their own children, either due to our long bitter experience that education 'isn't for the likes of us' or a simple inability to understand the nature of certain abilities or to comprehend their value? Or maybe even simpler social wealth gaps and gulfs of expectation and opportunity are the answer? Nothing points more clearly to the mismatch between culture and society, or to the urgent necessity of holding cultural and political representations in both their widest and most particular senses to some sort of public account.

And what of David Storey's baleful claim that the idea of education turning people into something different, better, something they weren't, was the greatest, most pernicious myth of its times? Is it just the last despairing gasp of a class that had been brought up with deeply ingrained feudal attitudes, or is there something in his view? The disturbing figures on social stagnation may only reflect organic limits to what can be achieved in terms of genuine social equality; on the other hand it seems clear to me that the British educational system with its feudal privileges, bought university places, and drastic inequalities, as well as a generally polite view of being cultured that hasn't really shifted much in higher education since Raymond Williams inveighed against 'the culture of the teashop' and Kingsley Amis enthusiastically praised J.G. Ballard's science fiction for being 'literature without the little finger raised'. My opinion is that the working-class were simply dumped by a metropolitan literary elite that had grown bored with their real problems, their conservatism and their reluctance to turn into some sort of revolutionary vanguard. Kingsley Amis seems to have done just this by the time he declared that left-wing intellectuals were suffering from 'social romanticism' in 1958. The same newspaper article from which I drew my account of the Sutton Trust's report on the stagnation of social mobility noted an 11% rise in applications to Oxford from black students in 2007. This is of course to be welcomed, but one can't help suspecting that this new agenda of inclusion is just another fashion moment, and that the more established immigrant communities had better jump up that ladder while the sun shines, before the cultural, educational and political establishments of this country grow nervous of the social consequences of politically empowering their more articulate children and go looking for another group to break in as temporary cultural fodder.

Former Labour Party leader Neil Kinnock explained in a recent radio interview that the increased relative poverty gap between the lower working-class and the middle class is accentuated by the massive expansion of the middle class in the postwar era. He told BBC Radio Two listeners that when he was growing up (in a prefab) many other people were in the same predicament; they had a solidarity and a culture of shared aspirations, and the expanded education system was there to transport him and his contemporaries up the social ladder. Contemporary lower working-class people are more culturally isolated as well as relatively poorer. The Labour Party's commitment to education was honoured by an expansion of higher-education places. But what will the qualifications such young working-class people so obtain be worth compared to a middle-class provenance and a degree from an established institution? The ladder is still there, and politicians may be sincere about helping everyone who can to step onto it; but the sense of possibility out of which Raymond Williams wrote his books, if it ever truly existed, that of a culturally and politically articulate working-class, has all but disappeared. David Storey and Bill Naughton, both writers from the Northern working-class: a writer who tracked that experience into education, and a populist writer who played for a working-class audience; complementary voices from a moment when both experiences were deemed important, even central, to British culture.

Chapter Fourteen

Doris Lessing: Odd Man Out

Doris Lessing arrived in London in 1949 from what was then Southern Rhodesia with little to her name except a young son, a few contacts in the Communist Party, and her first novel, *The Grass is Singing*, in the publishing pipeline. *In Pursuit of the English* (1960), written immediately after her five-volume *Children of Violence* sequence about the life and intellectual development of Martha Quest, deals with her early experiences in London as a single mother, and particularly with her desire to 'meet the English', which can be a difficult task for visitors to London to this day. Lessing found herself in a middle-class Communist enclave in Knightsbridge, dependent on the good graces of people she hardly knew, and uncomfortable with the politics of the postwar British CP, whose leader, Harry Pollitt, was seized by, among other things, a zeal to abolish working-class consumerism in a context where rationing was still very much in force and there was precious little in the shops for working-class people to consume, even if they'd had the money to do so.

Lessing makes this sound slightly amusing in her much later autobiography, or at least perfectly ridiculous.[1] *In Pursuit of the English*, written after she had been resident in London for a decade, strikes much the same note even as it conveys an outsider's discovery of a popular point of view as well as her resilient belief that she will be able to see and express the truth of what is really going on with the English working-class, and exudes a confidence which sustained her through her subsequent long career as a writer. *In Pursuit of the English* is a fascinating documentary (although quite as much a novel as the Martha Quest epic) of London in the immediate postwar years—peopled by spivs, shop-girls, prostitutes and others, all of whom she encounters with a brisk confidence, and who accept her own (to them not unusual) predicament as a single mother without turning a peroxide or brylcreemed hair. This minor book of Lessing's is a unique compendium of London working-class women's lives and attitudes in its early postwar period. A year in a boarding house and the intersecting lives of a few men and women—abortions, beatings, a spiv's scheming machinations, the gross sexual demands of some men and women's attempts to trap them into marriages few would envy, the coquettishness of a romantic virgin who fears marriage, the sunny disposition and self-acceptance of a well-heeled prostitute, vignettes of fearsome old crones, crying children who are beaten to sleep or merely tolerated—these are

Lessing's matter. For Lessing maybe it's a document of the lives of people who don't know how to live, who have had to muddle through the war on fear and ignorance, custom and tradition, on bad ways usually, making do and mend; but however naïve they may be, it's also perfectly clear to all of these people that Doris is living amongst them to gather material for a book, a circumstance out of which she makes comic capital from time to time.

She begins with an amusingly stereotypical definition of the elusive English male character: 'At first glance I knew he was the real thing. Tall, asthenic, withdrawn; but above all, he bore all the outward signs of the inwards, intestine-twisting prideful melancholy. We talked about the weather and the Labour Party.'[2] But this particular party also denies being English; he had a Welsh grandmother, leading Lessing to reflect that the English must be the most persecuted minority on earth and that 'like Bushmen in the Kalahari, that doomed race, they vanish into camouflage at the first sign of danger.' Later, following her experiences in the boarding house, she is told that the people she lived with were not the real working-class but 'lumpen proletariat, tainted with petty bourgeois ideology', and that likewise some miners she had met on another occasion were hardly typical of the English working-classes. Not only do the English hide themselves away, they are particularly sensitive about outsiders making generalisations about 'their' working-class, who seem to vanish before the observer's gaze, a trick of the light, or a category mistake, and Lessing is apparently foiled, like an earlier Polly Toynbee, all dressed down but with no-one truly significant to meet and report upon earnestly for the enlightenment of the *Guardian*-reading middle-classes.

After a false start flat-sharing with a bossy Australian in Bayswater Road, Lessing strikes out on her own by asking a girl at a shop counter if she happens to know of anywhere to live. It is the few streets of the Bayswater area that we come to know, full of bomb damage, prostitution and poverty, but also full of bustling ground-level enterprise and a spirit of recovery. So begins her relationship with Rose, with Flo, her husband Dan, and with an extravagantly drawn con-man variously known as Bobby Brent, Mr MacNamara and Alfred Ponsonby, whose scheming and one-upmanship provides a kind of foil for Lessing's writerly guile as the book progresses. As a battle of wits between a man and a woman, Lessing's encounters with Bobby Brent are particularly amusing for her justified confidence that she has seen through his various and relentless subterfuges, and her technique of completely going along with anything he suggests in order to gather yet more material on the mindset of the criminal classes. At first blissfully unaware of whom is on whose baited hook, he is painted as sufficiently cunning to at least slightly know when he is being outmanoeuvered. But it seems all-important to him to think he has taken her in. Lessing plays him along most of the time, and is fascinated by what she sees as the psychology of the spiv:

> He was not in the least like any of the rogues or adventurers I had known in Africa. They had all had a certain frankness, almost a gaiety, in being rogues. Mr MacNamara had nothing whatsoever in common with them. His strength was—and I could feel just how powerful that strength was, now I was recovering from my moment of being mad—his terrible, compelling anxiety that he should be able to force someone under his will. It was almost as if he were pleading, silently, in the moment when he was tricking a victim: please let me trick you; please let me trick you; please let me cheat you; I've got to; it's essential to me.[3]

Her moment of madness was to give him two guineas—which he generously commutes to pounds—as a flat-finder's deposit, but this transaction turns out not to have been so foolish after all, since he does indeed find her a flat, she signals her acceptance of his *raison d'être* and initiates a cat-and-mouse game that is to provide her with much material. Lessing apparently has little money, but the social relationships of *In Pursuit of the English* appear to be underpinned by her hosts' calculations of how much and in what ways they can cheat her—this is a *sine qua non* of her relationship with these working-class (or lumpen proletarian) Londoners. Like all social tourists she knows that you have to pay to be accepted and this she is eager to achieve: by paying her way she negotiates a space in the social economy of the household, which may be no more than to say that she must (like everyone else) pay the rent; but as in all boarding-house novels, it seems, the cost of a room can soar or shrink depending on what the landlady thinks of you, and a grudging respect must be earned by refusing to be stiffed by these cunning, rapacious harridans.

Rose, her main female informant and the person to whom she becomes closest, has scarcely stepped out of West London since birth, as appears to be the case with many of Bayswater's denizens, and you might think that such a settled community would run on rails, but it seems that everyone must renegotiate their place in it on a day-to-day basis, cavilling over trivial rights and wrongs and living out their lives in a world that remains largely mysterious to them as they trundle around on these ancestral tracks. At least, so it appears to Lessing as an observer of their tribal ways. The reader is stuck again and again by her sense that these people have forgotten what happened yesterday, what was said a moment ago, only to repeat it all, to say the same things, and bump up against the same obstacles or people with the same oaths or truisms on their lips. Lessing likes Rose's girlishness and is dismayed by her melancholy, her reliance on traditional wisdom, her self-denying approach to sex and her self-destructive fixation on a man who plainly cares little for her. Rose resents Doris' well-travelled middle-class attitudes, it's 'all very well for her' to think such and such, and has little real understanding of her new housemate's point of view. Flo and Dan have a fractious relationship based on her continual Italian cooking and his relentless demands for sex; their little girl Aurora has seemingly refused to learn to read, talk or eat, and despite the attentions of a social worker, a clip round the ear remains Flo's cure all for her daughter's ills. The little girl upstairs, Rosemary, has little more luck. Her parents, the Skeffingtons, have an even more violent marital relationship: 'I'm not naughty, I'm not naughty,' she is heard to wail night after night before being silenced with blows. When Lessing suggests calling in the NSPCC Rose says, 'I didn't know you was one of them nosey-parkers.'[4] and may have a point that Mrs Skeffington's imprisonment and her daughter's being put in a home wouldn't really improve the situation. Nevertheless, Lessing insists that they love the children deeply. Everyone in this household is a true blue Tory, because they're 'doing all right' and all are thoroughly contemptuous of Lessing's socialism, except for the ne'er-do-well Skeffingtons, who proudly display a Labour Party poster in their taped window when election time comes around, only to have it torn down by Flo.

It is a world in which men are usually brutal, duplicitous and feckless and women are kept firmly in their place. Rose's bargaining chip of withheld sex is a way of hanging onto her girlish romanticism, and once she has been persuaded to relinquish it by the other women, including Lessing, she soon finds herself ill-treated and neglected by the man she has so doggedly loved to distraction. But Rose feels herself as deeply betrayed when Lessing befriends a 'filthy' but well-heeled prostitute who briefly moves into the house, finding her predictably cynical approach to men far more sensible and just as 'interesting' as Rose's tormented romanticism, and their friendship never really recovers from this lapse of morality. Lessing underlines this to point out her sincerity—it as though Rose thinks she has seen through her own lack of this quality—but it is plain that Rose's stick-in-the-mud clinging to her delusions about love is far from healthy for this sympathetically-drawn young woman. Sexuality can be extremely expensive for women, and Rose's reluctance to indulge is perfectly understandable: home-made abortions are commonplace, and after the pain is over and the foetus flushed, Flo remarks to it: 'That fixed you.'

Wandering around the area's bombsites with Rose, Lessing spies a man with a typewriter propped up in the ruins, apparently some sort of official from 'Bomb Damage', an optimist Rose calls him, but whether he is a convenient invention or not (and this is a question one must ask about many of Lessing's observations) he is a useful figure for the paper thin fragility of London's streets and houses at this time: a man who must write in all the blanks, fill up the gaps between buildings, either by imagining what was there before or inventing something new to take its place; a task that parallel's Lessing's own efforts of interpretation and interpolation. Lying in her room at night she listens to dripping taps, arguments, radios, and traffic:

> I put my ear to the wall and heard how, as the trains went past and the buses rocked their weight along the street, shock after shock came up through brick and plaster, so that the solid wall had the fluidity of dancing atoms, and I felt the house, the street, the pavement, and all the miles and miles of houses and streets as a pattern of magical balances, a weightless structure, as if this city hung on water, or on sound. Being alone in that little box of ceiling board and laths frightened me.[5]

It is as though London, beaten to airy thinness by the German bombs, yields up the Platonic idea of itself, and the flesh and blood people with whom she shares her life are likewise abstracted, mere shadows acting out parts they have memorised some time earlier. Lessing listens to Flo's 'dramatised emotions' and tries to come up with the required 'exaggerated reactions of delight, complaint or shock' to her stories; Rose communicates her points more effectively by means of a drooping mouth or a folded hand, disapproval or disbelief by a querulous 'Yes?' Lessing is half in love with her, especially when she lets her hair down at night and talks freely and uninhibitedly, becoming 'a dozen women':

> With each turn of her head, each movement of her hands, she changed, and races and peoples flowed through her. When she spoke of her mother, who had spent her life cleaning other people's houses, she unconsciously smoothed down an imaginary apron; or she would fold her hands in a gesture of willing service, and she looked twenty years older—she was a working woman, with a tired body and ironic eyes. Then she would talk of Flo; and her whole pose changed, and became sceptical and knowing: Flo represented something she must fight, and so she was combative and watchful.[6]

Her memory is bodily and in these conversations she physically expresses the past. For these two women—who are highly critical of one another—everything is 'mark my words' and 'sugar is food', composed of truths they will assert with the utmost conviction, and which often, usually at their most critical, are not entirely baseless or stupid. The men are relatively mobile, they move around London to work: Flo and Rose largely creatures of the few streets they know, unwilling to travel even as far afield as the river (which Flo has apparently never seen), because 'I like what I'm used to'. What Flo is used to is the basement and her cooker; Rose sometimes ventures out to a Lyons corner house in the West End, always wearing plenty of make up because when she doesn't her man, Dickie, thinks she is 'flying the red flag'. Pleasure is important to her, enjoying the rituals of sitting near the window on the bus, and especially spending her hard-earned money—according to Lessing it is the justice of paying for them that makes her small simple enjoyments all right, permissible. The women are sad, driven people, and Lessing's pity and affection for them, her acceptance, cannot conceal that in her view there is nothing much to be done about their condition. All she can do is go along with Rose's favourite going-out game of spending the money she is going to win on the football pools next week: a pastime that many millions are still enjoying to this day.

Lessing's determination to scotch myths about the working-classes and especially to have the women answer back to them leads her to allow them to discourse at length about representations of themselves, an open invitation to dismissiveness to which Rose rises with a devastating critique of the offerings of the British media that still rings true. Certain radio programmes offend her to the point where she has to walk out of the room, while most British films seem to her to consist of people putting on funny voices to mock the working-classes, 'just because someone uses the wrong grammar', and Lessing sees her return from films 'so angry she would smoke several cigarettes before she could bring herself to speak about it':

> They make me sick. It was a British film, see. I don't know why I ever go to them sometimes. If it's an American film, well they make us up all wrong, but it's what you expect from them. You don't take it serious. But the British films make me mad. Take the one tonight. It had what they call a cockney in it. I hate seeing cockneys in films. Anyway, what is a cockney? There aren't any, except around Bow Bells, so they say, and I've never been there. And then the barrow boys or down in Petticoat Lane. They just put it on to be clever, and sell things if they see an American or a foreigner coming. 'Watcher, cock,' and all that talk all over the place. They never say Watcher, cock! Unless there's someone stupid around to laugh. Them film people just put it in to be clever, like the barrow-boys, it makes the upper-class people laugh. They think of the working-class as dragged up. Dragged

up and ignorant and talking vulgar-ugly. I've never met anyone who spoke cockney. I don't and no one I know does, not even Flo, and God knows she's stupid enough and on the make to say anything.[7]

Rose has 'got the 'ump' with British films (getting the 'ump with people and things is a recurring human constant in this book), and her dismissive attitude offers evidence of a London working-class eager to be demobilised from cockneyism, but no such luck was to be ours. She prefers American cinema and films about rich people, where you can 'go and have a nice sit down just put your feet up and think: I wish that was me' rather than be mocked by the cawing voices of your supposed facsimiles. Perhaps this shows that Rose is unrealistically aspirational, but this ersatz 'working-class' culture seems to her (or to Lessing) a way of keeping the real working-classes in their place. Rose has fairly recent memories of the camaraderie of wartime factory life and of the Blitz when people of different classes were sometimes thrown together in shelters on terms of equality and managed to find a common language of courtesy and kindness. Conversations with such kindly middle-class men sustained her through the bombing as her family cowered under a mattress and her dying father hacked his lungs out in the final stages of T.B. Her dislike of what socialism seems to be to her is rooted in these utopian moments of class-mixing under German fire, and her dislike of the working-class in films is borne of a sense of betrayal of the notion of equality that these degraded portrayals seem to represent to her. During the war 'People liked each other. Well, they don't now, do they? And so don't talk to me about your socialism, it just makes me tired, and that's the truth.'[8] A sense that the working-class has been kept in the dark pervades *In Pursuit of the English*. A retired bricklayer who has been studying in the Thinker's Library whispers a recently discovered truth to Lessing in the street: 'There's no God. We aren't anything but apes. They don't tell the working-man in case we get out of hand.'[9]

Doris Lessing may be knowing enough to realise that the revelation of the origin of species will not be quite enough to get the British working-man out of hand. She is not unprepared for the household's incomprehension of her activity as a writer, but for the sheer disappointment, hostility and downright dislike this appears to trigger off in Rose. *In Pursuit of the English* is a highly patterned and constructed book. Men and women come in paired contrasting types and she sustains her account of a year in Bayswater with a novelist's sense of rhythm and, more than this, a deep sense of underlying recurrences and repeating figures of speech and thought. For Lessing existence has a plot that her companions can only dimly guess at, yet she has a respect for their intuitions, their working knowledge of human relationships and their ability to muddle through. Conflicts can only be negotiated by having a good row about it: the strongest side wins. Near the end of the book Flo asks: 'Why does everything have to happen together, can you tell me that?' To which Rose replies: 'Because people make them happen together, that's why.'[10] There is mystery in the women's outlook, and Lessing isn't quite arrogant enough to entirely dismiss it as false-mystery. We feel she is learning or trying to learn things about people she hadn't quite known before. Her potential value as a writer to Bobby Brent comes at the end of the book. Bobby's canniness in seeing thorough of the ways of the world results in a scheme of his for getting her to write a story slandering him so that they he can sue the publisher and split the money with her. He tries to bully her into signing a contract drawn up by his lawyer to agree to do this, but Lessing guesses that his true motive is to set her up as a victim of his blackmail. This preposterous invention may well be Lessing's own, but whether real or not it is a laugh at the expense of the spiv, as nasty as that Rose complains of at the hands of the British cinema; Rose is only an ignorant snob herself and hasn't seen—or understood—any of the Ealing comedies designed to lift her spirits.

'I don't think my head for business is highly enough developed yet,' Lessing demurs to Bobby Brent's scheme, with a superciliousness that he never gets. Lessing is always pointing to a reality gap between the working-classes and conceptions of them enjoyed by middle-class leftists—although it is rare for her to write at length about working-class characters as she does here. It is her stock in trade as a writer, and her great strength, to appear to stand above and arbitrate between the social attitudes of a variety of characters, and in a similar vein, to be a tribune for women's consciousness who is not averse to taking on a male attitude or two: a seeming conservative amongst the unanchored radicals, a radical spy in the houses of reactionaries who take her into their confidence. She is always playing both sides against the middle, so that her elusive point of view, which is politically that of a kind of moderate middle-class socialist-feminist, remains alive and sinewy—at her best she is brilliant in her orchestration of this play of sympathies and opposing principles.

The closing pages of *In Pursuit of the English*, written like the rest of the book with the help of ten years hindsight, witness the emergence of a new generation of working-class Londoners. These young men, nephews of Rose, have failed to resist the bombardment of film and radio and early television, which has brewed up in their consciousness and conversation a rapid-fire Goon-show associative surrealist banter. Speaking in tongues and nonsense, they illustrate Lessing's view that the media-world will not raise the ideological level of the masses but encourage them to reduce everything to the level of comic fantasy, much to Rose's distress and Lessing's amusement:

> 'The Dalai Lama breeds them,' said Mick. 'He's not like old Ben Nevis, he has a real feeling for minks.'
>
> 'Sympathy,' said Len.
>
> 'Peculiar habits they have since they mutated,' said Mick. 'What is it now? I've forgotten.'
>
> 'Monks' habits,' said Len.
>
> 'Naah. You've got it wrong. I remember: each mink has to live inside a magic circle all his life. Because it mustn't move too much or it'll get thin and tough, no good for mink pie when they get like that.'
>
> 'A magic circle drawn by spirits.'
>
> 'Spirit of turpentine.'[11]

Mutation is of course a result of the atomic bomb, but Lessing here is an early proponent of the theory of a mutation in working-class consciousness supposed to have been produced by the bombardment of the deadly poisonous cathode rays and the prospect of world immolation, writing along with Spike Milligan, Allen Ginsberg and Colin MacInnes, with the best of them. 'There are two kinds of pointed sense of humour now,' one of the gabbling boys remarks. But are these two boys able to quite see the consequences of the concatenations of imagery they throw up so inventively, is there an attempt to shovel a glimpse into the ditch of what each juxtaposition means? Rose listens for a while uncomfortably before offering her verdict: 'Ah, shut up.' Consciousness, language, and human existence is proliferative, forever mutating and deathlessly opportunist. Lessing as a writer and an alien mutated intelligence is exactly as opportunist, removed from her own womanly values, as her friend Rose fears, and way ahead of Bobby Brent's schemes by a thousand miles. Her adoptive working-class household is kind to her and her young son, possibly because they fear her relentless intelligence and her mysterious power to prey on them. Bobby Brent preys on those around him with great success, despite their utter conviction of having seen through him. Lessing is close kin to the spiv, but has more sympathy for his marks—as much as the Dalai Lama did for those mutated Tibetan minks that Flo will one day be baking into a tasty mink pie. *In Pursuit of the English* is a somewhat condescending book, but can't very well avoid being so. What redeems it is its sense of the pain and confusion broiling on the hobs of ordinary women, underneath the enforced cheery surfaces of struggling postwar working-class life.

Once upon a time, before Marilyn French's *The Women's Room* commercialised the genre, a woman's room invariably contained a paperback copy of Doris Lessing's celebrated slab of socialist feminist consciousness, *The Golden Notebook*. Its cover was a rich shiny brown and the lettering curly and, well, yellow. Much thumbed or brand new, this hardy perennial was understood to contain everything you needed to know about being a woman—her nature was fourfold rather than merely dual, and in order to understand her you had to reread the same events of her life from multiple perspectives, and even then, there was some essence of a complete understanding of womanhood that was likely to slip through the gaps between those four colour-coded notebooks. Owners of the book would sometimes press it on you, their putative male reader, prefaced by a brief showing of these different coloured facets of womanhood. Bob Dylan might well have been crooning away on the record player with the dramatic steel-guitar phrase that punctuates 'Lay Lady Lay' with its seductive promise of perfect union, understanding, completion.

Doris Lessing was far more likely to shed some real light on your problems and groping self-conceptions than any real-life man optimistically tipping his hat at you with a broad smile and a fretboard at the ready in his left hand. *The Left Hand of Darkness*, Ursula LeGuin's brilliant science-fiction novel about the contingency of masculinity and femininity, came and went in the twenty-year time frame commanded by Lessing's most famous and popular novel, as did Marge Piercy's *Woman on the Edge of Time*, Joanna Russ' *The Female Man*, Rita-Mae Brown's *Rubyfruit Jungle* and many other novels and polemical works by and about women. If it sounds as if I'm trying to be funny about this, not so. I suspect many men of my age have had a special Doris Lessing reader in their lives. *Memoirs of a Survivor* or *Shikasta* were pressed upon us with the assurance that here was a truly brilliant woman writer who understood everything. I tend to think those women were more or less right. My own special Doris Lessing reader happened to be black. Lessing had a particular authority for her as a black woman and a feminist, because she was an anti-imperialist African writer who didn't mess about, who tried to describe things as they were, and was completely on your side. I believed her. This is why I have a special affection for Doris Lessing, and also why, reading even unfamiliar books by her for this essay, I have the uncanny sense of being addressed by an old friend: I have heard most of it before somewhere, sometime long ago.

My old girlfriend, my special Doris Lessing reader, Lola, was born and brought up in Manchester but had lived long in London, where she had been, somewhat reluctantly, an NHS nurse. *The Golden Notebook* is something of a handbook to class in London, among other things, and as such would seem to be very useful reading to a socially aspirant outsider—it glances down many streets and into many of those famous sub-divided, hierarchical worlds of the capital with an all-seeing, all-assessing eye. Lessing, whatever else she conveys, is always able to convince you that she is on your side (if you are an outsider) and that she is offering a truthful report of how things are, one that will help you understand the world you are living in, as well as yourself, your sexuality, your inner life, and free you from the mind-forged, man-forged manacles that have been holding you back, keeping you in your place. Lessing will help you, that is if she doesn't exhaust you first, cancelling all possibilities, judging and emptying them of excitement or meaning: according to Lola there was not much left to be discovered once you had read her, and perhaps those still tempted to lift a few of her readable but weighty tomes to see what real life might have in store for them should be reminded that idle curiosity is not to be recommended when consulting oracles, curiosity particularly killed the cat. Another friend of mine, Irene, tells me that Lessing was a great favourite of her mother, but that she herself has never tried any of her books, and was surprised to think that her own strong inner sense of being all-knowing as well as her penchant for ad-hoc dream-interpretation might have had a source in this unread, dusty author.

The Golden Notebook opens with a conversation between the two female protagonists of the short novel, 'Free Women', that frames the fictionalized autobiographical notebooks which make up the rest of this ambitious, self-conscious attempt to define women's consciousness at the mid-century. The four notebooks, Black, Red, Yellow, Blue, are to be assembled into a giant portmanteau of received ideas about women and men, sex and family life, personal and social psychology, socialist and international politics, memory and the art of the novel, as well as philosophy and general nostrum-mongering from the curriculum of those once fascinating decades. The women's lives, modern life in general, are said to be fragmented, and the purpose of the notebooks is to record the proliferating ramifications of this fragmented experience and conceptions that don't quite fit it. The scheme is to be kept tidy by this small novel, largely of conversations and affairs, about a pair of middle-class Communist friends Anna and Molly, and the novel is finally summated and supposedly integrated by the brief, closing 'Golden Notebook'. The women's conversation sounds a bit absurd at first, so obvious, so middle-class is it, and so absurdly by rote is the way their talk flags up the what are to be the major themes of the coming novel. After a chat with the milkman about how his son has won a scholarship to Oxford and will now be talking different to his ignorant father, the ladies purchase some fresh strawberries from a passing vendor, and one of them, Molly, attempts to persuade him to join them for a cup of coffee:

> 'Oh go on, don't be such a sourpuss. Come up and eat some of your strawberries with us. On me.'
>
> He didn't know how to take her. He stood, frowning, his young face uncertain under an over-long slope of greasy fairish hair. 'I'm not that sort if you are,' he remarked, at last, offstage as it were.
>
> 'So much the worse for you,' said Molly, leaving the window, laughing at Anna in a way that refused to be guilty.[12]

Over the course of the novel, especially its early part, Lessing tests the senses of class she has inherited from Marxism and the culture of the Communist Party against the real social lives and hierarchies she has lived in, mainly growing up in Africa and as part of a group of mainly upper-class Communist intellectuals in wartime Rhodesia, and in post-war England, mainly London. Over a couple of summer holidays spent at the roadside inn of Mashopi, Rhodesia, this intensely serious would-be vanguard group discuss politics, have affairs, carouse to homemade jazz provided by the taciturn Johnny and drink beer opened by his cheerfully parasitic sidekick, Stanley Lett, an earlier prototype of the spiv Bobby Brent. The young comrades pay so much solicitous attention to the politically aware and overworked African cook, Jackson, that they wind up getting him the sack. She is interested by the micro-dynamics of the group. Anna Wulf's boyfriend and the group's central intellectual force is Willi, a marooned German intellectual from a conventional upper-middle-class background, another member is Paul Blackenhurst, a pilot who will be killed in the early days of the war, another, the florid Scottish Jimmy, 'was no more ambitious than to become a professor of history in some university, which he has since become.'[13] This makes it plain that Lessing's own notions of what constitutes high ambition are not everyone's. Other colonial Communists later become successful businessmen. Here and elsewhere Lessing draws characters who have risen from the working-class with a special lively warmth and sympathy, like a trainee pilot, Ted Brown, an Oxford scholarship boy who puts so much of his energies into helping others from his own background, encouraging them to read, to study and aspire, and of course to join the political struggle for a better world. Lessing says he had much success at this, but it is clear she is laughing at him a little when she comments that he deliberately failed his final tests 'because he was wrestling with the soul of a young ox from Manchester'[14] and she views Ted and people like him as a particularly to be valued kind of exception to the rules of the class society she sees around her as a living, organic phenomenon. She is fascinated by the intelligent road-mender George Hounslow, with his stubby sensual body, his affair with the cook's wife, his deference to the upper-class Willi and his anguish about his illegitimate black child. Nearly all these men are condescending towards the two women in the group, Anna and the pretty young Maryrose, the latter who has been spoilt for love by an incestuous relationship with her dead brother. Lessing anatomises and places them all, but you feel there is a tendency to pigeonhole and create ready-made types running through this process of social mapping.

There is also the question of where she and her various interchangeable personae stand in relationship to all these people. It is clear she always regards herself as one of the elect, and also that this is more or less assented to in the groups (and woe betide any doubters, although none are recorded), but her power-seeking is best indicated by Anna's attachment to the relatively sexless but powerful Willi. Her eventual betrayal of him with Paul is justified by Willi's attitude of judgemental heartlessness towards those he leads. He despises nothing more fiercely than a sentimentalist, is capable of being helpful and kind, but only on condition of subordinating others, of being leader and continually bending them to his will. Anna notes all this, but Wulf will move on, move up, as did Lessing, and so she will end up not as an adjunct to the top banana of the social hierarchy, but eminent in her own right, and her unstoppable ability to rise in the world is predicated not only upon her talents but upon a certain ruthlessness in annexing and using others and what seems to the reader to be an innate sense of social elevation. Later on in her life she will become Willi, borrowing his intellectual matrix of social ideas, his German name, his high-handed manner of disposing of others and their petty problems. This worrying sense of *The Golden Notebook* as an attempt to produce a sort of compendious (but somewhat airless) handbook of the entire social and world system, makes her come to seem uncomfortably like a sort of socialist Ayn Rand, compelled to exalt mind and power and achievement in spite of her professed egalitarian beliefs: it is as though *Atlas Shrugged* had deeply make sense to her and got under her skin to the extent that she was unable or unwilling to shrug it off.[15] *The Golden Notebook* has a kind of gargantuanism and ambition, and like Rand's crowning novel, it is trying to be objective about society and human affairs.

Class hierarchies for Lessing are we suspect totally ineluctable, more or less natural, and based on given intelligence: scarcely a single example of a displaced person, in that particular sense, is given; although there are a number of people who have changed classes in *The Golden Notebook*, the main effort of their lives has been to achieve that and they are now something else. Aside from the mention of this, there is little sense of real human struggle in the novel, only of one particular case—the struggle to be a woman artist. Class itself as a social fact is unchangeable, and it is clear that for Lessing being middle-class is largely and positively to be the possessor of an intelligence that puts gay colours in the windows and tries to live a little more stylishly instead of crumbling under stultifying and insoluble unhappiness, like the inhabitants of the scruffy terraces she visits as a Communist canvasser in the 1950 general election. There is a mighty iceberg of human failure jutting under the surface of London life, sitting behind dull brownish curtains, women abandoned or surrounded by their screaming kids, like the 'Mrs Browns' who write letters to Ella at her women's magazine desk (these passages remind me of the American Communist fellow-traveller Nathaniel West's brilliant short novel of the thirties, *Miss Lonelyhearts*)[16] or the helpless patients of another Paul, the married doctor, a working-class medical psychologist, with whom Ella has an unhappy affair in a draft novel that forms part of the Yellow notebook. Paul, we are told, in this further fiction within fictions, tends to associate everything positive, progressive and democratic with the working-classes and everything stultifying, backward and benighted with the middle-classes—conservative members of the medical establishment and the hospital administrators who so often oppose him, and yet, like Ted in Africa, he is deluded in the way he has this view, and just as likely to share a divided consciousness with the middle-class leftists between their compassionate view of those they perceive to be the masses and their cynicism about their own class and about each other. Their nobility, it seems, has its severe limits, and may not apply at all where their own interests are involved. But to be fair they may not be altogether aware of this.

Ella is herself writing a novel, about a suicide, which is supposed to illustrate that the suicide doesn't know he is going to commit the act until the last minute, at which point it has become clearly inevitable, an illustration that social coercion as well as the logic of a psychological breakdown can operate as both an invisible and an inevitable pressure on the mind of the living. Hers is indeed a fiendish plot, but so is society itself, channelling human energies to ends and consequences of fixed, and predetermined, outcomes. The dreams she tells to her analyst, Mrs Marks, known as Mother Sugar to her clients, are of a doll-like world in which doll-like people take action but might as well do one thing as another. Should Julia's son be a conscientious objector to national service or not? Go to university or enter his father's firm? It doesn't seem to matter to Ella/Anna/Doris, and her dreams offer no escape, no ways out, but themselves replicate hierarchies in which doll-like people are forever betrayed into the preformed stories they must perforce act out. Her overarching sense of herself as a writer who wants to define reality is beset by this sense of unreality that is in fact an inescapable meta-reality. Once the social order is put through the ordering processes necessary for a novel, its inevitability is felt as a crushing weight—but is unreal still—people are doll-like, mannikins, tokens, pawns in some greater societal or psychological plot. And her characters do indeed have a doll-like quality, at least of having been freely drawn from some central casting warehouse of received social types.

The world of dreams and of social and political reality are sometimes brought hard up against one another in sections of the Notebooks where passages of psychoanalysis are juxtaposed with newspaper clippings relating to the end of the Korean war, the death of Stalin, the invasion of Hungary and other key events of the fifties as they undermine the Communist cause or world-view; but where dreams and social reality truly meet is in the area of cultural representations, particularly those of television and film, and it is clear that despite a notional ambition to reach out to the masses, Anna/Ella/Doris so despises mammon that she is unable to contemplate her racy African novel of interracial sex, here called *Frontiers of War* (and loosely based on her communist friends and the experience with the African cook at Mashopi) being turned into a film without a shudder of contempt and a heavy dose of irony at the expense of the TV and film producers who are so eager to traduce her integrity with their capitalist blandishments. They are unable to understand or respect the seriousness of her project as she is unable to contemplate dealing with them except as a sell-out. The lure of a mass audience is apparently non-existent for this writer, and yet she seems to have found one without any serious difficulty.

Her writing seems to work by a kind of negative capability, as John Keats describes it, consisting of the poet's ability to hold two or more opinions simultaneously in his mind without choosing between them. Except of course she does choose between them, or seems to, but, poet-like, maintains them all in equilibrium. Thus she is an anti-communist communist who can't do without that tragic history out of which to elaborate her critique, and in general a progressive politics to both endorse and nay-say; a trenchant feminist who maintains a view of women that is traditional in many respects, and who describes men and their dilemmas and qualities with far livelier insight and sympathy than she does women: her men are strikingly individual characters, her women tend to be interchangeable versions of herself; a radical psychologist who draws (without acknowledgement) on the major schools without feeling beholden to them; and a Sufi mystic whose religiosity tends more to an affirmation of me and mine, and by and large on quite profane values, than anything to do with transcendence, mystery or a higher being. It is perfectly clear that there is no higher being than Doris Lessing. In this sense it appears that, despite all the kerfuffle, what we are left with is just the perfectly sensible view of the North London middle-classes. And yet Lessing continues to affirm the absolute value and necessity of being political, and her way of being political seems to be a good way of being political because it doesn't give everything away to politics: neither to a particular party or authority, nor to a completely political way of being. Instead she always holds back, surveys, holds her judgement of herself for herself, and subjects others to it.

This judgement is bent to the overall cause of progress, democracy, socialism and a personal self-realisation which cannot be achieved without politics—both personal and public—without triumphing over others, for example, or being aware of the traps that certain systems of ideas propose. In this she is particularly useful to women—and thoroughly feminine: removed, judgemental, socially weighing. She is in a way as snobbish as Sandra, Ralph Singh's English wife in V.S. Naipaul's *The Mimic Men*, except that although an *arrivant* she is not an arriviste. Her confidence stems in part from being born at the top of a self-conscious racial hierarchy and having been arrogant enough to want to overthrow it—but even there, at her political beginnings, we suspect that she was playing upward games: getting out of the homestead, into the company of more interesting people, political people, and testing them and their milieu to its upward limits. It may seem odd to compare Lessing to Naipaul, a revolutionary woman to a male accepter and beneficiary of the inevitability of colonial hierarchies, but their predicaments are rather similar, especially in postwar Britain, and their contrasting takes on English social hierarchies are underlyingly alike.

One of the main reasons for the mental breakdown in *The Golden Notebook* is that a deeply held world of representations is being vanquished by a sort of reality principle, one which has powerful counter-representations at its disposal, fanciful though they may seem; but the symbolic-personal world—mostly derived from Marx and her early experiences—into which Lessing's real social observations are drawn up, continually reasserts itself, is determined to dispose of everything to its own order and its own satisfaction. This is why the world becomes doll-like, and this is a case of the ego reasserting itself and vanquishing the world—which may be ultimately a good thing and a necessary one for the empowered female subject. Doris Lessing's strength lies in the combination of the oceanic quality of her ego-world with her sense of a plot and she is highly impressive in the extent to which she maintains the clarity of her complexly articulated doll-world of representations whilst holding messy counter-evidence presented by observation and fuzzy logic on equally poised display.

Lessing's every invocation of socialist values calls forth its opposite, its pure negation, its counter-example: a kind of counter-factual truth drawn from a perceived reality principle that tests the hopeful aspirations of the socialists to destruction, and largely because of the nature of the urban middle class about which she is writing, makes howling nonsense of these progressivist beliefs. She appears to believe that, as with the Communists, do-gooders can only continue with their belief-system by refusing to witness the social realities around them; but whereas the actual London middle class is somewhat flexible and changeable in complexion, Lessing's version of it is largely drawn from a very traditional strata, and as an outsider to this apparently eternal class, a reader could only add that she is unable to fully factor in the barriers to understanding created by what can only be described as a remote and highly privileged perspective. But all the same she tries to get all the way around class in the way that the nineteenth century English and European novelists she most admires tried to get all the way around their own social systems and their ruling ideas. Lessing is aiming very high: at the level of Dostoyevsky, Stendhal, or Thomas Mann; but reading her we can't help but feel that too many ideas, too many questionable conceptions, world-historical events and significances are being brought to bear on too narrow a social range of characters. One of her paradoxes is that in taking on the English class system she tends to completely replicate its hierarchies and thus to show it is impossible to defeat; and this English sense of class as a vertically defined social place is overdetermined by her earlier African experience, which is of course itself influenced by English conceptions and also includes the further ineluctable hierarchy of race—which of course everyone in her circles is on principle against—but which is also shown to be more or less inevitable in reality. Politics can therefore only be gestural, guilt-ridden, and if pursued too vigorously by people who should have better things to worry about, destructive of the personality and of personal happiness. Irony isn't her strongest suit, but surely there is some in that scene in which her two middle-class Communist women inviting a passing strawberry-seller in for a cup of coffee. He is embarrassed and apparently sees their invitation as somehow wrong. Does he take it as a sexual invitation? Or simply as a waste of time? Anna believes he thinks this pair of posh women is simply laughing at him, and maybe he is right, they are; but perhaps also there is a kind of hope in the strawberry-seller's allergy to being patronised by chattering women. They, however, are quite unstoppable, incorrigible, and will find their own way forward:

> 'Do you remember Dr North?' said Anna.
> 'Of course.'

'He's starting a sort of marriage welfare centre—half official, half private. He says three-quarters of the people who come to him with aches and pains are in fact in trouble with their marriages. Or lack of marriages.'

'And you're going to dish out good advice.'

'Something like that. And I'm going to join the Labour Party and teach a night-class twice a week for delinquent kids.'

'So we're both going to be integrated with British life at its roots.'

'I was carefully avoiding that tone.'[17]

Conclusion

Down the Hatch

Colin MacInnes' capture of the feel of early-mod Soho and the idiom of his narrator is so complete and convincing that you can't help wondering how anyone could write so well about teenagers without actually being one. *Absolute Beginners* so much partakes of the glamour of Soho at this late fifties moment that it provides a kind of factitious instant micro-history through which anyone can re-experience being there for ever after—if they so wished, and perhaps that is what the novel is about: you do want to be there, in the fragile circumference of their certainty of their centrality that its teenage style-leaders seem to inhabit. It is surprising in a way that this book wasn't made into a film much earlier, but on reflection it fits into the culture of the eighties so well, fits like a glove onto that decade's sense of a newness arrived at by writing the embellished cultural memories of the fifties on a wiped slate in a bubble: the memory-blank of the Thatcher years, when it came to seem that almost anything could and would be more and more intensively remembered as a style while its original contexts were forgotten. Why did it have to wait so long before being made into a film? Arguably because it truly reflected on its times rather than simply exploiting a youth craze, and what it had to say about youth and its sense of being in the eye of the moment was too disturbing for a film aimed at sentimentalised teenagers: it would have needed Nicholas Ray, James Dean. And, despite the sophistication of the London pop art moment at whose christening party it appeared, Cliff Richard or Tommy Steele probably couldn't have played the leading man… but a late night viewing of *Expresso Bongo* will show that film to have said all the same things about the exploitation of youth and its ruthlessness and the downright phoniness of the music business.

Absolute Beginners had to wait its turn, to be turned into an item of eighties retro, a musical, an ostentatiously reinvented version of the past, an example of the style reinvention of the fifties (motivated by an agenda of temporarily forgetting the sixties and seventies) by the instant pop culture of the eighties. David Bowie and Roxy Music, still going now, were already nostalgia items for those of us who had come of age in the early seventies. I remember groaning faintly when the film was announced and friends began talking about exciting new things called 'scratch video' and how this was going to be the style of it and make it absolutely modern. I scratched my crisply gelled head. Another instant mismemory, I thought, and I wasn't absolutely wrong. Okay, probably slightly wrong, but the book itself is a compendium of mismemories, and is in part about the ersatz and makeshift constructions of which popular culture consists. I avoided the film at the time, but when eventually caught up with on late night television it seemed to exemplify the way fashion borrows from the past while emptying it of meaning—but also to be one of the last examples of those times reaching out into the cultural present. It was a product made by and for people who'd lived through those times, featuring artists who'd made and been made by them. Early post-war pop culture was still powering the career of David Bowie, for example, but the youth culture and visual style of the eighties—its 'ironic' glossed up gloss—meant that *Absolute Beginners* couldn't seamlessly rejoin the past in the way that American films like *The Last Picture Show* had attempted, but had instead to remake the past in terms of the present: no bad thing if you wanted to carry forward a celebratory banner of liberation and rebellion into what were, synths and glitterballs aside, grey, compromised times.

Yet in that eighties context any film remembering the rebellious past was almost sure to be a disappointment when it came out, and *Absolute Beginners* did poorly at the box office. It was too old fashioned, too political, maybe too unwieldy and unfocused as well. It owed something to Ken Russell's bright politicised pop video approach to rock and roll history in *Tommy*, which took the mickey out of cheesy glitz and phony teen rebellion but tried to draw out some underlying histories—particularly of the second world war—also mining the social power of the quasi-religious images thrown up by rock: Clapton is God, Tina Turner's hypersexualised performance as the Acid Queen. Perhaps the late influence of Russell's approach meant that the belated film of MacInnes' novel had a bit too much of the atmosphere of the mid-seventies about it: *Tommy* was a kind of auto-critique of fifties and sixties myths, their last gasp, before punk blew in and blew all of that away, at least for a time.

Absolute Beginners ends on an apocalyptic high of England's burning in the Notting Hill riots, an occurrence that effectively reveals the adolescent solipsism of the teenage mod outlook, but although the latency of apocalypse, Allen Ginsberg's sense of 'listening to the crack of doom on the hydrogen jukebox' (a phrase from *Howl* later used to define the whole of post-war youth culture by Jeff Nuttall in his study *Bomb Culture*[1]) had continued to echo throughout the British eighties, with the Brixton riots, the Irish hunger strikes, the sight of British ships sailing off to war in the Falklands, the miners' and printers' strikes, the poll tax riots, the apocalypse per se was a scenario that had by then turned curiously hollow. No-one any longer believed in it, except for the Greenham Common women protesting against American missiles on our soil and the people on the mass CND marches: even in cinema it had turned into a plot-element in a sci-fi action movie, a sort of McGuffin everyone was running after to start to stop, but what did it matter anyway since it had apparently already happened? Of sixties cultural figures only Bob Dylan seemed still committed in the eighties to the idea of apocalypse; for him the notion that we were living through the last days seemed to be part of a deep seated belief-system, or at least to be a rhetoric that he couldn't let go of: it guaranteed an ultimate messianic meaning to his art and to his political stance, whether calling the sky fire down on us on his born-again Christian albums, or gloating about the end to a young soon-to-be-immolated lover on the synth-laden 'When the Night Comes Falling from the Sky' in a voice that had become a screeching reedy wail of unhappiness.[2] But nobody except me liked those albums very much, and, even in a musical, a sort of woozy, cheesy mini-apocalypse and a fiery letting go of an English past to affirm a new identity was too much like 'history' to please an eighties audience: too urgent, too political. Didn't make sense any more. It wasn't what was going to happen anyway: a last gasp of mid-century political culture that seemed only a worn-out plot-shape for the *Terminator* movies, it no longer had any relevance or predictive reach.

If the film of *Absolute Beginners* is one example of the wholesale remembering of the styles of the fifties and sixties that occurred as the British twentieth century drew to a close, it also shows pretty clearly that such decontextualised misappropriations serve the purpose of legitimising something in the present—in this case providing a myth history for the eighties pop stars who thronged the streets of glammed up Soho and Napoli: the very emptiness of MacInnes' view of youth culture was one element that did translate in the film, and that particular return to the late fifties was widely taking place in pop culture: manufactured boy bands, the pretty youth cult, and the glorious incandescent meaningless moment of being in the eye of consumer culture. It was the moment in which the term 'postmodernism' first gained wide currency as an important new description of a contemporary cultural condition, and *Absolute Beginners* might have served a useful purpose of putting a lot of people off it—interesting for the appearance of Slim Gaillard in one of the party scenes, but they didn't do anything particularly good with him. A glance in the mirror at the retreating unfilmed fictions of yesteryear suggests only *The Lonely Londoners* as a gross oversight. Think of the Calypso soundtrack. Why was this particular film never made?

In other words, novels of the fifties and sixties—particularly those that were filmed—have had a great afterlife, and you can't help but notice that in many cases those fictions which enter popular memory and so define their period for a later day don't particularly deserve unquestioned authority, any more than do the songs which are even more definitive of their times in retrospect, and whose charm has also rubbed away with the passage of years. John Lennon's 'Working-Class Hero' (1970) encapsulated much of the feeling of *Room at the Top*, his impulse at this time to thoroughly shred the fictional, 'phony' world of the Beatles' songs, to demystify the band and denigrate its achievements by saying they were 'just the biggest bastards, that's all' and, more positively, to use the fame he had won to embrace a more political role and to identify himself with great causes like working-class revolution, ending the Vietnam war, the British occupation of the North of Ireland, the Black Panthers and, most horrifyingly, of course, feminism. Not only did fifties and sixties novels influence pop music, pop culture encapsulated them as false memories that, ever thinning out, ever cartoonised, would soon be all that remained of their turbulent times: self-serving emoticons of an era.

When I was a boy we ate very much in the modern way. We had Birds Eye hamburgers, frozen peas and the newly-introduced fabulous exotic delicacy of crinkle-cut chips. There was mince, steak and kidney pies, and on Fridays we enjoyed a row of four cod fish fingers. On Sundays we sat down to roast chicken or beef. In the long hot summers we trotted down to the sweet shop clutching fourpence, if we were lucky, to buy a three-stage Thunderbirds ice-lolly. We lived in a small block of flats on a newly built council estate, and thought ourselves lucky to have evaded the prefabs where my best friend and his family were domiciled. I remember a girl telling me later that some local children, protesters against the encroachment of modernity on traditional village ways, tried to impede the building of the flats by stealing bricks in a spontaneous protest against the uprooting of the orchard that had previously stood on the site. Our flat was filled with things my hard-working parents were buying on the never-never: carpets, a TV, a radiogram, a coffee table (we didn't drink coffee) with a cheerful print of a Spanish dancer trapped under its glass top, and, eventually, a proper spin dryer. The kitchen was too small for a twin-tub. We were a relatively poor family, but fairly average for the estate. And so we swung on through the swinging sixties while I watched the television plays, and a couple of years after release, the films that had been made about our kinds of lives. My grandfather even appeared in one of them. He came with the car, a Bristol (or an Alfa?) that he drove expertly through a puddle, splashing Lucinda Curtis' mini-dress in an unjustly forgotten film, *Nothing But The Best*.[3]

It has been a long process, slightly random and cumulative, that has led me to the particular novels and novelists I have written about in this study. There's a sort of molten core of writers I read as a teenager, around which are gathered a lot of scorched books discovered since by a process that involved them just falling into my hands, or being forced upon me by someone else, or which pressed themselves upon my attention simply by being considered important. A book sometimes hailed me by being obviously part of some ill-defined project of my own—that's one for the pot, I might have vaguely thought, that'll do, and ended up with a group of books that tried to define experiences which I thought important probably because I could relate them to my own. But if that were my sole measure it would be a poor one, and such a haphazard process reveals the poverty of one's own conceptions as well as revealing, in the cold light of a second look, that quite a lot of these books were not all they were cracked up to be, and that some neglected gems deserved to be just that. Nearly everything that manages to find its way into 'culture' will find its strong adherents who want to be defined by it and be just like it. My own aims in trawling the half-forgotten pages of so many out-of-print novels is not merely to reinforce well-worn senses of what the sixties were about—how would I know, I was a child?—but to glance down a few less well trodden pathways in hopes of discovering something new about a culture that offered to define my emerging sense of myself and led to self-conceptions that may well have been erroneous and unhelpful. Another of my aims is to scotch the commonplace rubric of 'working-class realism' that these novelists are so often lumped together under by dismissive critics who thereby diminish the craft and sophistication of many able novelists. Anyway, these books and their period can't be satisfactorily re-entered in wondering nostalgia, only in the probing spirit of American modernist poet William Carlos Williams in 'The Descent':

> Memory is a kind
> of accomplishment,
> a sort of renewal
> even
> an initiation, since the spaces it opens are new places
> inhabited by hordes
> heretofore unrealised,
> of new kinds—
> since their movements
> are toward new objectives
> (even though formerly they were abandoned).[4]

An early form of postmodernism was Jürgen Habermas' notion of a legitimation crisis. For Habermas the political ideals of the Enlightenment—liberty, equality, fraternity and the notions of political and human rights that went with these slogans—had laid the foundations of bourgeois political democracy but had run out of steam, because, he argued, such abstract slogans were essentially static where Capitalism was dynamic, expansive, and of course exploitative. The Enlightenment's ideals were ignored when inconvenient and tended to function as what he called legitimation for imperial, economic and social realities that were very different: they legitimised an unequal society in two ways—as a future towards which capitalist societies were supposed to be moving and as terms in which public political language was couched, as something that was already supposed to have been achieved in some measure. The so-called legitimation crisis arose when capitalism and imperialism could no longer credibly claim that their expansive operations were directed towards the greater good and the achievement of Enlightenment rights and ideals for everybody.[5] Struggles against colonialism all over the world, the Vietnam war and the exploitation of cheap labour in the third world were overwhelming evidence that this was so, and yet there was no other credible political language available—except that of Marxist revolution, believed in by a few, including Habermas himself. This sense of hypocrisy, or something like it, was at the root of sixties disaffection and of its seeking of new ways amongst the politicised young, as well as a retreat from politics by those who were doing okay. In Britain the sixties was a period of sharpening industrial militancy, which despite the best efforts of its best spirits, tended to be economically directed and to grow out of the confidence of prosperity. The economic bubble, when it burst, led to spasms of working-class struggle in defence of jobs and living standards that continued throughout the seventies, until the Conservatives came to power in 1979 and Prime Minister Margaret Thatcher launched her multi-pronged attack on working-class organisations, on the welfare state and the ideas that had nurtured these things in the early postwar period.

The flipside of what is seen as the political idealism of the fifties and especially the sixties was a kind of prosperous cynicism, added to which the prosperity of those who had never had it so good scarcely touched those at the bottom of society, either in the cities where waves of new immigrants lived in appalling social conditions and worked for way below union rates or in rural areas like those described in Ronald Blythe's *Akenfield* and John Berger's *A Fortunate Man* where wages remained traditionally low and the great 24-hour party of consumerism and youth culture was something to be witnessed on television, picked up in hairstyles and dance crazes, but in general happening elsewhere in a studio fantasy irrelevant to the real expectations of those people. Mass phenomena of the times like thousands of local rock and roll bands, dance clubs and an ongoing folk music revival speak warmingly of a homemade kind of rebellion and creativity that kept many people going well into old age. But Jack Trevor Story's novels—and many living memories—suggest that much of sixties prosperity was superficial, precarious, and bought on the never-never. In the sixties the expansion of higher education had yet to touch very many working-class young people and despite the rhetoric and the much resisted introduction of comprehensive schools, educational provision for the working and middle-class young remained brutally unequal as it does to this day. It's all just propaganda, as Arthur Seaton said, a truth likely to be wearily or gleefully embraced in the glitterball decade of the Thatcherite 1980s.

In the 1980s English novel culture was belatedly Europeanising, Americanising, or Latin Americanising itself. Magic realism was the thing, as done by Salman Rushdie, or else louche comedies about nightclubbing, or sex between career women with padded shoulders, or that Milan Kundera novel about his fascination with women going to the toilet and how it reminded him of Beethoven's late Quartets: anything but that dreary so-called realist stuff on television. This was our reality right now: the glitterball, the haircut, female desire projected in close-up over the grainy Falklands newsreel. We didn't want to look at the past, only to dress up in some of its styles as connoisseurs of fifties retro, and even if we were genuinely interested there were always strong political motives—as there always are—for encouraging people to live in the present and forget what has gone before. They need no encouragement, quite rightly, to live their own lives. And what better way to knock the claims of the recent past on the head than to demonstrate that 'realist' texts were actually 'patronising', voyeuristic, provincial, and, to the middle-class critic, worst of all: middle-class. And then there is the factor that culture is nearly always a way of living somewhere else, a somewhere that at best throws its own elevating light on your mundane reality, more usually a distraction, a way of romanticising yourself, an escape. They fell victim, on the one hand to a critique of representations, and on the other to a post-modernist aesthetics that ruled the truth claims of realism out of court.

The 'Bad New Working-Class' enjoyed a notable revival at the end of the British twentieth century with the creation of 'Essex Man' and 'Essex Girl', Loadsamoney, Wayne and Waynetta, and the personae of a host of other TV comedians, often enjoyed by working-class people themselves, and issuing finally in the creation of the stereotypical 'chav': the working—or usually benefit-claiming—class as incorrigibly stupid, reactionary, selfish and degraded. Whether such people have actually proliferated as greatly as we are led to believe or have been called into being as the 'folk devils' of our moment in social democracy is a question I will try to answer. Enjoyable as the creations of comedians like Catherine Tate sometimes are, I can't help but see their wit as borrowed from those she parodies, and their current predominance as a knock-on effect of a liberal middle-class response to the destruction of working-class organisations by Thatcherism: a response that amounted to a kind of chastened celebration of the curbing of the unions (something had to be done, after all) followed by a wholesale revival of 'mass society' horror as the victims of social exclusion were again and again blamed for their own problems. A website called Chavtowns shows that they may well have forced sterilisation to fear: 'They should sell White Lightning flavoured condoms for chavs, and instead of spermicide they could have sterilising fluid to stop them breeding for good,' suggests one correspondent. But if chavdom is seen by some as a genetic condition, other recognise it as a cultural phenomenon: 'I saw a young woman—I'd been to university with her, quite an intelligent girl, but she'd turned into a chav—probably had a minge on her like an elephant's arse—hanging around outside McDonald's like the rest of them.' On another site, dedicated to the opinions of the far-right, chavs are what working-class youth have degenerated into—nowadays the hearts of oak are no more than 'drug-dealing scum talking in negroid lingo.'

But the nineties and early twenty-first century have seen a new impetus towards realism—if indeed it can truly be said to be new. In every generation, as surely as there will be a new crop of art students who are attracted by Dada, there will be new-old experiences to define in realist art, springing up spontaneously, occasionally in the novel (*Trainspotting, Morvern Callar, The Football Factory*) more commonly in urban pop music (The Streets, Dizzee Rascal, The Enemy and many others) and in those most carefully staged interactions between so-called real people on so-called 'reality television'. New Labour's appeal to the aspirational working-classes acknowledged what had been so carefully designed to appeal to them in Margaret Thatcher's rhetoric a decade and a half earlier, with just a little more emphasis on the notion of 'equality of opportunity': the ladder is always there to be climbed by the bold and New Labour's first Prime Minister Tony Blair was about to helpfully place your best front foot firmly on the bottom rung of the social escalator. Remember that?

But what is it that legitimises fiction and makes us take its cultural yarn-spinning for truth? Its *vraisemblance*, its seeming truth to life, or its compelling allegories, whether sentimental or dark? The idea of a common culture as expounded by F.R. Leavis and Raymond Williams is, of course, a hopeful one that, in effect, and if successfully propounded, tended to shade away into the big lie of the level social playing field. First there were two cultures—not those of the whole of C.P. Snow's late fifties opposition between scientific and liberal humanist cultures, but as defined by the term of his equation which didn't consider science important at all: high culture and low culture, good high culture in which good values were enshrined and bad low vulgar culture in which they were traduced; then such values were partially inverted (by the Beatles! And the Stones!) and so-called mass culture became alternatively the bogey or the saviour of all we held dear, naturally depending on what we hold dear. If this is hard to follow, perhaps it will help to realise that the sixties and seventies revolutions in higher education were still administered by the sons and daughters of those types Kingsley Amis' Jim Dixon had failed to displace. There was nothing for it but to flee to London with that nice girl who was thinking of giving up men. Now, or perhaps the day before yesterday, we are enjoying a supposed plurality, a diversity of imagined communities who are supposedly making up their own versions of the world in a crazy quilt of multi-cultural diversity.

Such beautiful rainbow alliances rarely if ever genuinely spring from below—and cynics are apt to see the very language of diversity as an imposition policed by a handful of cultural, political and (in this case) literary pundits—who have an idea about what their readers or viewers want, what they will buy and the demographics of readership, which, if inaccurate and static and sometimes taking publishers by surprise, is based on 'experience' in a different sense: on commercial practices tried and true. So all this so-called diversity is brought to the table of the middle-class and its values and attitudes—and not even the real middle-class (which is diverse, has spent most of this century expanding and changing) but the older middle-class, who still dominate the culture industries in this country, notwithstanding that pop culture administration is sometimes left to the phony populism of a few upwardly mobile types. And they do like a bit of colour, they like to feel informed about what's going on out there, and they do like to have it safely neutralised, predigested. It's as Claud Cockburn put it in his perceptive *Bestseller: The Books Everybody Read 1890-1939*, and others have elaborated since—notably Franco Moretti in *Signs Taken for Wonders*, a study of nineteenth-century popular novels that reads both Bram Stoker's *Dracula* and Mary Shelley's *Frankenstein* for their anxiety value (fear of foreign blood and of the proletariat respectively)—the most useful trick is to articulate the anxieties of the middle-class, preferably in a lurid way, and to bring those fears to some reassuring, not-too-challenging conclusion; in other words, the would-be bestselling paperback writer must both incite and allay such fears in order to neutralise and incorporate them.

I believe this idea remains a useful one when considering more recent fiction. Take Irvine Welsh's *Trainspotting*. Who were its actual readers? Edinburgh junkies? Junkies everywhere? No. They were, on the whole, young people in general—or so appeared to me. I was living in a small town at the time it came out and everyone working-class under twenty-five seemed to instantly want to read it and identified with it. I was also teaching in a university, and there wasn't a student who didn't like it: the most unlikely people thought it defined their generation's experience in spite of having been written by somebody of my generation about people whose circumstances were remote form their own. I imagine that many of these young people—most of the hundreds of thousands of them—were recreational drug users, of a less 'serious' kind. They identified with the nihilism of the characters, were amused by their misadventures, and caught up in their acerbic world-view, yet we see that the consequences of such nihilism are not to be countenanced. It is a corrective for middle-class youth that panders to their selfish sense of disaffection but warns them not to take any of it too seriously. At the end of rebellion there is only death or the conventional trappings of lower middle-class life—which junkies so winningly disdain—to be striven for, and the heroic few who flout these goals are headed straight for a brick wall. *Trainspotting* is a more complex book that this suggests, Welsh's emergence as a writer of popular fictions that try to remain true to a bad new working-class sense of things is applaudable; but as a bestseller it is a morality tale for middle-class kids, and is I believe of more appeal to people who are in revolt against these backgrounds than working-class kids hoping to better themselves. Avoid drugs altogether, that's my advice. Let Irvine spin as many of his tales as he likes.

Martin Amis' professional interest in the bad working-class got underway in the mid-seventies with his first novel, *The Rachel Papers*, in which he sets up a triangle where a middle-class and working-class man amiably compete for the good things of life, including women, a formula he continued to exploit in book after book and brought to its most satisfactory culmination in his novels bracketing the eighties: *Money* and *London Fields*. John Self, Keith Tallent and their associates are vessels for Amis' righteous ire at the stupidity and greed of the Thatcher decade, but it might be objected that these avatars of avarice and lust are more emblematic of the attitudes of their creator towards the evils of democracy than faithfully rendered or even recognisable social types. His work is often powered by a massive disdain for people he has never met and knows little about, yet he envies them enough to document their worst excesses with an unmistakable sensuous enjoyment laced with the self-disgust of the hungover morning after transgressor of middle-class mores. He seems to love his nasty characters for being sensibility and guilt free. But how has he come to know so much about them?

A partial answer is that the contrasting types that Amis' novels are built around are a feature of novels he has read, and the form they take in his books is unmistakably English. Such an opposition between the man of intellect and the man of passion, whom the women must choose between, is a feature of Jane Austen's novels, of the Brontës' books, of the types represented by Jude and St John Rivers in Thomas Hardy's *Jude the Obscure*, between Birkin and Gerald in Lawrence's *Women in Love*. These are also class types, and in the English novel as such often demarked by a racially conceived contrast: Jude is dark, St John Rivers is fair; Birkin is a small, dark man, Gerald is a Germanic type: a big blonde bombshell. Of course there can be subtlety in the ways types are played: one can wage class war or point up social injustice; the apparent brute can be a man of sensitivity; the man of intellect can be a genuinely helpful nice vicar or another kind of charming manipulator. Lawrence reverses these polarities and makes one of his heroines, Gudrun, choose a capering, monkey-like half-Jew as beefy, elemental Gerald trudges off into the ice. Martin Amis takes racial and class types from the history of the English novel and plays them to the hilt: but with little in the way of subtlety. His middle-class characters are bloodless but sensitive, his working-class ones brainless leering sensualists. He is something of a Manichaean in the ways he pits these absolutely equal but opposite powers against one another. His approach to the rival claims of Apollo and Dionysus is far from being integrative: his working-class devils excite him, but he would have us believe he is on the side of the angelic host.

You might think it would be impossible for anyone who has never lived in his charmed circles to believe that Amis is writing about anyone except himself and his kind and their unpleasantly snotty attitudes to everyone else, but this would be to underestimate the hold that a sense of social hierarchy and middle-class authority still has on many English people. We seem to love being told how it is and what we are by people who sound like him, or some of us do. Later, in *The Information,* Amis attempts to write about the worlds of literary celebrity, reviewing, vanity publishing and even politics, contrasting success and failure and exploring the bile of the overlooked; but seems to know as little about these as anything else he has deemed himself expert on, and anyone who sees a biography of Stalin as an urgent political necessity fifty years after his death and twenty years after the collapse of Russian Communism is obviously stepping to a different political drum than anyone else, or maybe it's just the drum of a right-winger who will never quite admit it. His claims to be a writer of the left have always been preposterous, and that they were ever accepted is sad testimony to the remoteness of the so-called left-liberal literary Establishment from the lives of the people about whom they like so much to pontificate. Martin Amis should have got out more and written us all a letter about the nothing he was able to perceive about England. As it is, he is a facile writer, and most of his inventions are paper thin. Even his subtitle for *Money* suggests that he doesn't know much about suicide.

Money is still a good, highly readable novel that captures the febrile energy of a decade in waiting on the cusp of what would become an irresistible pressure to forget everything that had just occurred, but since it so enthusiastically gave in to a greed culture whilst wagging a disapproving finger at the Yanks it was one of the books that everybody read in the eighties. Everybody except me, who unfairly disapproved of its author. Coming to the book a couple of decades later it's not very difficult to relate the novel to the middle-class anxieties of that decade, particularly about the changing status of women, who come in for a lot of sexual abuse in the book: it offers itself as a critique of masculinity. It also speaks to the eighties' sense of living in an economic bubble that may soon burst (it did) and to an old-fashioned anxiety that money no longer guarantees class. Funny money seriously undermines class and badly impinges on the middle-class male's sense of ancestral superiority. John Self is a writer who has lost touch with reality. But is he a con-man, on top of the game, or is he himself being conned by the wily Americans? He lives in a transatlantic world that is taking over England and tries to insulate himself from it by means of booze, drugs and sex. It is all very redolent of the anxieties of the fifties, of his father's generation. Of course the novel enjoys John Self's enjoyment of excess and success, we lap it up with him, but it also offers the comforting moral of his downfall. The working-class characters in the book, whom the protagonist feels himself related to through his dodgy pub-owning Dad—a comical cameo appearance for Kingsley—are just as venal as everybody else but function as part of a reassuring world of Englishness and realness which we are led to feel may rescue Self from himself.

For a long time I thought Will Self had taken his pen name from Martin Amis' most famous character and his entire bearings from the man he perceived to be England's top novelist, but by the time *The Book of Dave*

(2006) appeared a considerable period had passed in which it seemed that the working-classes had been counted out as a subject for serious fiction by those at the top of the London hierarchy of Britain's culture-defining novelists. Self's book is a tour-de-force of his fiction's sense of Britain and where we are at right now, and in it the proletariat plays its always useful role as a diagnostic tool—a kind of weathervane—for where exactly we are all supposedly going so wrong. The highest authority that can be bestowed is to be permitted to speak about the people who apparently cannot speak for themselves. Self's book can be placed easily on a continuum of sociological or anthropological senses of the working-class since it makes gleeful use of both of these approaches and more. Intended in part as a critique of contemporary working-class fatherhood, and therefore ostensibly sociological—which is to say improving—he also takes the step of envisioning a whole far-future society in which surviving oiks have manufactured a religion and sense of history and a clan structure out of the recovered rantings of an early twenty-first-century cab driver. This is the anthropological approach with a vengeance, because the language of his London lost tribes, or at least of the lower orders, hasn't developed much beyond a pidgin—or at best only into the early stages of a creole—and unlike the Roman Catholic seminaries that based themselves on engineer Leibowitz's jottings in Walter M. Miller's science-fiction classic, *A Canticle for Leibowitz*, from which many of Self's ideas have been taken wholesale: the gender-separated clan societies of Ham, Chil and New London aren't dedicated to rebuilding Western civilisation but to maintaining a brutally unequal society whose administrators are enforcers of a world view that makes even less sense than that of the Holy Roman see. Will Self's contemporary cabbie, Dave Rudman, the unlikely source of their doctrines, is a bit like H.G. Wells' blowhard pub socialist in the thirties film that was made of his story 'The Man Who Could Work Miracles', except rather than mistakenly abolishing the world in his attempt to improve it, like Wells' character, the inheritors of his Word use it to construct a society based on an outlook gleaned from a mad book he has written. It works, horrifyingly enough, after a fashion, and just as he always said it would. But are the inhabitants of his comic dystopia descended of the good old working-class or of the bad new working-class? Or, as Will Self would no doubt put it, are they children or dwarves?

They are both. There are 'chavs' and 'bondsmen', all divided into clans of mummies and daddies, kept down by a priest caste of Drivers, a secret police of ceeceeteeveemen, and all ruled from London by the Davist church authorities, the PCO. Interleaved with these far-future doings on Ham are Dave's pained perambulations around contemporary London. He is a hard-working, rather sympathetic character who can't stand other cabbies, is only moderately racist and is anguished about his child-support case and his separation from his wife and his son. His interactions with his fares are marked by an italicised subtext that tells what he really thinks underneath the cheeky-chappie façade he manages to half-heartedly maintain most of the time. He has the knowledge but it has turned rancid under the impact of London's continual mutation and the nightmare thought that he won't be able to pass it all on to his son. We gradually discover that many features of far future life on Ham have their origins in his world. The Motos, for example, a species of giant mutant pigs who are both child-minders (and who speak an even more degraded language than the humans) and sacred animals who are ritually slaughtered as a food source, have somehow transferred themselves into reality from an origin as the repellant logo of a motorway services franchise.

Dave Rudman himself is an excellent character who never quite loses our sympathy. He is one of Will Self's more convincing creations largely because his cynical creator seems to love him as surely and deeply as do the inhabitants of Ham. As usual it is the emergent priest caste that have distorted his original message for their own repressive ends. There are two Daves—just as there turn out to be two Books of Dave, one whose rantings have come to form the basis of the awful religion of Ing, and the other, apparently discovered by The Geezer, the gifted, levitating Symun, composed of Dave's better thoughts—of the liberal beliefs ('awl wee gotta du iz luv eech uvvah… weer awl iz lads, an if we luv eech uvva iss lyke luvin im') which have a millenarian and Leveller flavour: these new edicts may be no less simplistic and pernicious but the Hamsters find them more congenial since they cut their Fourierian propensities a bit more slack. As for the first book: 'Dave sed ee roat i wen ee woz off iz rokkah, vass wy iss fulluv awl vat mad shit.' Symun's dangerous heresies turn out to be even more dangerous for The Geezer who has rashly uttered them.

An innovative novelist's originality is nearly always built out of a concatenation of previous writers, and Will Self is no exception. He is a magpie who has gathered widely, well able to patch together a nest out of his multiple borrowings. His spottable influences in *The Book of Dave* include John Lennon's *In His Own Write* and *A Spaniard in the Works*, for their comic Joyceanism and Lear-like linguistic invention (not to be underrated); William Golding's *Lord of the Flies* for its island setting and improvised religion ('piggy's got the conch'); Margaret Atwood's feminist dystopia *The Handmaid's Tale*; and most strikingly Russell Hoban's grim post-apocalyptic *Riddley Walker*, whose narrating character employs a degraded working-class speech not dissimilar to the funnitork (or Mokni) of the inhabitants of Ham. Symun is a bit like Hoban's Riddley: an intelligent boy who can read and write and might conceivably remake the ways of the tribe, but he is in effect crucified, and Carl, his son named after Dave's son, is left to challenge the ruling caste of lawyers of Chil and New London.

Unfortunately many of the book's main relationships don't make a great deal of sense. Is it plausible that Dave's estranged wife Michelle, another relentless social climber, would have married him in the first place a one-night stand she shagged to get her own back on her married boyfriend? Or is this Will Self's take on the hypergamy theme of the Angry Young Men? Women characters don't come off very well in this book, despite his aim to incriminate the attitudes of working-class men: attitudes which are by no means unique to them, as the fictions of Martin Amis and Will Self show. Both of these writers use working-class personae to explore—or simply to express—misogyny by projecting it onto bad working-class men whose attitudes they so disapprove of and so much enjoy. The Hamsters may describe women past childbearing age as 'boilers', but it is Will Self who relishes the physical disgust in his descriptions of them. He appears to be as disgusted by the supposed venality of women as Dave is—although he will never own up to this, only blame it on the working-classes and enjoy expressing his bile by proxy. Dave is his avatar. Perhaps he is a nostalgic romantic, like his confused protagonist. That there has been an impoverishment of relationships between men and women is one of his sharper themes. Some people think we are on a more equal footing than ever before. But what has caused this supposed degeneration? Child support legislation? The courts? Feminists in the civil service? Women's ill-spirited greed? After 500 odd pages of careless, unsympathetic women and their disturbed, violent men we are not really any the wiser, but we have had a laugh at their expense.

It may be obtuse or humourless to interrogate such a high-spirited tour de force of storytelling and linguistic inventiveness in this way, but since it claims to be saying something big about the working-classes it seems reasonable to ask whether or not *The Book of Dave* really makes any good sense of working-class problems. Or is it on the other hand a fantastically thoroughgoing critique of ways of looking at and writing about the working-class? It might be taken as attempting to do either of these things, but the answer to both questions must be a resounding no. He makes working-class self-definitions the sources of racism and misogyny, and a degraded language is, of course, *pace* Orwell, the principal means through which a population may be kept ignorant and manipulated as well as the main culprit out of which these regressive social forms have somehow sprung. If this were true, and it may be, there would be no possibility of rebellion. In his fantastic world of far-future Ing all earlier social hierarchies and institutions are left more or less intact, and so, as far as he is concerned, we feel they are immutable, natural and unchangeable ones. We suspect he thinks the Hamsters are just slightly more articulate versions of the moronic Motos. We are pig-fuckers one and all. But if the human impulse to create myths and allegories often does lend false authority to preposterous unprovable world-views, as happens with Dave's Book, then that is also true of the allegorical novel: for all its power it's a mode that can lend highly tendentious social descriptions too much authority too easily. Some adherents of post-modernism appear to believe that a mere realist or naturalist novel can only be understood as some sort of ill-bred throwback, possibly the puerile handprint of a trogloditic revert, and it might be assumed that the author of *The Book of Dave* is one of these; this is not necessarily the case, but post-modernist irony, parody and pastiche often provide cover for quite reactionary social attitudes.

James Kelman has a view of the state that is part Kafka and part DHSS claimant. His novels and stories privilege people's speech by taking it out of inverted commas and placing it at the top of the novel's hierarchy of discourses. *How Late It Is, How Late* was the culmination of his project to map the Glasgow working-class, its history, current state—and the end of its traditional sense of things. At the end of How Late Kelman's tenement-dwelling hero, who has gone blind in police custody and found himself in the arms of the modern caring state and on the outside of every understanding he ever had of the meaning of his life and class, takes a final coach to the Highlands in blind compulsive search of his Mary He then turned to the experience of migrancy and displacement in *Translated Accounts*, and, in a return to Scottish themes, to the last night in America of a returning emigrant in his most recent novel, but reading it I felt he was never going to get back to Glasgow, and that if he did he would find it so utterly changed that his insights would no longer play there. James Kelman's is a magnificent achievement, but he has been recording the last days, the end of a tenement culture and of working-class self-conceptions that no longer exist anywhere.

Tony Parsons, Essex boy, former punk journalist and former *Daily Mirror* columnist—like Keith Waterhouse before him—emerged in the later nineties as a novelist who would try to write about the predicaments of contemporary working-class men who were faced with long overdue changes in the position of women and new demands on their traditional sense of masculinity. The fact that one can trot this out so easily makes me uneasy as to his authenticity as a novelist and wonder if his bestselling books are likely to contain anything but a working-class celeb's pop-sociological platitudes about such subjects, or that his books might be no more than would-be improving apologetics driven by a narrowly political agenda. Even more disquieting, they seem to have found a massive audience that feels quite happy to be defined by them. Julie Burchill, another inveterate working-class columnist, trod an identical career path from music journalism to mainstream, and has written lively, sexy books about teenage lesbians and ambitious career women.

Martina Cole enjoyed heroine dump bins in Woolworth's for being 'the woman who tells it like it is' for as long as Woolworth's continued to exist. She escaped from an abusive marriage to tell her story and to write further adventures about a seventeen-year-old Essex girl who becomes the head of an international crime syndicate. Her stories are about a poor girl's triumph over adversity and ascent to power—economic power and power over men—and in this they draw on a strong tradition in women's popular fiction, present in many historical romances, bodice rippers and 'contemporaries'. She is a sort of Essex version of Barbara Taylor Bradford, with sales to match. Like Taylor Bradford her authority is predicated on the truth of her own story as a visible kind of working-class success story and this feeds her success with working-class readers who therefore think she knows something they don't, much as the early readers of Herman Melville's *Typee* were excited to think he had actually had it off with a South Sea island woman. Once, sitting in the waiting room of a small claims court with other people hoping for small scale justice over small amounts of owed money that were large to us supplicants, I noticed that an elderly man in a suit, there with his family, was holding a fat copy of one of her books in his hand. He held it indifferently, obviously hadn't read it, clearly preoccupied with the ordeal to come. He opened the book, glanced at the opening pages, and promptly shut it again. A large woman, his daughter, briefly took it from his hand and then passed it back to him, telling him again: 'You should read it, dad.' The book would help him through his difficulties, she seemed to think, whether these particular difficulties or others. Her father, pulling at his collar, nodded vague agreement. He held the book on his knee, as if it was a sort of bright talisman or a Holy Bible. I wondered if he was going to carry it into court as a way of insisting he should be given a fair hearing, and whether this family, nervous before the authority of the courts, were carrying their own counter authority with them, believing that their visible possession of a copy of a Martina Cole novel would make a just outcome more likely for them.

John King's *The Football Factory* is a novel of the London working-class that takes the part of the football hooligans Bill Buford tried to understand in his documentary book, *Among the Thugs*. King apparently feels a direct affinity with the men and boys who commit terrace mayhem, semi-Nazi skinheads and more or less decent blokes who like a bit of a ruck but nevertheless have their own standards and codes of behaviour. He also has the intelligence—and the distance from his characters—to use his books to create a portrait of the English male working-class psyche, its inherited myths and the historical truths that lie behind them, and has a keen sense of both loyalty and urgency in his mission to do this work. He also aims to appeal to hardcore football fans and to just the kinds of people who might be attracted to terrace or racial violence, and to set them straight in a sympathetic, truth-telling way. Tim Lott's first novel *White City Blue* is about a group of friends growing up in West London and their struggles to achieve a mature attitude to women. *Rumours of a Hurricane* remembers the Thatcher era and centres on the lives of striking print workers caught up in the bitter Wapping dispute that broke trades union power in the British newspaper industry. Both of these are part of a now rare attempt to write a London working-class experience in the contemporary English novel.

David Peace was a language teacher who lived in Japan and has written a number of novels with years as titles: *1974, 1977*, and *GB84* amongst them, reimagining his native land from a distant vantage point that has proved to be a highly effective way of creating gritty fictions. The first two are essentially crime novels, the third a semi-documentary exploration of the miners' strike of that year. A writer for whom these periods coincide with his childhood, they are works of reconstruction and imagination rather than memory—unless inherited memory—and in this they resemble those novels of Jonathan Coe that have explored the 1970s and 1980s (*The Rotters' Club* and *What a Carve Up!*) Peace's and Coe's novels are about slightly different social territories and dissimilar in tone, but their political agendas are somewhat similar and they are both writing about an English world they grew up in, or at least were alive in (just) and have subsequently failed to inherit. There's a curious kind of negative nostalgia about them, a feeling it might be better to call remorse for the crimes of others. This might seem slightly strange to those who were thinking adults or adolescents in the seventies, and sometimes, whether fairly or not, older readers may find it difficult to engage with such factitious, researched versions of the past. Everything is a bit too bang on. You walk into a pub and Marc Bolan is playing as two characters engage in a conversation about some flagged up subject that was in the newspapers that day. They are a little like the television detective series *Life on Mars* in which a present day detective is transported back to the world of 70s cop series *The Professionals* to unravel a crime or his own past, like the Victorian detective who time-travelled back to the 1960s in a well-known series of that era, *Adam Adamant*. In that series the contemporary world is seen though the eyes of a Victorian gentleman; in *Life on Mars* the television version of the seventies—the barbaric past with its tang of reality—are viewed through the eyes of a more liberal twenty-first century that may itself just be a world of representations into which the leading man disappears at the end of the series, running off the top of a high building. In a world so leached of meaning, can even this act be real, bring a real death, or will it (as he seems to believe) return him to the past he is so reluctant to leave behind?

The novels of Peace and Coe are more serious in intention, if no better or more engrossing than really good television, but all partake of a still mildly retro culture and represent a continuation—or updating—of those eighties films that remembered the fifties, and are therefore a feature of short range historical memory and generational succession through which senses of the immediate past are updated, reshaped and retransmitted cut to a current political agenda. Peace and Coe are mapping senses of the immediate past for their own and a succeeding, younger generation in a spirit that attempts to counter media trivialisations of historical memory.

A comparison of British 'novels of youth' from the sixties to the present reveals that little has changed in their handling of the condition of youth itself, nor of the adult world and of the media. Sex is more taken for granted, viewed more cynically but less as an all-consuming lure to the reader. Class is no longer seen in quite the same terms, or is rather hypocritically taken to no longer exist. Geoff Dyer's first novel *The Colour of Memory* apparently believe themselves to be working-class whilst actually living in a middle-class bubble, dripping with synaesthesia, which they assume to be also inhabited by all young Londoners. Dyer's is a kind of eighties retread of the earlier boarding house novel, but he approaches no experience as other to his own, apart from exhibiting an elaborate deference towards black people: there's a useful lesson on how to be cool about being mugged, but apart from this brush with one possible reality he attempts nothing as ambitious as Lynne Reid Banks or Nell Dunn or Doris Lessing. The representation of gender has changed a great deal, with many more young women novelists emerging every season, and many of their assumptions about love and romance might be thought to have changed beyond recognition to their sixties counterparts; but it should be pointed out that these are still their main preoccupations. As far as any dilemmas about being British is concerned, these are anxieties and identifications that appear to be confined, with an odd symmetry, to the sons and daughters of immigrants—and to the white working-class: in other words, to those whose identities have been previously called into question. But whilst the actual shapes and literary modes of most current novels are 'English' through and through, literary modernism is not as much a thing of the past now as it once seemed in the fifties to the Angry Young Men.

My readings of these few novels are not a fair or exhaustive survey of the British novel since the sixties or even of those elements in fiction that have taken their bearings from the fifties and sixties in my already tendentious and partial account of it. That task would be beyond the scope of this conclusion and I would risk losing the shape of what I am trying to say, particularly about representations of class, if I were to attempt it. There have been quite a number of successors to Samuel Selvon in Black British fiction, appearing patchily in little clutches: the telling of immigrant stories, important though it is perceived to be, is as much subject to the vagaries of fashion and perceived marketplaces as the telling of native working-class stories. To take one prominent example, Zadie Smith doesn't at all take her bearings from the West Indian novel but, in part at least, from English comic novelists like Evelyn Waugh and twentieth century American fiction. She has been understandably reluctant to be restricted by her perceived affiliations from only being allowed to tell certain kinds of stories. Perhaps what remains culturally black about her is this sense that she must begin again from scratch, and maybe her chafing against received definitions of immigrant experience. These dilemmas are perhaps similar to those of novelists who emerged during the working-class fashion moment of the late fifties and early sixties, and it will be interesting to see whether she remains prominent in the highly hemmed and symbolic world of British fiction, and in what capacity: as another middle-class London writer, I would guess.

China Miéville is an attempted summation of all inheritors of sixties science-fiction and fantasy, trans-genre if not trans-gender, a compendious and eloquent world-cruncher of tropes from Moorcock, Dick, Ballard, Kafka, and Bruno Schultz. You name it, Miéville has staked his claim as its liveliest practitioner, and his powers as an early twenty-first-century allegorist are indisputable. *The City and the City* (2009), a double-reality noir thriller, reprises so many ideas from other writers that it is difficult to start describing the book without heaping yet more unwitting praise on it. And perhaps that is the key to his success with this way of inheriting the fictional past and making a place for oneself in the present. It can be called the 'in the great tradition of' approach, and was, in the once oft-heard tongue of the ancient blurb writer, a quick way of flagging up the proposition that 'if you liked that, you'll like this'. Something was said to be 'in the great tradition of' Philip K. Dick or Herb Kastle or

H.P. Lovecraft only if there was nothing else that might be said of it—no reviews, no quotes, just a generic similarity, a storyline (*The Island of Dr Moreau,* anyone?), or a set of familiar characters (*Star Trek* novelisation here we come!) and an editor who knows how all books should go. Miéville has understood all this brilliantly, he is on top of the game, stealing and melding at will in a frenzy of appropriation and ingenuity whose governing ideas are not however as radical or as personal as those of the inventors of all these so-called genres: just a mulch-down of some late twentieth century academic commonplaces about identity, reality and their complete vanquishment by an imaginary realm. As I look at his author photos with his shaved head, big arms and tasty tats I'm tempted to dismiss him as a clonely replicant, but his writing is intelligent and it has soul.

Amongst other inheritors of fifties and sixties fictions are retro crime novelists. Crime was always a genre that had retro built into it. Poe's stories may have introduced the idea of modern scientific detection, but were always set in a European past; every incarnation of Sherlock Holmes seems always to have offered Conan Doyle's readers a frisson of looking into dark places in an officially bland period of history. Agatha Christie's twenties has grown in authority with each passing year; Georgette Heyer's Lord Peter Wimsey and other Cluedo protagonists have paved the way for a still thriving popular culture of perennial crimes and passions rigged out in the pristine fashions of yesteryear. Andrew Taylor's Lydmouth series, for example, is set in a perpetually drizzling fifties town; and Cathi Unsworth's most recent *noir* outing, *Bad Penny Blues* reanimates the fifties Soho many of my novelists evoked so beautifully. Back in the day. Stewart Home has evcavated painful cultural memories in his investigative memoir of his mother's friendship with Alex Trocchi, *Tainted Love*; and in a universe parallel to all these strands but informing some of them, Iain Sinclair, a writer rooted in the sixties like a particularly tenacious mandrake, is pursuing his own visions of an occluded past that might be stumbled upon at the outflow of any urban sewage pipe. Psychogeography, the zombie-evoking, urban botanising movement he and W.G. Sebald have spawned, sometimes attempts to remap the immediate cultural past, but seems to rather want to do away with fiction as such, which might be something of a double-blind. But Sinclair is all-defining for his adherents. His anthology *London: City of Disappearances* assembles a wide range of interesting writers who are tapping around the big city in his wake, and his own later books, such as *Hackney, That Rose-Red Empire*, have done plenty to excavate lost senses of histories unknown, to seize memories that may well be flashing up for the last time. But even a wildly enthusiastic reader of his work can find over time that a number of important landscape features have blinked out of existence in this town, which like Philip K. Dick's Millgate, Virginia in *The Cosmic Puppets*, lies paralysed under the stalemate grip of its warring giants.

It is a commonplace of some kinds of Marx-influenced literary theory that the wider social process always appears in the gaps, in the unsaid, in what is said to be implied by fictions and therefore particularly in what they cannot know about themselves. But if the novel depends too much on such an alert, active, decoding reader this turns out be a massive disadvantage for fiction: not because readers are so stupid but because fiction will be forgoing its own mission to explain, to supply its own context. If, like modern poetry, fiction is totally dependent on the cultural level of its reader, it will tend to find relatively few of them and will tend to leave those where they started. Novels may often be no more than cultural talismans or unreliable travelogues to exotic climes or unfamiliar social territories, but the best of them are surely more than that implies. 'The truth of fiction' is an oxymoron: unverifiable, and fairly sure to vapourise if we apply the usual rules of historical evidence to it; it is only slightly more peculiar than its counterpart 'the truth of poetry'. In both a kind of personation is involved. Fiction writers of the fifties and sixties were quite often social imposters, but they weren't the first to successfully try it on, nor will they be the last. James Curtis' *They Drive By Night* (1938) communicates a powerful sense of working-class life and language that is unique and various: old cockney, American importations, a variety of Northern and Scottish tongues; his novel is packed with closely-observed and lovingly recorded lore of long-haul lorry-drivers, memories of pay and conditions harking back to the twenties, evocations of the lives of road-girls of no fixed abode and Soho criminals, but its author (Geoffrey Basil Maiden) was an old boy of Canterbury School who rose to the rank of Major during the Second World War. Everything about our reading of his novel tends to change as soon as we know that; we trust it less and hopefully we are less naïve readers as a result. But it changes in another way too: we see that naivety is what makes this novel work: the naïve enthusiasm of its author for working-class life and speech, the directness with which he makes political points and identifies with his characters. What is called or experienced as 'authenticity' is only *vraisemblance*, research, colour, and the sympathies of an enthusiastic young man who has talked to the right people.

> 'Them days was all right round the Edgeware when we was chavvies, wasn't they?'
> 'Not arf.'[6]

Not only is 'authenticity' a mere jargon as analysed by Theodor Adorno in his demolition of Martin Heidegger's philosophy[7], in fiction it is often no more than an illusionistic practice of toff sprucers slumming in Soho, and the terms of its sympathy can seem unacceptable if we see these elements for what they are—simple impostures for fraudulent easy gain: low level breaking and entering. But, as we have seen, in writing about the working-classes, personation is a rule rather than an exception, and not altogether for discreditable reasons. Good fiction works because it provides a kind of transport to and between imagined towns; but it's not hard to guess the true colours of those witnessing eyes at the train or car window. Edna O'Brien wrote about a girl with green eyes; she is hardly a novelist of ideas but can dance you easily through two-hundred pages of her prose with no visible support except her charming narrative voice, sharp observation and her way of quickly disclosing a scene: and enough wit to subvert any kind of masculine pomposity. Does it matter that she's really Polish? As for the rest, and especially the unpublished ones, Doris Lessing writes interestingly of once being asked to judge a short story competition for *Reynold's News*, a leftward Sunday newspaper of the fifties, and of subsequently reading around thirty novels by the entrants:

> I had not done anything like this before and was surprised by what I now know is common. First, these novels were all *nearly* good. All writers—I have not met one who is different—go through the stage when what we write is nearly good: the writing lacks some kind of inward clinching, the current has not run clear. (…) To every one of these authors I wrote carefully, with advice, and saying, When you have rewritten this one or done another, send it to me. Not one of them was heard of again. There is a sad waste of talent going on.[8]

It has been argued that the role of the novel is no longer (if it ever was) to inform or misinform; but the kind of realism that deals in conceptions rather than only in surfaces remains more powerful in the fiction market than the descendents of naturalism or modernism, and is more likely to result in a novel that communicates widely. Allegory (or romance) has not been eliminated from fiction. The sheer expanse of smooth surface is more a phenomenon of electronic media than of the novel, which at its best remains a bit homespun and accidental. Novelists of ideas like Hermann Hesse and D.H. Lawrence were as much part of the culture of the fifties and sixties as anything contemporary being written then and were probably more influential on readers of those times than any of the books I have been discussing. Hesse's powerful critique of traditional education, his exploration of the claims of Apollo and Dionysus, and his commitment to spiritual values; Lawrence's anguished re-examination of class, sexuality and relations between the sexes, his search for kinds of knowledge that weren't safely contained in the moral precepts of the English middle-classes—all were very much still alive for readers in the fifties and sixties; Samuel Beckett was widely considered to be the most important living writer in English and the early part of the second half of the twentieth century was still avidly reading the mavericks of the first half: their combustible ideas were paraffin for its many rebellious contemporary writers. Is fiction better now? Has the legacy of the fifties and sixties novel been thoroughly exploited, subsumed and exhausted for good?

Whatever the answers to these questions, novels of the fifties and sixties must certainly be recommended as windows into the past, whether round, square, oval, or even pear-shaped, they bear a direct impress of the years and decades they were published in, and, as Moorcock saw, they appear to encapsulate a kind of wild account of current conceptions and obsessions scarcely regulated except by the vagaries of fashion or accident. But those two exceptions loom large in the world of literature. Received ideas and conceptions are all powerful in their historical moment and policed by powers that continue to hold a whip-hand in culture: the commissioning editors, TV producers, culture pundits, commercial interests, bookshop managers and, not least, those pesky, flighty, distraction-seeking readers. Buzz-words, the zeitgeist, and the absolute necessity to hit and ride the next wave, or perhaps the tail end of the current one: these are of course determining factors in what will appear on the shelves of bookshops and in the columns of newspapers at any given moment.

We the people may never again be the flavour of the month, and if 'we' are you can rest assured that some heavy-duty political manipulation is going on. But at least the working-class writers and sixties experimenters weren't bland; a number of the books I have discussed were bestsellers, or aiming to be, while others struggled to appear, hit the 'wrong' note and were snubbed by reviewers and readers, leading to careers which, from the point of view of those who lived them, were a continuous scrabble for existence and validity. People who set themselves up against genre or realist formulas: B.S. Johnson, Paul Ableman, Ann Quin, and many others, were frustrated if not silenced by the meanness of reviewers and the inhospitability of reading publics to unfamiliar forms and approaches, and the whole painful business of squeezing out the roses in their cheeks onto reams of crisp white paper. And yet the very 'realism' they attacked seems now also a trove of lost conceptions, promising beginnings, full of acute observation of social minutiae that would otherwise be lost to us and aided by a bracing honesty: a sense of the experiential in novel-writing.

Notes

Introduction

[1] Raymond Williams, *Culture and Society* (Penguin: Harmondsworth, 1979; first published by Chatto and Windus, 1958) p.313

[2] Ibid., p. 317

[3] Ibid., p. 317

[4] Ibid., p. 319

[5] Raymond Williams, *Politics and Letters* (London: New Left Books, 1979)

[6] William Faulkner, *Light in August* (London: Vintage Classics, 2000; first published 1932) p. 349

[7] Raymond Williams, *Border Country* (London: Readers Union, 1962; first published by Chatto and Windus, 1960) p. 12

[8] Ibid., p. 22-23

[9] W.D. Howells, 'Novel Reading and Novel Writing: An Impersonal Explanation' (1899) in *The Norton Anthology of American Literature, Volume One* (New York: Norton, 1989)

[10] Hamlin Garland, *Main-Travelled Roads* (Boston: Arena, 1891)

[11] Raymond Williams, ed. T Pinkney, *The Politics of Modernism* (London and New York: Verso, 1989) p. 195 my italics

[12] Raymond Williams, *Keywords* (London: Fontana, 1974)

[13] Vita Sackville-West, 'The Land' and 'A Saxon Song' in *Collected Poems: Volume One* (London: Hogarth Press, 1933)

> "Tools with the comely names,
> Mattock and scythe and spade,
> Couth and bitter as flames,
> Clean, and bowed in the blade,—
> A man and his tools make a man and his trade."

[14] D.H. Lawrence, *Women in Love*, ed. Charles L. Ross (Harmondsworth, Penguin, 1982; first published by Thomas Seltzer, privately printed, New York, 1920) pp.

[15] Richard Hoggart, *The Uses of Literacy* (Harmondsworth: Penguin, 1958)

[16] Kingsley Amis, 'Socialism and the Intellectuals' (first published by The Fabian Society) reprinted in *Protest: The Beat Generation and the Angry Young Men* (edited by Gene Feldman and Max Gartenberg; London: Panther Books, 1960; first published by The Citadel Press, 1958) p.261

[17] See Ulrich Beck, Anthony Giddens, Scott Lash, *Reflexive Modernisation: Politics, Tradition and Aesthetics in the Modern Social Order* (Cambridge: Polity, 1994) for a sketch of contemporary preoccupations in sociological theory

[18] Michael Young and Peter Willmott, *Family and Kinship in East London* (London:

Penguin, 2007; first published by Routledge and Keegan Paul, 1957) pp.108-109

[19] Franco Moretti, *The Way of the World: The Bildungsroman in European Culture* (London: Verso, 2000)

[20] Slim Gaillard, 'Romance Without Finance', on Charlie Parker, *The Complete Savoy Sessions 1945-48*

[21] Benedict Anderson, *Imagined Communities: Reflections on the Origin and Spread of Nationalism* (London: Verso, 1983)

Chapter One

[1] Alan Sillitoe, *Saturday Night and Sunday Morning* (London: Grafton Books, 1985; first published by W.H. Allen, 1958) p. 201

[2] Ibid., p. 28

[3] Ibid., p. 48

[4] Ford Maddox Ford, *Joseph Conrad: A Personal Remembrance* (New York: Little, Brown, 1924); Hugh Kenner, *Joyce's Voices* (Berkeley: University of California Press, 1978)

[5] *Saturday Night and Sunday Morning* p. 44

[6] Ibid., p. 51

[7] Max Stirner, *The Ego and His Own*, translated by Steven T. Byington, introduced by T.L. Walker (New York: Benj. R. Tucker, 1907)

[8] Brendan Behan, *Borstal Boy* (London: Corgi, 1965; first published by Hutchinson, London, 1958)

[9] Alan Sillitoe, *The Loneliness of the Long Distance Runner* (London: Grafton Books, 1984) p. 16

[10] Paul Willis, *Learning to Labour: How Working-Class Kids Get Working-Class Jobs* (Farnborough: Saxon House, 1977)

[11] Noli me Tangere: 'Touch me not' is said by the risen Christ to Mary Magdalene in John 20:17. Sir Thomas Wyatt, 'Sonnet 1', in *Silver Poets of the Sixteenth Century* (ed. Gerald Bullett; London: J.M. Dent, 1975) p 3

[12] 'Matty Groves' (Child ballad No. 81, 'Little Musgrave and Lady Barnard'); recorded in many different versions, including Joan Baez, 1963; Fairport Convention, 1969

[13] Geoffrey Gorer, 'The Perils of Hypergamy'. Reprinted as a conclusion to the British section of *Protest: The Beat Generation and the Angry Young Men*. John Holloway's, 'Tank in the Stalls: Notes on the School of Anger' (*The Hudson Review*, Vol. X,No. 3, Autumn 1957; reprinted by Feldman and Gartenberg), places these novels as a reaction against pre-war modernism and also relates their 'new' themes to H. G. Wells, Thomas Hardy and D.H. Lawrence. Holloway critically reads John Wain's Empson-influenced poetry as a retreat from the cold,

hard lessons of T.S. Eliot and Ezra Pound.

[14] Ibid., p. 156

[15] Ibid., p. 158

[16] John Wain, 'My Nineteen Thirties (part one)', *Evergreen Review*, Vol. 3, No. 9, Summer, 1959) pp. 76-89

[17] Feldman and Gartenberg, p. 188

[18] Ibid., p. 196

[19] Ibid., p. 199

[20] Ibid., p. 203-211

[21] Francis Thompson, 'The Hound of Heaven' in *The Hound and Heaven and Other Poems*, ed. G.K. Chesterton (New York: Brandon Books, 1978)

[22] George Scott, excerpt from *Time and Place*, in Feldman and Gartenberg, p. 237

[23] Tom Raworth to Edward Dorn 26/12/60, published in *Edward Dorn, American Heretic*: *Chicago Review* 49:3/4 & 50:1, Summer 2004 p. 31

[24] Robert Lowell, 'For the Union Dead' in *For the Union Dead* (New York: Farrar, Straus & Giroux, 1964)

[25] Kenneth Allsop, *The Angry Decade* (London: Peter Owen, 1958) p.19

Chapter Two

[1] Edna O'Brien, *Girl With Green Eyes* (London: Penguin, 2005; first published by Jonathan Cape as *The Lonely Girl*, 1962) p. 150

[2] *Housekeeping Monthly*, 13 May 1955

[3] Edna O'Brien, *The Country Girls Trilogy* (London: Jonathan Cape, 1983; first published as *The Country Girls*, 1960; *The Lonely Girl*, 1962; *Girls in Their Married Bliss*, 1966) p. 413

[4] Ibid., p. 432

[5] Ibid., p. 436

[6] Ibid., p. 493

[7] Ibid., p. 396

[8] Ibid., p. 474

[9] Lynne Reid Banks, *The L-Shaped Room* (London: Penguin, 1985; first published by Chatto and Windus 1960) p. 8

[10] Ibid., p. 46

[11] Anthony Giddens, *The Transformation of Intimacy: Sexuality, Love and Eroticism in Modern Societies* (Cambridge: Polity Press, 1993)

[12] *The L-Shaped Room*, p. 10

[13] Ibid., p. 25

[14] Ibid., p. 30

[15] Ibid., p. 32

[16] Ibid., p. 136

[17] Ibid., p. 140

[18] Ibid., p. 166

[19] Ibid., p. 89

[20] Ibid., p. 86

[21] Ibid., p. 112

[22] Ibid., p. 113

[23] Ibid., p. 125

[24] Ibid., p. 132

[25] Ibid., p. 83

[26] Ibid., p. 120

[27] Margaret Mead, *Coming of Age in Samoa: a Psychological Study of Primitive Youth for Western Civilisation* (New York: William Morrow, 1930)

[28] Nell Dunn interviewed by Virginia Ironside, *The Independent*, 2002

[29] Nell Dunn, with drawings by Susan Benson, *Up the Junction* (London: Virago, 1988; first published by MacGibbon and Kee, 1963) pp. 84-5

[30] Gertrude Stein, *Three Lives* (Harmondsworth: Penguin, 1990; first published by Random House, New York, 1909)

[31] Nell Dunn, *Poor Cow* (London: Virago, 1988; first published by MacGibbon and Kee, 1967) p. 123

[32] Raymond Williams, *The Long Revolution* (London: Chatto and Windus, 1961)

[33] Nell Dunn, *Talking to Women* (London: MacGibbon and Kee, 1965) pp. 133-4

[34] Nell Dunn, *Living Like I Do* (London: Futura, 1977)

[35] Nell Dunn, *The Incurable* (London: Jonathan Cape, 1971)

Chapter Three

[1] Colin MacInnes, *To the Victors, the Spoils* (Harmondsworth: Penguin, 1963; first published by MacGibbon and Kee, 1950) p. 42

[2] MacInnes, *June in Her Spring* (Penguin, Harmondsworth, 1964; first published by MacGibbon and Kee, 1952) p. 16

[3] Ibid., p. 20

[4] Ibid., p. 72

[5] Ibid., p. 74

[6] David Bowie, 'Fashion' from *Scary Monsters* (EMI, 1980)

[7] *June in her Spring*, p. 78

[8] Ibid., p. 92

[9] Ibid., p. 93

[10] Ibid., p. 98

[11] Ibid., p. 145

[12] Ibid., p. 99

[13] Colin MacInnes, *Absolute Beginners* (London: Allison and Busby, 1980; first published by MacGibbon and Kee, 1959) p. 12

[14] Ibid., p. 32

[15] Ibid., p. 37

[16] Ibid., p. 38

[17] Ibid., p. 80

[18] Ibid., p. 44

[19] Ibid., p. 44

[20] Ibid., p. 69

[21] Ibid., p. 78

[22] Ibid., p. 127

[23] Ibid., p. 61

[24] Ibid., p. 43

[25] Ibid., p. 82

[26] Ibid., p.175

Chapter Four

[1] CLR James, *Letters from London: Seven Essays* (Oxford: Signal Books, 2003; first published 1932, *Port of Spain Gazette*) p. 103

[2] Samuel Selvon, *The Lonely Londoners* (London: Longmans, 1998; first published by Wingate Ltd., 1956) p. 24

[3] Ibid., p. 35

[4] Ibid., p. 45

[5] Ibid., p. 45

[6] Ibid., p. 46

[7] Ibid., p. 67

[8] Ibid., p. 67

[9] Ibid., p. 73

[10] Ibid., p. 75

[11] Ibid., p. 75

[12] Ibid., p. 76

[13] Ibid., p. 78

[14] Tom Leonard, Poetry and Prose, in *Etruscan Reader 5* (with Bill Griffiths and Tom Raworth) (Buckfastleigh: etruscan books, 1997)

[15] *The Lonely Londoners*, p. 109

[16] Ibid., p. 141

[17] Samuel Selvon, *The Ways of Sunlight* (London: Longman, Green, 1957), p. 188

[18] Walter Benjamin, 'The Storyteller: Reflections on the Work of Nikolai Leskov', in *Illuminations* (London: Fontana 1973)

[19] Victor Headley, *Yardie* (London: X Press, 1992)

[20] W.R. Burnett, *Little Caesar* (1930), Edward G. Robinson memorably uttered these words in the film's classic death scene.

[21] Richard Wright, *Native Son* (Harmondsworth: Penguin, 1977; first published by Harper, New York, 1940)

[22] Samuel Selvon, *Moses Ascending* (London: Penguin, 2008; first published 1975)

[23] Benjamin, 'Theses on the Philosophy of History' in *Illuminations*

[24] V.S. Naipaul, *The Mimic Men* (Harmondsworth: Penguin, 1976; first published by Andre Deutsch, London, 1967) p. 5

[25] Ibid., p. 19

[26] Ibid., p. 37

[27] Ibid., p. 45

[28] Ibid., p. 64-5

[29] Ibid., p. 67

[30] Ibid., p. 83

[31] Ibid., p. 148

[32] Ibid., p. 149

Chapter Five

[1] In Jonathan Coe, *Like a Fiery Elephant: The Story of B.S. Johnson* (London: Picador, 2004) p. 393

[2] John Berger, *The Foot of Clive* (London: Methuen, 1962) p.133-4

[4] John Berger, *A Fortunate Man* (London: Readers Union, 1968; first published by Allen Lane: Penguin, Harmondsworth, 1967) p. 69

[5] Ibid., p. 151

[6] Walter Benjamin, *One Way Street* (London: New Left Books, 1979) p. 66

[6] B.S. Johnson, *Travelling People* (London: Constable, 1963) p.

[7] E.R. Braithwaite, *To Sir With Love* (London: Bodley Head, 1959); *Violent Playground* (1958), dir. Basil Deardon

[8] B.S. Johnson, *Albert Angelo* in *The B.S. Johnson Omnibus* (London: Picador, 2004) p. 133

[9] Ibid., p. 133

[10] *The B.S. Johnson Omnibus* (London: Picador, 2004) p.180

[11] B.S. Johnson, *Trawl* (London: Secker and Warburg, 1966) p.11

[12] Ibid., p. 17

[13] *The B.S. Johnson Omnibus*, p. 92

[14] *Ibid.*, p. 197

[15] Jeff Nuttall in *All Bull: The National Servicemen* (ed. Johnson) (London: Quartet, 1973) p. 20

[16] John Berger, *King: A Street Story* (London: Bloomsbury, 1999)

[17] John Berger, quoted in *Like a Fiery Elephant*, p. 415

Chapter Six

[1] Leslie Thomas, *The Virgin Soldiers* (London: Constable, 1966) p. 12

[2] Ibid., p. 10

[3] Ibid., p. 11

[4] John Ashbery, 'Decoy' in *Selected Poems* (London: Paladin, 1987) p. 105

[5] *The Virgin Soldiers*, p. 25

[6] Ibid., p. 35

[7] Ibid., p. 38

[8] Ibid., p. 49

[9] Ibid., p. 53

[10] Ibid., p. 60

[11] Ibid., p. 77

[12] Ibid., p. 128

[13] Ibid., p. 129

[14] W.D. Howells, in *The Norton Anthology of American Literature*, p. 238

[15] Robert Vincent Remini, *Daniel Webster: The Man and his Times* (New York: Norton, 1997)

[16] Leslie Thomas, *Orange Wednesday* (London: Constable, 1967) p. 31

[17] Ibid., p. 59

[18] Ibid., p. 177

[19] Ibid., p. 182

[20] Leslie Thomas, *Waiting for the Day* (London: Heinemann, 2003) p.50

Chapter Seven

[1] Colin Wilson, *The Outsider* (London: Victor Gollancz, 1956)

[2] Colin Wilson, *The Glass Cage: An Unconventional Detective Story* (London: Village Press, 1966) p. 169

[3] Alexander Trocchi, *Young Adam* (Paris: Olympia Press, 1961; London: NEL, 1966)

[4] Herman Hesse, *Klingsor's Last Summer* and other early novellas.

[5] Alexander Trocchi, *Cain's Book* (London: John Calder, 1964)

[6] *Cain's Film* (1969) dir. Jamie Wadhawan

[7] Alexander Trocchi, *Thongs* (Paris: Olympia Press, 1955)

[8] See Howard Slater's account of Trocchi's involvement with Project Sigma ('an organisation of a world wide linking up of intellectuals and poets to effect a revolutionary transformation of Western Society') in *Edinburgh Review 83,* Summer 1990 pp. 132-4

[9] Wallace Stevens, *Harmonium* (London: Faber, 2001; first published 1923, revised edition, 1931), p.7

[10] Pinter—in an early interview quoted in Michael Billington's excellent biography, *Harold Pinter* (London: Faber and Faber, 2007)

[11] Harold Pinter, *Various Voices: Prose, Poetry, Politics 1948-2005* (London: Faber 2005) p.138

[12] Harold Pinter, *The Dwarfs* (London: Faber, 1990) p.98

[13] Ibid., p. 114

[14] William Blake, 'A Poison Tree' from *Songs of Innocence and Experience* (1794)

[15] *The Dwarfs*, p. 176

[16] Paul Ableman, *I Hear Voices* (Paris: Olympia Press, 1958; London: New English Library, 1966) p.57

[17] Ibid., p. 11

[18] Ibid., p. 10

[19] Ibid., p. 18

[20] Ibid., p. 23

[21] Ibid., p. 24

[22] Ibid., p. 39

[23] Ibid., p. 51

[24] Ibid., p. 50

[25] Ibid., p. 80-2

[26] Ibid., p. 84

[27] J.H. Prynne, *Stars, Tigers and the Shapes of Words* (London: Birkbeck College, 1993)

[28] *I Hear Voices*, p. 94

[29] Ibid., p. 114

[30] Ibid., p. 119

[31] Ibid., p. 121

[32] Ibid., p. 128

[33] Paul Ricoeur, Time and Narrative (*Temps et Récit*), 3 vols. trans. Kathleen McLaughlin and David Pellauer (Chicago: University of Chicago Press, 1984, 1985, 1988)

[34] *I Hear Voices*, p. 149

[35] Ibid., p. 185

[36] St. Augustine, *Confessions* (London: Penguin, 1996)

[37] R.D. Laing, *The Politics of Experience* (Harmondsworth: Penguin, 1967)

[38] R.D. Laing and A. Esterson, *Sanity, Madness and the Family: families of Schizophrenics* (Harmondsworth: Penguin, 1990; first published by Tavistock Publications, 1964)

[39] Jacques Lacan, *Ecrits*, translated by Alan Sheridan (London: Tavistock, 1966)

Chapter Eight

[1] Percy Bysshe Shelley, *A Defence of Poetry* (1821)

[2] Michael Moorcock, *A Cure for Cancer* (London: Allison and Busby, 1968) p. 55

[3] Ibid., p. 7

[4] Michael Moorcock, *The Condition of Muzak* (London: Allison and Busby, 1976) p. 186

[5] Michael Moorcock, *The English Assassin* (London: Allison and Busby, 1972) p. 43

[6] Michael Moorcock, *The Eternal Champion* (St Albans: Mayflower, 1970)

[7] Joseph Campbell, *The Hero with a Thousand Faces* (London: Fontana, 1993; New Jersey, Princeton University Press, 1949)

[8] Michael Moorcock, *Elric of Melnibone* (London: Hutchinson, 1972)

[9] Michael Moorcock, *Behold the Man* (London: Grafton Books, 1986; first published by Allison and Busby, 1969)

[10] Michael Moorcock, Introduction, *New Worlds 1* (London: Victor Gollancz, 1991) p. 9

[11] Angela Carter, *Shadow Dance* (London: Victor Gollancz, 1966)

[12] Lorna Sage (ed), *Flesh and the Mirror* (London: Virago, 1995)

[13] Michael Moorcock, *The Transformation of Miss Mavis Ming* (London: W.H. Allen, 1977)

[14] Angela Carter, *The Passion of New Eve* (London: Virago, 1982; first published by Victor Gollancz, 1977)

[15] Angela Carter, *The Magic Toyshop* (London: Virago, 1987; first published by Victor Gollancz, 1967) p. 9

[16] Ibid., p. 97

[17] Ibid., p. 69

[18] Ibid., p. 106

[19] Ibid., p. 152

[20] Brian Aldiss, *Barefoot in the Head* (London: Faber and Faber, 1969)

[21] Philip K. Dick, 'Expendable', in *Beyond Lies the Wub: Volume One of the Collected Stories of Philip K. Dick* (London: Grafton Books, 1990; first published as 'He Who Waits' in *Fantasy and Science Fiction*, July 1953)

[22] John Clare, 'Insects'

[23] Alexander Pope, *Essay on Man*

[24] Brian Aldiss, *Hothouse* (London: Four Square, 1964; first published by Faber, 1962)

[25] Richard Dawkins, *The Selfish Gene* (Oxford: OUP,1976)

[26] J. G. Ballard, 'The Flowers of Time' in *The Four-Dimensional Nightmare* (The Science Fiction Book Club, 1963)

[27] Edmund Wilson, *Axel's Castle: A Study in the Imaginative Literature of 1870-1930* (London: Flamingo, 1984; New York, Scribners, 1931) pp 206-11

[28] Baudelaire, 'A Hemisphere in a Head of Hair' in *Spleen de Paris* (1862)

[29] Arthur Rimbaud, 'Apres le Deluge', the opening poem of Les Illuminations, in *Complete Works, Selected Letters*, translated by Wallace Fowlie (Chicago, 1967)

[30] J.G. Ballard, *The Crystal World* (London: Jonathan Cape, 1966) p. 101

[31] Arthur Schopenhauer, *The World as Will and Representation* (1819); one volume edition, *The World As Will and Idea* (edited by David Berman, translated by Jill Berman; London: J.M. Dent, 1998)

[32] J.G. Ballard, *Concrete Island* (London: Jonathan Cape, 1973)

[33] J.G. Ballard, 'The Greatest Television Show On Earth' in *Low Flying Aircraft* (London: Triad/Panther, 1978; first published by Jonathan Cape, 1976) p. 148

[34] Jean Baudillard, *Selected Writings*, ed. Mark Poster (Cambridge: Polity Press, 1988)

[35] J.G. Ballard, *Kingdom Come* (London: Fourth Estate, 2006)

[36] J.G. Ballard, postcard to the author, 22/9/06

Chapter Nine

[1] Jack Trevor Story, *Live Now, Pay Later* (Harmondsworth: Penguin, 1963) p. 14

[2] Ibid., p. 44

[3] Ibid., p. 35

[4] Ibid., p. 74

[5] Ibid., p. 105

[6] Ibid., p. 76

[7] Ibid., p. 97

[8] *Letters from London* (C.L.R. James), p. 120

[9] Jack Trevor Story, *I Sit in Hangar Lane* (London: Secker and Warburg, 1968) p.105

[10] Jack Trevor Story, *One Last Mad Embrace* (London: Allison and Busby, 1970) p. 8

[11] Ibid., p. 14

[12] Ibid., p. 52

[13] Ibid., p. 211

Chapter Ten

[1] Iona and Peter Opie, *The Lore and Language of Schoolchildren* (Oxford: Clarendon Press, 1959)

[2] Iona Opie, unidentified print article.

[3] Keith Waterhouse, *There is a Happy Land* (London: Michael Joseph, 1957) p. 6

[4] Ibid., p. 37

[5] Ibid., p. 49

[6] *Whistle Down the Wind* (1961) dir. Bryan Forbes

[7] *A Taste of Honey* (1961) dir. Tony Richardson

[8] *There is a Happy Land*, p. 38

[9] A.E. Housman, 'A Shropshire Lad' in *Collected Poems* (London: Jonathan Cape, 1974; first published 1896) p. 29

[10] Ibid., p. 9

[11] Raymond Williams, *Television: Technology and Cultural Form* (London: Fontana, 1974)

[12] Keith Waterhouse, *Billy Liar* (London: Michael Joseph, 1959) p. 41

[13] Ibid., p. 55

[14] William Empson, 'Aubade' in *The Complete Poems* (London: Penguin, 2001). 'Traditionally the song warning lovers to part before dawn.' (Empson) pp. 68-

9/316

[15] Keith Waterhouse, *Maggie Muggins, or, Spring in Earl's Court* (London: Michael Joseph, 1981)

Chapter Eleven

[1] Barry Hines, *A Kestrel for a Knave* (London: Penguin, 2005; first published by Michael Joseph, 1968) p. 20

[2] Ibid., p. 130

[3] D.H. Lawrence, *Birds, Beasts and Flowers* (1927) (Harmondsworth: Penguin, 1999)

[4]*A Kestrel for a Knave*, p. 106

[5] P.B. Shelley, 'Ode to a Skylark'

[6] *A Kestrel for a Knave*, p. 181

[7] Louis Althusser, *Lenin and Philosophy* (London: New Left Books, 1971) pp. 203-4

[8] Terry Eagleton, *Criticism and Ideology*, (London: New Left Books, 1976) p. 83

Chapter Twelve

[1] *The Leather Boys*, dir. Sidney J. Furie (1964)

[2] John Hill, *Sex, Class and Realism in British Cinema 1956-63* (London: BFI, 1986)

[3] Gillian Freeman, *The Leather Boys* (London: New English Library, 1969; first published by Anthony Blond, 1961, under the name Eliot George) p. 59

[4] Gillian Freeman, *Jack Would Be A Gentleman* (London: Longmans, Green, 1959)

[5] Iris Murdoch, *Under the Net* (London: Chatto and Windus, 1954) p. 111

[6] Iris Murdoch, *The Bell* (London: Chatto and Windus, 1958)

[7] Iris Murdoch, *Bruno's Dream* (London: Chatto and Windus, 1969) p. 146

[8] Iris Murdoch, *The Sea, The Sea* (London: Chatto and Windus, 1978)

[9] Samuel Taylor Coleridge, 'Frost at Midnight' (1798)

[10] Hartley Coleridge, 'Long Time a Child' and 'To a Deaf and Dumb Little Girl' (circa 1830s)

[11] Iris Murdoch, *The Sovereignty of Good* (London: Ark, 1970)

Chapter Thirteen

[1] Bill Naughton, *Late Night on Watling Street* (London: Panther Books, 1965; first published by MacGibbon and Kee, 1959)

[2] James Curtis, *They Drive By Night* (London: Ace Books, 1959; first published 1938, reissued by John Lehmann Ltd., 1948). Dedication: 'To SHIRLEY who drove me on to write this book, night after night.' At the time of writing three of

Curtis' novels, *The Gilt Kid, There Ain't No Justice* and *They Drive By Night* have been reissued by London Books.

[3] Bill Naughton, *Alfie* (London: Allison and Busby, 1988; first published by MacGibbon and Kee, 1966) p. 12

[4] Ibid., p. 11

[5] Ibid., p. 19

[6] Ibid., p. 18

[7] Ibid., p. 36

[8] Bill Naughton, *Alfie Darling* (London: MacGibbon and Kee, 1970) p. 165

[9] Robert Johnson, 'Terraplane Blues' on *King of the Delta Blues Singers* (Columbia Records, 1960)

[10] David Storey, *This Sporting Life* (London: Longmans, Green, 1960) *film,* dir. Lindsay Anderson, 1963)

[11] Robert Johnson, 'Come on in my Kitchen' (1936)

[12] David Storey, *Flight into Camden* (Harmondsworth: Penguin, 1964; first published by Longmans, Green, 1960) p.194

[13] Ibid., p. 54

[14] Ibid., p. 55

[15] Ibid., p. 107

[16] Ibid., p. 34

[17] Ibid., p. 124

[18] Ibid., p. 133

[19] Ibid., p. 138

[20] Ibid., p. 92

[21] Ibid., p. 165

[22] Bill Naughton, *Saintly Billy; On the Pig's Back: an autobiographical excursion* (Oxford: OUP, 1987, 1988)

[23] 'Children from poor families "doomed" as social mobility stalls', *Independent,* 13 Dec 2007

Chapter Fourteen

[1] Doris Lessing, *Walking in the Shade: Autobiography Volume Two* (London: Harper Collins, 1997)

[2] Doris Lessing, *In Pursuit of the English* (London: MacGibbon and Kee, 1960) p. 9

[3] Ibid., p. 53

[4] Ibid., p. 91

[5] Ibid., p. 87

[6] Ibid., p. 115

[7] Ibid., p. 122

[8] Ibid., p. 124

[9] Ibid., p. 138

[10] Ibid., p. 203

[11] Ibid., p. 238

[12] Doris Lessing, *The Golden Notebook* (London: HarperCollins, 2007; first published by Michael Joseph, 1962) p. 33

[13] Ayn Rand, *Atlas Shrugged* (New York: Random House, 1957)

[14] *The Golden Notebook*, p. 90

[15] Ibid., p. 91

[16] Ibid., p. 576

Conclusion

[1] Jeff Nuttall, *Bomb Culture* (London: Paladin, 1968)

[2] Bob Dylan, 'When the Night Comes Falling from the Sky', from *Empire Burlesque* (Columbia, 1985)

[3] *Nothing But the Best* (1964), dir. Clive Donner

[4] William Carlos Williams, 'The Descent', in *Pictures from Brueghel* (New York: New Directions, 1962; first published in *The Desert Music*, 1954) p. 73

[5] Jürgen Habermas, *Legitimation Crisis* (London: Heinemann, 1976)

[6] *They Drive By Night*, p. 143

[7] Theodor Adorno, *The Jargon of Authenticity* (London: Routledge and Keegan Paul, 1973)

[8] *Walking in the Shade*, p. 221

Select Bibliography

Fiction

Paul Ableman	*I Hear Voices, As Near As I Can Get, Green Julia* (play), *The Twilight of the Vilp, Vac, Tornado Pratt, Tests, Arthur Daley Straight Up: The Autobiography, Porridge*
Brian Aldiss	*Non-Stop, Hothouse, Barefoot in the Head*
Richard Allen	*Skinhead, Suedehead, Skinhead Farewell, Teeny Bopper Idol*
Margaret Atwood	*The Handmaid's Tale, Oryx and Crake*
Kingsley Amis	*Lucky Jim, Girl, 20, Jake's Thing, The Old Devils*
Martin Amis	*The Rachel Papers, Other People, Money, London Fields, The Information*
J.G. Ballard	*The Drowned World, The Drought, The Crystal World, The Atrocity Exhibition, Crash, Concrete Island, The Disaster Area, Myths of the Near Future, Empire of the Sun, The Day of Creation, Cocaine Nights, Super-Cannes, Kingdom Come*
Lynn Reid Banks	*The L-Shaped Room*
Alexander Baron	*From the City, from the Plough*
Stan Barstow	*A Kind of Loving*
John Berger	*A Painter of Our Time, The Foot of Clive, Corker's Freedom, A Fortunate Man, G, A Seventh Man, Into Their Labours, To the Wedding, King, Here Is Where We Meet* (autobiography), *A to X*
Julie Burchill	*Ambition, Sugar Rush, I Knew I Was Right*
John Braine	*Room at the Top, The Vodi, Life at the Top, The Jealous God*
Anthony Burgess	*A Clockwork Orange*
Alan Burns	*The Angry Brigade*
Angela Carter	*Shadow Dance, The Magic Toyshop, Several Perceptions, Heroes and Villains, The Passion of New Eve, The Infernal Desire Machines of Dr Hoffman, Black Venus, Nights at the Circus, Wise Children*
Peter Cave	*Chopper, Mama, Rogue Angels*
Jonathan Coe	*The Rotters' Club, What A Carve Up!*
Martina Cole	*Dangerous Lady, The Ladykiller, The Jump, Maura's Game, The Take*
Jack Common	*Kiddar's Luck*
James Curtis	*The Gilt Kid, There Ain't No Justice, They Drive By Night*
Len Deighton	*The Ipcress File, Horse Under Water, SSGB*
Charles Dickens	*Hard Times, Great Expectations, Oliver Twist, Bleak House*
Nell Dunn	*Up the Junction, Poor Cow, The Incurable, Living Like I Do*
George Eliot	*Middlemarch, Adam Bede*
William Faulkner	*Light in August, As I Lay Dying, Go Down, Moses, The Sound and the Fury, Sanctuary, The Wild Palms*
Margaret Forster	*Georgy Girl*

Gillian Freeman	*The Liberty Man, Jack Would Be A Gentleman, The Leather Boys, The Leader, The Campaign, Nazi Lady, His Mistress' Voice, But* Nobody *Lives in Bloomsbury, The Undergrowth of Literature* (criticism)
Janice Galloway	*The Trick is to Keep Breathing*
William Golding	*Lord of the Flies, Pincher Martin, The Spire*
Graham Greene	*Brighton Rock, A Gun for Sale, The Confidential Agent, The Heart of the Matter, Our Man in Havana*
Walter Greenwood	*Love on the Dole*
Patrick Hamilton	*Twenty Thousand Streets Under the Sky, Hangover Square, The Slaves of Solitude*
James Hanley	*Drift, Boy, The Last Voyage, Stoker Bush, The Furys, Our Time is Gone, A Secret Journey, No Directions, Hollow Sea, Levine, A Woman in the Sky, Don Quixote Drowned* (essays)
Thomas Hardy	*Jude the Obscure, Tess of the D'Urbervilles*
Victor Headley	*Yardie*
Herman Hesse	*Klingsor's Last Summer, Narziss and Goldmund, Steppenwolf, The Glass Bead Game*
Barry Hines	*The Blinder, A Kestrel for a Knave, First Signs, The Gamekeeper, Looks and Smiles*
Russell Hoban	*Riddley Walker*
Stewart Home	*A Hundred Things to do with a Dead Princess, Tainted Love*
C.L.R. James	*Minty Alley*
B.S. Johnson	*Travelling People, Albert Angelo, Trawl, The Unfortunates, House Mother Normal, Christie Maldry's Double Entry, See the Old Lady Decently, Aren't You A Bit Young To Be Writing Your Memoirs?* (essays)
James Joyce	*Dubliners, A Portrait of the Artist as a Young Man, Ulysses, Finnegans Wake*
James Kelman	*Not Not While the Giro, The Bus Conductor Hines, Greyhound for Breakfast, A Disaffection, How Late It Is, How Late, Translated Accounts, You've Got to Be Careful in the Home of the Free*
Gerald Kersh	*Night and the City*
John King	*The Football Factory, England Away, The Prison House*
D.H. Lawrence	*Sons and Lovers, The Rainbow, Women in Love, The Lost Girl, Lady Chatterley's Lover*
John Lennon	*In His Own Write, A Spaniard in the Works*
Doris Lessing	*The Grass is Singing, The Black Madonna, This Was The Old Chief's Country, Children of Violence* (tetralogy), *In Pursuit of the English, The Golden Notebook, Briefing for a Descent into Hell, The Summer Before the Dark, Memoirs of a Survivor, Canopus in Argos* (tetralogy), *Under My Skin, Walking in the Shade*

Tim Lott	*White City Blue, Rumours of a Hurricane*
Colin MacInnes	*To the Victors the Spoils, June in her Spring, Absolute Beginners, City of Spades, Mr Love and Justice, England, Half-English*
Julian MacLaren-Ross	*Of Love and Hunger, Selected Stories*
W. Somerset Maugham	*Liza of Lambeth, The Moon and Sixpence, Here and There*
China Miéville	*Perdido Street Station, The City and The City, Un Lun Dun*
Walter M. Miller Jr	*A Canticle for Leibowitz*
Magnus Mills	*The Restraint of Beasts, The Scheme for Full Employment*
Michael Moorcock	*Elric of Melniboné, Stormbringer, The Jerry Cornelius Quartet, The Eternal Champion, Behold the Man, The City in the Autumn Stars*
Arthur Morrison	*A Child of the Jago*
Iris Murdoch	*Under the Net, The Bell, The Red and the Green, Bruno's Dream, The Sea, The Sea*
V.S. Naipaul	*The Mystic Masseur, A House for Mr Biswas, The Suffrage of Elvira, The Middle Passage, Miguel Street, Mr Stone and the Knight's Companion, The Mimic Men, In a Free State*
Bill Naughton	*One Small Boy, Late Night on Watling Street, Alfie, Alfie Darling, On the Pig's Back, Saintly Billy*
Courttia Newland	*The Scholar, Society Within, Snakeskin*
Edna O'Brien	*The Country Girls, The Lonely Girl, Girls in Their Married Bliss, A Fanatic Heart*
George Orwell	*Keep the Aspidistra Flying, Coming Up For Air, 1984, Animal Farm*
Agnes Owens	*Gentlemen of the West*
Tony Parsons	*Man and Boy, One for My Baby*
David Peace	*1974, 1977, GB84*
Chris Petit	*The Hard Shoulder*
Jim Phelan	*Ten A Penny People*
Christopher Priest	*Fugue for a Darkening Island*
Ann Quin	*Berg, Passages, Three, Tripticks*
Will Self	*The Quantity Theory of Insanity, My Idea of Fun, Big Tough Toys for Big Tough Boys, The Book of Dave, Umbrella*
Samuel Selvon	*A Brighter Sun, The Lonely Londoners, The Housing Lark, The Ways of Sunlight, Moses Ascending*
Mary Shelley	*Frankenstein, The Last Men in London*
Alan Sillitoe	*Saturday Night and Sunday Morning, The Loneliness of the Long Distance Runner, Travels in Nihilon, The Death of William Posters*
Iain Sinclair	*Lud Heat, Suicide Bridge, White Chappell, Scarlet Tracings, Downriver, Lights Out for the Territory, (ed) London: City of Disappearances* (anthology)
Zadie Smith	*White Teeth, The Autograph Man, On Beauty, NW*
Muriel Spark	*The Ballad of Peckham Rye, Memento Mori, The Prime of Miss Jean Brodie*

Gertrude Stein	*Three Lives*
Alex Stewart	*The Bikers*
Bram Stoker	*Dracula, The Lair of the White Worm*
David Storey	*This Sporting Life, Flight into Camden, Radcliffe, Pasmore, A Temporary Life, Saville, A Prodigal Child, Present Times, A Serious Man*
Jack Trevor Story	*Live Now, Pay Later, Something for Nothing, The Urban District Lover, I Sit in Hangar Lane, One Last Mad Embrace, Littledog's Day*
Leslie Thomas	*This Time Next Week, The Virgin Soldiers, Orange Wednesday, The Love Beach, The Magic Army, Tropic of Ruislip, Other Times, Waiting for the Day*
Alexander Trocchi	*Young Adam, Cain's Book*
Cathi Unsworth	*Bad Penny Blues, Weirdo*
John Wain	*Hurry on Down*
Keith Waterhouse	*There is a Happy Land, Billy Liar, Jubb, Office Life, Thinks, Maggie Muggins, Soho*
Irvine Welch	*Trainspotting, The Acid House, Filth, Porno, Bedroom Secrets of the Master Chefs*
H.G. Wells	*Selected Short Stories, The Time Machine, The First Men in the Moon, The History of Mr Polly, Love and Mr Lewisham, Kipps, Tono-Bungay*
Robert Westerby	*Wide Boys Never Work*
Raymond Williams	*Border Country, The Fight for Manod*
Colin Wilson	*The Glass Cage: An Unconventional Detective Story*
Virginia Woolf	*Mrs Dalloway*
Michael Young	*The Rise of the Meritocracy*

Criticism

Stanley S. Atherton	*Alan Sillitoe: A Critical Assessment*
Ian A. Bell (ed.)	*Peripheral Visions: Images of Nationhood in Contemporary British Fiction*
Malcolm Bradbury	*The Modern British Novel* His chapters 'The Sixties and After' and 'Artists of the Floating World: 1979–Present' are high-speed surveys, but contain useful critical and political/historical bibliographies.
Geoff Dyer	*Ways of Telling: The Work of John Berger*
A. Robert Lee (ed.)	*Other Britain, Other British*
Lorna Sage (ed.)	*Flesh and the Mirror: Essays on Angela Carter*

On the Sixties — *written at the time*

Nell Dunn	*Talking to Women*
George Melly	*Revolt into Style*
Jeff Nuttall	*Bomb Culture*

On the Novel — *traditions and contexts*

John Carey	*The Intellectuals and the Masses*
Claud Cockburn	*Bestseller: The Books That Everyone Read 1900-1939*
Stephen Connor	*The British Novel in History: 1950-1995*
F.R. Leavis	*The Great Tradition*
Q.D. Leavis	*Fiction and the Reading Public*
Franco Moretti	*Signs Taken for Wonders, The Way of the World*
Raymond Williams	*The Country and the City*
Ian Watt	*The Rise of the Novel*
Colin Wilson	*The Outsider*
Ken Worpole	*Dockers and Detectives, Reading By Numbers*

Theories

Theodor Adorno	*Minima Moralia, The Jargon of Authenticity*
Louis Althusser	*Lenin and Philosophy*
Benedict Anderson	*Imagined Communities*
M. M. Bahktin	*The Dialogical Imagination*
Walter Benjamin	*Illuminations, One-way Street and Other Writings*
Marshall Berman	*All That Is Solid Melts Into Air: The Experience of Modernity*
George Dangerfield	*The Strange Death of Liberal England*
Terry Eagleton	*Criticism and Ideology, Literary Theory*
Frantz Fanon	*Black Skin, White Masks, The Wretched of the Earth*
Anthony Giddens	*The Consequences of Modernity, The Transformation of Intimacy*
Jürgen Habermas	*Legitimation Crisis*
Jean François Lyotard	*The Postmodern Condition*
Georg Lukacs	*History and Class Consciousness, Studies in European Realism*
Pierre Macherey	*A Theory of Literary Production*
Iris Murdoch	*The Sovereignty of Good*
Raymond Williams	*Culture and Society, The Long Revolution, Television and Cultural Form, Politics and Letters,The Politics of Modernism, Resources of Hope*
Edmund Wilson	*Axel's Castle: A Study in the Imaginative Literature of 1870-1930*
David Morley & KenWorpole (eds.)	*The Republic of Letters: Working-Class Writing and Local Publishing*

Social History/General

Ronald Blythe	*Akenfield*
Peter Hennessey	*Having it so Good: Britain in the Fifties*
Christopher Hill	*The World Turned Upside Down*
Eric Hobsbawm	*Captain Swing, The Age of Extremes 1914-1991*
Richard Hoggart	*The Uses of Literacy: Aspects of Working-Class Life*
C.L.R. James	*Letters from London*
Richard Jefferies	*Hodge and his Masters*
A.L. Morton	*A People's History of England*
Iona & Peter Opie	*The Lore and Language of Schoolchildren*
	Children's Games in Street and Playground
Andrew Salkey	*Georgetown Journal*
Dominic Sandbrook	*White Heat: A History of Britain in the Swinging Sixties*
E. P. Thompson	*The Making of the English Working-Class*
Michael Young & Peter Willmott	*Family and Kinship in the East End*

Acknowledgements

I wish to thank the helpful staff of Hornsey Library, where most of the research for this book was done; Tom Raworth for directing me towards Paul Ableman and for sending me copies of *I Hear Voices* and Leslie Thomas' *The Virgin Soldiers* he had bought for a penny each on the internet; Clair Wills for reading great chunks of the first draft in progress; Herbie Butterfield and Richard Gray for commenting favourably on its first completed form; Terry Eagleton for admiring its steady political focus but noting that it wasn't exactly subtle; Iain Sinclair for pointing me towards Jack Trevor Story and pointing out that he has never liked Colin Wilson; Dave Cook for his continued enthusiasm; and finally, Tony Frazer, my publisher, for his willingness to take a chance on something out of his usual area. None of the above is responsible for anything I say about post-war British novels: the errors, as they say, are all my own. This study quotes generously, often from neglected writers, but care has been taken to remain within the Society of Authors' guidelines regarding fair use.

www.ingramcontent.com/pod-product-compliance
Ingram Content Group UK Ltd.
Pitfield, Milton Keynes, MK11 3LW, UK
UKHW041949190726
13854UKWH00004B/1867